Logic Programming

International Series in Logic Programming

Series Editor
Keith Clark, Imperial College of Science and Technology

Associate Editors
Bob Kowalski, Imperial College of Science and Technology
Jean-Louis Lassez, IBM, Yorktown Heights, USA

Editorial Board
K Furukawa (ICOT, Japan)
H Gallaire (Bull Systems, France)
J W Lloyd (Bristol University, UK)
J Minker (Maryland, USA)
J A Robinson (Syracuse University, NY, USA)
S-A Tärnlund (Uppsala University, Sweden)
M H van Emden (University of Waterloo, Canada)
D H D Warren (Bristol University, UK)

Other Titles in the Series
Parallel Logic Programming in PARLOG: The Language and its Implementation   Steve Gregory

Programming in PARLOG   Tom Conlon

Advanced Prolog: Techniques and Examples   Peter Ross

Logic Programming

Systematic Program Development

Yves Deville
University of Namur

ADDISON-WESLEY PUBLISHING COMPANY

Wokingham, England · Reading, Massachusetts · Menlo Park, California
New York · Don Mills, Ontario · Amsterdam · Bonn · Sydney
Singapore · Tokyo · Madrid · San Juan

Cover designed by Hybert Design and Type, Maidenhead and printed by The Riverside Printing Co. (Reading) Ltd.
Typeset by Times Graphics, Singapore.
Printed in Great Britain by T. J. Press (Padstow), Cornwall.

First printed 1990

British Library Cataloguing in Publication Data
Deville, Yves *1960–*
  Logic programming: systematic program development.
  1. Computer systems. Programming languages: Prolog
  I. Title
  005.13′3

  ISBN 0–201–17576–2

Library of Congress Cataloging in Publication Data
Deville, Yves *1960–*
  Logic programming: systematic program development/Yves Deville.
    p.   cm. — (International series in logic programming)
  Includes bibliographical references.
  ISBN 0–201–17576–2
  1. Logic programming.   I. Title.   II. Series.
QA76.63.D48   1990
005.1 — dc20

89–18349
CIP

Foreword

As logic programming nears its twentieth anniversary the proposition that *logic can and should be used as a programming language* has become widely accepted and finds daily confirmation in the experience of thousands of Prolog users around the world.

The idea of logic programming originally emerged from fruitful intellectual turmoil in the late 1960s and early 1970s. About that time various attempts were under way to apply the ideas and techniques of machine-oriented logic – such as those underlying the resolution system – to problems of artificial intelligence and natural language processing.

Already in 1967 Ted Elcock and his colleagues at the University of Aberdeen had experimented in their Absys system with the concept of a purely assertional programming formalism based on logical principles. Earlier still, in John McCarthy's 1957 paper 'Programs with Common Sense' we find the thesis plainly stated that in order to write a successful problem-solving program exhibiting artificial intelligence one must represent the relevant knowledge as a collection of assertions expressed formally in first-order logic, and adjoin to this *knowledge base* an efficient *proof procedure*. Such a computer program would then be able to solve problems by formally deducing suitably posed theorems from the assertions in the knowledge base. Many groups began research projects following McCarthy's prescription. This approach was, however, controversial and vigorously debated.

The McCarthyite view that knowledge is best represented as a collection of *assertions* found itself pitted against the Minskyite view that knowledge is better represented as a collection of *procedures*. There ensued a serious but entertaining 'logic war' over the question: is knowledge declarative or procedural?

The war reached a peak at the first International Joint Conference on Artificial Intelligence, held in May 1969, where we heard Cordell Green's important McCarthyite paper on his resolution-based QA2 and QA3 systems, in which he clearly laid out the main conception of logic programming as we now have it, except for the crucial limitation to Horn

v

clauses. This was followed by Carl Hewitt's equally memorable Minskyite paper describing his PLANNER system, which also pointed in the same general direction but with a completely different set of principles. We did not realize it at the time, but it was these two papers which prepared the way for the settlement of the issue, and by the end of 1971 the logic war was essentially over.

On the procedural side, the final blast came from Marvin Minsky and Seymour Papert in the vivid 'anti-logic' passages of their 1971 MIT Artificial Intelligence Progress Report. On the declarative side it fell to Robert Kowalski and Alain Colmerauer to establish the basis of the peace: the elegant modern formulation of the idea of logic programming and its powerful embodiment in Prolog. In the January 1988 issue of the *Communication of the Association for Computing Machinery* Kowalski tells of his first interactions with Colmerauer in 1971, the year of Prolog's birth. The logic war was ended because logic programming removed its underlying cause. As Kowalski showed, both sides were right. The assertions in a logic program also have a perfectly natural interpretation as procedures. In Prolog, this distinction disappears.

Today logic programming is a standard paradigm in the methodology of computing. Its attractions are immediate. Kowalski's apothegmatic equation ALGORITHM = LOGIC + CONTROL sums up the most striking of them: the clean separation of the knowledge required to solve a problem from the way this knowledge is to be deployed to solve it. Indeed Prolog invites (but does not require) the programmer to forget entirely about the control and concentrate on the logic, with a default control regime which systematically explores the programmer's assertions in a uniform left-to-right and top-to-bottom order. Prolog programs written in such a carefree spirit typically maximize intelligibility and clarity at the expense of some loss of efficiency in execution. Ways are therefore provided in Prolog for the programmer optionally to influence the execution of the program. By exploiting these a skillful practitioner can increase the efficiency of the program without changing its meaning or net effect. That is to say, given any Prolog program there are many other Prolog programs which are semantically equivalent to it and differ from it in their relative efficiency.

The overall task of the Prolog programmer thus falls intuitively into three natural phases:

(1)   to specify the problem to be solved;
(2)   to formulate a suitable method for its solution;
(3)   to select, from the many equivalent programs, one which is most efficient.

Yes, indeed. But how in practice does one do this? Can one learn to do it well? Can the skill be taught? Are there principles involved which can be recognized and organized into a discipline?

In this admirable and unashamedly evangelical book Dr Deville undertakes to answer these questions and leaves little room for doubt that the process of arriving at correct and efficient Prolog programs can indeed be analysed and understood. He explains his analysis lucidly and in considerable detail, developing on its basis a natural yet systematic way of going about the task of programming in Prolog. The resulting discipline is a rigorous elaboration of the above three-phase scheme, presented with a convincing rationale and an infectious enthusiasm.

It is a pleasure to greet so lively and valuable a contribution and to felicitate its author.

J.A. Robinson
Syracuse University
April 1989

Preface

Aims and objectives of the book

Although Prolog is now widely used for the development of programs or software, there is nevertheless a need for a discipline of Prolog programming or software development with the Prolog language. This book is aimed at being a first step in this direction. A systematic methodology for logic program development is proposed, covering the entire development process: from an informal specification to an efficient logic program. Our subject is thus the *rigorous* construction of logic programs which are both *correct* and *efficient*. Our goal is not to reject Prolog programmers' techniques, but rather to induce the programmers to be more rigorous, and to help them in the development of reliable logic programs. The book also has a broader aim in the development of program construction techniques.

Approach

In order to get the spirit of our approach, let us paraphrase Dijkstra's statement on program correctness (Dijkstra, 1968). The problem of program correctness is usually tackled as follows: 'Given a specification and given a program, prove that the program meets the given specification'. But this can be tackled from the other side: 'Given a specification, how do we construct, from the given specification, a program meeting it?' The approach taken here is much inspired from this second statement. We also take the position that the specification of a problem is initially a non-formal statement. This is much closer to the reality of programming, and does not pass in silence over the difficult task of constructing such a formal specification.

Since both logic programming and Prolog are based on logic, it is interesting to use the logical framework when constructing a logic program. It is however well known that the actual behaviour of logic programming languages shows some characteristics that make these languages differ from logic. We therefore separate these two aspects. The development of logic programs can be based on the following three steps:

- elaboration of a specification,
- construction of a logic description,
- derivation of a logic program in a logic programming language.

Structure and content of the book

The book is divided into three major parts, one for each of the three steps of the development process. Parts II and III are structured similarly in order to systematize the presentation.

Introduction

Chapter 1 underlines the need for a methodology and shows that programming in Prolog is different from programming in logic. Following on from this, the problems of programming in Prolog are dealt with. The methodological framework is then introduced.

Part I   Specifications

Chapter 2 describes the first step of the development process: the elaboration of a specification.

Part II   Logic descriptions

This part handles the second step, that is the construction of a logic description of the problem, from the specification. It is the central part of the development process and requires much creativity.

   Chapter 3 introduces the declarative semantics of first-order logic and explains what logic descriptions are.

   Chapter 4 answers the following question: 'What does it mean for a logic description to be correct with respect to a specification?'

   Chapter 5 handles the creative task of constructing a logic description. In this central chapter, a general construction method is proposed and various construction techniques and heuristics are analysed.

   The transformation of logic descriptions is investigated in *Chapter 6*.

Part III   Logic programs

The last step of the development process is dealt with in this part, that is, the derivation of a correct and efficient logic program (in Prolog) from a logic description.

   Chapter 7 introduces the procedural semantics of a logic program.

Correctness criteria of a logic program are described in *Chapter 8*. An explanation is given of what the user can expect from the execution of a program with respect to its specification.

Chapter 9 handles the derivation of a correct logic program (in Prolog) from a logic description. Techniques for analysing and solving the possible problems for achieving correctness are presented.

Chapter 10 investigates the transformation of Prolog programs into more efficient ones, by means of the suitable introduction of control information.

Conclusion

The overall methodology is evaluated in *Chapter 11* and a future for logic programming is investigated.

Most of the material presented is independent of our methodological framework, and can thus be used successfully in other approaches to logic program development.

Readership

This book is intended for Prolog programmers, students, and those interested in logic programming, as well as researchers in logic programming. It will be assumed that the reader has some knowledge of the Prolog language and some programming practice can also be useful. The Prolog language will not be described here. We refer the reader to the classic Clocksin and Mellish (1984), or to the well-developed Sterling and Shapiro (1986). No particular prerequisite on logic or on the theory of logic programming is required.

Using the book

Except for the description of the Prolog language, this book is intended to be self-contained. Exercises are presented throughout the text. They illustrate the material covered and also sometimes extend it. A summary is given at the end of each chapter, as well as a background section where references can be found for further development of the material. In order to facilitate access to the various parts of the developed examples, Tables of Specifications, of Logic Descriptions and of Procedures have been included in an Appendix, as well as a general Table of Problems.

Theoretical justifications and foundations of the methodology, as well as some technical aspects, are included in starred sections or starred exercises (∗). Some double starred sections and exercises (∗∗) make digressions requiring some knowledge about logic or about the theory of logic programming.

The text can be used in many different ways. Starred sections can be skipped by the non-interested reader, or in a first reading, without affecting the applicability of the methodology. The text can also serve as a basis, or as a complementary book, for courses on logic programming, Prolog programming or programming methodology. Depending on the level of the course, starred sections and parts of the material could be skipped. For instance, a possible consistent subset of the book, more oriented towards practice, would include Chapters 2, 5, 8, 9 and 10.

Acknowledgements

This work was based on the research for my MS degree (Syracuse University, USA) and PhD degree (Facultés Universitaires N.D.P. Namur, Belgium).

I am particularly grateful to Alan Robinson. This work benefitted from his advice. His interest in my research as well as his encouragement to make it into a book were deeply appreciated.

I am indebted to Baudouin Le Charlier who provided continous help. Much of this work has been influenced by our discussions and his pertinent remarks.

Other people who deserve my thanks for commenting on drafts and suggesting improvements include Axel van Lamsweerde, Pascal Van Hentenryck, Jean-Marie Jacquet and the members of the FOLON research project, especially Pierre Flener and Pierre De Boeck who provided a careful reading of the text. My thanks go also to Bruno Delcourt who smoothed my access to formatting tools.

Special thanks are due to Chris Hogger who took the trouble carefully to revise the text. His detailed suggestions and criticisms greatly benefitted this book. I am also grateful to Addison-Wesley, notably to Simon Plumtree, Stephen Bishop and to Sheila Chatten.

Finally, I wish to thank P. & I., my anonymous supporters.

The author is supported by the Belgian National Fund for Scientific Research as a Research Associate.

The publisher wishes to thank the M. C. Escher heirs, Cordon Art and the Haags Gemeentemuseum for permission to reproduce the lithographs on pages xviii, 24, 58, 186 and 302 of this book.

Yves Deville
Namur
February 1990

Contents

PART II   Logic Descriptions

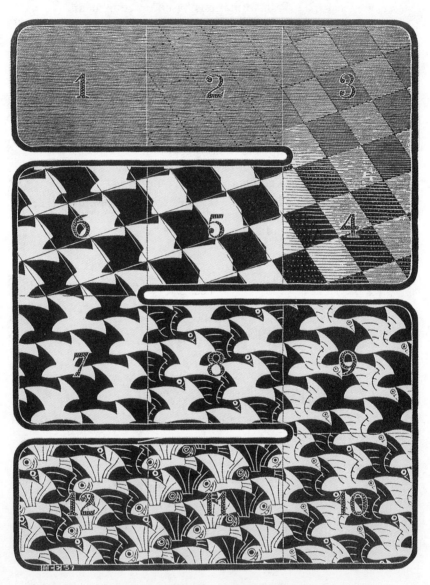

Regular division of the plane, M. C. Escher (1957). Collection Haags Gemeentemuseum, The Hague. © 1989 M. C. Escher Heirs/Cordon Art, Baarn, Holland

1
Introduction

PREVIEW   In this chapter, the need for a methodology in logic programming will be underlined by means of a short example (Section 1.1), which stresses some of the major problems that can arise in the development of Prolog programs. Next, the question 'PROLOG = PROgramming in LOGic?' is analysed in detail; not only from a theoretical point of view, but also from a practical programming point of view (Section 1.2). Four paradigms for programming in Prolog, which cover the possible approaches to programming in logic, are then presented and analysed (Section 1.3). A methodology for systematic logic program development based on one of these paradigms is introduced in Section 1.4 and illustrated in Section 1.5. Finally, some alternative methodologies are outlined and compared with the proposed one (Section 1.6).

Logic Programming had its beginnings in the early 1970s. It was mainly introduced by Kowalski (1974) and Colmerauer *et al.*, (1973), following earlier work in Automated Theorem Proving and Artificial Intelligence (AI). The construction of automated deduction systems is one of the aims of AI. Major developments in Automated Theorem Proving arose from the work of Herbrand in 1930 (Herbrand, 1930) and the introduction of the resolution principle by Robinson in 1965 (Robinson, 1965). Kowalski and Colmerauer's fundamental idea was that *logic could be used as a programming language.* It is also worth mentioning earlier papers (Footer and Elcock, 1969; Green, 1969; Hayes, 1973) that introduced a similar idea. Thus the concept of logic programming arose. The Prolog language (PROgramming in LOGic) was conceived and Colmerauer and Roussel implemented a first interpreter (Colmerauer *et al.*, 1973). Shortly afterwards, Hill (1974) proved the completeness of the resolution method used in logic programming (usually called SLD-resolution). Next, Van Emden and Kowalski (1976) defined various types of semantics for logic programs and subsequently Clark (1978) suggested how to deal with negation as failure in this context.

While in Automated Theorem Proving the goal is to prove theorems, in logic programming the objective is to *compute results* from specific input data. One of the main concepts behind logic programming is that an algorithm can be described in Horn clause logic. This logic has a *procedural interpretation* which makes it very effective as a programming language. It seems unlikely that more general forms of logic could achieve this effectiveness.

So far, one of the most important results of logic programming has been the development of the Prolog language. However, logic programming is not limited to Prolog, but includes many other research topics: the theoretical foundations of logic programming; languages (for example, design, implementation, parallelism, the integration of functional programming); methodology; logic and databases; knowledge representation; natural language processing; applications (for example, expert systems); architecture and hardware; and so on.

It is often claimed that PROLOG = PROgramming in LOGic. It is however well known that the declarative semantics of the Prolog language differs somewhat from the procedural semantics. From these facts, several attempts have been made to improve or enrich the Prolog language: IC-Prolog (Clark and McCabe, 1979), EPILOG (Porto, 1982), METALOG (Dincbas and Le Pape, 1984), MU-Prolog (Naish, 1985a) and Prolog II (Giannesini *et al.*, 1986) and so on.

An opposite point of view can be adopted. Given the imperfections of Prolog, is it possible to construct a correct Prolog program, using the logic programming framework? Although the design of better logic programming languages is a fundamental issue, it is also important to present methodologies of logic program construction for actual, widely used programming languages. Understanding this can help programmers in Prolog program development. By stressing the imperfections of the language, a helpful basis for the development of logic programming language can also be achieved. Such an approach is taken in this book where a methodology for systematic logic program development is proposed. It proceeds from the specification phase towards efficient Prolog programs. However, it is aimed at being as language-independent as possible. Only the last few steps deal explicitly with the Prolog language so that the major part of this proposal can be applied to any logic programming language.

1.1 The need for a methodology

The need for a methodology is illustrated by a short example. The reader is advised to try and solve the problem before looking at the proposed

Prolog code. This is not so as to criticize the reader's Prolog programming style but only so as to underline some of the problems encountered in the development of a Prolog program. The objective here is thus to justify the necessity of the methodological aspects of logic program development.

The problem

The following problem belongs to logic programming folklore (see, for example, Clocksin and Mellish (1984) or Sterling and Shapiro (1986)).

> Write a Prolog procedure efface(X, L, LEff) which removes the first occurrence of X from the list L, giving the list LEff. If there is no such X in the list L, it should fail.

Let us call this statement a specification of the problem. At this stage of the example, we are not concerned with the quality of the specification (some readers may find it ambiguous or incomplete).

Prolog programs

```
efface( X, [X | T], T ) ←
efface( X, [H | T], [H | TEff] ) ← efface( X, T, TEff )
```

Procedure 1.1   efface(X, L, LEff)

```
efface( X, [X | T], T ) ← !
efface( X, [H | T], [H | TEff] ) ← efface( X, T, TEff )
```

Procedure 1.2   efface(X, L, LEff)

```
efface( X, [X | T], T ) ←
efface( X, [H | T], [H | TEff] ) ← not( X = H ), efface( X, T, TEff )
```

Procedure 1.3   efface(X, L, LEff)

These three proposed Prolog programs, although representative, do not cover all the possible recursive solutions (that is, without auxiliary procedures such as member). Two other solutions will be given at the end of the chapter.

Test data

Once a program has been given, it is usual to test it on some simple representative data. If the reader has a different Prolog program, he or she should also test it on the data of Table 1.1, and compare its behaviour

Table 1.1 Test data efface(X, L, LEff).

	X	Test data L	LEff	Intended behaviour	Procedure 1.1	Actual behaviour Procedure 1.2	Procedure 1.3
1	2	[1,2,3,2,4]	[1,3,2,4]	yes	correct	correct	correct
2	2	[1,2,3,2,4]	[1,2,3,4]	no	yes	yes	correct
3	2	[2|3]	3	?	yes	yes	yes
4	2	[1,2,3,2,4]	LEff	LEff=[1,3,2,4]	also LEff=[1,2,3,4]	correct	correct
5	0	[1,2,3,2,4]	LEff	no	correct	correct	correct
6	X	[1,2,3,2,4]	[1,3,2,4]	X=2	correct	correct	no
7	X	[1,2,3,2,4]	[1,2,3,4]	no	X=2	X=2	correct
8	2	L	[1,3,2,4]	L=[2,1,3,2,4] L=[1,2,3,2,4] L=[1,3,2,2,4]	also L=[1,3,2,4,2]	L=[2,1,3,2,4]	correct
9	X	[1,2,3,2,4]	LEff	X=1 LEff=[2,3,2,4] X=2 LEff=[1,3,2,4] X=3 LEff=[1,2,2,4] X=4 LEff=[1,2,3,2]	also X=2 LEff=[1,2,3,4]	X=1 LEff=[2,3,2,4]	X=1 LEff=[2,3,2,4]
10	2	[2,1|L]	L	no	yes	yes	yes
11	X	L	[1,3]	L=[X,1,3] X≠1 L=[1,X,3] X≠1,3 L=[1,3,X] X≠3	L=[X,1,3] L=[1,X,3] L=[1,3,X]	L=[X,1,3]	L=[X,1,3]
12	2	L	LEff	L=[2|LEff] L=[E1,2|T] LEff=[E1|T] E1≠2 ⋮ ⋮	L=[2|LEff] L=[E1,2|T] LEff=[E1|T] ⋮ ⋮	L=[2|LEff]	L=[2|LEff]
13	X	L	LEff	L=[X|LEff] L=[E1,X|T] LEff=[E1|T] E1≠X ⋮ ⋮	L=[X|LEff] L=[E1,X|T] LEff=[E1|T] ⋮ ⋮	L=[X|LEff]	L=[X|LEff]

with the intended behaviour. In the table, the *actual* behaviour is marked 'correct' when it is the intended behaviour. Otherwise, the actual behaviour is explicitly described.

The reported actual behaviour is obtained from any 'classical' Prolog system (left-to-right and depth-first search, negation as failure without delay mechanism, and unification without occur check and constraint).

The intended answer for test data 3 is difficult to deduce from the specification because [2 | 3] and 3 are not lists! However, it can be decided that such a goal should fail or that such a goal should not be given. The intended behaviour of test data 11–13 cannot be obtained from the usual Prolog systems (where inequalities are not given as answer substitutions). For instance, if we restrict the problem to lists of positive integers, the intended behaviour L = [1, X, 2], X ≠ 1 could be described as L = [1, 0, 2], X = 0; L = [1, 2, 2], X = 2; L = [1, 3, 2], X = 3 and so on.

From Table 1.1, it can be seen that the actual behaviour of Procedure 1.1 is often in contradiction to the intended behaviour. This is not surprising since the procedure actually removes *any* occurrence of X (and not only the *first* one). The actual behaviour of Procedures 1.2 and

1.3 are not the same. For instance, test data 2 is (surprisingly) incorrect with Procedure 1.2. Thus Procedure 1.2 cannot be seen as an optimized version of Procedure 1.3. The actual behaviour with test data 10 shows the effect of the absence of occur check in Prolog implementations (this will be further developed in Section 1.2).

EXERCISE

1.1   What happens if the second clause of Procedure 1.2 is modified as follows:

efface(X, [H | T], LEff) ← efface(X, T, TEff), LEff = [H | TEff]

Is it correct with more test data? What about the following goal?

← efface(1, [1, 2, 1], [1, 2])

Comments

The above example serves to illustrate the difficulty of constructing a Prolog program which behaves correctly for all the proposed test data. Does it mean that the possible uses of a procedure should be restricted to special cases (for example, a variable can only appear in the third parameter of any goal with efface)? Such a restriction ought to have been stated in the specification anyway. The given specification of the problem is also somewhat dynamic and imperative. The parameter LEff is *constructed* from X and L. Would it be better to express this in more relational terms? What would be a good convention when types are not respected in a goal: should the procedure fail or should such goals be prevented?

This efface example also illustrates that without construction methods it is difficult to imagine *a priori* for which test data a Prolog program is correct. Procedure 1.3 is certainly more declarative than Procedure 1.2 but seems less efficient. Is it possible to obtain a correct and efficient Prolog program while thinking logically? How can an elegant correct logic program be found or constructed? Since Prolog's execution mechanism is simple but rigid, does the introduction of new mechanisms facilitate the construction of correct Prolog programs?

The example considered underlines the need for a methodology in the development of logic programs. It also points out that other mechanisms could perhaps enhance the quality of the Prolog language. The question of designing a better logic programming language is not expressly tackled here, but limitations of the Prolog language will emerge in the chapters that follow.

1.2   PROLOG = PROgramming in LOGic ?

In this section, the following equation is analysed:

programming in Prolog = programming in logic.

Such an analysis is essential for the introduction of a methodology for Prolog program development based on logic. Some of the logical foundations of logic programming will be used. These concepts are not defined here because the objective is to get an idea of possible problems. The concepts will be introduced and defined precisely in the chapters that follow. The discussion here is based on the Prolog language, but is also extended to any sequential logic programming language. In what follows, the term 'logic programming language' will refer to a sequential logic programming language. A brief characterization of what programming in logic is will be given first.

1.2.1   Logic programming

One of the attractive features of logic programming is the duality of its semantics. The declarative semantics is based on first-order logic and deals with the logical consequences of a logic program. The procedural semantics is based on execution mechanisms (SLD-resolution + computation rule + search rule) and deals with the derivation or computation of answer substitutions. From a theoretical point of view, two major theorems ensure some equivalence between the two semantics. Here we will consider programs and goals without negations (called **definite programs** and **definite goals**).

A **soundness theorem** tells that any result obtained by computation (an answer substitution) is also correct from the declarative semantics point of view. Conversely, a **completeness theorem** expresses that for any correct answer substitution from the declarative point of view, there exists a derivation, based on the procedural semantics, which computes that answer substitution (or a more general one).

The equivalence of these two semantics is the core of logic programming. The concept of programming in logic can be explained as the construction in logic of a description of a problem (using the declarative semantics). This description can then be executed in order to compute results (using the procedural semantics). In the construction of the logic description of a problem, it is thus possible to focus upon only the declarative semantics. Moreover, given that the problem is described in terms of relations (predicates), the corresponding logic program can be used whatever the instantiation of the parameters (some arguments being input data while others are output results). This is called **multidirectionality**. These concepts are specific to logic programming and do not have any counterpart in imperative or functional programming.

For the Prolog programming language, the above equation does not hold. In the sections that follow, gaps between the declarative and the procedural semantics are underlined.

1.2.2 Incompleteness

Even if completeness is theoretically achievable in logic programming, this is not the case in Prolog. The following example demonstrates this.

EXAMPLE 1.1

> p(a, b) ←
> p(c, b) ←
> p(X, Z) ← p(X, Y), p(Y, Z)
> p(X, Y) ← p(Y, X)

It is obvious that p(a, c) is a logical consequence of this logic program. Unfortunately, Prolog will never find it (incompleteness). There is a successful derivation in the derivation tree for the goal ← p(a, c), but Prolog's search rule will never reach it.

More generally, if a logic programming language has a depth-first search rule, then it is incomplete. In the above example, no matter how the clauses are ordered, how the literals in the bodies are ordered or what the computation rule is, a logic programming language with a depth-first search rule with a fixed order for trying the clauses will never find p(a, c) as a logical consequence of this program. In order to obtain completeness, a breadth-first search rule (or some variant of one) is necessary.

From a programming point of view, a breadth-first search rule is restrictive in a (sequential) logic programming language because it is too inefficient. Some variant of a depth-first search rule is required. It is therefore in the nature of any practical logic programming language to be incomplete.

1.2.3 Unfairness

If an existential variable (that is, a variable occurring in the scope of an existential quantifier) occurs in a logical consequence of a logic program, Prolog's execution is required not only to succeed, but also to compute values for that variable. With a depth-first search rule, not all the possible values will necessarily be found eventually. Such behaviour is called **unfair**. Consider the following example.

EXAMPLE 1.2

> append([ ], L, L) ←
> append([H | T], L, [H | TApp]) ← append(T, L, TApp)
> append3(L1, L2, L3, LApp) ← append(L1, L2, L1_2),
>   append(L1_2, L3, LApp)

This example shows procedures implementing the append and append3 relations (the latter holds when the list LApp is the concatenation of the lists L1, L2 and L3). Table 1.2 presents the sequence of successive instantiations resulting from the goal ← append3(X, Y, [2], LApp) where the variables X, Y and LApp are implicitly existentially quantified.

Table 1.2   ← append3(X, Y, [2], LApp).

X	Y	LApp
[]	[]	[2]
[]	[H1]	[H1, 2]
[]	[H1, H2]	[H1, H2, 2]
.	.	.
.	.	.

This shows the unfairness of the execution. X is always an empty list whilst other correct instantiations also exist. Note that unfairness can lead to incompleteness. For example, the goal

   ← append3(X, Y, [2], LApp), X = [1]

will never succeed whereas append3([1], Y, [2], LApp) is a logical consequence of this logic program.

Unfairness, like incompleteness, can only be solved with a breadth-first search rule (or some variant). Therefore, unfairness also lies in the nature of any practical (sequential) logic programming language.

1.2.4 Unsoundness

Unsoundness occurs when there is a successful computation of a goal which is not a logical consequence of the logic program.

Most Prolog implementations, for efficiency reasons, use an unification algorithm without occur check. This means that when testing whether or not a variable X unifies with a term t, no check is made to detect whether X occurs in t, or not. It is therefore possible in Prolog to unify X and f(X) to produce an infinite term f(f(f(...))) while it should be impossible to unify them. This omission can lead to unsoundness. Consider the following program.

EXAMPLE 1.3
```
test ← p( X, X )
p( Y, f( Y ) ) ←
```

Given the goal ← test, a Prolog system without occur check will succeed (with the empty answer substitution). The predicate test is therefore considered as a logical consequence, but this is quite wrong! The problem arises because the unification algorithm of Prolog mistakenly unifies p(X, X) and p(Y, f(Y)).

A more concrete example will show that this problem can arise with useful procedures.

EXAMPLE 1.4

```
append( [], L, L ) ←
append( [H | T], L, [H | TApp] ) ← append( T, L, TApp )
```

Here, the goal ← append([], L, [1|L]) will succeed (with some possible trouble in printing out the answer)! But the list [1|L] is not the concatenation of the empty list and the list L. Prolog mistakenly considers append([], L, [1|L]) as a logical consequence of the program and soundness is therefore destroyed. Test data 10 of Table 1.1 is another example. Whenever some feature of Prolog destroys soundness, it also destroys completeness whenever negation as failure is also supported (see below).

There are two major solutions to this unsoundness problem. The first one is to change the logic and to consider that X and f(X) should actually unify. This leads to the concept of infinite terms (see, for example, Prolog II (Giannesini *et al.*, 1986)). A second solution consists of reconsidering the implementer's choice and introducing the occur check in Prolog interpreters, but this may reduce their efficiency.

1.2.5 Negation

All computable functions are computable in Horn clause logic. Therefore, the use of negation does not increase the power of expression. However in practice, the construction and the expression of a problem in Prolog is often simplified by the possible introduction of negative subgoals.

It is worth noticing that negative information cannot be expressed with definite Horn clauses (also called definite program clauses), even if negative subgoals are allowed in the body of the clauses. Negative information can be introduced in many ways. On the one hand, program clauses can be further extended by allowing the head of such clauses to be a positive or a negative literal (as with classical clauses). With such a form, the necessary conditions for a relation to be true and the necessary conditions for the same relation to be false can thus be described. Such clauses can be handled procedurally by a full resolution system, or by an extension of the Horn clause proof procedure. There is, however, an extra efficiency cost in using such a negation. On the other hand, a new inference rule can be added for program clauses. A very simple and efficient one is the **negation as failure** inference rule. The idea of the negation as failure rule is to conclude ¬q if it is impossible to derive q from the logic program. Let us first analyse the problems caused by this inference rule.

Since it is impossible to express negative information with program clauses, the negation as failure inference rule is unsound by nature.

EXAMPLE 1.5

    p(a) ←
    r(b) ← not(p(Y))

In this Prolog example, the goal ← not(p(b)) succeeds since it is impossible to derive ← p(b) from the program. However, ¬p(b) is not a logical consequence of this logic program. Instead of considering the logic program, Clark (1978) suggested that the completion of the program is considered when interpreting the result from such a computation. Completion is obtained, roughly speaking, by replacing the implications by equivalences. The completion of Example 1.5 is shown in Example 1.6. With such a form, the necessary and sufficient conditions for a relation to be true can thus be described, these also implicitly describe when it is false. The major difference with the above clausal approach is that the computation does not take place on the completion of a program, but in the program itself, which reduces the efficiency cost.

EXAMPLE 1.6

    p(X) ⇔ X = a
    r(X) ⇔ X = b & (∃Y) ¬p(Y)
    (+ some axioms for equality)

Now ¬p(b) is a logical consequence of the completion of the logic program. Soundness is achieved for this goal. But completion is not a sufficient condition for obtaining soundness. For instance, the goal ← not(r(b)) succeeds but ¬r(b) is not a logical consequence of the completion. Unsoundness can be avoided by restricting the form of the computation rule to a safe computation rule. The general idea is to select negative subgoals only when they are **ground** (that is, without variables). With a safe computation rule, the goal ← not(r(b)) no longer succeeds. Note that the Prolog computation rule is not safe.

Completeness is a more important issue because it cannot be achieved with a negation as failure rule. First, the restriction to a safe computation rule introduces incompleteness because the goals for which a safe computation rule cannot be applied have to be forbidden in order to avoid unsoundness. Such goals are often known as **floundering** goals. In the above example, the goal ← not(p(X)) is not accepted because the negative subgoal is not ground when selected. But this goal should succeed since ¬p(b) is a logical consequence of the completion.

EXAMPLE 1.7

q(a) ← r(a)
q(a) ← not(r(a))
r(X) ← r(f(X))

Example 1.7 illustrates another aspect of incompleteness. Obviously, q(a) is a logical consequence. But whatever the computation and search rules are, there is no successful derivation of q(a). In order to conclude ¬r(a), negation as failure tries to show the impossibility of deriving r(a). But here, it has to search an infinite derivation tree. This is a consequence of the undecidability of first-order logic. If p is not a logical consequence, the derivation of p will not always terminate. Incompleteness can occur in such cases.

The incompleteness problem is in the nature of negation as failure, and cannot be suppressed. In spite of its incompleteness, negation as failure is a very suitable solution to the introduction of negative information because of its efficiency and its simplicity. Negation as failure also has the advantage of supporting default reasoning, which is likely to be problematic in any computational logic system. Therefore, a practical (sequential) logic programming language should at least propose a negation as failure rule in order to handle negation. This does not exclude other forms of negation for particular problems, or particular negative subgoals (≠ in Prolog II for example (Giannesini *et al.*, 1986)).

1.2.6 Control information

By **control information**, we mean the choice of search rule and computation rule, and any non-logical information (provided by the programmer or deduced by the interpreter) used to reduce the search space during the execution of a logic program. The set of available control primitives is usually called the **control language**. If control information can be provided by the programmer, other forms of control can be handled by an interpreter or compiler, such as search strategy, the selection order of clauses and literals, or intelligent backtracking.

In Prolog, the cut is the main control primitive. It allows the search in the derivation tree to be pruned. Misplaced cuts can therefore lead to incompleteness and unfairness since some solutions can be missed.

Are control primitives necessary for the programmer? Theoretically, no: a logic programming language does not need such primitives. But in practice, is it possible to have a reasonably efficient programming language without control primitives being introduced by the programmer? An automated system cannot deduce all of the relevant control information that the user is able to produce for each particular program so as to achieve efficiency. Therefore, part of the control must be the programmer's responsibility. Hence, control primitives must be part of any practical logic programming language. But misplaced control primitives increase the gap between the declarative and the procedural semantics.

1.2.7   Extralogical features

Input–output primitives (such as file handling or terminal handling) cannot be fully described in first-order logic although every practical programming language must offer such primitives; as does Prolog. These primitives produce input–output by side–effects. Side–effect primitives increase the gap between the declarative semantics and the procedural semantics.

Other extralogical primitives are also available in most logic programming languages. The classical ones include bagof, setof, assert, retract, univ. These are outside the scope of first-order logic but can be useful from a pragmatic point of view.

1.2.8   Multidirectionality

It is often claimed that Prolog procedures can be used in more ways than one (the arguments being either input data or output results). This may be the case in applications with very few algorithmic aspects (such as databases), however multidirectionality is very seldom possible within the general framework of algorithmic applications (see the example in Section 1.1). Given the incompleteness of Prolog, some input–output patterns can loop whilst being a logical consequence of the logic program. Problems can also arise because of unfairness and negation as failure. Moreover, for efficiency reasons, some built-in Prolog procedures are not multidirectional (arithmetic built-ins for example).

What about multidirectionality in other logic programming languages? There are some limitations. Some logic programs must be used with a restricted directionality in order to avoid incompleteness and unfairness. Other limitations arise if negation as failure is used. A program (with negations) can be correct for some directionalities but incorrect for others (unsoundness or incompleteness). Moreover, as in Prolog some built-in primitives (for example, arithmetics and comparisons) must have a restricted directionality for efficiency reasons.

But there are two more fundamental restrictions on multidirectionality: efficiency and undecidability. Let $P(x, y)$ denote a logic program computing y as the application of a total function f to an input x.

Suppose that $P(x, y)$ is constructed with this functional mode in mind. For example, f could be the symbolic derivation of an arithmetic expression x, or the decomposition of an integer x into its prime factors. So if $P(x, y)$ is used with x as input and y as output, it will compute $f(x)$. But let us take y as input, and x as output. Here, $P(x, y)$ is now supposed to compute the inverse function (which is at least a relation). In the above example, the inverse function will be the symbolic integration, or the multiplication of the (prime) integers. In most cases, $P(x, y)$ will only be able to enumerate all possible x, eventually stopping if there is an x such that $y = f(x)$. Such an enumeration is usually too inefficient to be acceptable. Imagine how inefficient it will be in these two examples! But in general, if such an x does not exist, the undecidability of first-order logic implies that termination will not always occur. $P(x, y)$ is thus not acceptable for computing the inverse function. These limitations of multidirectionality illustrate the classical, difficult problem of obtaining the inverse algorithm from a given one (Gries, 1981; Dijkstra, 1970). The above restrictions on multidirectionality arise in particular with programs referring to infinite relations.

1.3 Programming with Prolog
With the many differences between the declarative and the procedural semantics, it could be concluded that

programming in Prolog $\neq$ programming in logic

But most of these differences (beside the occur check unsoundness) also hold for any practical (sequential) logic programming language. As observed earlier, by 'practical' we mean a logic programming language with at least the negation as failure inference rule and a depth-first search rule (or a similar rule) for efficiency reasons. Thus, if IDEAL were the name of another practical (sequential) logic programming language (based on SLD-resolution), the equation would become:

programming in IDEAL $\neq$ programming in logic

Given these two inequalities, what does it mean to program in logic? How do you program in Prolog or in another (sequential) logic programming language? Four possible solutions are now described.

Paradigm 1: programming in DREAMLOG = programming in logic
A first idea is to design yet another logic programming language (say, DREAMLOG) which would not suffer from this gap between the declarative and procedural semantics. This approach is unrealistic: for instance, the completeness of DREAMLOG will make it too inefficient to be useful. A DREAMLOG answer is thus hopeless for a general

purpose (sequential) logic programming language. This severe conclusion is certainly not applicable in the context of prototyping where such an approach could be helpful.

Paradigm 2:   *programming in Prolog = programming in NEWlogic*
If the procedural semantics is different from the declarative, why not change the declarative aspect (and perhaps also the procedural one)? On the one hand, if the new declarative semantics is close to first-order logic, then the problems of completeness *versus* efficiency and extralogical features are still present. On the other hand, NEWlogic can be very different from first-order logic. For instance, NEWlogic can be very close to the procedural semantics. In that case, many of the ideas of logic programming are lost, which brings us to the next paradigm.

Paradigm 3:   *programming in Prolog = programming in Prolog*
In this approach, the logical aspects of the logic programming language are completely ignored. Here, the gap between the declarative and the procedural semantics is considered to be so enormous that the construction of a correct Prolog program is supposed to be simplified by using only the procedural aspect. This gives the above equation which holds trivially. This approach requires some consideration, it is actually how most Prolog programmers do write programs, and it is the approach taken in most Prolog textbooks. With such a perspective, however, the concept of logic programming is missing, which is unfortunate.

Paradigm 4:   *programming in Prolog = programming in logic + ...*
A final solution consists of separating the logical aspects from the non-logical ones: this gives the above equation. The two semantics are reconciled by adding something onto the right hand side of the equation. The logic programming paradigm can therefore be used in the construction process of a logic program. But it has to be combined with something else in order to obtain a correct Prolog program. The problem here consists of defining what this 'something' should be. The methodology described in this book is based on this approach and is presented in the following section.

1.4   Overview of the methodology

The contention of this book is that the logic programming paradigm is very powerful and can be used advantageously when programming in Prolog. The main objective of the book is to present a methodology for logic program development. In order to obtain reliable and efficient Prolog programs, the logic framework will be used extensively while taking advantage of the power of Prolog as a target programming language. In practice, such a methodology is applicable for solving

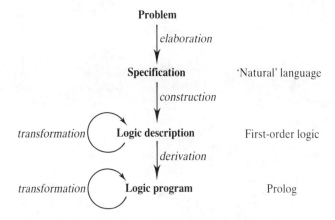

Figure 1.1   Logic program development.

general programming problems and not just specifically Artificial Intelligence problems. It is especially adapted for solving problems by means of recursion, or some kind of 'loop'.

In order to use the logical framework for constructing Prolog programs, the development of a program is decomposed into several steps. As usual, the first one is the elaboration of a specification of the problem. The second step consists of constructing a logic description in pure logic from the specification, independent of any programming language or procedural semantics. The last step deals with the derivation of a logic program (in Prolog) from the logic description. This step handles the issues that make programming in Prolog different from programming in logic. Convenient and simple solutions must therefore be found for all the problems outlined in the previous sections. Note that only the last step deals with a particular logic programming language (here, Prolog). Two transformation levels are also included in the general schema as shown in Figure 1.1. The above steps systematize the logic programming adage 'think logically first, then consider the procedural behaviour'.

The methodology is detailed in Figure 1.2. These figures will be described and the basic choices made in the design of the methodology underlined.

In the elaboration of a specification, no particular specification language is imposed. The specification is basically an informal description of a relation. Type information is added, as well as the directionalities for which the program has to be correct. If some side-effects need to be specified, they will be described in an extra part of the specification. In this framework, the transformations of a specification are not explicitly considered.

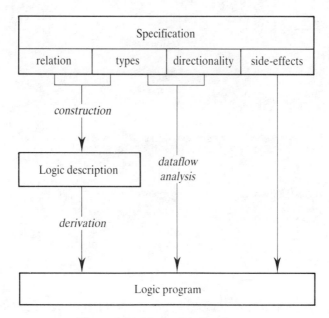

Figure 1.2   Methodology schema.

The second step consists of constructing from the specification what is called a logic description. A **logic description** is a formula in typeless first-order logic. More precisely, it is an *if and only if* definition of a predicate. With logic descriptions of this form, the completion of the derived logic programs will be logically equivalent to the logic descriptions. This approach allows the negation as failure rule to be seen as real negation at the logic description level. This construction is independent of the chosen programming language as well as of the procedural semantics. It is based on the declarative semantics of pure logic. This simplifies the construction process. This construction is performed using the informal description of the relation and the type information stated in the specification. The construction process is mainly based on structural induction and the generalization paradigm. At this level, logic descriptions can be transformed within first-order logic, by means of fold/unfold transformation techniques for instance. The name 'logic description' was chosen instead of 'formal specification' because the words 'formal specification' could be confused with the previous specification step (where there could be informal or formal specifications). Moreover, within the proposed framework, the logic description will be constructed (inductively) from a (non-recursive) specification. The resulting recursive logic description will be closer to an algorithm solving the problem than to a specification of the problem.

The last step deals with the derivation of a logic program (in Prolog) from the logic description. It starts with the translation of the logic description into program clauses. In order to obtain a correct Prolog program, an abstract interpretation or a dataflow analysis (using the type and directionality information of the specification) has to be performed to determine a permutation of the clauses and of the literals such that incompleteness, unfairness, unsoundness and negation problems do not occur. An independent termination proof must sometimes be carried out. If side-effects are specified, the Prolog program should be modified in order to include this aspect. Thus, this step has to solve all the problems that make the procedural semantics different from the declarative semantics used at the logic description level. The Prolog code can finally be transformed by the introduction of control information and by optimizations based on Prolog's execution mechanism.

   It should be noted that the above methodology is not always applicable, especially for programs with few logical aspects such as input–output procedures, file handling, and so on. In such cases, the development could be based on the procedural semantics alone, without any concern for first-order logic.

1.5   Example

The proposed methodology for logic program development is illustrated using the problem encountered in Section 1.1. Not all the justifications will be given here since this example is aimed at introducing the construction process.

> procedure   efface(X, L, LEff)
>
> *Type*:   X : Term
>   L, LEff : Lists
>
> *Relation*:   X is an element of L and LEff is the list L without the first occur-
>   rence of X in L.
>
> *Application conditions*:
> in(any, ground, any) : out(ground, ground, ground)
> in(ground, any, ground) : out(ground, ground, ground)
>
> **Specification 1.1**   efface(X, L, LEff)

   In Specification 1.1, type information is explicitly stated and the procedure is specified in a relational and non-recursive way. The application conditions describe the possible uses of the procedure (directionalities). They specify the allowed forms of actual parameters before the execution of the procedure (the *in* part). The form of the parameters after execution is also specified (the *out* part). The above directionalities are assumed to be given with the problem. In this example, the *in* part specifies that the second parameter, or the first and the third one, must be ground before the execution of the procedure. The *out* part expresses here that all the actual arguments will be ground after a successful execution. The constructed efface procedure has thus to be correct with respect to both directionalities.

Logic description

The form of the constructed logic description will be as follows:

$$\text{efface}(\text{X}, \text{L}, \text{LEff}) \Leftrightarrow \begin{aligned} &\vee \; C_1 \; \& \; F_1 \\ &\vee \; C_2 \; \& \; F_2 \\ &\quad\vdots \\ &\vee \; C_n \; \& \; F_n. \end{aligned}$$

where C_i and F_i are formulae.

The logic description is constructed in several steps:

(1)   *Choice of an induction parameter* : L

(2)   *Choice of a well-founded relation* : $l_1 < l_2$ iff l_1 is a proper suffix of l_2

(3)   *Structural forms of the induction parameter*

C_1 : L empty : L = []
C_2 : L non-empty : L = [H | T]

(4)   *Construction of the structural cases*

F_i must be a necessary and sufficient condition to have efface(X, L, LEff) when C_i is true:

- For L = [], it is impossible to have a list LEff which is the list L without the first occurrence of X.
  We obtain F_1: false.

- For L = [H | T], there are two possibilities depending on whether H = X or not:

  (i)   For H = X, the necessary and sufficient condition is LEff = T, because T is the list L without the first occurrence of X.

  (ii)   For H ≠ X, the necessary and sufficient condition is that LEff must be of the form [H | TEff], where TEff is the list T without the first occurrence of X.

  We obtain F_2:

  (H = X & LEff = T
  ∨ H ≠ X & efface(X, T, TEff) & LEff = [H | TEff]).

Note that T < L according to the well-founded relation when L is any ground list since T is a proper suffix of L.

The constructed logic description is thus:

efface(X, L, LEff) ⇔
        L = [] & false
     ∨ L = [H | T] & (H = X & LEff = T
                        ∨ H ≠ X & efface(X, T, TEff) & LEff = [H | TEff])

where the variables H, T and TEff are assumed to be existentially quantified on the right hand side of this logic description.

Logic program

A logic program now has to be derived from the logic description. The logic description is first translated into program clauses. In this example the resulting clauses are:

efface(X, L, LEff) ← L = [H | T], H = X, LEff = T
efface(X, L, LEff) ← L = [H | T], LEff = [H | TEff], efface(X, T, TEff),
          not(H = X)

In order to obtain a correct Prolog procedure, a permutation of the literals must be found such that Prolog's computation rule is safe, and the directionality of the recursive call efface(X, T, TEff) respects the specification. In this example, the above permutation meets these requirements. Termination is also achieved since in the recursive call, some ground term (T or TEff, depending on the directionality) is decreasing.

This Prolog procedure can then be transformed into a more efficient version, giving Procedure 1.4.

efface(X, [X | T], T) ←
efface(X, [H | T], [H | TEff]) ← efface(X, T, TEff), not(X = H)

Procedure 1.4   efface(X, L, LEff)

Procedure 1.4 is not correct for test data 11 of Table 1.1 which does not respect the specified directionalities. For instance, the goal

    ← efface(X, L, [1]), L = [1, 2].

will fail whereas efface(2, [1, 2], [1]) succeeds.
    If the only specified directionality were

in(ground, ground, any): out(ground, ground, ground)

then another correct permutation for the clauses would be:

efface(X, L, LEff) ← L = [H | T], H = X, LEff = T
efface(X, L, LEff) ← L = [H | T], not(H = X), LEff = [H | TEff],
        efface(X, T, TEff)

This procedure can then be transformed into the more efficient Procedure 1.5. Observe that the literal LEff = T cannot be compiled into the head (see Exercise 1.4).

> efface(X, [X | T], LEff) ← !, LEff = T
> efface(X, [H | T], [H | TEff]) ← efface(X, T, TEff)

Procedure 1.5   efface(X, L, LEff)

EXERCISES

1.2   Consider the test data 12 of Table 1.1 for Procedures 1.4 and 1.5. How could they be modified to incorporate type checking?

1.3   For which test data of Table 1.1 must the actual behaviour of Procedure 1.4 be the same as the intended behaviour, according to the specified directionalities? And for Procedure 1.5?

1.4   For which test data of Table 1.1 do Procedures 1.2 and 1.5 differ?

1.6   Background

The gap between the declarative and the procedural semantics is well known; Examples 1.1, 1.3 and 1.7 are taken from Lloyd (1987). Unfairness and the append3 example are also analysed in Vasak and Potter (1985).

In Tärnlund (1977) and Sebelik and Stepanek (1982), it is shown that all computable functions are computable in Horn clause logic. Beside the negation as failure rule, other solutions have been proposed to handle negation; see, for example, Reiter (1978), Sakai and Miyachi (1983), Gabbay and Sergot (1984), Voda (1986) and Poole and Goebel (1986).

Examples of control information can be found in some Prolog dialects: annotations in IC-Prolog (Clark and McCabe, 1979), meta-rules (Gallaire and Lasserre, 1982; Dincbas and Le Pape, 1984), wait declarations in MU-Prolog (Naish, 1985b), and clausal annotations in UNSW-Prolog (Vasak and Potter, 1985). Intelligent backtracking, an example of control handled by a compiler or interpreter, is described in Bruynooghe (1978) and in Pereira and Porto (1982).

An example of the application of Paradigm 2 is the logical reconstruction of Prolog II (Van Emden and Lloyd, 1984). The unsoundness of Prolog due to the occur check problem is solved there by modifying the equality axioms.

Paradigm 3 ignores the declarative aspects and focusses on only the procedural semantics. This approach to Prolog program construction is illustrated using the procedure efface(X, L, LEff) specified in the previous section. It is constructed here for X and L ground, and LEff as a variable. Two cases are considered:

(1)   If X is the first element of the list L, then unify LEff with the tail of L.
(2)   Otherwise, unify the head of LEff with the head of L, and the tail of LEff with a variable (say TEff) that will become, by a recursive call, the tail of L without the first occurrence of X.

In Prolog, this gives:

```
efface( X, [X | T], T ) ← !
efface( X, [H | T], [H | TEff] ) ← efface( X, T, TEff )
```

which is Procedure 1.2. The cut here is the Prolog implementation of *otherwise*. In such a procedural construction, the order of the clauses and of the subgoals, the form of the parameters, and the backtracking are very important from the beginning of the construction process. The 'logic' of the problem is thus mixed with procedural considerations.

Methodologies based on the procedural semantics are somehow related to imperative programming techniques. For instance, at the various points of the procedure, what has already been done could be described by means of assertions. An interpretation should also be given to such assertions in the backtracking process. The above procedural construction of efface is simple because for X and L ground and LEff a variable, there is at most one solution for LEff. A procedural approach can be very convenient for problems where the procedural aspect is crucial (for example, side-effect procedures). However, for other problems, especially those with multiple solutions and non-determinism, the procedural approach requires some skill and debugging. A technique of assertions for Prolog programs is used in Drabent and Maluszynski (1987) to describe properties of the program.

In Prolog textbooks, the presented programming techniques are mainly based on the procedural approach (see, for example, Clocksin and Mellish (1984), Bratko (1986) and Giannesini *et al.* (1986)). It should be noted that Sterling and Shapiro (1986) separate the concept of logic programs from the Prolog language.

The methodology proposed in this book can also be compared with more formal approaches to logic program development. If the starting point is a given first-order logic specification, formal techniques can be applied so as to deduce a logic program. Such an approach is taken in Clark (1979), Hogger (1984), Hansson (1980) and Dayantis (1987). The proposed techniques are powerful but the problem of program develop-

ment is premised upon the construction of a formal first-order specification. This construction is however not usually considered. A formal
first-order specification corresponds to the logic description presented
here, but with a more general form.

The proposed methodology is of course inspired from Kowalski's
equation 'Algorithm = Logic + Control' (Kowalski, 1979). The final
executable algorithm results from the addition of control to the logic
description.

SUMMARY

- The construction of a Prolog program that behaves properly is not a
  trivial task.

- Programming in Prolog ≠ programming in logic. There are major gaps
  between the declarative and the procedural semantics:
  incompleteness, unfairness, unsoundness, side-effects, and so on.

- From the above inequality, programming in Prolog can be handled in
  four different ways:
  - by designing a perfect logic programming language (generally a
    hopeless task),
  - by changing the declarative semantics,
  - by considering only the procedural semantics,
  - by separating the logical aspects from the non-logical ones in the
    construction process.
  This last approach is the basis of the proposed methodology.

- The development of a Prolog program is decomposed into three steps:
  - the elaboration of a specification,
  - the construction of a logic description in first-order logic,
    independent of any procedural semantics,
  - the derivation of a Prolog program from the logic description.

PART I

Specifications

Waterfall, M. C. Escher (1961). Collection Haags Gemeentemuseum, The Hague. © 1989 M. C. Escher Heirs/Cordon Art, Baarn, Holland

2

Specification

PREVIEW   The first step in the development of a logic program is the elaboration of a specification. A complete discussion of the concept of specification is beyond the scope of this book. In this chapter, the concept of specification is introduced (Section 2.1) and a precise and standard form for specifying logic procedures is presented and justified (Section 2.2). A description is then given of how a specification can be elaborated (Section 2.3).

2.1   The concept of specification

The word 'specification' can be used in many different ways in software engineering as well as in logic programming. It is therefore worth locating the proposed methodology, especially the specification stage, within the more general framework of the software life cycle. This section also presents the concept of a logic procedure, the basic block in the construction of logic programs.

2.1.1   Specification in the software life cycle

The phrase 'software life cycle' became popular in 1975–6. Before presenting this concept, let us first explain what software engineering is, using Boehm's definition (Boehm, 1976):

> 'Software engineering is the practical application of scientific knowledge in the design and construction of computer programs and the associated documentation required to develop, operate, and maintain them.'

This definition can be completed by saying that software engineering usually involves several people and programs that will be maintained in several versions (Parnas, 1983).

The development of large systems takes a considerable time and afterwards they are in use for an even longer time. Distinct stages in their development and usage can be identified. Together, they make up what is called the 'software life cycle'. There are many presentations of this life cycle, most of which can be encompassed in the following life cycle model (Sommerville, 1985).

(1)   *Requirement analysis*   The first stage of the software life cycle is to establish the requirement definition, that is, to set out the services provided for the user and the constraints under which the software must operate. The requirement definition (also called the requirement specification) describes what the software will do (but not how it will do it!).

(2)   *Design*   In the design phase, the requirement definition is analysed and the software components to provide the user services are designed. The internal structure of a software system is usually a decomposition into modules, each one of which is the responsibility of an individual or a small group. The design is expressed in such a way that these modules are relatively independent, more manageable than the complete requirement definition, and may be subsequently realized in some programming language. The result of the design phase is called the software design or the design specification.

(3)   *Implementation*   The implementation phase turns the design specification into code executable in the runtime environment (program development process). This entails defining the internal mechanisms by which each module will meet its specification.

(4)   *Testing*   The individual program units or programs are integrated and tested as a complete system to ensure that the software requirements have been met. Testing is usually broken down into three steps: **module testing**, which subjects each module to the test data supplied by the programmer; **integration testing**, which tests groups of components together, and **system testing**, which involves the test of the complete system by an outside group.

(5)   *Maintenance*   The system is installed and put into practical use. Maintenance involves correcting errors that were not discovered in earlier stages of the life cycle, improving the implementation of system units, and enhancing the system's services as new requirements are perceived.

A distinction is often made between **programming-in-the-small** (that is, the development of moderate-size programs within a few months), and **programming-in-the-large** (that is, the development of a large software system (DeRemer and Kron, 1975; Barstow, 1987)). Techniques for developing logic programs should be seen in a programming-in-the-small perspective although programming-in-the-large also includes program development.

In the above model, the word 'specification' is used in different phases with different meanings. The elaboration of the specification of a logic program is essentially part of the design phase of the software life cycle. The development of a logic program from the design specification of a component of the system (which, here, is called the 'specification') is mainly connected with the implementation phase of the software life cycle. In a multi-person perspective, four classes of people are concerned with such specifications. Firstly, the **specifier** him- or herself: that is, the person who elaborates the specification from a description of the problem. Secondly, the **implementer**: that is, the person who has to construct a logic program that respects the specification. Thirdly, the **user**: usually the person who wants to use the specified logic program when designing or implementing other parts of the system. Finally, let us not forget the **modifier** who is not necessarily the same person as the implementer.

Parnas' characterization of a specification (Parnas, 1972) is also especially instructive.

> 'The specification must provide
> > to the *intended user*
> > **all** the information that he will need to use the program correctly,
> > and **nothing more**.
>
> The specification must provide
> > to the *implementer*
> > **all** the information about the intended use that he needs to
> > complete the program,
> > and **no additional information**.'

A specification is an interface between the user and the implementer. For the user, a specification is a useful statement explaining how to utilize the program adequately and how to use it correctly, especially when designing others. A good specification should facilitate reasoning when constructing and proving other programs. The major qualities of a specification are simplicity and intelligibility.

2.1.2   Procedures in logic programming

The design phase of the software life cycle analyses the requirement specification and deduces objects, their types, and relations between these objects. In a logic programming perspective, the implementation step will construct logic procedures for the specified relations. It is therefore fair to consider the specification of a logic procedure as a specification unit in the implementation stage.

In this chapter, it will be sufficient to rely on the following characterization of a logic procedure. A **logic procedure** p (with arity *n*), or simply a **procedure**, is a sequence of program clauses (with or without negations) with the same predicate *p* (with arity *n*) in the head of each of these clauses. By extension, built-in procedures of the programming language are also called procedures. A logic program is then a set of logic procedures. The execution of a logic procedure for a given goal can be seen as computing a sequence of answer substitutions, called computed answer substitutions. This statement will be developed in detail in Chapter 7. At this specification level, the definition of substitutions and answer substitutions is necessary. These concepts are well known to Prolog programmers.

> **Definition 2.1** A **substitution** θ is a finite set of the form $\{V_1/t_1, \ldots, V_k/t_k\}$ where each V_i is a variable, each t_i is a term distinct from V_i, and the variables $V_1, \ldots, V_k$ are distinct. When E is an expression, Eθ is the expression obtained by simultaneously replacing each free occurrence of the variable V_i in E by the term t_i ($1 \leq i \leq k$).

> **Definition 2.2** An expression E is an **instance** of F iff there exists a substitution θ such that $E = F\theta$.

EXAMPLE 2.1

$\theta : \{X/f(Y), Y/a, Z/g(W)\}$
E : p(h(X), Y, W)
Eθ : p(h(f(Y)), a, W)
p(h(a), Y, a) is an instance of p(h(X), Z, X)

In Example 2.1, Eθ is *not* p(h(f(a)), a, W) since the replacement of X and Y by f(Y) and a in E is done simultaneously, and only once.

> **Definition 2.3** An **answer substitution** θ for a goal $\leftarrow$ p($A_1, \ldots, A_n$) is a substitution for variables occurring in $A_1, \ldots, A_n$.

An answer substitution is thus not necessarily the result of some computation. When this is the case, such a substitution will be called a **computed answer substitution**.

> **Definition 2.4** An expression E is **ground** if it does not contain variables. (By convention, variables begin with an uppercase letter.)

2.2 The general form of a specification

A framework for specifying logic procedures is described in Figure 2.1. It should be noticed that we are not concerned here with specifying a problem (requirement analysis level), but rather with specifying a procedure that solves the problem (design level).

The different parts of the specification act as preconditions or postconditions. A **precondition** is a condition that must be fulfilled before the execution of the procedure. A **postcondition** is a condition that will be fulfilled after the execution.

Specifications will sometimes be expressed differently (for example, in exercises), using an abbreviated form such as: $p(T_1, \ldots, T_n)$ holds iff $T_1, \ldots$ and T_n belong to p. The general specification schema will now be described and justified. A justification can be made at two levels. Firstly, each part of the specification can be justified on its own: does it contain pertinent information within the framework of logic programming? Secondly, the overall schema can be justified as a whole: does it contain sufficient information (complete specification)? Is there useless information (redundancy, noise, and so on)? Is this specification format useful in practice for specifying logic procedures and for constructing logic procedures from such specifications? A definitive answer can only be given after a complete description of the process of logic program development. The above questions are however discussed in the following subsections.

---

procedure $p(T_1, T_2, \ldots, T_n)$

Type: T_1 : type$_1$
       T_2 : type$_2$
       $\vdots$ $\vdots$
       T_n : type$_n$

Restriction on parameters:

Relation: Description of a relation p between the parameters T_1, $\ldots, T_n$.

Application conditions:
- directionality
- environment precondition

Side-effects:
- side-effects description

Figure 2.1   General form of a specification.

2.2.1 Types

The first part of a specification deals with type information. A type is assigned to each parameter. Let us now describe the role of type information and its utility.

The role of types

In the general form of a specification, type$_i$ is the name of a type set.

> **Definition 2.5**   A **type set** (or, briefly, a **type**) is a non-empty set of ground terms.

Examples of type sets are integers, lists, trees, booleans, and so on. This definition of a type set makes type information independent of the language used for describing types. There are no *a priori* constraints on different type sets; they are not necessarily disjoint, which allows subtypes (that is, subsets). The most general type set is of course the set of all the ground terms.

The type of parameters plays a dual role; it is a precondition and a postcondition on a goal $\leftarrow p(A_1, \ldots, A_n)$, where the A_i are the actual parameters, which may thus contain variables.

Types as precondition

When an actual parameter A_i is ground, it should respect the specified type (that is, $A_i \in$ type$_i$). For an actual parameter A_i containing variables, the weakest constraint is the existence of a ground instance of A_i belonging to type$_i$. Since variables can be shared between parameters, the precise type precondition can be stated as follows:

> Before the execution of the procedure, there must exist a ground instance of $\langle A_1, \ldots, A_n \rangle$ belonging to (type$_1 \times \ldots \times$ type$_n$).

If this type precondition is not fulfilled, then the convention adopted here is that the effect of the procedure execution is undefined. It is thus the user's responsibility to ensure that the type precondition is fulfilled before the execution of a procedure.

EXAMPLE 2.2

> $\langle X, [X \mid T] \rangle$ respects the types *integer* and *list*
> since, for instance $\langle 2, [2, a] \rangle \in (integer \times list)$
> $\langle T, [X \mid T] \rangle$ does not respect the types *integer* and *list*
> since no ground instance belongs to (*integer* $\times$ *list*); T cannot be instantiated to both an integer *and* a list with a single substitution.

Types as postcondition

The execution of a procedure produces answer substitutions, thus yielding instantiations (not necessarily ground) of the actual parameters

$A_1, \ldots, A_n$. Type information acts as a postcondition; it gives information about the type of the parameters after a successful execution of the procedure. More precisely:

> If θ is a computed answer substitution, then at least one ground instance of $\langle A_1, \ldots, A_n \rangle \, \theta$ belongs to ($type_1 \times \ldots \times type_n$).

Here it is the implementer's responsibility to make sure that this postcondition is respected. It is thus a characteristic of correct logic procedures, as described in more detail in Chapter 7.

The utility of types

The type specification of procedure parameters provides useful information. Without it, the relation described in the specification should be meaningful for any ground term. This may be difficult or even impossible in some cases (for example, the concatenation of non-list terms). For the user of a procedure, type specification describes the form of the parameters and thereby simplifies the reasoning about the procedure. For the implementer, types facilitate the construction of the procedure because they restrict the possible forms of the parameters (types as preconditions) and thereby avoid unnecessary and sometimes complex tests.

The necessity of types is sometimes a controversial issue. In the proposed specification framework, if types are not necessary or useful to a particular procedure, the type part of that procedure can be passed over. This expresses that all the parameters are terms, the most general type.

*Alternative conventions

The definition of type set could be extended to convey more formally the role of type information in a specification.

> **Definition 2.6**   Let t be a type set. The set t^* is the set of terms (ground and not ground) which have a ground instance belonging to t. More formally
>
> $$t^* = \{A \mid \exists \theta \quad A\theta \in t\}.$$

EXAMPLE 2.3

> $2 \in integer$, since 2 is a ground term which is an integer.
> $[a, b] \in list$, since $[a, b]$ is a ground term which is a list.
> $X \in integer^*$, since there exists a ground instance of X which is an integer.
> $[a \mid T] \in list^*$, since there exists a ground instance of $[a \mid T]$ which is a list (for example, $[a, b]$).

The type precondition can then be re-expressed as

$$\langle A_1, \ldots, A_n \rangle \in (\text{type}_1 \times \ldots \times \text{type}_n)^*$$

If θ is a computed answer substitution, the type postcondition can also be re-expressed as

$$\langle A_1, \ldots, A_n \rangle \, \theta \in (\text{type}_1 \times \ldots \times \text{type}_n)^*$$

Other conventions can be adopted for types as preconditions and postconditions. As a first choice of convention, it is the user's responsibility to ensure that the type precondition is fulfilled. Another convention could be that the procedure fails. This implies explicit type checking in the implementation. This is the traditional difference between a permissive and defensive programming style.

The definition of the set t^* is very general since it only requires at least one ground instance belonging to the set t. It could be required that *all* ground instances belong to t. The following set t^+ captures this distinction:

$$t^+ = \{A \mid \forall \theta \;\; A\theta \text{ ground} \Rightarrow A\theta \in t\}$$

As an alternative type precondition on the actual parameters, it could then be required that $\langle A_1, \ldots, A_n \rangle \in (\text{type}_1 \times \ldots \times \text{type}_n)^+$. As an alternative type postcondition, it could be required that, for every computed answer substitution θ, $\langle A_1, \ldots, A_n \rangle \, \theta \in (\text{type}_1 \times \ldots \times \text{type}_n)^+$. Such conventions could be taken as the type postconditions. They are, however, too restrictive for the type preconditions. For instance, if the type is *list of integers*, or even *integer*, then variables will be excluded as input parameters.

EXERCISES

2.1 Does the goal $\leftarrow p(X, [X \, 0 \, Y], f(X, Y))$ respect the type precondition of a procedure $p(\,T1, T2, T3\,)$ with type T1 integer, T2 list and T3 term?

Give examples of possible answer substitutions for this goal, assuming that the type postcondition is respected.

What about the goal $\leftarrow p(\,X, [X, Y \, 0 \, Y], Y\,)$?

*2.2 Show that, in general, the set $(\,t1^* \times t2^*\,)$ is different from the set $(\,t1 \times t2\,)^*$, where $t1$ and $t2$ are type sets.

*2.3 Find examples of type sets t such that $t^* = t^+$, and examples where $t^* \neq t^+$.

2.2.2　The domain of a procedure

Type information is not always sufficient for expressing that some *relation* between parameters must hold before the execution of a procedure. This can be handled by describing some *restrictions on the parameters*. For instance, it could be required that $A_1 > A_2$, where the type of A_1 and A_2 is integer. Such relations can be viewed as an extension of type information, thus acting as preconditions as well as postconditions. Such restrictions on parameters are of course optional. Type information and the restrictions on parameters define the *domain* of the procedure.

> **Definition 2.7**　The **domain** of (a procedure) p is the set of ground n-tuples $\langle t_1, \ldots, t_n \rangle$ such that
> - $\langle t_1, \ldots, t_n \rangle \in (\text{type}_1 \times \ldots \times \text{type}_n)$
> - $\langle t_1, \ldots, t_n \rangle$　satisfies the restrictions on the parameters

When there are no restrictions on the parameters, the domain of a procedure reduces to the types. Let us now systematize the role of the domain of a procedure.

> **Definition 2.8**　Let $A_1, \ldots, A_n$ be terms. $\langle A_1, \ldots, A_n \rangle$ is **compatible** with the domain of (the procedure) p iff there exists a ground instance of $\langle A_1, \ldots, A_n \rangle$ which is in the domain of p.

Henceforth, it will be assumed that the domain of a procedure is not empty. Note that in the above definition, the same ground instance verifies both the type *and* the restrictions on the parameters.

Domain as precondition
Before a procedure p can be excecuted, the actual parameters $\langle A_1, \ldots, A_n \rangle$ must be compatible with the domain of p. If this precondition is not fulfilled, the adopted convention is that the effect of the procedure is undefined.

Domain as postcondition
After a successful execution of a procedure, for a computed answer substitution θ, it is the case that $\langle A_1, \ldots, A_n \rangle \theta$ is also compatible with the domain of p. This characterizes the postcondition aspect.

2.2.3　Directionality

The directionality part of a specification is a description of the possible uses of the procedure. It describes the form of the actual parameters before and after the execution of a procedure. For each parameter, three possible forms have been retained: ground, variable and neither ground nor variable. They are represented by *ground*, *var* and *ngv*, respectively.

A **directionality** is denoted by

$$\text{in}(\ m_1, \ldots, m_n\ ) : \text{out}(\ M_1, \ldots, M_n\ )$$

where

- $m_i, M_i \neq \{\}$
- $m_i, M_i \subseteq \{\text{ground, var, ngv}\}$

For readability, each singleton $\{f\}$ will be notated as *f*. *Novar* is also defined as {ground, ngv}, *noground* as {var, ngv}, *gv* as {ground, var} and *any* as {ground, var, ngv}.

The **directionality of a procedure** p is a list of directionalities.

EXAMPLE 2.4

in(ground, var) : out(ground, ground)
in(var, ngv) : out(novar, ground)
in(ground, noground) : out(ground, novar)
in(ground, any) : out(ground, any)

The role of directionalities

Definition 2.9   Let $A_1, \ldots, A_n$ be terms. $\langle A_1, \ldots, A_n \rangle$ **satisfies the *in* part or *out* part of a directionality** in($m_1, \ldots, m_n$) : out($M_1, \ldots, M_n$) iff each A_i has one of the forms of the set m_i or M_i, respectively.

EXAMPLE 2.5

$\langle [H \mid T], [3] \rangle$ satisfies in(ngv, ground).
$\langle 8, [8, X], L \rangle$ satisfies out(any, noground, var).

Directionality as precondition

The directionality of a procedure forms a precondition on the possible patterns of actual parameters $A_1, \ldots, A_n$. They must satisfy the *in* part of at least one specified directionality. The adopted convention is that the effect of the procedure is undefined if this precondition is not fulfilled.

Directionality as postcondition

The directionality of a procedure also gives information on the form of the parameters after a successful execution. If the actual parameters $\langle A_1, \ldots, A_n \rangle$ satisfy the *in* part of a specified directionality, then $\langle A_1, \ldots, A_n \rangle \theta$ will satisfy the corresponding *out* part, where θ is a computed answer substitution.

It must be emphasized that the concept of directionality is different from Warren's modes which describe the ways in which a procedure is used in a particular Prolog program (Warren, 1977). Warren's modes are an *a posteriori* statement deduced (automatically or not) from the program. Modes are not related to specifications nor to the correctness of a procedure, but usually rather to code optimization.

The utility of directionalities

The necessity of a directionality description within a specification comes from the observation that fully multidirectional procedures are very rare in logic programming languages such as Prolog. The *in* parts of the specified directionalities of a procedure are therefore necessary because they specify for which directionalities the procedure is applicable. The *out* part provides helpful information when designing other procedures making use of this one. For instance in the clause

$$p(X, Y) \leftarrow q(X, Y), r(X, Y)$$

the *out* part of the directionality of q is necessary for showing that the procedure r(X, Y) is used correctly according to its directionality. The *out* part of a directionality can sometimes be deduced from the *in* part and the description of the relation. It is, however, more convenient to have it explicitly described. This simplifies the verification of logic procedures and allows some automation of the verification process.

Directionality has some similarities with type information. They both act as precondition as well as postcondition. However, a major difference is that type information is part of the logical aspect of the procedure whilst directionality is part of its procedural aspect.

The chosen form of the directionality description is a compromise between simplicity and expressive power. The choice of *ground, var* and *ngv* is not the only possible one. *Ground* and *var* were chosen because these two forms correspond to input and output parameters. They are theoretically sufficient to construct useful procedures. But they do not take into account one of the particularities of logic programming languages: a result can be partially computed (neither ground nor variable). This aspect is included in the directionality concept through the *ngv* form. More elaborate forms of parameters cannot be described with the proposed notation. For instance: 'Constant', 'Ground term but not constant', 'Structure whose arguments are all variables', 'Ngv term with only one variable', 'Ngv term whose variables are all different', and so on. Such information can sometimes be useful. Another limitation is that relations between the forms of parameters cannot be described. For instance: 'These two parameters do not have any variables in common', 'All the variables appearing in that parameter appear in this other one', and so on.

The possible forms of directionality were chosen for their simplicity and will be sufficient for most logic procedures. More elaborate directionality descriptions could not cover every possible case. Uncovered but useful distinctions will always subsist. If the directionality specification of a procedure requires a more elaborate description than can be expressed in the proposed notation, this can always be given by adding extra information in the directionality part to describe that particular case.

The consistency and minimality of a directionality

From the definition of a directionality, it can easily be seen that some combinations are impossible or contain useless information. For instance, in the directionality

in(ground, ground) : out(var, gv)

a first parameter which is ground cannot become a variable. The associated procedure is thus always required to fail. Besides this, the *out* part of the second parameter contains useless information. Gv is the abbreviation of {ground, var}, it thus specifies that after a successful execution of the associated procedure, the second parameter can be ground or a variable. But it cannot be a variable since it is known to be ground before the execution. Such a directionality will be called inconsistent and non-minimal, as formalized hereafter.

A total ordering $\leq_{ins}$ (reflexive, antisymmetric and transitive) can be defined over the set {ground, var, ngv} as follows:

$$\text{var} \leq_{ins} \text{ngv} \leq_{ins} \text{ground}$$

It expresses that a variable is 'less instantiated' than a term that is neither ground nor variable, which is in turn 'less instantiated' than a ground term. Since $\leq_{ins}$ is a total relation, every non-empty subset S of {ground, var, ngv} contains a minimum and a maximum denoted by min(S) and max(S), respectively.

> **Definition 2.10**   A directionality $in(m_1, \ldots, m_n) : out(M_1, \ldots, M_n)$ is **consistent** iff $\forall 1 \leq i \leq n : max(m_i) \leq_{ins} max(M_i)$.

Property 2.1

The consistency criterion can be restated as follows:

$$\forall 1 \leq i \leq n \; \forall x \in m_i \; \exists y \in M_i : x \leq_{ins} y$$

Proof

This condition is necessary since $\forall x \in m_i : x \leq_{ins} max(m_i)$ and $max(m_i) \leq_{ins} max(M_i)$ with $max(M_i) \in M_i$. Thus y can be taken as max(M_i). The condition is sufficient. Take max(m_i) as x, then max(m_i) $\leq_{ins} y_0$ for some $y_0 \in M_i$. Hence max(m_i) $\leq_{ins}$ max(M_i) since $y_0 \leq_{ins}$ max(M_i) by the definition of max. ∎

EXAMPLE 2.6

> in(ground) : out(ngv)   is inconsistent
> in(novar) : out(noground)   is inconsistent
>   (that is, in({ground, ngv}) : out({ngv, var}))
> in(any) : out(noground)   is inconsistent
> in(gv) : out(any)   is consistent

Inconsistent directionalities should be prevented. By the definition of a substitution, if A is a ground term, then so is Aθ, for any θ. If A is a variable, then Aθ can be a variable, a ground term or an ngv term, depending on θ. Finally, if A is an ngv term, Aθ is either a ground term or an ngv term. Therefore, if a condition max(m_k) $\leq_{ins}$ max(M_k) is not respected for some k, then $\exists x \in m_k$ such that $\forall y \in M_k : x >_{ins} y$. It can thus be said that, for some actual parameters satisfying the *in* part of this inconsistent directionality (that is, when A_k has the form x of M_k), there exists no substitution θ such that $\langle A_1, \ldots, A_n \rangle \theta$ satisfies the corresponding *out* part (that is, $A_k \theta$ cannot have one of the forms of M_k). Thus, the corresponding procedure always fails in such cases. This behaviour is very unlikely to be the intended one.

> **Definition 2.11**   A directionality in($m_1, \ldots, m_n$) : out($M_1, \ldots, M_n$) is **minimal** iff $\forall 1 \leq i \leq n : $ min(m_i) $\leq_{ins}$ min(M_i).

Property 2.2

The minimality criterion can be restated as follows:

> $\forall 1 \leq i \leq n \ \forall y \in M_i \ \exists x \in m_i : x \leq_{ins} y$

Proof
Similar to the proof of Property 2.1. ∎

When minimality is not achieved, one of the forms of a parameter in the *out* part of the directionality is 'less instantiated' than its corresponding form in the *in* part description. This form can therefore be suppressed without any loss of information. The suppression of such useless forms is called minimalization. It consists of suppressing all the elements of each M_i that are strictly smaller than the corresponding min(m_i). Minimalization should be restricted to consistent directionalities to avoid suppressing *all* the elements of M_i.

> **Definition 2.12**   Let $m, M \subseteq$ {ground, var, ngv}.
> **minimal(m, M)** = $\{y \in M : $ min(m) $\leq_{ins} y\}$

Definition 2.13 The **minimalization** of a consistent directionality in($m_1, \ldots, m_n$): out($M_1, \ldots, M_n$) is the directionality in($m_1, \ldots, m_n$): out($M'_1, \ldots, M'_n$) with $M'_i = $ minimal(m_i, M_i).

The above minimalization can also be used to extract more information from the *out* part of a directionality when the corresponding *in* part is satisfied by some actual parameters. For example, $\langle 3, \mathsf{X} \rangle$ satisfies the *in* part of the consistent and minimal directionality

    in(any, var) : out(novar, ground)

For any answer substitution θ computed by the associated procedure, $\langle 3, \mathsf{X} \rangle\,\theta$ will thus have the form $\langle$novar, ground$\rangle$. It is, however, obvious that this can be restricted to $\langle$ground, ground$\rangle$ since the first actual parameter is known to be ground.

More formally, when the actual parameters $\langle A_1, \ldots, A_n \rangle$ with forms $\langle f_1, \ldots, f_n \rangle$ satisfy the *in* part of a directionality

    in($m_1, \ldots, m_n$) : out($M_1, \ldots, M_n$)

then, for any answer substitution θ computed by the associated procedure, $\langle A_1, \ldots, A_n \rangle\,\theta$ will satisfy out($M'_1, \ldots, M'_n$) where $M'_i = $ minimal(f_i, M_i). Note that this statement can be immediately extended for f_is that are non-singletons.

*The compatibility of directionalities

In some cases, the actual parameters $\langle A_1, \ldots, A_n \rangle$ may satisfy the *in* part of more than one specified directionality. From the definitions, it is known that for every computed answer substitution θ, $\langle A_1, \ldots, A_n \rangle\,\theta$ will satisfy *all* the corresponding *out* parts. However, this can lead to another form of inconsistency, called incompatibility, between directionalities. The two simple directionalities that follow illustrate such an incompatibility.

    in(var) : out(ground)
    in(var) : out(ngv)

More formally, when the actual parameters $\langle A_1, \ldots, A_n \rangle$ with forms $\langle f_1, \ldots, f_n \rangle$ satisfy the *in* part of the directionalities

    in($m_1^1, \ldots, m_n^1$) : out($M_1^1, \ldots, M_n^1$)
       $\vdots$ $\vdots$ $\vdots$ $\vdots$
    in($m_1^p, \ldots, m_n^p$) : out($M_1^p, \ldots, M_n^p$)

then, for any answer substitution θ computed by the associated procedure, $\langle A_1, \ldots, A_n \rangle \theta$ will satisfy the form out$(M'_1, \ldots, M'_n)$ with

$$m'_i = \text{minimal}(f_i, \bigcap_{1 \leq k \leq p} m_i^k).$$

This statement can also be immediately extended for f_is that are non-singletons. If some M'_i is empty, the directionalities are said to be **incompatible**. No answer substitution can satisfy all the corresponding *out* parts.

The correctness of directionalities

The criteria that have been introduced can be used to define a notion of correctness for the specified directionality of a procedure.

> **Definition 2.14**   The directionality of a procedure (that is, a list of directionalities) is **correct** iff
>
> (1)   All the directionalities are consistent and minimal.
>
> (2)   The directionalities are not incompatible.

The correctness of directionalities can be verified automatically. Minimality is not essential, but minimal directionalities simplify the specification.

EXERCISES

*2.4 Prove Property 2.2.

*2.5 For each of the following directionalities, determine whether they are consistent and minimal.

> in(ground) : out(var)
> in(ngv) : out(noground)
> in(var) : out(any)
> in(novar) : out(gv)
> in(gv) : out(noground)
> in(noground) : out(ngv)
> in(any) : out(any)

*2.6 Show that the minimalization of a consistent directionality yields a consistent, minimal directionality.

*2.7 Determine the minimalization of the following directionalities:

> in(ground, ngv, novar) : out(novar, gv, any)
> in(ground, ngv, novar) : out(any, noground, gv)
> in(ngv, ground) : out(any, gv)

*2.8 What are all the possible values of m and M in the directionality in-(m) : out(M) in order that it be consistent and minimal?

2.2.4 Multiplicity

Another useful kind of information is the number of answer substitutions for a given procedure call. Such information can be used for proving termination and fairness of other procedures using the specified one. The convention taken here is to attach multiplicity information to each directionality by means of a couple $\langle Min–Max \rangle$ where *Min* and *Max* are, respectively, a *lower bound* and an *upper bound* to the number of answer substitutions for this directionality. The chosen possible values of the lower bound are the positive integers and infinity (denoted by ∞). The chosen possible values of the upper bound are the positive integers, the symbol * and infinity. For the upper bound, a positive integer also specifies that the execution terminates, the symbol * specifies that no upper bound is given, but the execution terminates, while ∞ specifies that the sequence of answer substitutions may be infinite. It is the implementer's responsibility to ensure this termination criterion. Multiplicity thus acts as a postcondition.

> **Definition 2.15**   Let *Subst* be a sequence (of length *Lg*) of answer substitutions. *Subst* **satisfies the multiplicity** $\langle Min–Max \rangle$ iff
>
> - $Min \leq Lg$
> - If $Max = *$, then *Lg* is finite, otherwise $Lg \leq Max$.

A multiplicity does not have to be attached to every directionality although an implicit (useless) $\langle 0–\infty \rangle$ can always be considered to be attached to the directionalities without any explicit multiplicity description. Example 2.7 presents some of the principal uses of multiplicity. In practice, integers other than 1 are seldom used.

EXAMPLE 2.7

    in(ground, var) : out(ground, ground) $\langle 1–1 \rangle$
        that is, total function characterization.
    in(ground, var) : out(ground, ground) $\langle 0–1 \rangle$
        that is, partial function characterization.
    in(any, ground) : out(any, ground) $\langle 0–* \rangle$
        that is, finite execution characterization.
    in(ngv, ground, var) : out(ground, ground, ngv) $\langle 2–2 \rangle$
        that is, fixed number of answer substitutions.
    in(any, var) : out(any, ground) $\langle 1–\infty \rangle$
        that is, always a solution.
    in(var, var) : out(ngv, ground) $\langle \infty–\infty \rangle$
        that is, infinite number of answer substitutions.

Multiplicity information is especially useful when the upper bound is not infinite. It is then known that the execution will terminate, which is essential for proving the termination of other procedures. In some cases, multiplicity can be deduced from the directionality and the description of the relation. However, multiplicity can show that an infinite number of possible solutions is actually covered by a finite sequence of answer substitutions. Multiplicity can also be used to express some functionality between parameters as shown in Example 2.7.

2.2.5 Relations

The central part of the specification of a logic procedure is of course the definition of the relation to be verified by the parameters. It is denoted p in the general specification form. This relational aspect is very specific to logic programming and relational programming. By a **relation** p, we mean a set of ground n-tuples. The specified relation will usually be a subset of the domain, but this is not required.

Role of relations

If the utility of the relation within the specification framework is obvious, it is worth detailing its role. Roughly speaking, the relation can be seen as a postcondition. It gives information on the parameters after a successful execution of the procedure: namely, that they belong to the specified relation. This should be further refined since there often exists more than one solution for a given goal, and variables may appear within the resulting parameters. Hence, every computed answer substitution yields correct solutions (**partial correctness** property), and all the possible correct solutions are covered by some computed answer substitution (**completeness** property). More precisely:

Let $\langle A_1, \ldots, A_n \rangle$ be actual parameters respecting the preconditions of the procedure, that is

- $\langle A_1, \ldots, A_n \rangle$ is compatible with the domain of the procedure, and
- $\langle A_1, \ldots, A_n \rangle$ satisfies the *in* part of a specified directionality.

The **correct solutions** are the ground instances of $\langle A_1, \ldots, A_n \rangle$ belonging to the domain and to the specified relation.

    Partial correctness: every computed answer substitution θ yields correct solutions, that is every ground instance of $\langle A_1, \ldots, A_n \rangle \theta$ belonging to the domain of the procedure also belongs to the specified relation.

    Completeness: all the correct solutions are covered by some computed answer substitution θ, that is every correct solution is a ground instance of $\langle A_1, \ldots, A_n \rangle \theta$ for some completed answer substitution θ.

It is the implementer's responsibility to ensure that the procedure satisfies these criteria. It is thus a characteristic of correct logic procedures.

    The role of the specified relation on the procedure efface(X, L, LEff) specified in Section 1.5 (Specification 1.1) will be illustrated. The goal

← efface(X, [1, 2, 3, 2, 4], [1 | T]) is compatible with the domain of efface and satisfies the *in* part of the directionality in(any, ground, any) : out(ground, ground, ground):

- A ground instance of $\langle X, [1, 2, 3, 2, 4], [1 | T] \rangle$ belongs to (term $\times$ list $\times$ list)
- [1, 2, 3, 2, 4] is ground

The set of correct solutions is the set

$$\{ \langle 2, [1, 2, 3, 2, 4], [1, 3, 2, 4] \rangle,$$
$$\langle 3, [1, 2, 3, 2, 4], [1, 2, 2, 4] \rangle,$$
$$\langle 4, [1, 2, 3, 2, 4], [1, 2, 3, 2] \rangle \}.$$

If the computed answer substitutions are

$$\theta_1 = \{ X/2, T/[3, 2, 4] \}$$
$$\theta_2 = \{ X/3, T/[2, 2, 4] \}$$
$$\theta_3 = \{ X/4, T/[2, 3, 2] \},$$

then every computed answer substitution yields correct solutions and all the correct solutions are covered by some computed answer substitution.

As another example, let us take the classical append(L1, L2, LApp) procedure which holds iff LApp is the concatenation of L1 and L2 (L1, L2 and LApp are lists). For the sake of simplicity, directionalities are not considered in this example. The goal ← append([X], L, LApp) is compatible with the domain of append: a ground instance of $\langle [X], L, LApp \rangle$ belongs to (list $\times$ list $\times$ list). The set of correct solutions is the set

$$\{ \langle [t], l, [t | l] \rangle \mid t \text{ is a ground term and } l \text{ is a ground list} \}.$$

Let the computed answer substitution be

$$\theta = \{ LApp/[X | L] \}.$$

Every computed answer substitution yields a correct solution: all ground instances of $\langle [X], L, LApp \rangle \theta = \langle [X], L, [X | L] \rangle$ belonging to the domain of efface (that is, L being instantiated to a list) are correct solutions. This illustrates the necessity of restricting the ground instances to those belonging to the domain of the procedure because some ground instances of $\langle [X], L, [X | L] \rangle$ are outside the specified types (that is, when L is instantiated to a non-list).

All the correct solutions are covered by some computed answer substitution. Obviously, any correct solution is an instance of $\langle [X], L, [X | L] \rangle$.

Definition of a relation

In the specifications proposed in this book, relations will be specified in natural language (together with some adequate notation depending on the application domain). It will now be argued that natural language is well-suited for such a task.

Prolog is not a specification language
It is generally admitted that programming languages like Pascal or LISP cannot be specification languages (Meyer, 1984; Liskov, 1975). There are no major differences between Prolog code and code in other programming languages. The understanding of a Prolog program requires the procedural semantics (because of the differences between the declarative and the procedural semantics). This is not easy for a complex Prolog procedure with control information and extralogical features. Moreover, to understand such a procedure requires a knowledge of the procedures used inside its code. But then their 'specification' also reduces to Prolog code! Such a specification concept is far away from the idea of specification as a useful statement explaining how to utilize a procedure adequately and correctly, especially when designing other procedures.

Formal versus informal specification
The approach taken for specifying relations (natural description augmented with appropriate notations) may appear controversial and is apparently opposed to the current trend of making program specifications more and more formal, and of introducing such formalism earlier in the development process (Balzer *et al.*, 1983; Zave, 1984). It is often argued that a specification should be written in a formal specification language (Liskov, 1975; Parnas, 1977; Balzer *et al.*, 1983). Examples of formal specification languages are Z (Abrial, 1980), Clear (Burstall and Goguen, 1980), Larch (Guttag, 1977), Msg (Berzins and Gray, 1985), Gist (Feather, 1983) and others (Guttag, 1977; Goguen *et al.*, 1978; Thatcher *et al.*, 1982; Nordström and Smith, 1984; etc.). A formal specification language has a precise and unambiguous semantics and is thereby easy to communicate. A formal specification allows automatic analysis such as completeness and consistency verification. Formal specifications can even be their own prototypes and can become implementations (Balzer *et al.*, 1983). At the very least, a prototype can be deduced and code generation thereby simplified. Finally, formal proof techniques can be used to verify the correctness of a program with respect to its formal specification.

Let us clarify some common misunderstandings. The words 'informal statements' are often understood to mean imprecise statements. But this is not correct. An informal statement is just a statement in a *non-formalized* language. Another misconception associates an informal statement or a statement in natural language with a text in plain

English. But natural language does not exclude the definition of appropriate concepts and notations, developed on an *ad hoc* basis. Finally, a formal language is not just a set of notations; its syntax and semantics must be defined precisely. Moreover, if it allows the definition of new notations, this must be done within the formal language using only its semantics. If this is not the case, it is not a formal language any more.

It should first be noted that the semantics of a formal specification language must be defined. Such a definition must use natural language (another formal language defining the specification language only postpones the problem to the definition of this new definition language). Natural language is precise enough to describe the 'specification' of the formal language without ambiguity. Moreover, whatever formalization stages might be used later, in practice natural language is almost always the medium in which an application is first conceived.

If a formal language is unambiguous and precise, the price to pay is the limitation of its power of expression. If something can be expressed, it is often differently from the way the specifier wanted to express it. As pointed out in Balzer *et al.* (1978), the creation of a formal specification involves spreading implicitly specified information throughout the specification and increasing the complexity by structuring the specification into parts and establishing the necessary interface between them. This greatly impedes the ability to understand and modify the specification. The expression of a relation in a formal specification language will not be easy. Some conventions must be used to represent objects not belonging to the language. The specification is thus 'coded' in the particular formal language. The construction of a specification is almost as difficult as the construction of a program. In an evaluation of the formal specification language Gist, it has been said that the experience with Gist has not always reflected the expectations. Although Gist was designed to be a specification language, formal specifications written in it, like those in all other formal specification languages, tend to be hard to understand (Feather, 1984).

By this argument, formal specification languages do not appear to be the ultimate solution for writing specifications. But is natural language better adapted for this difficult task? Natural language can be augmented by any appropriate notations useful for the given problem, and it has no limitations of expression. The specification therefore does not have to be encoded in a particular formalism, and so the resulting specification will be closer to the idea the specifier has in mind. Such a specification will be easier to understand than a formal one. If it is possible to use natural language ambiguously, it is also possible to use it very precisely. So informal statements can be at least as precise as formal ones.

The concept of specification is related to program correctness. A program is correct *with respect to* its specification. A correctness proof tries to show the consistency of a program with respect to its specification. But with an informal specification, is it possible to establish the correctness of a program with certainty? Of course not. If a proof of its correctness is given, it should also be proven that the proof is correct, and so on. The goal of a correctness proof is thus to convince oneself that a program is correct with respect to its specification. With a formal specification, it is possible to define a formal system such that the correctness proof of the program is reduced to a formal proof in that system. But there is also some uncertainty here. This uncertainty does not lie in the fact that the program is correct with respect to its formal specification, but rather in whether the formal specification really represents what it is intended to represent. As pointed out in Liskov (1975), there is no formal way of establishing that a formal specification captures a concept. The difficulty with correctness proofs is also developed in Mills (1975).

Logic specifications
The use of formal logic as a specification language is common in logic programming. Such formal specifications are called **logic specifications**. In Winterstein *et al.* (1980), for instance, the derivation of different unification algorithms from a logic specification is presented. The main emphasis is to show that predicate logic may also serve as a specification language for software engineering. But the logic specification is a translation in Horn clauses of Robinson's unification algorithm. The use of Horn clauses to describe an algorithm cannot transform it into a specification! In the logic programming community, distinctions are rarely made between a description in logic of an algorithm and a specification as a statement of *what* the algorithm is expected to do.

The concept of a logic specification is misleading. On the one hand, it is regarded as a real specification, so that it is the description of the problem to be solved. On the other hand, a logic specification is a partial description of an algorithm solving the problem. So it can be executed by introducing suitable control information, and only needs to be transformed for efficiency reasons, yielding the final program. Thus a logic specification has the double property of defining a problem and solving it. A logic specification reduces the problem of program construction to the introduction of control and program transformation, thus skipping one of the major steps: the construction of that first formal logic description of a solution. Note that it is not being argued that formal languages (and thus logic) are useless, only that they are not always well-adapted as *specification* languages. An informal specification can be transformed into a formal one in order to analyse some of its contents, or to facilitate the construction of a program. But then it cannot be considered as a specification any more, but rather as the result of a first programming step. The construction of a first-order logic statement from an informal specification is thus seen as a first programming step.

2.2.6   Environment precondition and side-effects description

In Chapter 1, the necessity of input–output logic procedures was pointed out. It is impossible to specify them only in terms of a relation between their parameters, a description of their input–output side-effects is also required. Side-effects are expressed in a separate part of the specification to point out the non-logical aspect of such procedures. Procedures with side-effects will receive special attention in their construction.

The side-effects description acts as a postcondition since it specifies a condition that will be satisfied after the execution of the procedure. The specification of side-effects is a difficult task, especially when the sequence of answer substitutions has more than one element. In such cases, is the side-effect related to the first of them, or to all of them? What about infinite sequences of answer substitutions? For simplicity, the multiplicity of procedures with side-effects could be described by $\langle 0–1 \rangle$ or $\langle 0–* \rangle$, it will simplify their construction. This is only a suggestion, as some side-effect procedures could require more than one answer substitution or even an infinite number of answer substitutions. Given that only a few procedures have side-effects, the omission of the side-effect part of a specification will imply no side-effects.

The environment of a procedure contains other logic procedures as well as non-logical aspects such as files, input–output devices, and so on. The environment precondition specifies conditions that the environment of the procedure must satisfy before the execution of the procedure. This is often necessary for side-effect procedures but also for some procedures without side-effects (for example, a coherent database as an environment precondition for procedures dealing with databases). If these preconditions are not satisfied before the execution of the procedure, the effect of the procedure will be undefined.

2.2.7   The role of a specification: summary and examples

Table 2.1 summarizes the role of the different parts of a specification. Substitutions θ within the table symbolize answer substitutions computed by a procedure implementing the specification. Examples of specifications will appear throughout the book. It is shown here that system predicates can also be specified using the proposed framework.

In Specification 2.1, a well-defined arithmetic expression is an arithmetic expression without division by 0. The effect of the execution of the goal $\leftarrow$ X is 3/0 is thus undefined. This specification assumes that the Prolog system under consideration has no error recovery in the case of division by 0. The given multiplicity $\langle 0–1 \rangle$ is somehow redundant with the rest of the specification but underlines the deterministic behaviour of this procedure. Specification 2.2 illustrates the specification of environment preconditions and side-effects. In order to be complete in the

Table 2.1   Role of a specification: summary.

Specification part	Role	
Domain (Type + restrictions on parameters)	*precondition*:	$\langle A_1, \ldots, A_n \rangle$ compatible with the domain of p
	postcondition:	$\langle A_1, \ldots, A_n \rangle \theta$ compatible with the domain of p
Relation	*postcondition*:	**Partial correctness**: all ground instances of $\langle A_1, \ldots, A_n \rangle \theta$ in the domain of p belong to the specified relation **Completeness**: every correct solution is a ground instance of $\langle A_1, \ldots, A_n \rangle \theta$ for some computed answer substitution θ
Directionality	*precondition*:	$\langle A_1, \ldots, A_n \rangle$ satisfies the *in* part of a specified directionality
	postcondition:	$\langle A_1, \ldots, A_n \rangle \theta$ satisfies the corresponding *out* part
Multiplicity	*postcondition*:	The sequence of computed answer substitutions satisfies the specified multiplicity
Environment precondition	*precondition*	
Side-effects	*postcondition*	

specification of get0(C), the concept of current character, current input stream and the type character should be defined precisely.

> procedure   X is Exp
>
> *Type*:   X : Integer
>   Exp : Arithmetic expression
>
> *Relation*:   X is the value of Exp.
>
> *Application conditions*:
> in(any, ground) : out(ground, ground) $\langle 0-1 \rangle$
>
> **Specification 2.1**   X is Exp

> procedure   get0(C)
>
> *Type*:   C : Character
>
> *Relation*:   C is the current character of the Current Input Stream (CIS).
>
> *Application conditions*:
> • in(any) : out(ground) $\langle 0-1 \rangle$
> • The current character of the CIS must be defined

Side-effects:
- If the current character of CIS is not the special character *end_of_file*, then the character following the current character becomes the new current character
- If the current character of CIS is the *end_of_file* character, the current character becomes undefined

Specification 2.2 get0(C)

2.2.8 Limitations and extensions

The proposed specification framework is not always suited to the specification of logic procedures. The concepts introduced have to be adapted and extended in some cases. Other notations or conventions can be used provided they can simplify the specification. Of course, notations and conventions must be described precisely. It is not claimed that the chosen conventions are always the best ones. The chosen approach has been to keep the specification framework general but simple, covering most procedures. Here follow some extensions that can be useful in certain procedure specifications.

- Extension of the possible different forms of parameters within ngv.
- Combination of type information and directionality (for example, in([any, . . . , any]) specifies that before execution, the actual parameter is a list of fixed length whose arguments are terms of any form).
- Relation between the form of a parameter in the *in* part and in the *out* part of a directionality (for example, in(ngv) : out(unchanged) could specify that computed answer substitutions do not affect this parameter).
- Definition of pre- and postconditions for each directionality.
- Definition of pre- and post environment conditions.
- Insertion of examples within the specification.

Specification 2.3 illustrates how the defined concepts can be applied to specify a procedure for which the specification framework, as presented, is not particularly adapted.

procedure var(T)

The behaviour of this procedure is characterized by the following directionalities:

in(var) : out(var) $\langle 1-1 \rangle$ with answer substitution $\theta = \{\}$
in(novar) $\langle 0-0 \rangle$

Specification 2.3 var(T)

2.3 Elaboration of a specification

Specification writing is not the ultimate goal, it is only a step towards the realization of a program. The elaboration of a specification will not only appear in the first stage of program development, it will also take a prominent part recursively in the construction process. The design of a program is actually a sequence of specification and construction steps. The top-down model characterizing such a sequence is presented first. Then the concept of data abstraction, which is also important in the elaboration of specifications, will be described through a small example. Finally, the elaboration of suitable directionalities within a specification is dealt with.

2.3.1 Top-down methodology

Why do we need specifications? It is easy to understand the role of a specification for a procedure or program that will be constructed, used, or modified by someone else. But even if the programmer of a procedure is the only user, a specification is useful. Of course he or she knows what the procedure is expected to do. But a specification is a memorandum so that the code need not be reanalysed every time in order to discover some forgotten details that are necessary if the procedure is to be used correctly or modifed (for example, the order and semantics of the parameters, correct directionality, and so on). This shows the utility of a specification for an existing procedure.

Specifications are also necessary within the construction process. Observe first that it is easier to develop a 'small' correct program than a 'big' one. 'Small' programs represent the limit of what it is possible to do rigorously. In fact, the construction of a 'big' program is not manageable if an attempt is made to do it directly. A possible way of constructing a 'big' program is to decompose it into smaller pieces. The construction of the program is then possible because the specification of these pieces allows them to be used as primitive procedures of the language, independently of the complexity of their implementation. The construction of the initial program is therefore conceptually as easy as the construction of a 'small' program. This is the basic idea behind **top-down** programming. The construction of a program requires the specification of procedures which will be considered as atomic actions when designing the program. These new procedures will be developed similarly until the procedures obtained are so simple that it is possible to construct them directly by means of the built-in primitives of the language.

The top-down approach describes a recursive application of specification and construction steps. In the construction of a procedure, useful subproblems must be 'guessed'. The choice of these subproblems can be guided by two criteria. Firstly, the subproblems should be helpful when constructing either the initial procedure being considered or other ones in a reusability perspective. Secondly, it must be possible to construct procedures that realize the specified subproblems.

A top-down methodology is in fact not a pure top-down decomposition. There is an inevitable intertwining of specification and implementation as described in Swartout and Balzer (1982). A specification must sometimes be reconsidered during the implementation phase for two major reasons. When a procedure satisfying a specification cannot be constructed, the previous steps of the global construction process have to be reconsidered; either specifications must be modified or new specifications must be designed. Specifications should also be modified when a specified subproblem has some undesirable effects or is useless for constructing a procedure. This is possible since it is sometimes difficult to foresee all the implications and interactions of the specified subproblems. There are thus more intertwined relationships between specification and implementation than the traditional top-down model would have us believe. An explicit separation of specification and implementation, together with a pure top-down presentation, can only be made afterwards. Hence the maxim

'Everything should be built top-down, except the first time.'

The implementation of a top-down design methodology in a particular programming language principally depends on two things. Firstly, a written procedure should not be significantly changed if the context in which it is used is modified. Secondly, the interface between the procedure and its users must be simple. Like most programming languages, logic programming languages are well-adapted to supporting a top-down approach. The interface for a procedure is simple, and there are no syntactic or semantic differences between constructed procedures and built-in procedures. Thus, every procedure can be seen as a new primitive of the language. Concerning the independence of a procedure from the environment in which it is used, the only problem is the possible conflict of procedure names. A careful choice of procedure names can overcome this, but an ideal solution is the concept of modules within the logic programming language.

A top-down approach is not the only possible one. Another model is the **bottom-up** construction process, which starts by constructing 'small' pieces that realize useful operations. Other pieces can then be constructed using the smaller ones, until the initial problem to be solved is reached. The bottom-up approach puts the emphasis on the general utility and reusability of the pieces, sometimes to the detriment of the initial problem to be solved. A top-down decomposition underlines the utility of a subproblem in constructing a particular procedure, sometimes at the expense of generality and reusability.

2.3.2 Data abstraction

Procedural abstraction is very useful in program development. It allows the subproblems to be seen as primitives of the language, independently of the complexity of their implementation. Since programs manipulate objects, the development of programs also involves the definition of objects or data types. If the programming language possesses the required data types, the developer's task is simplified. But such data types are usually more abstract than those available in the language, and depend on the application domain. The extension of the primitive data types with new types (just as procedural abstraction extends the primitives of the language) is called **data abstraction**. The definition of these abstract objects (called **abstract data types**) usually also involves the specification of operations manipulating these objects.

As with the decomposition of procedures, abstract data types must be refined into existing or concrete data types. This process is often called **data refinement** or **data reification**. The relationship between abstract data types and their representation can be expressed by a function mapping the concrete objects to the abstract ones. This **abstraction function** is also sometimes called the **retrieve function**. In order to obtain an adequate representation, it must be possible to represent every abstract data type by a concrete one. Two different abstract objects are always represented differently because the retrieve mapping is a function.

Data abstraction is parallel to the top-down decomposition of procedures. A programmer using an abstract object does not need to know how it is represented nor how its associated operations are implemented. The internal details of object representation and manipulation can then be modified or changed without affecting the other components of the system. Data abstraction is thus also particularly useful during program modification and maintenance.

EXERCISES

2.9 Consider the abstract data type *Rational*. Assuming that your Prolog handles integers, specify useful operations for this abstract data type. Define different Prolog representations for rationals and their corresponding retrieve function. Discuss the advantages and disadvantages of the different representations.

*2.10   What are the advantages and disadvantages of one-to-one compared to many-to-one retrieve functions in the context of logic programming? (*Hint*: what about equality and unification?)

2.3.3   Specifying a directionality

Since the concept of directionality is specific to logic programming, it is worth considering how an appropriate directionality can be attached to a specification. Two cases are analysed, depending on the existence of a given specification.

Suppose, first af all, that a specification exists and that the implementer's task is to construct a procedure respecting the given specification. In such a case, the specification already contains the *in* part of the directionalities for which the procedure is required to be correct. The *out* part, as well as the associated multiplicity, are usually added by the implementer after the completion of the construction, in order to give useful information to the potential users of the procedure. If the constructed procedure is also proven to be correct for other directionalities, these can be added to the initial ones, thus extending the possible uses of the procedure.

Next suppose that a subproblem is being specified during the construction of a procedure. The directionality to be attached to this specification will usually depend on how and where this subproblem will be used within the procedure under construction. Since the actual position of a subproblem in procedure clauses is a procedural feature, such a directionality can be specified only during the last step of the construction of the procedure (that is, the derivation of a logic procedure from a logic description). However, the temporary absence of a directionality for the subproblem does not prevent its logical construction since the construction of a logic description is independent of directionalities.

*2.4   Background

Rather than referring to the literature of software engineering and program correctness where the concept of specification is mainly developed, this section is oriented towards the logic programming literature. It is worth underlining that the viewpoint given here on the concept of specification, its nature and its role is inspired by Le Charlier's thesis on program correctness (Le Charlier, 1985). Classical papers on software specification techniques can be found in Gehani and McGettrick (1986). For further developments on data abstraction, see Hoare (1972), Guttag (1979), Jones (1980, 1986), Fairley (1985) and Liskov and Guttag (1986).

Life-cycle models

The described life-cycle model was first proposed by Royce (1970). For further development and variants of the model, see Boehm (1976, 1981), Zelkowitz (1978), Janssen and Tonies (1979), Fairley (1985), Sommerville (1985) and Macro and Buxton (1987). Besides this conventional software life cycle, another approach (called the operational approach) has recently been proposed (Zave, 1984). A similar approach has also been described in Balzer *et al.* (1983). Their model is based on executable specifications and program transformation.

Examples of specification

Two specifications of the efface(X, L, LEff) procedure extracted from the Prolog programming literature are reproduced in Examples 2.8 and 2.9.

EXAMPLE 2.8

> 'Deleting one element: the goal efface(X, Y, Z) removes the first occurrence of element X from list Y, giving a new effaced list Z. If there is no such X in list Y, the predicate fails.' (Clocksin and Mellish, 1984, p. 151.)

EXAMPLE 2.9

> 'efface(X, Xs, Ys) ←
> Ys is the list obtained by removing the first occurrence of X in the list Xs.'
> (Sterling and Shapiro, 1986, p. 113.) (The original name *select-_first* has been changed for ease of comparison.)

The proposed code for the specification of Example 2.8 is equivalent to Procedure 1.2, and for the specification of Example 2.9 to Procedure 1.3. These two programs are correct for the directionalities

    in(ground, ground, var) : out(ground, ground, ground)
    in(ground, ground, any) : out(ground, ground, ground)

respectively. Other uses lead to incorrect results. This essential information is not included in these specifications, although it is stated elsewhere in Sterling and Shapiro's text, in the program analysis. If the procedure code has to be analysed to deduce such information, then the specification is incomplete. Notice that the specification in Example 2.9 is more relational than in Example 2.8 where it is essentially operational. The word 'predicate' is also somehow inappropriate in a specification. The notion of success or failure is relative to the execution of a procedure, not to a predicate.

Directionality

The concept of directionality in logic programming is not new. The originality of the approach taken here is its attachment to a specification. The notion of 'mode' was introduced by Warren (1977) in order to talk about the ways in which a procedure is used in a Prolog program. The initial objective was code optimization. Similar ideas are presented in Mellish (1981, 1985), Debray and Warren (1986a, 1986b), etc. Notations for describing some forms of directionality or multiplicity are also present in, amongst others, Bruynooghe (1982), Shoham and McDermot (1984), Reddy (1984), Dembinski and Maluszynski (1985) and Nakamura (1986). Here, directionality declarations expressing control information for the interpreter (for example, IC-PROLOG, MU-PROLOG and PARLOG) are not investigated.

Types

The introduction of types into logic programming has already been seen in Clark and Tärnlund, 1977). Some logic programming languages are typed languages. For instance, the EQLOG language is based on many-sorted Horn clause logic with equality (Goguen and Meseguer, 1984, 1985). Turbo PROLOG imposes types for very pragmatic reasons.

Types are mostly discussed in the logic programming literature through object-oriented and modular logic programming, as well as type inference. Research is currently under way to integrate an object-oriented approach or modules within a logic programming language (Feuer, 1983; Furukawa and Nakajima, 1983; Kawanobe, 1984; Zanioli, 1984; Mizoguchi *et al.*, 1984; Chomicki and Minsky, 1985; Aït-Kaci and Nasr, 1986b; Sannella and Wallen, 1987). Type inference systems have been developed within the context of functional programming (Milner, 1978; Mycroft, 1984; Mishra and Reddy, 1985). Within the framework of logic programming, types and type inference are discussed in, amongst others, Mycroft and O'Keefe (1983), Milner (1978), Kanamori and Fujita (1984), Bruynooghe (1982), Haridi and Sahlin (1983), Mishra (1984), Aït-Kaci and Nasr (1986a, 1986b), Gang and Zhiliang (1986), Naish (1987), Zobel (1987), Kluźniak (1987) and Yardeni and Shapiro (1987).

SUMMARY

- A specification is an interface between the implementer and the user, providing all the information needed to complete a program and to use it correctly.
- A procedure specification principally contains type information (defining the domain of the procedure), the definition of a relation and directionalities.

- Type information is used before and after the execution of a procedure.
- A directionality specifies a possible use of a procedure. It describes the possible forms of the parameters (ground, var, ngv) before and after the execution of the procedure.
- The specification of a relation can be made in natural language augmented with appropriate notations.
- A top-down methodology is appropriate for the elaboration of specifications.

PART II

Logic Descriptions

The second step of logic program development deals with the construction of a logic description from a specification. This step is one of the most creative ones. The construction of a logic description is based on the declarative semantics of logic and is independent of the target logic programming language as well as of the procedural semantics. Therefore, only the logical parts of a specification (types, other preconditions, and relations) will be used in this construction process. Thus, in the specifications to be considered here, neither application conditions nor side-effects are dealt with.

Chapter 3 introduces first-order logic and its declarative semantics. The general form of a logic description is also presented. As soon as the construction of logic descriptions is considered, the concept of correctness must also be dealt with: what does it mean for a logic description to be correct with respect to its specification? Such a definition of correctness is presented in Chapter 4. The major chapter of this part, Chapter 5, is concerned with the construction of logic descriptions. This construction is based on structural induction and the generalization paradigm. It will be shown that the constructed logic descriptions are correct by construction. They can then be transformed by means of transformation rules (Chapter 6). The construction techniques presented are independent of the overall methodology in the sense that they can successfully be applied to logic program construction in other methodological approaches.

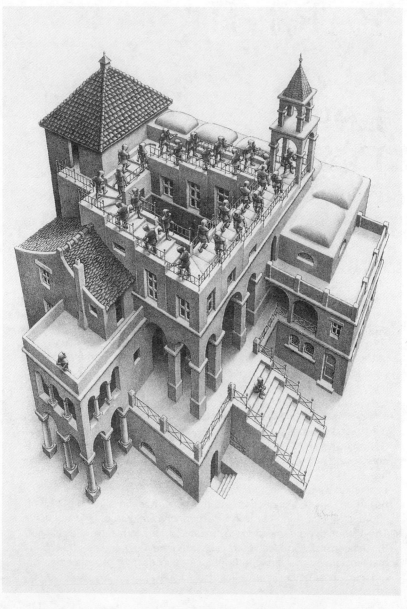

Ascending and descending, M. C. Escher (1960). Collection Haags Gemeentemuseum, The Hague. © 1989 M. C. Escher Heirs/Cordon Art, Baarn, Holland

3

Declarative semantics
of first-order logic

PREVIEW   Logic is often defined as the study of reasoning. It is used to formalize and symbolize reasoning. First-order logic is without doubt one of the oldest and most developed logic formalisms. It will be used here to formalize algorithms.

There are two aspects to first-order logic: model theory and proof theory. Model theory is the study of the meaning of logic sentences (semantical study). It is concerned with 'what follows from what'. Proof theory is the study of axioms and theorems as logic sentences (syntactical study). It is concerned with 'what can be deduced'. The declarative semantics of logic programming languages is in the model theory while the procedural semantics is in the proof theory. At this logic description level, we adopt a pure model-theoretic approach. This chapter is structured as follows:

- First-order language: definition of the form of sentences (Section 3.1).

- Interpretations and models: definition of the meaning of sentences (Section 3.2).

- Logical consequences: analysis of 'what follows from what' (Section 3.3).

- General form of a logic description (Section 3.4).

The approach taken here, which differs from that of the classical first-order logic used in logic programming, is as follows:

- A first-order language is defined outside particular first-order theories. Therefore, every logic description will have the same underlying first-order language. This simplifies the theory of the construction of logic descriptions.

- Interpretations are restricted to Herbrand interpretations since general interpretations are not required within the context of algorithm formalization.

59

3.1   First-order language

Let us first define the form of the sentences, called formulae, in first-order logic. A **first-order language** consists of well-formed formulae constructed with the symbols of the language (called the alphabet). The following definitions are partly based on Lloyd (1987).

Alphabet

An **alphabet** is composed of six disjoint sets of symbols: variable symbols, function symbols, predicate symbols, connectives, quantifiers and punctuation symbols. The sets of function and predicate symbols are usually decomposed into n-ary function symbol sets and n-ary predicate symbols sets, where n is a positive integer. These sets are fixed here once and for all, as is the first-order language.

> **Definition 3.1**
> - The **set of variable symbols** is composed of finite strings of letters and digits beginning with an uppercase letter.
> - The **sets of n-ary function symbols** and **n-ary predicate symbols** are composed of finite strings of letters, digits and special characters, not beginning with an uppercase letter. Each string will be subscripted with $\langle \text{function}, n \rangle$ in the n-ary function symbol set, and with $\langle \text{predicate}, n \rangle$ in the n-ary predicate symbol set. 0-ary function symbols are also called **constants**. The set of binary predicate symbols is augmented with the symbol '=' (for equality), the set of constants with the symbol '[]' (for the empty list), and the set of binary function symbols with the symbol '•' (for lists).
> - The **set of connectives** is $\{\neg, \&, \vee, \Rightarrow, \Leftrightarrow\}$.
> - The **set of quantifiers** is $\{\forall, \exists\}$.
> - The **punctuation symbols** are '(',')' and ','.

Note that for each n, the set of n-ary function symbols and the set of n-ary predicate symbols are infinite but countable. In what follows, variable symbols, function symbols and predicate symbols will simply be called variables, functions and predicates.

Well-formed formulae

Definition 3.2   A **term** is defined inductively as follows:

- A variable is a term.
- If f is an n-ary function and $t_1, \ldots, t_n$ are terms then $f(t_1, \ldots, t_n)$ is a term.

Definition 3.3 A **(well-formed) formula** is defined inductively as follows:

- If p is an *n*-ary predicate and $t_1, \ldots, t_n$ are terms
  then p($t_1, \ldots, t_n$) is a formula (called an **atomic formula** or **atom**).
- If F and G are formulae
  then $\neg$F, (F & G), (F $\vee$ G), (F $\Rightarrow$ G) and (F $\Leftrightarrow$ G) are formulae.
- If F is a formulae and X is a variable
  then ($\forall$X)F and ($\exists$X)F are formulae.

Definition 3.4 A **literal** is an atom, or the negation of an atom. A **positive literal** is an atom. A **negative literal** is the negation of an atom.

Definition 3.5 The **first-order language** is the set of all formulae.

The informal semantics of connectives and quantifiers is as follows: $\neg$ means negation (not), & means conjunction (and), $\vee$ means disjunction (or), $\Rightarrow$ means implication (implies, or if... then), $\Leftrightarrow$ means equivalence (is equivalent to, or iff). $\exists$ is the existential quantifier (there exists ... such that) and $\forall$ is the universal quantifier (for all).

Conventions
- For a 0-ary function f (constant) and 0-ary predicate p, we will write f and p rather than f( ) and p( ).
- For readability the _ character can be inserted anywhere in the middle of variables, functions and predicates.
- The sets of *n*-ary functions and *n*-ary predicates are disjoint (because of their subscripts). When writing formulae, these subscripts will be dropped. The distinction between functions and predicates will be clear in every formula. Moreover, the arity is also unambiguous. But if the same string stands for a predicate and a function (or two predicates or functions with different arity) they are conceptually different because of their virtual subscripts.
- The terms $\bullet$(t1, t2) will be written as [t1 | t2] and $\bullet$(e_1, $\bullet$(e_2, ..., $\bullet$(e_n, [ ]) ...)) as [e_1, e_2, ..., e_n], where t1, t2, e_1, ..., e_n are terms.
- The literals =(t1, t2) and $\neg$=(t1, t2) will be written as t1 = t2 and t1 $\neq$ t2 where t1 and t2 are terms.
- The formula (F $\Rightarrow$ G) can also be written as (G $\Leftarrow$ F).

- To avoid having formulae cluttered with brackets, the following precedence hierarchy will be adopted, with the highest precedence at the top. A left to right precedence is also adopted for connectives on the same level.

$$\neg, \forall, \exists$$
$$\&$$
$$\vee$$
$$\Rightarrow, \Leftrightarrow$$

- **w, x, y, z** will denote n-tuples of variables and **s, t** n-tuples of terms. x_i and s_i denote the ith element of **x** and **s**, respectively.

EXAMPLE 3.1

> X, Toto, Y32aB, Head_of_List   are variables
> a, 18, toto, y32aB, void, [ ]   are constants
> f(a), gag_1(8, Y), [Head | T], [a, b, c]   are terms
> p, q(f(a)), minus(X, s(18), Y32ab)   are atoms
> p & q(f(Y)) $\Rightarrow$ p   is a formula
> ($\forall$X) (X $\neq$ f(a) $\Leftarrow$ $\neg$r(X, f(a)))   is a formula
> ($\forall$X $\exists$Y $\forall$Z) (q(X) & r(Y, Z))   is a formula

We will need some other definitions.

Definition 3.6   The **scope** of ($\forall$X) (or ($\exists$X)) in a formula ($\forall$X)F (or ($\exists$X)F, respectively) is the formula F.

Definition 3.7   An occurrence of a variable X in a formula F is a **bound occurrence** (in F) if it occurs in a part of F of the form ($\forall$X)G or ($\exists$X)G; otherwise it is a **free occurrence** (in F).

Definition 3.8   A variable X is **bound** (or **free**) in a formula F iff some occurrence of X is bound (or free, respectively) in F.

Definition 3.9   A formula F is **quantifier free** iff it does not contain any quantifiers.

Definition 3.10   A **closed formula** is a formula with no free occurrence of any variable.

Definition 3.11   An **expression** is either a term, a set of terms, a quantifier-free formula or a set of quantifier-free formulae.

EXAMPLE 3.2

> The scope of ($\exists$X) in ($\exists$X)(X $\neq$ f(a) $\Leftrightarrow$ $\neg$r(X, f(a))) is the formula (X $\neq$ f(a) $\Leftrightarrow$ $\neg$r(X, f(a))).

In the formula $(\forall X) q(X) \Rightarrow r(X, f(Y))$, the first two occurrences of X are bound while the third is free as well as the occurrence of Y. This formula is thus not closed.

Definition 3.12 Let F be a formula. We denote the closed formula obtained by adding a universal (or existential) quantifier for every free variable in F by $\forall(F)$ (or $\exists(F)$, respectively). $\forall(F)$ is called the **universal closure** of F and $\exists(F)$ the **existential closure** of F.

EXAMPLE 3.3

The existential closure of the formula $(\forall X) q(X) \Rightarrow r(X, f(Y))$ is the formula $(\exists X \, \exists Y)((\forall X) q(X) \Rightarrow r(X, f(Y)))$.

EXERCISES

3.1 Can a variable be bound *and* free in a formula F?

3.2 What is the existential closure of a closed formula?

3.3 Show that the universal closure of a formula is a closed formula.

3.2 Interpretations and models

An **interpretation** assigns a *meaning* to the terms and the formulae. Generally speaking, an interpretation consists of a domain of discourse (over which the variables range), an assignment of each ground term to an element of the domain and an assignment of each atom to the truth value *true* or *false*. Given an interpretation, the truth value of any closed formula can be deduced. Given a set of formulae, the interpretations for which these formulae are true are of particular interest. Such interpretations will be called **models**.

A theorem is a formula that can be deduced from a set of formulae by means of inference rules (proof theory). Gödel's completeness theorem expresses that given a set of formulae, a formula is a theorem if and only if it is true in all the models of the given set of formulae. Usually, some interpretation (called the **intended interpretation**), by which the formulae are interpreted, is distinguished. The intended interpretation should of course be a model of the considered set of formulae. A formula which is true in the intended model is not necessarily a theorem since it can be false in some other (bizarre) models. Gödel's incompleteness theorem states the existence of formulae which are true in the intended model but which are not theorems (assuming the intended model is not trivial). This reduces somewhat the power of inference rules and deduction.

In the specification of a logic procedure, the relation is defined over ground terms. Therefore, we are interested here in interpretations for which the domain of discourse is the set of ground terms; each term being interpreted as itself. Such interpretations are called **Herbrand interpretations**. Other interpretations are outside the specification and thus outside the construction process. Thus, within the framework of logic program construction considered here, interpretations can be restricted to Herbrand ones. Since logic descriptions and logic programs are closed formulae, only closed formulae will be considered in what follows.

Herbrand interpretations

> **Definition 3.13**   The **Herbrand universe** is the set of all ground terms.

> **Definition 3.14**   The **Herbrand base** is the set of all ground atoms.

By the definition of the first-order language, the Herbrand universe and the Herbrand base are uniquely defined. In a Herbrand interpretation, the domain is the Herbrand universe and ground terms are interpreted as themselves. Herbrand interpretations vary in the way they assign truth values to ground atoms. Such an assignment can be characterized by splitting the Herbrand base into two complementary sets: the first is the set of ground atoms which are true in the interpretation, and the second is the set of ground atoms which are false in the interpretation. A Herbrand interpretation can thus be identified as a subset of the Herbrand base, that is, the set of all ground atoms which are true in the interpretation (the other ground atoms being then false in the interpretation). This justifies the following definition.

> **Definition 3.15**   A **Herbrand interpretation** (or **H-interpretation**) is a subset of the Herbrand base.

EXAMPLE 3.4

H-interpretation a = {p(a), q(b), p(f(a)), q(f(b)),
$\qquad\qquad$ p(f(f(a))), q(f(f(b))), . . .}
In this H-interpretation, p(f(f(a))) is true as is q(f(b)), but p(c)
is false in a as is r(a).

By convention the 0-ary predicate true belongs to every H-interpretation, and the predicate false does not.

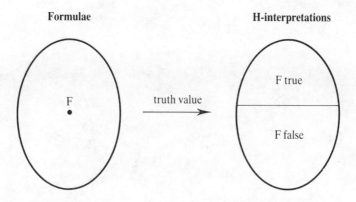

Figure 3.1 Truth value of a formula.

Truth value

Given an H-interpretation a, it is possible to assign a truth value to every closed formula. A closed formula is either true in a, or false in a; but never true and false simultaneously (see Figure 3.1).

> **Definition 3.16** Let a be an H-interpretation. The **truth value** (in a) of a closed formula F is defined as follows:
>
> - If F is a ground atom, then F is true in a iff $F \in a$.
> - If F is a formula of the form $\neg G$, $(G \& H)$, $(G \vee H)$, $(G \Rightarrow H)$ or $(G \Leftrightarrow H)$, then the truth value of F in a is given according to Table 3.1.
> - If F has the form $(\forall X)G$, then F is true in a iff, for every ground term t, $G\{X/t\}$ is true in a. (Remember that, by Definition 2.1, $G\{X/t\}$ is the formula obtained by replacing all free occurrences of X in G by t).
> - If F has the form $(\exists X)G$, then F is true in a iff there exists a ground term t such that $G\{X/t\}$ is true in a.

Table 3.1 Truth values of formulae.

G	H	$\neg G$	$(G \& H)$	$(G \vee H)$	$(G \Rightarrow H)$	$(G \Leftrightarrow H)$
true	true	false	true	true	true	true
true	false	false	false	true	false	false
false	true	true	false	true	true	false
false	false	true	false	false	true	true

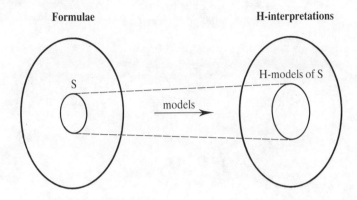

Figure 3.2   Models of formulae.

EXAMPLE 3.5

H-interpretation $a = \{p(\,t, t\,)\,|\,t \text{ is a ground term}\}$.

Formula $F : (\,\forall X\,\forall Y\,)\,(\,\neg p(\,X, Y\,) \lor p(\,f(\,X\,), f(\,Y\,)\,)\,)$.

F is true in a

iff for any ground terms t1, t2 :
   $(\,\neg p(\,t1, t2\,) \lor p(\,f(\,t1\,), f(\,t2\,)\,)\,)$ true in a

iff for any ground terms t1, t2 :
   $p(\,t1, t2\,)$ false in a or $p(\,f(\,t1\,), f(\,t2\,)\,)$ true in a

iff for any ground terms t1, t2 :
   $p(\,t1, t2\,) \notin a$ or $p(\,f(\,t1\,), f(\,t2\,)\,) \in a$

iff true (since if $p(\,t1, t2\,) \in a$, then t1 and t2 are the same ground
term; $f(\,t1\,)$ and $f(\,t2\,)$ are thus also the same ground term. Hence
$p(\,f(\,t1\,), f(\,t2\,)\,) \in a$).

Models

A **model** of a set of formulae is an interpretation in which all the formulae
of the set are true. See Figure 3.2.

Definition 3.17   Let a be an H-interpretation. a is a **Herbrand
model** (or **H-model**) of a closed formula F iff F is true in a. a is an
H-model of a set S of closed formulae iff a is an H-model of each
formula in S.

Definition 3.18   A closed formula or a set of closed formulae is
H-satisfiable iff it has an H-model. Otherwise, it is **H-unsatisfiable**.

Definition 3.19   Two (sets of) closed fomulae are **H-equivalent**
iff they have the same H-models.

EXERCISES_____

3.4 Show that the truth values of (G & H), (G ∨ H) and (G ⇔ H) can be expressed in terms of ¬ and ⇒.

3.5 Let # be a new binary connective such that (G # H) is true iff both G and H are false. Show that every connective can be defined in terms of # alone.

3.6 Show that the truth value of (∀X)G in **a** is equivalent to the truth value of ¬(∃X) ¬G in **a**, for any H-interpretation **a**.

3.7 Let F be the formula (∀X ∃Y)p(X, Y). Give an H-interpretation which is an H-model of F, and another one which is not an H-model of F.

3.8 Give an example of an H-unsatisfiable formula.

3.9 Show that if a formula has an H-model, then it has infinitely many H-models.

3.10 Let S = {$F_1, \ldots, F_n$} be a finite set of closed formulae. Show that for any H-interpretation **a**, **a** is an H-model of S iff **a** is a model of the formula (F_1 & . . . & F_n).

_____

3.3 Logical consequences

Logical consequences deal with the question 'which formulae logically follow from given formulae'. The models of a formula give its meaning. It is therefore natural to define that a formula logically follows from (or is a logical consequence of) a given formula when the first formula is true in all the models of the given formula. In other words, a logical consequence of a given formula agrees with the meaning of the given formula. See Figure 3.3.

> **Definition 3.20** Let S be a set of closed formulae and F be a closed formula. F is a **Herbrand logical consequence** (or **H-logical consequence**) of S iff F is true in every H-model of S. Such a property is denoted as
>
> S ⊨$_H$ F

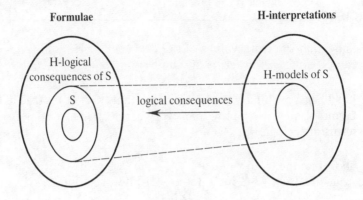

Figure 3.3   Logical sequences of formulae.

It is very important to note that, in general, $S \not\models_H F$ (that is, F is not an H-logical consequence of S) is different from $S \models_H \neg F$ (see Exercise 3.12).

EXERCISES

3.11   Show that $S \models_H F$ iff every H-model of S is an H-model of F.

3.12   Find examples for which:

    (a) $S \models_H F$ and $S \not\models_H \neg F$

    (b) $S \not\models_H F$ and $S \not\models_H \neg F$

    (c) $S \models_H F$ and $S \models_H \neg F$

3.13   Given an H-unsatisfiable set of closed formulae S, show that $S \models_H F$, for any closed formula F.

3.14   Do the following equivalences hold?

$$\{(F \,\&\, G)\} \models_H H \quad \text{iff} \quad \{F\} \models_H H \quad \text{or} \quad \{G\} \models_H H$$

$$\{(F \lor G)\} \models_H H \quad \text{iff} \quad \{F\} \models_H H \quad \text{and} \quad \{G\} \models_H H$$

where F, G and H are closed formulae.

**H-interpretations versus interpretations

Since we are focussing our attention on Herbrand interpretations, the set of Herbrand logical consequences is a superset of the set of logical consequences (relative to all models). The restriction from the interpretations point of view is thus an extension from the logical consequences point of view.

The relation between Herbrand logical consequences and logical consequences (denoted $\models$) can be further refined. On page 34 of Shepherdson (1988) it is said that the set of Herbrand logical consequences of a definite Horn clause program coincides with the set of its logical consequences. This relation can be generalized as stated in Theorem 3.1.

Theorem 3.1

Let:

- S be a set of closed formulae such that an infinite number of constants of the language does not occur in S, and
- F be a closed formula,

then

$$S \models F \quad \text{iff} \quad S \models_H F$$

Proof
(Deville, 1988.)   ∎

For S finite, the set of Herbrand logical consequences and the set of logical consequences are thus equivalent. Note that Theorem 3.1 is not applicable for completed programs since the equality theory uses all the constants of the language. It can be shown that for completed programs, the set of Herbrand logical consequences is not recursively enumerable (Shepherdson, 1988).

Since the proposed logic is not pure first-order logic, the attentive reader may object that the methodology is based not only on Paradigm 4 (Section 1.3), but also on Paradigm 2, where NewLogic is considered. This is certainly true. However, this slight change does not affect our general approach, which is definitely based on Paradigm 4.

3.4 The general form of a logic description

The logic descriptions that will be considered for developing logic programs are formulae with a particular form.

Definition 3.21 A **logic description** is a closed well-formed formula of the following form:

$$(\forall X_1 \ldots \forall X_n)(\, p(X_1, \ldots, X_n) \Leftrightarrow \text{Def})$$

where $n \geq 0$ and Def is a formula. A logic description which has p as predicate symbol on its left-hand side will be denoted as **LD(p)**. The formula Def on the right-hand side of the equivalence is called the **definition part** of LD(p).

For notational convenience, the universal quantifiers $\forall X_i$ will be implicit. In the definition part, Def, free variables (different from the X_i) are allowed and are then assumed to be existentially quantified over Def.

EXAMPLE 3.6

length(List, Nb) ⇔
        List = [ ] & Nb = 0
        ∨ List = [H|T] & length(T, Nb_T) & add(Nb_T, 1, Nb)

stands for the formula

(∀List ∀Nb)(length(List, Nb) ⇔
        (∃H ∃T ∃Nb_T)(List = [ ] & Nb = 0
             ∨ List = [H|T] & length(T, Nb_T)
                 & add(Nb_T, 1, Nb)))

The form of a logic description is a good compromise between generality and closeness to logic programs. On the one hand, it will be possible to transform it automatically into a logic program. On the other hand, such a form also facilitates the construction of correct logic descriptions because it is natural to describe the necessary and sufficient conditions for $p(X_1, \ldots, X_n)$ to be true.

*3.5 Background

Further developments of first-order logic can be found in Kleene (1952), Schoenfield (1967), Chang and Lee (1973), Levin (1974), Ebbinghaus *et al.* (1984) and Lloyd (1987).

In logic programming, it is usual to have different possible sets of variable, function and predicate symbols, and thus to have different languages for different theories (Van Emden and Kowalski, 1976; Apt and Van Emden, 1982). A different approach is taken here since the Herbrand universe is defined independently of any particular program. All the logic descriptions and logic programs will thus have the same underlying Herbrand universe. A similar approach is taken in Kunen (1987), Maher (1988) and Topor and Sonenberg (1988). Some comparison between these two approaches is made in Shepherdson (1988) and Deville (1988).

The proposed declarative semantics of first-order logic is based on Herbrand interpretations. This model theory is simpler than that of classical logic. It is also appropriate in the context of logic program development, as will be shown in the next chapter. The definition of a semantics in terms of special classes of models is not unusual in logic programming. Examples can be found in Minker (1982), Apt *et al.* (1988), Przymusinski (1988a, 1988b) and Maher (1988).

SUMMARY

- A first-order language consists of the formulae constructed with the symbols of the language.
- An H-interpretation assigns a meaning to the formulae. A formula is either true or false in an H-interpretation.
- An H-model of a set of formulae is an H-interpretation in which these formulae are true.
- A formula is an H-logical consequence of a set of formulae if it is true in every H-model of this set.
- A logic description is a formula of the form

    $p(\mathbf{x}) \Leftrightarrow$ Def

    where $\mathbf{x}$ is a tuple of variables and Def is a formula.

4

Correctness of a logic description

PREVIEW   When constructing a logic description from a specification, the question of its adequacy with respect to its specification, that is its **correctness**, must be faced. But what does it mean for a logic description to be correct with respect to its specification?

This chapter introduces the concept of correctness for a logic description. As we are concerned here with the declarative semantics of first-order logic, the definition of correctness will be based on the model theory. Informally, a logic description will be correct if there is an 'equivalence' between the relation described in the specification and the logical consequences of the logic description. Thus, there are no procedural aspects.

It is important to note that, from a pragmatic point of view, the correctness definition becomes less relevant within the construction process as soon as the applied construction process is proved to yield correct logic descriptions. Such an approach is taken here. However, it could be interesting for the reader to have a general understanding of the correctness criteria presented in Section 4.1. The precise justification of the correctness definition (Section 4.2), the properties of correct logic descriptions (Section 4.3) as well as an example of a correctness proof (Section 4.4) are presented in starred sections.

4.1   Definition of correctness

The correctness of a logic description refers to the relation described in the specification and its domain (the types and parameter restrictions). Therefore, given the specification of a procedure, the associated specification of a logic description will be composed of the type information, the restrictions on the parameters and the described relation.

73

From a constructive point of view, it is important to be able to discuss the correctness of a logic description without having to consider the logic descriptions associated with its subproblems. When construct- ing or proving the correctness of a logic description, only the specifica- tion of these subproblems should be involved. Otherwise, a correctness proof could only be achieved if all the subproblems had been completely solved. The abstraction principle would then be lost. Therefore, in the concept of correctness, all the subproblems of a logic description will be considered as primitives and the existence of correct logic descriptions will thus be assumed for all of them. The problem of the correctness of a logic description is thus reduced to the correctness of a logic description in a set of logic descriptions. The concept of correctness in a set of logic descriptions is presented first followed by a definition of the correctness of a logic description.

4.1.1 Correctness in a set of logic descriptions

As mentioned earlier, the idea behind the correctness criteria is to establish an equivalence between the relation described in the specifica- tion and the H-logical consequences of a set of logic descriptions. At this logic description level, the verification of the domain membership will be made explicitly. Thus, when a ground n-tuple **t** is in the domain and belongs to the specified relation, then p(**t**) should be 'true'. When **t** either is not in the domain or does not belong to the specified relation, then p(**t**) should be 'false'. Given the declarative semantics of first-order logic, 'p(**t**) true' means 'p(**t**) is an H-logical consequence'; and 'p(**t**) false' means '¬p(**t**) is an H-logical consequence'. Hence the following defini- tion, illustrated in Figure 4.1.

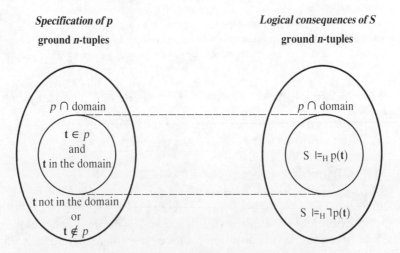

Specification of p   *Logical consequences of S*

ground n-tuples   **ground n-tuples**

$p \cap$ domain $p \cap$ domain

$t \in p$
and
t in the domain

$S \models_H p(t)$

t not in the domain
or
$t \notin p$

$S \models_H \neg p(t)$

Figure 4.1 Correctness of a logic description.

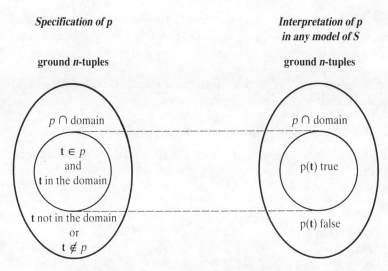

Figure 4.2 Correctness of a logic description.

Definition 4.1
Let:

- S be a finite set of logic descriptions containing LD(p), and
- *p* be the relation described in the specification of p.

LD(p) is **(totally) correct in S** with respect to (w.r.t.) its specification iff for any ground *n*-tuple **t**, the following conditions hold:

$$S \vDash_H p(t) \quad \text{iff} \quad t \in p \quad \text{and} \quad t \text{ is in the domain of } p \qquad \textbf{(C1)}$$

$$S \vDash_H \neg p(t) \quad \text{iff} \quad t \notin p \quad \text{or} \quad t \text{ is not in the domain of } p \qquad \textbf{(C2)}$$

It will be shown in Section 4.3 (Property 4.2) that when LD(p) is correct in S, then the truth value of a ground atom p(**t**) is the same in all the H-models of S (see Figure 4.2). This property is particularly interesting when constructing or reasoning with a logic description since thus any single H-model can be focussed on.

If we replace 'iff' by 'implies' in C1 and C2, LD(p) is said to be **partially correct in S** w.r.t. its specification. If we replace 'iff' by 'is implied by' in C1 and C2, LD(p) is **complete in S** w.r.t. its specification. The partial correctness defined here is similar to the classical concept of partial correctness in programming: a program is partially correct if it only computes correct results (if any). Note however that there is no computational aspect here. Partial correctness is sometimes called 'soundness' in logic programming. Completeness expresses that any correct result (according to the specification) should be an H-logical consequence of the logic descriptions. There is no exact counterpart of completeness in deterministic programming languages. Because these deal with functions rather than relations, it is sufficient to show that a program terminates (when it is partially correct). But here, the relation concept suggests a completeness requirement.

4.1.2   Correctness of a logic description (in a set of specifications)

Let us now define the correctness of a logic description, but independently of the logic descriptions associated with its subproblems. The following definition of correctness involves the specification of the subproblems.

Definition 4.2
Let:

- LD(p) be a logic description,
- $q_1, \ldots, q_n$ be all the predicate names appearing in LD(p) and distinct from p, and
- $Spec_1, \ldots, Spec_n$ be the specifications of $q_1, \ldots, q_n$.

LD(p) is **correct** w.r.t. its specification (in $\{Spec_1, \ldots, Spec_n\}$) iff for any finite set S of logic descriptions, such that

- LD(q_j) is correct in S w.r.t. its specification $Spec_j$ ($1 \le j \le n$), and
- S contains no occurrences of p,

It is the case that
LD(p) is correct in $S \cup \{LD(p)\}$ w.r.t. its specification.

In the above definition, the set S represents a correct implementation (in logic) of the subproblems involved in LD(p). Such a set cannot contain any occurrence of p. Otherwise the introduction of LD(p) in S could destroy the correctness of some logic description, as illustrated in the next section. The correctness of mutually recursive logic descriptions must thus be established simultaneously. The following definition expresses the correctness criterion for k mutually recursive logic descriptions.

Definition 4.3
Let:

- LD(p_1), $\ldots$, LD(p_k) be mutually recursive logic descriptions,

- $q_1, \ldots, q_n$ be all the predicate names appearing in LD(p_1), ..., LD(p_k), and distinct from $p_1, \ldots p_k$; and
- $Spec_1, \ldots, Spec_n$ be the specifications of $q_1, \ldots, q_n$.

LD(p_1), ..., LD(p_k) are **correct** w.r.t. their specification (in $\{Spec_1, \ldots, Spec_n\}$) iff
for any finite set S of logic descriptions, such that

- LD(q_j) is correct in S w.r.t. its specification $Spec_j$ ($1 \leq j \leq n$), and
- S contains no occurrences of $p_1, \ldots, p_k$,

It is the case that
LD(p_i) is correct in $S \cup \{LD(p_1), \ldots, LD(p_k)\}$ w.r.t. its specification ($1 \leq i \leq k$).

Definition 4.2 is thus a particular case of Definition 4.3 (that is, $k = 1$) for non-recursive and simply recursive logic descriptions.

*4.2   Justification

The above definitions raise some questions that will be answered hereafter. Why consider ground terms only? Is this realistic? Should the logic description verify domain membership (that is, type and restrictions on parameters)? Are both criteria C1 and C2 needed? Is C2 necessary or is it redundant with C1? Why can mutually recursive logic descriptions not be considered separately? Why consider H-logical consequences?

Restriction to ground terms

The correctness definition is restricted to *ground* terms because there is no directionality aspect at this logic level. Considering ground terms simplifies the correctness definition, the construction process and the correctness proofs. A logic description could be seen as 'testing' if the domain precondition is respected and if the relation holds for given ground terms. This approach is realistic if a correct logic description can be used with some variables as actual parameters. This will be a property of correct logic descriptions.

Verification of domain membership

In the correctness criteria, the position is taken here that a logic description has to verify that the parameters are in the domain of the procedure. Although an opposite approach is taken at the logic program level, our choice facilitates the derivation of correct logic procedures from correct logic descriptions. Assuming the parameters are in the domain would yield the following correctness definition:

> LD(p) is correct in S w.r.t. its specification iff
> for any ground *n*-tuple t in the domain of p, we have:
>
> $$S \vDash_H p(t) \quad \text{iff} \quad t \in p \tag{NC1}$$
> $$S \vDash_H \neg p(t) \quad \text{iff} \quad t \notin p \tag{NC2}$$

Negative information

In the correctness criteria, condition C2 is necessary because negations can be used within a logic description, as illustrated in Example 4.1.

EXAMPLE 4.1

> p(L)
>   specification: L list; $p = \{\}$ (that is, the empty relation)
>   logic description:
>   p(L) ⇔   L = [] & false
>   ∨ L = [H | T] & p(T)
>
> q(T)
>   specification: T term; $q = \{t \mid t \text{ ground term}\}$
>   logic description:
>   q(T) ⇔ ¬p([])
>
> r(T)
>   specification: T term; $r = \{\}$
>   logic description:
>   r(T) ⇔ ∃X p(X)
>
> S = {LD(p), LD(q), LD(r), LD(=)}
> (LD (=) is the usual syntactical equality)

It is easy to see that the logic description LD(p) in this example is correct in S. For any ground term t, we have:

$$S \vDash_H p(t) \quad \text{iff} \quad t \in p \quad \text{and} \quad t \text{ is a list} \tag{C1}$$
$$S \vDash_H \neg p(t) \quad \text{iff} \quad t \notin p \quad \text{or} \quad t \text{ is not a list} \tag{C2}$$

The logic description LD(q) is also correct in S. Its correctness depends crucially on the correctness of LD(p) (not C1, but only C2). For $t \in q$, by the correctness of LD(p) (C1 alone), we have $S \nvDash_H p(t)$ while $S \vDash_H \neg p(t)$ is actually needed in order to prove the correctness of LD(q). That is what C2 expresses. Criterion C2 is necessary as soon as negations are allowed in logic descriptions.

Mutually recursive logic descriptions

In the definition of correctness for non-mutually recursive logic descriptions, the set S cannot contain any occurrences of p, in order to prevent the occurrence of mutually recursive logic descriptions not explicitly considered.

EXAMPLE 4.2

append3(L1, L2, L3, LApp) ⇔   append(L1, L2, L1_2)
                                & append(L12, L3, LApp)
append(L1, L2, LApp) ⇔ append3(L1, L2, [], LApp)

In Example 4.2, if append is assumed to be correct, then append3 is correct with respect to its specification (append3 holds iff the list LApp is the concatenation of the lists L1, L2 and L3). If append3 is assumed to be correct, then append is correct. But append and append3 are no longer correct in {LD(append), LD(append3)}. For instance, the H-interpretation in which the append and append3 predicates are always false is an H-model. It is therefore impossible to have $S \vDash_H$ append(t_1, t_2, t_3), for any terms t_1, t_2 and t_3. In other words, correctness would not be monotonic if such a condition were not imposed. The only way to prove the correctness of mutually recursive logic programs is to prove them correct together.

**Restriction to Herbrand interpretations

When programming in logic, the concern is actually not with non-Herbrand interpretations, or at least not with interpretations with a domain non-isomorphic to the Herbrand universe. The results of a computation are substitutions. The domain under consideration is the set of all ground terms (the Herbrand universe). From a computational point of view, when a formula $\exists X\, p(X)$ is true, a *witness* should exist in the Herbrand universe (say a) such that p(a) is true. Moreover, if p(t) is false for every ground term t, $\exists X\, p(X)$ should be false. But this is not always the case since $\exists X\, p(X)$ can be true in some non-Herbrand models. In Example 4.1, it could be verified that, for any ground term t,

$S \vDash p(t)$ iff $t \in p$ and   t is a list   (C1′)
$S \vDash \neg p(t)$ iff $t \notin p$ or   t is not a list   (C2′)

For this logic description, the restriction to Herbrand interpretations is of no consequence.

This however is not the case with LD(r). This logic description contains a fair use of p. It can be verified that LD(r) is actually correct in S. Indeed, for any term t, we have:

$$S \vDash_H r(t) \quad \text{if} \quad t \in r \tag{C1}$$
$$S \vDash_H \neg r(t) \quad \text{iff} \quad t \notin r \tag{C2}$$

When considering all models (rather than simply the Herbrand models) we also have:

$$S \vDash r(t) \quad \text{iff} \quad t \in r \tag{C1'}$$

However, we *do not have*:

$$S \vDash \neg r(t) \quad \text{iff} \quad t \notin r \tag{C2'}$$

C2′ does not hold because, even if $p(t)$ is false for any ground term t (that is, $S \vDash \neg p(t)$), $\exists X\, p(X)$ is not false (that is, $S \nvDash \neg \exists X\, p(X)$). In order to show this, a (non-Herbrand) model $\mathbf{a}$ of S can be shown for which $\exists X\, p(X)$ is true, and hence $r(t)$ is true in $\mathbf{a}$. We thus have $S \nvDash \neg r(t)$ since $t \notin r$ (since r is empty). The description of such a model $\mathbf{a}$ follows.

> Domain D of $\mathbf{a}$: Herbrand universe of the language augmented with the new constants $a, \heartsuit_1, \ldots, \heartsuit_h, \ldots$. The interpretation of the terms is the usual Herbrand one. The interpretation of the predicate is as follows:
>
> - $p(\heartsuit_i)$ and $p([d_1, \ldots, d_m | \heartsuit_i])$ true in $\mathbf{a}$ ($i \geq 1, m \geq 1,$ $d_j \in D$)
> - $d = d$ true in $\mathbf{a}$ ($d \in D$)
> $\heartsuit_i = [a | \heartsuit_{i+1}]$ and $[a | \heartsuit_{i+1}] = \heartsuit_i$ true in $\mathbf{a}$ ($i \geq 1$)
> $[h | t] = [h' | t']$ true in $\mathbf{a}$ iff $h = h'$ and $t = t'$ true in $\mathbf{a}$ ($h, t, h', t' \in D$)
> - $r(d)$ true in $\mathbf{a}$ ($d \in D$)
> - $q(d)$ true in $\mathbf{a}$ ($d \in D$)

It can be shown that $\mathbf{a}$ is a model of S (and thus of the equality theory LD(=)). In this model, $\exists X\, p(X)$ is true in $\mathbf{a}$. (For example, $p(\heartsuit_i)$ is true in $\mathbf{a}$.) It is easy to build an example where C2′ holds but not C1′.

This example shows the necessity of restricting our attention to Herbrand interpretations only. Otherwise, LD(r) (like most logic descriptions) would not be considered correct.

*4.3 Properties

In this section, properties of correct logic descriptions are stated and proven. The first property shows the satisfiability of correct logic descriptions.

Property 4.1 *Satisfiability of correct logic descriptions*
Let S be a set of logic descriptions
If LD(p) is correct in S
then S is H-satisfiable.

Proof

Let p be the relation described in the specification of p, and t be ground in the domain of p. Suppose S has no H-model. By the definition of $\vDash_H$, we have $S \vDash_H p(\ t\ )$ and $S \vDash_H \neg p(\ t\ )$. Since LD(p) is correct in S, we obtain $t \in p$ (by C1) and $t \notin p$ (by C2). This is impossible. Therefore, S has an H-model and so it must be H-satisfiable.   ∎

The next property shows that any single H-model can be focussed upon as soon as a logic description is correct.

Property 4.2

Let:

* S be a set of logic descriptions,
* p be the relation described in the specification of p,
* LD(p) be correct in S, and
* **a** be an H-model of S

For any ground n-tuple **t**,

p(t) is true in **a**   iff $t \in p$ and   t is in the domain of p

Proof

Let t be ground. If $t \in p$ and t is in the domain of p, then $S \vDash_H p(\ t\ )$ (by C1). Hence, p(t) is true in **a**. If $t \notin p$ or t is not in the domain of p, then $S \vDash_H \neg p(\ t\ )$ (by C2). Hence, p(t) is false in all H-models of S. Therefore, if p(t) is true in **a**, it must be the case that $t \in p$ and t is in the domain of p.   ∎

From Properties 4.1 and 4.2, the so-called **Herbrand rule** is applicable for a correct logic description: if $S \cup \{p(\ t\ )\}$ has no H-model, then infer $\neg p(\ t\ )$. Note that CWA (that is, the closed world assumption) is also applicable: if a ground atom p(t) is not a logical consequence of S, then infer $\neg p(\ t\ )$. This results from the fact that $S \nvDash_H p(\ t\ )$ is equivalent to $S \vDash_H \neg p(\ t\ )$ when the logic description is correct. Thus, either $S \vDash_H p(\ t\ )$ or $S \vDash_H \neg p(\ t\ )$ holds. S is also complete for the predicate p(t).

Next comes an equivalent characterization of correctness in a set of logic descriptions which may simplify correctness proofs.

Property 4.3   *Equivalent correctness criterion*

Let:

* S be a set of logic descriptions, and
* p be the relation described in the specification of p.

LD(p) is correct in S w.r.t. its specification iff:

(1)   S has an H-model
(2)   For every H-model **a** of S, for any ground *n*-tuple **t**,
       (2.1) If **t** is in the domain of p,
              then   p(**t**) is true in **a**   iff   **t** ∈ *p*.
       (2.2) If **t** is not in the domain of p,
              then   p(**t**) is false in **a**.

Proof
See Exercise 4.1.   ■

The concept of correctness has to be monotonic. When a logic description LD(p) is correct in a set S, it should also be correct in extensions of S (for example, S ∪ {LD(r)}). The following property states conditions sufficient to ensure monotonicity of correctness.

Property 4.4   *Monotonicity of correctness*
Let:

*   S and S′ be two sets of logic descriptions, and
*   S ⊆ S′.

If:

*   LD(p) is correct in S w.r.t. its specification, and
*   S′ has an H-model,

then LD(p) is correct in S′ w.r.t. its specification.

Proof
Every model of S′ is also a model of S since S ⊆ S′. The result is then established by using Property 4.3.   ■

When constructing a logic description, the literals used are usually not ground, but existentially quantified. If ∃(p(**u**)) is true in all H-models, a ground instance **s** of **u** should exist such that p(**s**) is also true. The ground instance **s** is a **witness** of ∃(p(**u**)). This outcome is quite natural since the aim is actually to compute results. Property 4.5 states the existence of such a witness.

Property 4.5   *Existence of a witness*
Let:

*   S be a set of logic descriptions,
*   *p* be the relation described in the specification of p, and
*   LD(p) be correct in S.

For any **u**, we have each of the following:

$S \vDash_H \exists(p(\mathbf{u}))$ iff   (E1)
    there exists some ground instance **s** of **u**
    such that $\mathbf{s} \in p$ and **s** is in the domain of p

$S \vDash_H \exists(\neg p(\mathbf{u}))$ iff   (E2)
    there exists some ground instance **s** of **u**
    such that $\mathbf{s} \notin p$ or **s** is not in the domain of p

$S \vDash_H \neg\exists(p(\mathbf{u}))$ iff   (E3)
    there exists no ground instance **s** of **u**
    such that $\mathbf{s} \in p$ and **s** is in the domain of p

$S \vDash_H \neg\exists(\neg p(\mathbf{u}))$ iff   (E4)
    there exists some ground instance **s** of **u**
    such that $\mathbf{s} \notin p$ or **s** is not in the domain of p

Proof

    if part of E1
    There exists some ground instance **s** of **u**,
    such that $\mathbf{s} \in p$ and **s** is in the domain of p

  $\Rightarrow$ there exists some ground instance **s** of **u**
        such that $S \vDash_H p(\mathbf{s})$ (by C1)

  $\Rightarrow$ $S \vDash_H \exists(p(\mathbf{u}))$

    if part of E3
    $S \nvDash_H \neg\exists(p(\mathbf{u}))$

  $\Rightarrow$ $\exists(p(\mathbf{u}))$ is true in some H-model of S (say $\mathbf{a}$)

  $\Rightarrow$ there exists some ground instance **s** of **u**
        such that $p(\mathbf{s})$ is true in $\mathbf{a}$
        (because the domain of an H-model is the set of ground terms)

  $\Rightarrow$ there exists some ground instance **s** of **u**
        such that $\mathbf{s} \in p$ and **s** is in the domain of p
        (by Property 4.2)

    only if part of E1
    $S \vDash_H \exists(p(\mathbf{u}))$

  $\Rightarrow$ $S \nvDash_H \neg\exists(p(\mathbf{u}))$
        (since S is H-satisfiable: Property 4.1)

  $\Rightarrow$ there exists some ground instance **s** of **u**
        such that $\mathbf{s} \in p$ and **s** is in the domain of p
        (by the *if* part of E3)

    only if part of E3
    $S \vDash_H \neg\exists(p(\mathbf{u}))$

  $\Rightarrow$ $S \nvDash_H \exists(p(\mathbf{u}))$
        (since S is H-satisfiable: Property 4.1)

$\Rightarrow$ there exists no ground instance **s** of **u**
                  such that $s \in p$ and   **s** is in the domain of p
                  (by the *if* part of E1)

The proofs of E2 and E4 are similar.   ∎

In Property 4.5, (E3) and (E4) can be re-expressed as follows:

$S \vDash_H \forall(\neg p(\mathbf{u}))$ iff   **(E3)**
   for all ground instances **s** of **u**
   $s \notin p$ or   **s** is not in the domain of p

$S \vDash_H \forall(p(\mathbf{u}))$ iff   **(E4)**
   for all ground instances **s** of **u**
   $s \in p$ and   **s** is in the domain of p

When existentially quantified variables occur in a negative literal $\neg p(\mathbf{u})$, it is sometimes useful to add extra literals verifying domain membership. This is because it is usually ground instances **s**, such that $s \notin p$ but **s** is in the domain of p, that are of interest. Assuming the existence of LD(p_dom(**t**)) which holds iff **t** is in the domain of p, it can easily be proven that

$S \vDash_H \exists(p\_dom(\mathbf{u}) \,\&\, \neg p(\mathbf{u}))$ iff   **(E2′)**
   there exists some ground instance **s** of **u**
   such that $s \notin p$ and   **s** is in the domain of p

$S \vDash_H \neg\exists(p\_dom(\mathbf{u}) \,\&\, \neg p(\mathbf{u}))$ iff   **(E4′)**
   there exists no ground instance **s** of **u**
   such that $s \notin p$ and   **s** is in the domain of p

In practice, LD(p_dom) does not have to be used explicitly. The domain to be verified actually depends on the form of the *n*-tuple **u**. Note that (E4′) can also be re-expressed as:

$S \vDash_H \forall(p\_dom(\mathbf{u}) \Rightarrow p(\mathbf{u}))$ iff   **(E4′)**
   for all ground instances **s** of **u** in the domain of p
   $s \in p$

EXERCISES

*4.1   Prove Property 4.3.

*4.2   Suppose that in the definition of correctness in a set of logic descriptions, conditions C1 and C2 are replaced by NC1 and NC2

(see Section 4.2), which only consider ground terms in the domain of p. What would Property 4.5 become? (*Hint*: use the same idea as in (E2′) and (E4′)).

---

*4.4   Example

In this section, it is illustrated how a logic description can be proven to be correct. The specification of the relation is informal and the concept of *reverse list* is supposed to be well understood. This assumption is made to underline the general idea of such correctness proofs without any reference to a particular specification language used for describing the relations.

> procedure   reverse(L, LRev)
>
> *Type*:   L, LRev : Lists
>
> *Relation*:   LRev is the reverse list of L.
>
> Specification 4.1   reverse(L, LRev)

The specification of append is given in Specification 4.2. The specification of T1 = T2 is that it holds iff T1 is syntactically equal to T2.

> procedure   append(L1, L2, LApp)
>
> *Type*:   L1, L2, LApp : Lists
>
> *Relation*:   LApp is the concatenation of L1 and L2.
>
> Specification 4.2   append(L1, L2, LApp)
>
> reverse(L, LRev) $\Leftrightarrow$ L = [] & LRev = []
> $\lor$ L = [H | T] & reverse(T, TRev)
>   & append(TRev, [H], LRev)
>
> Logic Description 4.1   reverse(L, LRev)

The following correctness proof may appear cumbersome for such an easy logic description. But the purpose of the proof is to show the underlying principles of the proof method. In the next section, a construction method will be presented where such proofs are no longer needed. This method will guarantee that the constructed logic descriptions are correct *by construction*.

Correctness criteria
By the correctness definition and Property 4.3, LD(reverse) is correct w.r.t. its specification iff
for any finite set S of logic descriptions such that

- LD(append) and LD(=) are correct in S, and
- S contains no occurrences of reverse,

it is the case that:

(1) $S' = S \cup \{LD(\text{ reverse })\}$ has an H-model

(2.1) For any H-model **a** of S', for any ground lists
$[e_1, \ldots, e_n], [f_1, \ldots, f_m]$ (with $n, m \geq 0$):
reverse($[e_1, \ldots, e_n], [f_1, \ldots, f_m]$) is true in **a** iff
"$[f_1, \ldots, f_m]$ is the reverse list of $[e_1, \ldots, e_n]$"

(2.2) For any H-model **a** of S', for any ground terms t1 and t2 not
both lists:
reverse(t1, t2) is false in **a**.

Correctness proof

Proof of (1)
By Property 4.1, S has an H-model **a**. Since S has no occurrence of
reverse, any modification of the value of the reverse predicate in **a** still
yields a model. Take **a**′ as **a** but with reverse(l1, l2) ∈ **a**′ iff l1, l2 are lists
and l2 is the reverse list of l1. **a**′ is thus an H-model of S. It can easily be
verified that **a**′ is also an H-model of S'.   ∎

Proof of (2.1)
Proof by induction on the length of the list $[e_1, \ldots, e_n]$. Let **a** be any
H-model of S'

For n = 0
reverse([], $[f_1, \ldots, f_m]$) is true in **a**
iff [] = [] & $[f_1, \ldots, f_m]$ = [] is true in **a**
  (because (∃H ∃T)[]=[H|T] is false in **a** (correctness of = in S'), and
  Property 4.5)
iff $[f_1, \ldots, f_m]$ = [] is true in **a**
  (because [] = [] is true in **a**)
iff m = 0
iff "[] is the reverse list of []"
iff "$[f_1, \ldots, f_m]$ is the reverse list of $[e_1, \ldots, e_n]$"

For n > 0
reverse($[e_1, \ldots, e_n], [f_1, \ldots, f_m]$) is true in **a**
iff ((∃H ∃T) $[e_1, \ldots, e_n]$ = [H | T] & (∃TRev)reverse(T, TRev)
  & append(TRev, [H], $[f_1, \ldots, f_m]$)) is true in **a**
  (because $[e_1, \ldots, e_n]$ = [] is false in **a** (n > 0))

iff   ((∃TRev)reverse([e₁, . . . , eₙ], TRev)
   & append(TRev, [e₁], [f₁, . . . , fₘ])) is true in a
   (because (∃H ∃T)[e₁, . . . , eₙ] = [H | T] is true in a, and ⟨e₁, [e₂, . . . , eₙ]⟩
   is the only witness for ⟨H, T⟩ respecting the specification of = (Property
   4.5))
iff   append ([eₙ, . . . , e₂], [e₁]), [f₁, . . . , fₘ]) is true in a
   (because of the induction hypothesis and Property 4.5)
iff   "[f₁, . . . , fₘ] is the concatenation of [eₙ, . . . , e₂] and [e₁]"
   (because append is correct in S′)
iff   "[f₁, . . . , fₘ] is [eₙ, . . . , e₂, e₁]"
iff   "[f₁, . . . , fₘ] is the reverse list of [e₁, . . . eₙ]"   ■

Proof of (2.2)
Let a be an H-model of S′.
If LRev is not a list
then LRev = [] is false in a, as also is append(TRev, [H], LRev).
If L is not a list (induction on the form of L)
then L = [] is false in a; if L = [H | T] is true in a, then reverse(T, TRev) must
be false in a since T cannot be a list and because of the induction
hypothesis.   ■

    These proofs make use of knowledge associated with the 'reverse
list' concept. A formal proof however should use a formal description of
this concept in the last steps of the basis and of the induction part of the
proof. The purpose here was not to give a formal specification or a formal
correctness proof, but rather to illustrate how the definition of correctness can be used in a correctness proof.

*4.5   Background

Logic and program correctness

Logic has already been used to define the correctness of imperative
programs. In 1967, Floyd (1967) pointed out that symbolic logic can be
used for analysing programs. However, the idea of describing static
conditions existing whenever the execution of a description reaches
particular points had already been stated in Naur (1966) (general
snapshots). Later, Manna (1969a, 1969b) related the correctness of
programs and the satisfiability of certain formulae in first-order logic.
Following this approach, formulae describing correctness can be me-
chanically deduced (by resolution) if and only if the program is correct
(Chang and Lee, 1973).

    Another approach is taken by Hoare (1969, 1971). A logical system
is defined in which the correctness of a program can be formally proven.
This formal system has some similarities with Floyd's method. However,

while Floyd describes forward-evaluation axioms, Hoare uses backward ones. Moreover, the concept of a procedure is introduced. Dijkstra's weakest-precondition (wp) calculus is inspired by Hoare's formal system, but wp calculus includes the concept of termination (Dijkstra, 1975, 1976). These approaches usually require a formal specification to start with, as does Manna's.

In the definition of correctness given here, the correctness of a logic description can be proven without having explicit logic descriptions for its subproblems. A correctness proof only uses their specifications. This idea of abstraction in correctness proofs has already appeared in Hoare (1971, 1972), by means of procedures and data representation. Programs can also be seen as levels of abstraction, each level being described by a specification (Robinson and Levitt, 1977). Such a program structure simplifies correctness proofs.

Clark and Tärnlund

Clark and Tärnlund (1977) proposed one of the first formulations of correctness criteria in logic programming. It was developed and systematized in Clark's thesis (Clark, 1979).

Given a relation p* and a definite program P, the problem of proving correctness consists of showing that $p^* = \{t \mid P \vDash p(t)\}$. The basic idea is to consider P as first-order axioms formalizing p*. An axiom set A is constructed with P, together with axioms about the data structures and induction schema. Before defining correctness criteria, some specific notations have to be introduced.

> Let x_i, y_i be variables
> $p(x, y)$ denote $p(x_1, \ldots, x_m, y_1, \ldots, y_n)$
> $x^{\smallfrown} y$ denote a permutation of x, y
> $i(x)$ denote some m-ary (input) relation over terms
> $o(x, y)$ denote some $m + n$-ary (output) relation over terms
> $\langle p(x^{\smallfrown} y), i \rangle$ be called a **use** of P

Partial correctness
The use $\langle p(x^{\smallfrown} y), i \rangle$ is partially correct for an output relation o
iff $A \vDash (\forall x \, \forall y)(i(x) \, \& \, p(x^{\smallfrown} y) \Rightarrow o(x, y))$

Completeness
The use $\langle p(x^{\smallfrown} y), i \rangle$ is complete for an output relation o
iff $A \vDash (\forall x \, \forall y)(i(x) \, \& \, o(x, y) \Rightarrow p(x^{\smallfrown} y))$

Partial correctness and completeness together mean that, under the restriction that certain arguments are bounded by some input relation i, the relation p computed by P is the output relation o. This can be written as:

Total correctness
The use $\langle p(x^{\smallfrown} y), i \rangle$ is totally correct for an output relation o
iff $A \vDash (\forall x)(i(x) \Rightarrow (\forall y) \, p(x^{\smallfrown} y) \Leftrightarrow o(x, y)))$

A termination criterion is also defined as follows:

Termination
P terminates for the use $\langle p(\,x\hat{}\,y\,),\,i\rangle$
iff $A \models (\,\forall x\,)(\,i(\,x\,)\,\Rightarrow\,(\,\exists y\,)p(\,x\hat{}\,y\,))$

The concepts of completeness and termination may overlap. Termination together with partial correctness imposes the existence of at least one correct solution p(s^ t) for some correct inputs. If the output relation is a function, this is equivalent to completeness and partial correctness (total correctness).

For the classical quicksort description, a partial correctness theorem of the use $\langle$quicksort(L, LS), list_int(L)$\rangle$ for the output relation perm(L, LS) & ordered(LS) would be:

$$(\,\forall L \;\forall LS\,)\,(\,\text{list\_int}(\,L\,)\,\&\,\text{quicksort}(\,L,\,LS\,)\,\Rightarrow\,\text{perm}(\,L,\,LS\,)$$
$$\&\,\text{ordered}(\,LS\,)\,)$$

Axioms should be given in order to formalize list_int(L) (expressing that L is a list of integers), perm(L, LS) (expressing that LS is a permutation of L) and ordered(LS) (expressing that LS is an ordered list of integers).

In this example, a termination theorem of the use $\langle$quicksort(L, LS), list_int(L)$\rangle$ would be :

$$(\,\forall L\,)(\,\text{list\_int}(\,L\,)\,\Rightarrow\,(\,\exists LS\,)\text{quicksort}(\,L,\,LS\,)\,)$$

The above definitions of correctness introduce the idea of preconditions (expressed in the input relation). In the quicksort example type preconditions are used. A directionality concept is suggested, specifying a particular form for the parameters. In practice, therefore, the quicksort program should be used with its first parameter ground. The expression of correctness for multidirectional procedures usually requires more elaborate correctness criteria.

A second remark concerns the formulation of the input and output relations. In this setting, they should be formalized in first-order logic. The specification language is thus fixed, but has the advantage of being the same as the programming language. However, first-order logic is not always as well adapted as the specification language. Program verification consists here of showing some formal equivalence between two logic formulae. Program construction will be the derivation/transformation of one logic description (specification) into another in Horn clause logic (program) (Clark, 1979; Hansson and Tärnlund; 1979; Hogger, 1981). It should also be pointed out that Clark's correctness definition can also be used for proving other properties of logic descriptions, associativity, output parameter type, and so on.

In Clark's approach, correctness is established by proving theorems in first-order logic. However, such correctness criteria require a complete inference system when actual computation takes place. This is not the case in most logic programming language interpreters, thus reducing the effectiveness of these correctness criteria.

Finally, we should note that Clark's correctness definitions deal with definite program clauses. There is thus no negation in the body of the clauses and therefore, $\neg p(\ x \hat{}\ y\ )$ does not have to be considered in the correctness criteria. The correctness proofs can thus be made in the unique least Herbrand model of the definite logic program.

Hogger

Hogger (1981, 1984) introduced interesting correctness definitions. The correctness of a pair (P, G) where P is a definite program and G is a goal ← p(t), is defined with respect to a first-order specification S as follows.

> *Total correctness*
> The pair (P, G) is totally correct with respect to S
> iff $\forall \theta : S \vDash p(\ t\theta\ ) \Leftrightarrow P \vDash p(\ t\theta\ )$ where θ is a substitution
>
> *Termination*
> The pair (P, G) terminates (or is solvable, using Hogger's terminology)
> iff $\exists \theta : P \vDash p(\ t\theta\ )$ where θ is a substitution

There are three major differences between this approach and the one presented in this book. Firstly, the above definitions are goal dependent (form of **t**). This corresponds to the introduction of directionalities or preconditions in the correctness criteria. But a more general form of correctness is obtained if **t** is an *n*-tuple of variables. Secondly, P is a definite program. Without negation, the correctness of $\neg p(\ t\theta\ )$ does not have to be captured. The third difference is the form of the specification. Given that the specification S is a first-order statement, Hogger can discuss the logical consequences of S. This corresponds to the criterion given here that tθ belongs to the relation described in the specification.

Others

In Balogh (1978) partial correctness is defined for definite programs. A definite program P is **partially correct** with respect to the pre-assertion i and post-assertions o1 and o2, iff o1 is a sufficient condition and o2 is a necessary condition for the fulfillment of p(x) for each input satisfying i, on which the program terminates. That is:

$$(\ i(\ x\ )\ \&\ termin(\ p, x\ )\ ) \Rightarrow (\ o1(\ x\ ) \Rightarrow p(\ x\ )) \ \&\ (p(\ x\ ) \Rightarrow o2(\ x\ )))$$

This definition is not a first-order characterization of partial correctness since p appears as a parameter of the *termin* predicate. Without this termination characterization, when o1 and o2 are the same, this definition corresponds to Clark's total correctness. Balogh uses this definition to prove the partial correctness of Prolog programs, using Hoare-like inference rules. A formal verification system is also presented.

In Kanamori and Seki (1986), a specification S is expressed in a subset of first-order logic. The verification of a definite program P with respect to S consists of showing that $M_0 \models S$, where M_0 is the minimal Herbrand model of P. Another verification consists of proving S from comp(P) (completion of P). Once again, specifications are restricted to (a subset of) first-order logic, and programs are restricted to definite programs.

In Sterling and Shapiro (1986), a definite program is defined to be *correct* with respect to an intended meaning M (that is, a Herbrand interpretation) if M_0 (the minimal Herbrand model) is contained in M. P is *complete* with respect to M if M is contained in M_0. A termination criterion is also defined.

SUMMARY

- The correctness of a logic description establishes an equivalence between the relation described in the specification and the H-logical consequences of the logic description.

- When a logic description LD(p) is correct w.r.t. its specification, any single H-model can be focussed upon, since the truth value of a ground atom p(t) is the same in all the H-models of LD(p).

- A correct logic description remains correct when new logic descriptions are introduced.

5
Construction of a logic description

PREVIEW   This chapter handles the creative task of constructing a logic description: one of the major tasks in the global process of solving a problem with logic programming. This is also the case for any kind of programming language and method. The design of a correct algorithm is one of the truly creative aspects of programming. There is no miracle recipe, and tricks cannot overcome this need for creativity. Construction techniques presented in this chapter are based on structural induction and the generalization paradigm. They are mostly independent of the methodological framework proposed. They can be applied successfully in other methodological approaches as well as in imperative or functional programming languages.

Before describing a general construction method (Section 5.4), the concept of primitive logic descriptions, the representation of data structures, and well-founded relations are introduced (Sections 5.1, 5.2 and 5.3). It is shown that the logic descriptions obtained with this construction method are correct by construction and the construction process actually contains an implicit correctness proof (Section 5.5). Various heuristics for the construction process are presented, covering the choice of a well-founded relation (Section 5.6) and of an induction parameter (Section 5.7). It is then shown that the construction of an algorithm can be performed by means of different strategies of generalization of the problem (Section 5.8). Finally, the inductive construction technique is briefly compared with two others (Section 5.9), and possible automations of the construction process are sketched (Section 5.10).

This chapter contains many examples illustrating the various aspects of the construction process.

5.1 Primitive logic descriptions

A top-down construction of a logic description consists of expressing the description in terms of specified subproblems. The logic descriptions of these specified subproblems are then constructed in another step, and so on. But when does this process stop? The answer is when primitive logic descriptions are reached. These are supposed to be defined already and to have a specification. What the primitive logic descriptions actually are depends on the target logic programming language. This is not unusual. When an algorithm is designed in an abstract imperative or functional language, the existence of some primitive operations or functions which depend on the target programming language must also be assumed.

In logic programming, the basic primitive is equality, which has the same specification in every logic programming language. It has already been used in some of the examples earlier in this book. Besides I–O primitives, there are also primitive logic descriptions for operations on integers and for the comparison of terms and integers. But the syntax and the specification of these primitives may differ slightly from one language to another.

The equality used in logic programming is the syntactical equality (which is not the equality encountered in first-order logic). Its specification is:

> procedure   T1 = T2
>
> *Type*:   T1, T2 : Term
>
> *Relation*:   T1 is syntactically identical to T2.
>
> **Specification 5.1**   T1 = T2

The relation described in this specification is the set $\{\langle t1, t1 \rangle \mid t1$ is a ground term$\}$. The use of LD(=) as a primitive can be viewed as restricting the H-interpretations to those in which = is interpreted as syntactical equality. A similar view can also be taken for other primitives (for example, addition, comparison, and so on).

*Construction of LD(=)

Although syntactical equality can be considered as a primitive, it is interesting to construct its logical description. Even if it does not have the form of a logic description (it is an infinite set of formulae), it is called LD(=) anyway.

The construction of LD(=) proceeds in two parts: the necessary and the sufficient conditions for $t_1 = t_2$ for t_1, t_2 ground terms. In other words, we will determine when $t_1 = t_2$ should hold (that is, when t_1 is syntactically equal to t_2), and when $t_1 \neq t_2$ should hold (that is, when t_1 is not syntactically equal to t_2).

Let us first consider when $t_1 = t_2$ should hold.

(1)   For t_1, t_2 being the same constant (say c): $c = c$

(2)   For t_1, t_2 being two terms of the form $f(s_1, \ldots, s_n)$ and $f(s'_1, \ldots, s'_n)$:

$$f(s_1, \ldots, s_n) = f(s'_1, \ldots, s'_n) \text{ if } s_i = s'_i \text{ for all } 1 \leq i \leq n$$

Secondly, when does $t_1 \neq t_2$ hold:

(3)   for t_1, t_2 being two different constants (say c and d): $c \neq d$

(4)   For t_1, t_2 being two terms of the form $f(s_1, \ldots, s_n)$ and $g(s'_1, \ldots, s'_m)$, where f and g are different functions:

$$f(s_1, \ldots, s_n) \neq g(s'_1, \ldots, s'_m)$$

(5)   For t_1, t_2 being two terms of the form $f(s_1, \ldots, s_n)$ and $f(s'_1, \ldots, s'_n)$:

$$f(s_1, \ldots, s_n) \neq f(s'_1, \ldots, s'_n) \quad \text{if} \quad s_i \neq s'_i \quad \text{for some } 1 \leq i \leq n$$

The above description cannot be formalized in a single formula (or a finite number of formulae). For instance, (2) expresses that for all function symbols f, and for all ground terms $s_1, \ldots, s_n, s'_1, \ldots, s'_n$, we have:

$$f(s_1, \ldots, s_n) = f(s'_1, \ldots, s'_n) \Leftarrow s_1 = s'_1 \& \ldots \& s_n = s'_n$$

The quantification over ground terms can be made with universal quantifiers since the domain of discourse in H-interpretations is the set of ground terms (that is, the Herbrand universe). However, a quantification over function symbols is impossible in first-order logic. This can be overcome by expressing formula schemata yielding an infinite number of formulae, one for each function symbol and arity. (1) and (2) can be encompassed in the following schema:

$$\forall(f(X_1, \ldots, X_n) = f(Y_1, \ldots, Y_n) \Leftarrow X_1 = Y_1 \& \ldots \& X_n = Y_n)$$
                                                                                      (Eq1)

for each function f ($n \geq 0$).

For 0-ary functions (that is, constants), Eq1 reduces to (1). (5) can be described as follows:

$$\forall(X_1 \neq Y_1 \vee \ldots \vee X_n \neq Y_n \Rightarrow f(X_1, \ldots, X_n) \neq f(Y_1, \ldots, Y_n))$$

for each function f ($n \geq 0$)

or equivalently:

$$\forall(f(X_1, \ldots, X_n) = f(Y_1, \ldots, Y_n) \Rightarrow X_1 = Y_1 \& \ldots \& X_n = Y_n)$$
                                                                                      (Eq2)

for each function $f(n \geq 0)$.

(3) and (4) are described in the last schema:

$$\forall(\, f(\, X_1, \ldots, X_n\,) \neq g(\, X_1, \ldots, X_m\,)\,) \qquad\qquad \textbf{(Eq3)}$$

for each pair f, g of distinct functions ($n, m \geq 0$).

LD(=) is thus composed of the schemata Eq1, Eq2 and Eq3 (Logic Description 5.1). It can easily be shown that LD(=) is correct with respect to its specification (see Exercise 5.1). It is also important to notice that LD(=) actually formalizes the unification of terms (see Exercise 5.3). The schemata Eq1 and Eq2 can be gathered together in a single schema with an equivalence instead of the two implications. Conditions (1) and (2) could also be formalized by the following single formula instead of the schema Eq1. Using Eq1 leads to Logic Description 5.2:

$$(\,\forall X\,)\,(\, X = X\,) \qquad\qquad \textbf{(Eq1')}$$
$$\forall(\, f(\, X_1, \ldots, X_n\,) = f(\, Y_1, \ldots, Y_n\,)\, \Leftarrow\, X_1 = Y_1\, \&\, \ldots\, \&\, X_n = Y_n\,)$$
for each function f ($n \geq 0$) $\qquad\qquad \textbf{(Eq1)}$
$$\forall(\, f(\, X_1, \ldots, X_n\,) = f(\, Y_1, \ldots, Y_n\,)\, \Rightarrow\, X_1 = Y_1\, \&\, \ldots\, \&\, X_n = Y_n\,)$$
for each function f ($n \geq 0$) $\qquad\qquad \textbf{(Eq2)}$
$$\forall(\, f(\, X_1, \ldots, X_n\,) \neq g(\, X_1, \ldots, X_m\,)\,) \qquad\qquad \textbf{(Eq3)}$$
for each pair f, g of distinct functions ($n, m \geq 0$)

Logic Description 5.1   T1 = T2

$$(\,\forall X\,)\,(\, X = X\,) \qquad\qquad \textbf{(Eq1')}$$
$$\forall(\, f(\, X_1, \ldots, X_n\,) = f(\, Y_1, \ldots, Y_n\,)\, \Rightarrow\, X_1 = Y_1\, \&\, \ldots\, \&\, X_n = Y_n\,)$$
for each function f ($n \geq 0$) $\qquad\qquad \textbf{(Eq2)}$
$$\forall(\, f(\, X_1, \ldots, X_n\,) \neq g(\, X_1, \ldots, X_m\,)\,) \qquad\qquad \textbf{(Eq3)}$$
for each pair f, g of distinct functions ($n, m \geq 0$)

Logic Description 5.2   T1 = T2

****LD(=) and the identity theory**

The above LD(=) is part of the so-called identity theory or equality theory (Clark, 1978; Lloyd, 1987). The identity theory is formed by Eq1, Eq1', Eq2, Eq3 and the two following axiom schemata Eq4 and Eq5.

$$(\,\forall X\,)\,(\, X \neq t_{[X]}\,) \qquad\qquad \textbf{(Eq4)}$$

where $t_{[X]}$ is a non variable term containing X

$$\forall(\, X_1 = Y_1\, \&\, \ldots\, \&\, X_n = Y_n\, \Rightarrow$$
$$(\, p(\, X_1, \ldots, X_n\,)\, \Rightarrow\, p(\, Y_1, \ldots, Y_n\,)\,)\,) \qquad\qquad \textbf{(Eq5)}$$

for each predicate p (including =)

From a model theoretic point of view, Eq1, Eq2 and Eq3 ensure that the domain of any model of the identity theory contains an isomorphic copy of the Herbrand universe. Different ground terms are also interpreted as different elements of this subdomain, and the ground atom s = t is true if and only if the interpretation of s is the same as the interpretation of t. The predicate = is thus interpreted as the identity relation on this subdomain. The identity theory does not restrict the domain of its models to an isomorphic copy of the Herbrand universe, nor does it impose that the predicate = be interpreted as the identity relation on the whole domain of its models. These two requirements are actually impossible to formalize by means of a first-order theory. Schemata Eq1′, Eq1 and Eq5 force = to be an equivalence relation.

From a proof theoretic point of view, the identity theory can be characterized as follows: $\exists (s = t)$ is a theorem iff s is unifiable with t; and $\neg\exists (s = t)$ is a theorem iff s is not unifiable with t.

When restricted to H-interpretations, schemata Eq1′, Eq4 and Eq5 of the identity theory are useless (see Exercise 5.4).

EXERCISES

*5.1 Show that LD(=) is correct w.r.t. its specification (*Hint*: proof by induction).

*5.2 Show that {Eq1, Eq2, Eq3} and {Eq1′, Eq2, Eq3} are H-equivalent, but that Eq1 and Eq1′ are not H-equivalent.

**5.3 Prove that, if s and t are terms (not necessarily ground),

$$\text{LD}(=) \vDash_H \exists (s = t) \quad \text{iff} \quad \text{s is unifiable with t}$$
$$\text{LD}(=) \vDash_H \neg\exists (s = t) \quad \text{iff} \quad \text{s is not unifiable with t}$$

**5.4 Prove that the identity theory is an H-logical consequence of LD(=).

5.2   Data structures

The proposed construction method is independent of the complexity of the problem. However, in order to simplify the presentation, the constructed logic descriptions will handle simple data structures such as lists or integers. This section describes briefly the representational aspect of abstract objects.

In an abstract data type approach, procedures for manipulating abstract objects must be specified. For logic descriptions these objects are logical terms. Consider, for example, the abstract data type **Association-list**, where an association-list (or AL) is a list of pairs $\langle e_1, v_1 \rangle, \ldots, \langle e_n, v_n \rangle$, such that

- $e_i \neq e_j$ for all $i \neq j$
- e_i is a constant called an element of AL
- v_i is a ground term called the associated value of the element e_i.

Some operations on association-lists are specified below.

> procedure   assoc(A_List, Elem, Value)
>
> *Type*:   A_List : Association-list
>   Elem : Constant
>   Value : Term
>
> *Relation*:   Elem is an element of A_List, with Value as associated value.
>
> **Specification 5.2**   assoc(A_List, Elem, Value)

> procedure   add_elem(A_List, Elem, Value, New_A_List)
>
> *Type*:   A_List, New_A_List : Association-list
>   Elem : Constant
>   Value : Term
>
> *Relation*:   Elem is not an element of A_List, and New_A_List is the association-list A_List with the additional pair $\langle$Elem, Value$\rangle$.
>
> **Specification 5.3**   add_elem(A_List, Elem, Value, New_A_List)

> procedure   drop_elem(A_List, Elem, Value, New_A_List)
>
> *Type*:   A_List, New_A_List : Association-list
>   Elem : Constant
>   Value : Term
>
> *Relation*:   Elem is an element of A_List, with Value as associated value, and New_A_List is the association-list A_List without the pair $\langle$Elem, Value$\rangle$.
>
> **Specification 5.4**   drop_elem(A_List, Elem, Value, New_A_List)

When choosing a representation for an abstract object in logic programming, it is usual to distinguish two possible forms of data representation: terms and relations (Kowalski, 1979). In **term representation**, structured data is formed by using function symbols to collect components into groups. For example, the association-list ($\langle c, 15 \rangle, \langle f, 2 \rangle, \langle a, 8 \rangle$) could be represented by the term [a [c, 15], [f, 2], [a, 8]]. Constants and structured terms are passive objects which are manipulated by procedures. This representation of data is compact and elegant. However, the computational effort required to access their components leads to some potential inefficiency at run time.

The alternative to term representation is **relation representation** in which objects are represented by logic descriptions. For example, the association-list associst_1 ($\langle c, 15 \rangle, \langle f, 2 \rangle, \langle a, 8 \rangle$) could be represented as proposed in Specification 5.5 and Logic Description 5.3.

procedure   assoc_list(Associst_Name, Elem, Value)

Type: Associst_Name : Constant
        Elem : Constant
        Value : Term

Relation: Value is the associated value of the element
          Elem in the association-list Associst_Name.

Specification 5.5   assoc_list(Associst_Name, Elem, Value)

assoc_list(Associst_Name, Elem, Value) ⇔
    Associst_Name = associst_1 & (Elem = c & Value = 15
                    ∨ Elem = f & Value = 2
                    ∨ Elem = a & Value = 8)

Logic Description 5.3   assoc_list(Associst_Name, Elem, Value)

The major drawback of relation representation is that the objects cannot be modified unless logic descriptions are allowed to modify other logic descriptions. The advantage of relation representation is its efficiency in accessing its components (when a 'good' relation is chosen). It will be seen in Part III how a relation representation can be obtained by meta-programming while preserving the correctness of the logic program. The relation representation will not be used within a logic description because it would affect the logical foundations of the logic description.

5.3   Well-founded relations and induction

The construction of logic descriptions can be achieved by structural induction, that is, induction on the structural form of the parameters. This section presents the concept of well-founded relations and the induction principle.

Definition 5.1   Let E be a set, and $<$ be any binary relation over E. A sequence $x_1, x_2, \ldots, x_{i-1}, x_i, x_{i+1}, \ldots$ of elements of E is a **decreasing sequence** iff $x_1 > x_2 > \ldots > x_{i-1} > x_i > x_{i+1} > \ldots$

Definition 5.2   A relation $<$ is **well-founded** over E, or (E, $<$) is a **well-founded set**, iff there is no infinite decreasing sequence of elements of E.

Definition 5.3   An element e of E is a **minimal element** of (E, <)
iff there is no element e' in E such that e' < e.

EXAMPLE 5.1

- The classical 'less than' relation is well-founded over the set of positive integers, but not over the set of positive and negative integers.
- The relation 'is the tail of' is well-founded over the set of ground lists. The minimal elements of the set {[a], [d, f, a], [f, a], [c, d]} are [a] and [c, d].

The following induction principle is an elegant and powerful way
of proving certain properties of the elements of a well-founded set.

Theorem 5.1   *The induction principle*
Let:

- (E, <) be a well-founded set, and
- W(x) be some property of the elements of E.

If $\forall x \in E\,(\,[\forall y \in E : y < x \Rightarrow W(y)] \Rightarrow W(x)\,)$
then $\forall\, x \in E : W(x)$.

Proof (by contradiction)
Let I be the subset of E for which W(x) is false. Suppose I is not empty,
then I has a minimal element $x_0 \in I$ because (E, <) is well-founded (see
Exercise 5.5). All the elements of E smaller than x_0 thus belong to E\I. By
the definition of I, we have: $(\forall e \in E : e < x_0 \Rightarrow W(e))$. Applying the
hypothesis, W(x_0) holds and $x_0 \notin I$. Hence we have a contradiction. So I
is empty.   ∎

In general, the induction principle can be applied as follows:

- Define a well-founded relation < over E;
- Prove that W(x_0) is true for every minimal element x_0 of (E, <);
- For an arbitrary non-minimal x, prove that W(x) is true assuming that W(y) is true for some y < x;
- Conclude that W(x) is true for all the elements of E.

The above induction principle is more general than that which is
usually called generalized induction or complete induction, where
(E, <) has to be well-ordered. Well-founded sets do not require the
relation to be transitive (see Exercise 5.7). In the induction principle it is
not stated that the induction hypothesis (that is, W(y) holds for all y < x)
must be used in order to prove W(x). It just states that any of these
assumptions *may* be used. The discovery of an adequate well-founded
relation is part of the creative aspect of an induction proof. This is
especially true when this principle is applied to algorithm construction
(in logic or otherwise).

EXERCISES

5.5   Prove that $(E, <)$ is a well-founded set iff every non-empty subset of E has a minimal element.

5.6   Find well-founded relations over the set of positive and negative integers, and over the set of rational numbers.

5.7
- $(D, <)$ is **partially ordered** (or **linearly ordered**) iff
  - $<$ is irreflexive (that is, $\forall x \; \neg x < x$)
  - $<$ is asymmetric (that is, $\forall x, y \quad x < y \Rightarrow \neg y < x$)
  - $<$ is transitive (that is, $\forall x, y, z \quad x < y \;\&\; y < z \Rightarrow x < z$)
- $(D, <)$ is **well-ordered** iff $(D, <)$ is partially ordered and well-founded.

(a)   Show that if a relation $<$ is asymmetric, then it is irreflexive.

(b)   Prove that $(D, <)$ is well-ordered iff $(D, <)$ is well-founded and transitive.

(c)   Let $(D, <)$ be well-founded. Define $x <^* y$ iff $x < e_1 < \ldots < e_n < y$ with $e_1, \ldots, e_n \in D$ and $n \geq 0$. Show that $(D, <^*)$ is well-ordered.

5.8   Let $(D1, <_1)$ and $(D2, <_2)$ be well-founded. Show that the following $(D, <)$ are well-founded:

(a) $D = D1 \cup D2$
$x < y$ iff $x \in D1$, $y \in D1$ and $x <_1 y$
            or $x \in D2$ and $y \in D2$ and $x <_2 y$
            or $x \in D1$ and $y \in D2$

(b) $D = D1 \times D2$
$\langle x1, x2 \rangle < \langle y1, y2 \rangle$ iff $x1 <_1 y1$
                      or $x1 = y1$ and $x2 <_2 y2$

Show that $(D, <)$ is also well-ordered when $(D1, <_1)$ and $(D2, <_2)$ are well-ordered.

5.4   A general construction method

This section presents a general method for constructing logic descriptions. Its use can help in many problems, but it is not claimed to be universal or applicable in all situations, nor does it produce algorithms automatically. The presentation is restricted to problems requiring recursive logic descriptions. Problems that can be solved without any recursivity (or any kind of 'loop') are usually straightforward and the logic description is constructed by composing some subproblems.

The proof of program properties, and thus of program correctness, can be carried out in many different ways. Induction is certainly a good candidate since it has been applied successfully in imperative and functional programming. A distinction is often made between computational induction (that is induction on the course of the computation) and structural induction (that is induction on the structure of the parameters).

Structural induction has been chosen here as the basis of the construction method. Computational induction has not been retained because it requires a computation model, which is counter to our purely logical approach. This choice is also justified as follows. Firstly, structural induction is well-adapted to the construction of programs since the induction is done on an already existing parameter whose structure is usually well-known by the programmer. Secondly, structural induction can successfully be applied when using informal specifications. Finally, as in imperative programming, structural induction will also turn out to be capable of handling the termination aspect at the logic program level.

The objective of the construction process is to obtain a logic description which is correct by construction. An independent correctness proof will not have to be carried out separately, since it will be implicit in the construction process. The resulting logic descriptions will have the following form:

$$p(\mathbf{x}) \quad \Leftrightarrow \quad
\begin{aligned}
& C_1 \;\&\; F_1 \\
\lor\; & C_2 \;\&\; F_2 \\
& \vdots \quad \vdots \\
\lor\; & C_m \;\&\; F_m.
\end{aligned}$$

where F_i and C_i are formulae.

Following our conventions, all the free variables over the C_i and F_i not appearing in $p(\mathbf{x})$ are existentially quantified over the definition part (that is, the right-hand side of the equivalence) of the logic description. Typically, each $C_i \;\&\; F_i$ will deal with one of the various cases of the induction parameter. Each C_i will thus determine a possible case of the induction parameter while the corresponding F_i will verify that the relation holds in this particular case. In practice, each C_i will often be a literal and the F_i a conjunction of literals.

Construction process

(1) *Choice of an induction parameter*
Choose a parameter x_j (or some parameters), called the **induction parameter(s)**.

(2) *Choice of a well-founded relation*
Define a well-founded relation over the type of the induction parameter x_j (or the set of tuples of the chosen parameters).

Suppose that for any subproblem q that will be used (including p itself),

q(t) true   iff $t \in q$ and   t is in the domain of q

Construct the logic description for p(x) such that for x ground,

p(x) true   iff $x \in p$ and   x is in the domain of p

The construction proceeds as follows:

(3)   *Structural forms of the induction parameter*
Construct a C_i for each structural form (including the minimal ones) of the induction parameter x_j, assuming that x_j has the correct type.

(4)   *Construction of the structural cases*
Construct the corresponding F_i as follows:

(4.1)   Suppose that x is in the domain of p. Construct the F_i such that when C_i is true, C_i & F_i is true iff $x \in p$. The formula F_i can be constructed by reducing the problem to simpler subproblems (because of the particular structural form of x_j) and/or by a recursive use of p(t) such that it is possible to show that $t_j < x_j$ (where $<$ is the well-founded relation defined in Step 2).

(4.2)   Verification of the domain membership. Verify or modify F_i such that C_i & F_i is false when x is not in the domain of p.

The above construction process serves to develop recursive logic descriptions and can easily be extended for mutually recursive logic descriptions. In this process, a relation is tested to see whether or not it holds for a given ground term. This simplifies the construction since other forms of parameters (such as variables) are not considered at this level. The creative aspect of algorithm construction is focussed on the choice of the induction parameter, the choice of a well-founded relation and the construction of the C_i and F_i, although the latter is mainly determined by the two former choices. The induction parameter must be chosen first followed by the well-founded relation. The choice of an induction parameter is more important than in functional or imperative programming, since in logic or relational programming there is *a priori* no input parameter. The definition of a well-founded relation is sometimes refined while constructing the F_i. For minimal elements, the problem must be solved without any occurrence of p. For non-minimal elements, the problem may be reduced to something 'smaller' or 'simpler' according to the well-founded relation. So p can be used or combined with some other procedures such that the given case of the global problem is solved. Domain membership (4.2) is verified afterwards and within each particular structural case, because most of the verification will already have been carried out by the subproblems involved. Thus this avoids unnecessary testing.

Construction steps 3 and 4 could be made more precise by relating them to the declarative semantics, that is H-interpretations.

Let:

- LD(q_1), ... , LD(q_k) be the subproblems that will be used in LD(p) which is under construction, with $q_i \neq p$

- a be an H-interpretation with
  - $q_i(t) \in a$ iff $t \in q_i$ and t is in the domain of q_i $(1 \leq i \leq k)$
  - $p(t) \in a$ iff $t \in p$ and t is in the domain of p
  where q_i is the relation described in the specification of q_i
  p is the relation described in the specification of p

- x be a ground n-tuple.

(3)   *Structural forms of the induction parameter*
       Construct the C_i from all the different structural forms of x_j
       (with a form covering the minimal elements) such that
       $\exists(C_1 \vee C_2 \vee \ldots \vee C_n)$ is true in a when x is in the domain of p.

(4)   *Construction of the structural cases*
       Construct the corresponding F_i as follows:
       (4.1) Suppose that x is in the domain of p. Construct the F_i such
              that $\exists(C_i \& F_i)$ is a necessary and sufficient condition in the
              H-interpretation a to have $x \in p$ when $\exists(C_i)$ holds in a. For
              any recursive use of p(t) it should be shown that $t_j < x_j$.
       (4.2) Verification of the domain membership. Verify or modify F_i
              such that $\exists(C_i \& F_i)$ is false in a when x is not in the domain
              of p.

Some questions

The presentation of this structural induction method can raise several questions:

- Are the constructed logic descriptions correct w.r.t. their specification?
- How is the induction parameter chosen?
- How is the well-founded relation chosen?
- What is the influence of the chosen induction parameter on the construction process and on the resulting logic description?
- What is the influence of the chosen well-founded relation on the construction process and on the resulting logic description?

- What is the relation between these choices?
- Are these choices related to the directionality specification?
- What about the case where, given an induction parameter and a well-founded relation, it is impossible to reduce the problem to a smaller one which can be solved with a recursive use of p?
- Should this induction construction method be preferred to a simple decomposition into subproblems, without recursion?

These questions are addressed in detail in the following sections.

*EXAMPLE

The construction method has already been illustrated in Section 1.5 on the efface(X, L, LEff) example (Specification 1.1). However, Construction Step 4.2 has not been performed. Many other examples will be constructed throughout this chapter.

The efface example is reconstructed here in detail, using the more precise framework of H-interpretations. In practice, constructions will be much shorter. This example will also illustrate that the constructed logic descriptions are correct by construction.

(1)　*Choice of an induction parameter*
　　　Let us take L as induction parameter.

(2)　*Choice of a well-founded relation*
　　　L is a list, so a well-founded relation has to be defined over lists. A possible relation is: $l1 < l2$ iff $l1$ is a proper suffix of $l2$. This is a well-founded relation because lists are finite and so it is impossible to have an infinite decreasing sequence.
　　　Let $\mathbf{a}$ be an H-interpretation where $t_1 = t_2$ is true iff t_1 is syntactically identical to t_2; and efface(X, L, LEff) is true iff L and LEff are lists and LEff is the list L without the first occurrence of X.

(3)　*Structural form of the induction parameter*
　　　The C_i must cover all the different structural forms of L. A simple choice is:

　　　　　$C_1 : L = []$
　　　　　$C_2 : L = [H | T]$　　H and T are assumed to be existentially quantified
　　　　　　　　　　　　　　　　(definition part of a logic description)

C_1 and C_2 cover all the possible forms of L: for any ground list $[e_1, \ldots, e_n]$, we have $(\exists H \exists T)([e_1, \ldots, e_n] = [] \lor [e_1, \ldots, e_n] = [H | T])$ true in $\mathbf{a}$. C_2 is especially chosen such that $T < L$ when L is a ground list. We could also say that the well-founded relation was especially chosen such that $T < L$ when L is a ground list. These choices are not independent.

(4)   *Construction of the structural cases*

(4.1) Let L and LEff be ground lists, and X be a ground term.
$\exists(\,C_i\,\&\,F_i\,)$ must be a necessary and sufficient condition to
have efface(X, L, LEff) when $\exists(\,C_i\,)$ is true in **a**.

- For L = [], it is impossible to have a list LEff which is
  the list L without the first occurrence of X.
  We obtain F_1 : false

- For L = [H | T], there are two possibilities depending on
  whether H = X or not.
  For H = X, the necessary and sufficient condition is
  LEff = T, because T is the list L without the first
  occurrence of X.
  For H $\neq$ X, the necessary and sufficient condition is
  that LEff must be of the form [H | TEff] where TEff is the
  list T without the first occurrence of X.
  We obtain F_2 : (H = X & LEff = T
  $\qquad\qquad \vee\ H \neq X\ \&\ \text{LEff} = [\text{H} \,|\, \text{TEff}]$
  $\qquad\qquad\qquad\qquad \&\ \text{efface}(\,X,\,T,\,\text{TEff}\,)$

  Note that T < L according to the well-founded relation
  when L is any ground list, since T is a proper suffix of L.

(4.2) *Verification of the domain membership*
Suppose that the parameters are not in the domain of efface
(that is, either L or LEff is not a list).
We must verify that $\exists(\,C_2\,\&\,F_2\,)$ is false in **a** $((\,C_1\,\&\,F_1\,)$
being trivially false).

- $\exists(\,\text{L} = [\text{H} \,|\, \text{T}]\ \&\ \text{H} \neq X\ \&\ \text{LEff} = [\text{H} \,|\, \text{TEff}]\ \&\ \text{efface}(\,X,\,T,\,\text{TEff}\,)\,)$
  is false in **a**:
  if L is not a list, either L = [H | T] or efface(X, T, TEff) is
  false in **a**;
  if LEff is not a list, either LEff = [H | TEff] or efface(X, T,
  TEff) is false in **a**.
  (This holds because the recursive use of efface verifies
  the domain membership.)

- $\exists(\,\text{L} = [\text{H} \,|\, \text{T}]\ \&\ \text{H} = X\ \&\ \text{LEff} = \text{T}\,)$ is not necessarily false
  in **a**:
  For instance, efface(a, [a | b], b) is true in **a**. An extra
  literal such as list(T) must be added (where list(T)
  holds iff T is a list).

$$\begin{aligned}
\text{efface}(\,X,\,L,\,\text{LEff}\,) \Leftrightarrow \quad & \\
L = []\ \&\ & \text{false} \\
\vee\ L = [\text{H} \,|\, \text{T}]\ \&\ (\,\text{H} = X\ \&\ & \text{LEff} = \text{T}\ \&\ \text{list}(\,\text{T}\,) \\
\vee\ \text{H} \neq X\ \&\ & \text{LEff} = [\text{H} \,|\, \text{TEff}] \\
& \&\ \text{efface}(\,X,\,T,\,\text{TEff}\,)\,)
\end{aligned}$$

Logic Description 5.4   efface(X, L, LEff)

*5.5   Correctness of the construction method

In this section, it is shown that logic descriptions obtained with the construction method are correct *by construction*. The construction process actually contains an implicit correctness proof. The following theorem establishes a generic correctness proof for logic descriptions obtained with the construction method. This generic correctness proof is then illustrated on the efface(X, L, LEff) construction.

Theorem 5.2   *Correctness of constructed logic descriptions*

If LD(p) is obtained by the construction method
then LD(p) is correct w.r.t. its specification.

Proof
LD(p) has the following form:

$$p(\mathbf{x}) \Leftrightarrow \begin{array}{l} C_1 \,\&\, F_1 \\ \vee\, C_2 \,\&\, F_2 \\ \quad\vdots\quad\vdots \\ \vee\, C_m \,\&\, F_m \end{array}$$

By the definition of correctness and Property 4.3, LD(p) is correct w.r.t. its specification iff for any finite set S of logic descriptions such that:

- all the subproblems LD(q_1), . . . , LD(q_k) used in LD(p) (with $q_i \neq$ p) are correct in S, and
- S contains no occurrences of p.

It is the case that:

(1) $S' = S \cup \{LD(p)\}$ has an H-model

(2)   for every H-model $\mathbf{a}$ of S, for any ground n-tuple t

     (a)   if t is in the domain of p, then p(t) is true in $\mathbf{a}$ iff $t \in p$

     (b)   if t is not in the domain of p, then p(t) is false in $\mathbf{a}$
     where p is the relation described in the specification of p.

The construction process of LD(p) involves an H-interpretation $\mathbf{a}$ with the two following properties:

(i) $q_i(\mathbf{t}) \in \mathbf{a}$ iff $t \in q_i$ and t is in the domain of q_i ($1 \leq i \leq k$)

(ii) $p(\mathbf{t}) \in \mathbf{a}$ iff $t \in p$ and t is in the domain of p
    where q_i is the relation described in the specification of the subproblem q_i.

The proof of correctness of LD(p) amounts to the proof of (1) and (2).

Proof of (1)
The subproblems LD(q_i) are correct in S. By Properties 4.1 and 4.2, S has an H-model where (i) holds. Since S contains no occurrences of p, this H-model can be transformed into another H-model of S (say a') where (i) and (ii) hold. By Construction Step 4, a' is also a model of $S \cup \{LD(p)\}$ = S'. This holds because LD(p) introduces constraints only on the predicate p, not on the q_i.

As a consequence, LD(q_i) are correct in S' (Property 4.4). The above argument shows the existence of an H-model of S' where (ii) holds. In order to prove (2), we have to show that (ii) holds for *all* H-models of S'.

Proof of (2)
Let:

- **t** be a ground *n*-tuple
- a' be an H-model of S'
- x_j be the induction parameter chosen in the construction process
- < be the well-founded relation chosen in the construction process.

The proof is obtained by induction on type$_j$, with < as well-founded relation. The induction hypothesis is:

For any ground *n*-tuple **s** with $s_j < t_j$:
　　p(**s**) true in a'　iff　$s \in p$　and　s is in the domain of p.

(a)　Let **t** be in the domain of p.
　　By Property 4.1, (i) holds in a'. Thus by Construction Step 3, we have:

$$\exists(C_1 \vee C_2 \vee \ldots \vee C_m)\{x/t\} \text{ is true in } a'$$

　　That is, for some k:

$$\exists(C_k)\{x/t\} \text{ is true in } a'$$

By Construction Step 4.1, $\exists(C_k \& F_k)\{x/t\}$ is a necessary and sufficient condition to have $t \in p$ in any H-interpretation where (i) and (ii) hold.
　　But

(i)　holds in a',

(ii)　holds in a' for **s** with $s_j < t_j$ (induction hypothesis).

Since recursive uses of p are made with a parameter smaller than t_j, we have:

$t \in p$ iff $\exists(C_k \& F_k)\{x/t\}$ is true in a'
iff $\exists(C_1 \& F_1 \vee \ldots \vee C_m \& F_m)\{x/t\}$ is true in a'
iff $p(t)$ is true in a'

(b)   Let t not be in the domain of p.
By Construction Step 4.2, for every structural case, we have $\exists(C_k$ $\& F_k)\{x/t\}$ false in a'. Hence $\exists(C_1 \& F_1 \vee \ldots \vee C_m \& F_m)\{x/t\}$ is false in a'. Thus $p(t)$ is false in a'. ∎

EXAMPLE

The above generic correctness proof is now illustrated on the logic description efface(X, L, LEff) constructed in the preceding section (Logic Description 5.4). The same notation will be used as in Theorem 5.2. The following correctness proof is actually based on the arguments used in the construction of the logic description, especially Step 4.

Proof of (1): Similar argument as in Theorem 5.2.
Proof of (2): This part is an instance of the above generic proof.
Let:

- t be a ground term
- $[e_1, \ldots, e_n]$ and $[f_1, \ldots, f_m]$ be ground lists
- a' be an H-model of S'.

(2.1) efface(t, $[e_1, \ldots, e_n]$, $[f_1, \ldots, f_m]$) is true in a' iff 't is an element of $[e_1, \ldots, e_n]$, and $[f_1, \ldots, f_m]$ is the list $[e_1, \ldots, e_n]$ without the first occurrence of t'.
This is proven by induction on lists, using the well-founded relation in the construction process (proper suffix).

case 1   minimal element: $[e_1, \ldots, e_n]$ is an empty list ($n = 0$).
efface(t, [], $[f_1, \ldots, f_m]$) is true in a'
iff ([] = [] & false) is true in a'
iff false
iff 't is an element of [], and $[f_1, \ldots, f_m]$ is the list [] without the first occurrence of t'

case 2   non-minimal elements: $[e_1, \ldots, e_n]$ is a non-empty list ($n > 0$).
case 2.1 $e_1 = t$
efface(t, $[e_1, \ldots, e_n]$, $[f_1, \ldots, f_m]$) is true in a'
iff (($\exists H \exists T$) $[t, e_2, \ldots, e_n] = [H \,|\, T]$ & $H = t$ & $[f_1, \ldots, f_m] = T$
& list(T)) is true in a'

iff $[f_1, \ldots, f_m] = [e_2, \ldots, e_n]$

iff 't is an element of $[t, e_2, \ldots, e_n]$, and $[f_1, \ldots, f_m]$ is the list $[e_1, \ldots, e_n]$ without the first occurrence of t'

case 2.2 $e_1 \neq t$

efface$(t, [e_1, \ldots, e_n], [f_1, \ldots, f_m])$ is true in $\mathbf{a}'$

iff $((\exists H \exists T)\ [e_1, e_2, \ldots, e_n] = [H|T]\ \&\ H \neq t\ \&\ (\exists \mathsf{TEff})$
$[f_1, \ldots, f_m] = [H\,|\,\mathsf{TEff}]\ \&\ \mathsf{efface}(t, T, \mathsf{TEff}))$ is true in $\mathbf{a}'$

iff $((\exists \mathsf{TEff})\ [f_1, \ldots, f_m] = [e_1|\mathsf{TEff}]\ \&\ \mathsf{efface}(t, [e_2, \ldots, e_n],$
$\mathsf{TEff}))$ is true in $\mathbf{a}'$

iff 't is an element of $[e_2, \ldots, e_n]$, and $[g_1, \ldots, g_k]$ is the list
$[e_2, \ldots, e_n]$ without the first occurrence of t'
and $[f_1, \ldots, f_m] = [e_1, g_1, \ldots, g_k]$ is true in $\mathbf{a}'$
(by induction hypothesis and Property 4.3: existence of a
witness)

iff 't is an element of $[e_1, e_2, \ldots, e_n]$, and $[f_1, \ldots, f_m]$ is the
list $[e_1, e_2, \ldots, e_n]$ without the first occurrence of t'

(2.2) For nl1, nl2 ground terms that are not both lists, efface$(t, nl1, nl2)$
is false in $\mathbf{a}'$. This is a straightforward proof based on Construction
Step 4.2 in the construction of efface.

EXERCISE

*5.9 The proposed construction method allows *recursion through nega-
tion*. Let even(L) hold iff the list L has an even number of elements.
The following logic description can be obtained with the construction method.

$$\text{even}(L) \Leftrightarrow \quad L = [\,]$$
$$\vee\ L = [H\,|\,T]\ \&\ \text{list}(T)\ \&\ \neg\text{even}(T)$$

Show that the above logic description is correct w.r.t. its specification. Why is the literal list(T) necessary?

5.6 The choice of a well-founded relation

The choice of a well-founded relation (wfr) is one of the creative tasks in
the construction process. We discuss here how to make this choice, and
its influence on the construction process and the resulting algorithms.
The following discussion is also applicable in the context of imperative or

functional programming, as well as in other approaches to logic program development.

5.6.1   How to choose a well-founded relation

A well-founded relation is defined over the type of the induction parameter. If there is more than one such parameter, the well-founded relation must be defined over the Cartesian product of the types of these induction parameters. This is more difficult because such a well-founded relation is usually some combination of others. Let us focus the discussion on cases where there is a single induction parameter. Examples with multiple induction parameters will be given later.

When a type is defined inductively, it is always possible to define the well-founded relation *is a component of*. It is well-founded because a component contains strictly fewer symbols than the term itself. It is also possible to define a well-founded relation through a mapping from the considered type to positive integers. Induction proofs can become more complicated with this additional mapping.

Let us compare some well-founded relations over lists:

$l_1 <_1 l_2$ iff l_1 is the tail of l_2 **(wfr1)**
$l_1 <_2 l_2$ iff l_1 is a proper suffix of l_2 **(wfr2)**
$l_1 <_3 l_2$ iff the number of elements of l_1 is less than
                    the number of elements of l_2 **(wfr3)**

The relation wfr3 subsumes wfr2: $l_1 <_2 l_2$ implies $l_1 <_3 l_2$ and wfr2 subsumes wfr1. The relation wfr1 is not transitive, wfr2 is transitive but not total and wfr3 is transitive and total. When a well-founded relation subsumes another one, the induction hypothesis can be used for more elements than with the other. With wfr3, the induction hypothesis can be applied on any list of shorter length; with wfr2, for any proper suffix; with wfr1, only for the tail. On the other hand, wfr3 requires a mapping from lists to integers. This can obscure an induction proof, especially if this mapping is not trivial. The choice of a well-founded relation is related to the construction of a logic description or, more precisely, to the induction hypothesis needed in the construction process. In this example, wfr1 and wfr2 will be preferred to wfr3 for their simplicity and because they do not involve any mapping. In most problems, the induction hypothesis provided by these two well-founded relations will be sufficient in the construction process.

The choice of a well-founded relation for a given induction parameter can be guided by the following heuristics:

(1)   Define a simple well-founded relation over the *type* of the induction parameter. If a well-founded relation is defined over

another set (such as positive integers), a mapping from the type to the other set must be defined. Induction proofs can become more complicated with this additional mapping.

(2)   If necessary, strengthen the well-founded relation during the construction process (when a stronger induction hypothesis is required).

Heuristic (1) can be further refined. The definition of a well-founded relation influences the construction of the logic description. For non-minimal elements, the problem is usually reduced to an element 'just smaller' according to the well-founded relation. For a given type, a well-founded relation can reflect the structural form of the type. However, it is sometimes possible to define a well-founded relation reflecting another structural form. In such cases, the constructed logic descriptions can be very different. Therefore two classes of well-founded relations (and thus of logic descriptions) can be distinguished. In the first one, the logic descriptions are constructed with a well-founded relation reflecting the structure of the induction parameter. Such relations are called **intrinsic** since they do not come from outside, and belong to the nature of the type of the induction parameter. In the second class, the logic descriptions are constructed with a well-founded relation reflecting another structure (for example, the structure of another parameter). Such relations are called **extrinsic** since they originate from the outside and are not part of the nature of the induction parameter. This distinction gives a useful heuristic for choosing a well-founded relation.

Intrinsic heuristic: Choose a well-founded relation reflecting the structural form of the induction parameter(s).

Extrinsic heuristic: Choose a well-founded relation reflecting the structural form of some other parameter(s), or reflecting the structural form of the relation itself.

The difference between the intrinsic and extrinsic heuristics lies in the perception of the induction parameter. In an intrinsic approach, the well-founded relation is taken as it is. But in an extrinsic approach, the induction parameter is, if possible, perceived as a particular *coding* of some other parameter(s), or as a *representation* of a more abstract object. The construction process is based on the chosen well-founded relation. Therefore, the resulting logic descriptions will reflect that choice and can be very different. Such a distinction cannot be made for all problems.

5.6.2   Example: compress(L, CL)

The application of the intrinsic and extrinsic heuristics is illustrated on an example of simple data compression. The necessary concepts will be introduced with a small example before specifying the problem (Specification 5.6).

EXAMPLE 5.2

list of characters	[y, y, v, e, e, e,s, s]
compression	↓
compact list of characters	[y, 2, v, 1, e, 3, s, 2]

Definition 5.4 A **compact list of characters** is a list of the form $[c_1, n_1, c_2, n_2, \ldots, c_k, n_k]$ where:

- $k \geq 0$
- c_i are characters with $c_i \neq c_{i+1}$ ($1 \leq i < k$)
- n_i are strictly positive integers.

Definition 5.5 Let L be a list of characters $[c_1, \ldots, c_n]$ ($n \geq 0$). A **max-subsequence** of L is a sublist $[c_p, c_{p+1}, \ldots, c_q]$ of L such that:

- $1 \leq p \leq q \leq n$
- $c_j = c_{j+1}$ ($p \leq j < q$)
- $c_{p-1} \neq c_p$ if $p > 1$
- $c_q \neq c_{q+1}$ if $q < n$

In Example 5.2, [e, e, e] is a max-subsequence of [y, y, v, e, e, e, s, s], but [e, e] or [y, y, v] are not.

Definition 5.6 The **compression** of a list of characters L is a compact list of characters where each max-subsequence of L is replaced by the character occurring in the subsequence, and the length of this subsequence.

procedure   compress(L, CL)

Type: L : List of characters
CL : Compact list of characters

Relation: CL is the compression of L.

Specification 5.6   compress(L, CL)

In the construction process, L will be taken as the induction parameter. The choice of CL is developed later.

Construction with an intrinsic well-founded relation

(1)   *Choice of an induction parameter* : L

(2)   *Choice of a well-founded relation*
The intrinsic heuristic guides the choice to a well-founded relation reflecting the structural form of L, that is, the structural form of a list (of characters). We choose here:

$$l_1 < l_2 \quad \text{iff} \quad l_1 \text{ is a proper suffix of } l_2.$$

A well-founded relation reflecting the structural form of L induces the following idea of a solution:

$$[e_1, e_2, \ldots, e_n]$$
$$\underbrace{\qquad\qquad}$$
recursion

(a)   recursion with the tail of L (that is, reducing the problem to a 'just smaller' one according to the well-founded relation).

(b)   extend the result of the recursion in order to treat the first character.

(3)   *Structural forms of the induction parameter*
A first guess would classically be to take L = [] and L = [H|T]. But the construction would force us to backtrack in that choice. Lists of one character must be considered separately. The structural forms are thus L = [], L = [C] and L = [C1, C2|T].

(4)   *Construction of the structural cases*
(4.1) Suppose that L is a list of characters and CL is a compact list.
   •   For L = [], we immediately get CL = [].
   •   For L = [C], the compress relation is obviously verified iff CL = [C, 1].
   •   For L = [C1, C2|T], we can use compress recursively (with [C2|T] < L):

   (∃CL1) compress([C2|T], CL1)

Depending on whether C1 = C2 or not, we obtain:

C1 ≠ C2: The compress relation is verified iff
   CL = [C1, 1|CL1]

C1 = C2: The compress relation is verified iff
   CL1 = [C1, Lg|TCL] & add(Lg, 1, Lg1)
   & CL = [C1, Lg1|TCL]

(The specification of add is given in Specification 5.7).

(4.2) *Verification of the domain membership*
Two literals must be added. In the second structural case (that is, when L = [C]), it has to be verified that C is a character in order to have L as a list of characters and CL as a

compact list of characters. In the third structural case (that is, when L = [C1, C2 | T]), it also has to be verified that C1 is a character, but only when C1 ≠ C2. The recursive use of compress takes care of the other verifications (the specification of char(X) is given in Specification 5.8).

> procedure   add(A, B, AplusB)
>
> *Type*:   A, B, AplusB : Integers
>
> *Relation*:   AplusB is the sum of A and B.
>
> **Specification 5.7**   add(A, B, AplusB)

> procedure   char(X)
>
> *Type*:   X : Term
>
> *Relation*:   X is a character.
>
> **Specification 5.8**   char(X)

The above construction yields Logic Description 5.5 where the name of the procedure is suffixed in order to distinguish it from the other constructions.

> compress_int_L(L, CL) ⇔
>   L = [] & CL = []
>   ∨ L = [C] & CL = [C, 1] & char(C)
>   ∨ L = [C1, C2 | T] & compress_int_L([C2 | T], CL1)
>   & (C1 ≠ C2 & CL = [C1, 1 | CL1] & char(C1)
>   ∨ C1 = C2 & CL1 = [C1, Lg | TCL]
>   & add(Lg, 1, Lg1)
>   & CL = [C1, Lg1 | TCL])

Logic Description 5.5   compress int L(L, CL)

Construction with an extrinsic well-founded relation

(1)   *Choice of an induction parameter*: L

(2)   *Choice of a well-founded relation*
The extrinsic heuristic guides the choice to a well-founded relation reflecting the structural form of CL, or of the relation itself. A representation of compact lists has to be found in L. One possible idea is to see a list of characters as a list of max-subsequences of characters. An associated well-founded relation would be:

$$l_1 < l_2 \quad \text{iff} \quad l_1 \text{ is a proper suffix of } l_2, \text{with max-subsequences of } l_2.$$

This well-founded relation reflects the structure of the relation and induces the following idea of solution:

$$[e_1, e_2, \ldots, e_i, \quad e_{i+1}, \ldots, e_n]$$

$$\underbrace{} \qquad \underbrace{\phantom{e_{i+1}, \ldots, e_n]}}$$

first   recursion
max-sequence

(a)   What is the first max-subsequence of L?

(b)   What is the length of this first max-subsequence of L?

(c)   Recursion with the list L without its first max-subsequence (that is, reducing the problem to a 'just smaller' one according to our well-founded relation).

(3)   *Structural forms of the induction parameter*
The structural forms of the induction parameter L of compress are L empty (that is, L =[]) and L non-empty (that is, L = [C|T]).

(4)   *Construction of the structural cases*
The construction process will introduce two subproblems that are specified in Specifications 5.9 and 5.10.

> procedure   first_max_seq(L, F_Seq, Suf_L)
>
> *Type*:   L : Non-empty list of characters
> F_Seq, Suf_L : List of characters
>
> *Relation*:   L is the concatenation of F_Seq and Suf_L, with F_Seq the first max-subsequence of L.
>
> **Specification 5.9**   first_max_seq(L, F_Seq, Suf_L)

> procedure   length(L, Lg)
>
> *Type*:   L : List
> Lg : Positive integer
>
> *Relation*:   Lg is the number of elements of L.
>
> **Specification 5.10**   length(L, Lg)

(4.1)   Suppose that L is a list of characters and CL is a compact list of characters.
- For L = [], we immediately obtain CL = []
- For L = [C|T], the specified subproblems can be used:

$$(\exists Lg \; \exists F\_Seq \exists Suf\_L \,) \,(\, first\_max\_seq(L, F\_Seq, Suf\_L \,) \\ \& \; length(F\_Seq, Lg \,))$$

we now have that the compress relation holds iff

$$CL = [C, Lg \,|\, Tail\_CL] \,\&\, compress(Suf\_L, Tail\_CL \,)$$

(We have Suf_L < L)

Note that this construction could have been performed with the 'proper suffix' well-founded relation. But here, the chosen well-founded relation guided the general strategy of this algorithm.

(4.2)   *Verification of the domain membership*
No literal has to be added. The verification that L is a list of characters is done by first_max_seq. The verification that CL is a compact list is more subtle. In the second structural case (that is, when CL = [C, Lg | Tail_CL]), we know that Tail_CL has to be a compact list of characters because of the recursive use of compress. It is also verified that C is a character (because of first_max_seq), and Lg is an integer (because of length). In order to have a compact list of characters, C must be different from the first character of Tail_CL. This is verified by the combined two literals first_max_seq and compress.

Logic descriptions will not be constructed here for the subproblems first_max_seq and length. The resulting logic description for compress is Logic Description 5.6.

```
compress_ext_L( L, CL ) ⇔
    L = [] & CL = []
  ∨ L = [C | T] & first_max_seq( L, F_Seq, Suf_L )
                & length( F_Seq, Lg )
                & CL = [C, Lg | Tail_CL]
                & compress_ext_L( Suf_L, Tail_CL )
```

Logic Description 5.6   compress_ext_L(L, CL)

Comparison

The construction process and the logic descriptions resulting from the intrinsic and extrinsic well-founded relations will now be compared. For compress_int_L, a well-founded relation was easily found. The difficulty here was to imagine how to combine the result of the recursion on the tail of L, with the first character of L. Once this had been found, the construction was quite simple. For compress_ext_L, the well-founded relation was difficult to find because some representation of the relation had to be discovered within L. However, the construction was easily done and the subproblems first_max_seq and length provided a simple way to help.

What about the resulting logic descriptions? It is difficult to compare their simplicity because some people will prefer the first one and others the second. Nevertheless, the following observations can be made. The structure of compress_int_L reflects the structure of the list of characters L, while compress_ext_L reflects the structure of the compact list of characters CL. On the one hand, the description obtained with the extrinsic well-founded relation can appear simpler since the well-founded relation and the resulting description explicitly use the concept defined in the specification: max-subsequences. This is not the case with the intrinsic well-founded relation. On the other hand, the description obtained with the extrinsic well-founded relation can also appear more complex because the logic description for the subproblem first_max_seq is almost as complex as the description of the initial problem. Compress_ext_L is a 'two loops' algorithm: each max-subsequence is treated as a whole, and, within each subsequence, characters are handled separately (first_max_seq and length). Compress_int_L is a 'one loop' algorithm: each character is treated separately. This comparison is illustrated in Figures 5.1 and 5.2. In Figure 5.1, the first parameters of the successive recursive uses of compress_int_L are given for L = [p, p, d, d, d, e]. In Figure 5.2, the first parameters of the successive recursive uses of compress_ext_L are given in the left-hand column, together with the corresponding first parameters of the successive recursive uses of first_max_seq in the right-hand column (see Exercise 5.17 for a logic description of first_max_seq).

---

compress_int_L

[p, p, d, d, d, e]
[p, d, d, d, e]
[d, d, d, e]
[d, d, e]
[d, e]
[e]
[]

Figure 5.1   Example of recursive uses of compress_int_L.

---

compress_ext_L	first_max_seq
[p, p, d, d, d, e]	
	[p, p, d, d, d, e]
	[p, d, d, d, e]
	[d, d, d, e]
[d, d, d, e]	
	[d, d, d, e]
	[d, d, e]
	[d, e]
	[e]
[e]	
	[e]
	[]
[]	

Figure 5.2   Example of recursive uses of compress_ext_L.

The distinction between intrinsic and extrinsic well-founded relations is not appropriate for all problems. It is sometimes useless because the well-founded relations will be almost the same, as will be the construction processes and the resulting logic descriptions. For other problems an extrinsic approach can be impossible when no suitable representation of other parameters or of the relation can be found. When an intrinsic and an extrinsic approach are possible, there is no *a priori* reason, generally speaking, to believe that the construction process or the resulting logic description will be superior with one approach rather than the other.

EXERCISES_____

5.10 Let palindrome(L) hold iff the list L is a palindrome (that is, equal to its reverse). Construct a recursive logic description (without reverse). Define precisely the well-founded relation used in the construction process.

5.11 Let factorial(N, FactN) hold iff FactN is N! (that is, $N*(N-1)*\ldots*2*1$). The type of N and FactN is positive integer. Construct a logic description with N as induction parameter.

5.12 Let prefix(L, PrefL) hold iff the list PrefL is a prefix of the list L. Construct a recursive logic description with PrefL as induction parameter. What is the simplest well-founded relation?

5.13 Let sumlist(L, S) hold iff S is the sum of the elements of L. The type of L is list of integers and S in an integer. The sum of the elements of an empty list is defined to be 0. Construct a logic description with L as induction parameter.

5.14 Let minlist(L, Min) hold iff Min is the minimum of the elements of L. The type of L is non-empty list of integers and Min is an integer. Construct a logic description with L as induction parameter.

5.15 Let remove(X, L, LRem) hold iff the list LRem is the list L from which all the occurrences of the term X in L have been removed. Construct a logic description with L as induction parameter.

5.16 Let merge(L1, L2, LM) hold iff LM is the merging of the two lists L1 and L2. The type of L1, L2 and LM is ordered list of integers. Construct a logic description with an induction on the couple (L1, L2). Pay particular attention to verifying the domain membership.

5.17   Construct a logic description for first_max_seq(L, S_Seq, Suf_L) (see Specification 5.9) using L as induction parameter.

5.18   Let max_seq(L, Max) hold iff Max is the maximum length of all the max-subsequences of L. The type of L is list of characters and Max is a positive integer. By definition, 0 is the maximum length of all the max-subsequences of the empty list. Construct a logic description with L as induction parameter, using an extrinsic well-founded relation.

5.19   • Let partition(X, L, LInf, LSup) hold iff the list LSup contains all the elements of L which are greater than or equal to X, and only them; and the list LInf contains all the elements of L which are less than X, and only them. The type of L, LInf and LSup is list of integers, and the type of X is integer.

   • Let quicksort(L, SL) hold iff the list SL contains all the elements of L, and only them, in increasing order. The type of L and SL is list of integers.

   Construct a logic description for quicksort, with L as induction parameter, using partition as a subproblem. Define precisely the well-founded relation used in the construction process. Be sure the recursive literals have a smaller parameter.

5.20   • Let an **invoicelist** be a list of triplets of the form (Name, Num, Price) where Name is a constant, Num and Price are positive integers. This list is ordered on Name and on Num for equal Names.

   • Let a **client summary** be a triplet of the form (Name, ListInv, TotPrice) where Name is a constant, TotPrice is a positive integer and ListInv is a list of couples of the form (Num, Price) where Num and Price are positive integers. The list ListInv is strictly ordered by Num.

   • Let a **global summary** be a couple of the form (ListCliSum, TotPrice) where TotPrice is a positive integer and ListCli-Sum is a list of client summaries, strictly ordered by their first element (that is, Name).

   From the above definitions, it can easily be imagined how an invoice list can be turned into a global summary.

   (a)   Define precisely the concept of a global summary of an invoice list.

   (b)   Specify a procedure invoice(L, GS) which holds iff GS is the global summary of L.

(c)   Construct a logic description with L as induction parameter, using an intrinsic well-founded relation.

(d)   Construct a logic description with L as induction parameter, using an extrinsic well-founded relation.

5.7   The choice of an induction parameter

Is there really a choice for the induction parameter, or is it just a matter of the presentation of the construction yielding the same logic description anyway? Some examples will be presented first, illustrating the various cases. Then, how to choose an induction parameter is analysed. As for the choice of a well-founded relation, the following discussion is independent of the methodological framework used for developing logic programs. There is however much more freedom in the choice of an induction parameter in the relational programming framework than in the imperative or functional framework.

5.7.1   Examples

EXAMPLE   efface(X, L, LEff)

In Section 5.4, the construction method has been illustrated on the construction of a logic description for the problem efface(X, L, LEff) (Specification 1.1). In that construction, L was chosen as the induction parameter. We will now take another induction parameter.

(1)   *Choice of an induction parameter* : LEff
The parameter X cannot be taken as the induction parameter because its structure has nothing to do with the problem. A construction with L as induction parameter has been made in Logic Description 5.4.

(2)   *Choice of a well-founded relation*
$l_1 < l_2$ iff l_1 is a proper suffix of l_2

(3)   *Structural forms of the induction parameter*
The structural forms are LEff empty and LEff non-empty.

(4)   *Construction of the structural cases*
(4.1) Suppose that L and LEff are lists.
  • For LEff = [], the only possibility is L = [X]. LEff is then the list L without the first occurrence of X.
  • For LEff = [H | TEff], there are two possibilities:

Either L = [X, H | TEff] so that [H | TEff] is the list [X, H | TEff] without the first occurrence of X.

Or with H ≠ X, take efface(X, T, TEff). In that case, TEff is the list T without the first occurrence of X. Therefore [H | TEff] is the list [H | T] without the first occurrence of X (because H ≠ X).

(4.2) *Verification of the domain membership*
In the second structural case (that is, when LEff = [H | TEff]), a literal must be added to ensure that TEff is a list.

The resulting logic description (Logic Description 5.7) is very similar to the one obtained with L as induction parameter (Logic Description 5.4). In fact, their definition parts are logically equivalent and this description can be transformed to yield the first one. This will be shown in the section on transformations.

efface_ LEff(X, L, LEff) ⇔
    LEff = [] & L = [X]
    ∨ LEff = [H | TEff] & (L = [X, H | TEff] & list(TEff)
                  ∨ H ≠ X & efface_LEff(X, T, TEff)
                   & L = [H | T])

Logic Description 5.7   efface_LEff(X, L, LEff)

EXAMPLE   length(L, Lg)

The second example is the classical length problem (Specification 5.12). Two constructions can be done: one with L as the induction parameter, and a second with Lg. The well-founded relations are respectively 'proper suffix' and 'less than'. These two constructions being quite simple, only the resulting logic descriptions are given (Logic Descriptions 5.8 and 5.9). These are both correct, but not equivalent (greater(A, B) holds iff the integer A is greater than the integer B). It is worth noting that the well-founded relations used are both intrinsic and extrinsic because there is a simple correspondence between the two parameters.

length_L(L, Lg) ⇔
    L = [] & Lg = 0
    ∨ L = [H | T] & length_L(T, Lg_T) & add(Lg_T, 1, Lg)

Logic Description 5.8   length_L(L, Lg)

length_Lg(L, Lg) ⇔
    Lg = 0 & L = []
    ∨ greater(Lg, 0) & L = [H | T] & add(Lg_T, 1, Lg)
                        & length_Lg(T, Lg_T)

Logic Description 5.9   length_Lg(L, Lg)

EXAMPLE suffix(L, SufL)

    procedure   suffix(L, SufL)

    Type: L, SufL : Lists

    Relation: SufL is a suffix of L.

    Specification 5.11   suffix(L, SufL)

The construction of suffix(L, SufL) (Specification 5.11) cannot easily be achieved with SufL as the induction parameter. For SufL non-empty, assuming a 'proper suffix' well-founded relation, a recursive use of suffix with the tail of SufL does not help in verifying that SufL is a suffix of L. The 'proper prefix' well-founded relation is actually needed. But this requires the decomposition of a non-empty list into two parts: its last element and the list of all the other elements. Given the structure of a list, such a decomposition is very costly. We can thus say that SufL is not a good candidate as induction parameter because of the available primitives on lists. Two other constructions are now investigated.

Construction 1
In this construction of suffix(L, SufL), L is chosen as the induction parameter, using the 'proper suffix' well-founded relation. The construction is straightforward and the logic description is given in Logic Description 5.10.

    suffix_L(L, SufL) ⇔
        L = [] & SufL = []
     ∨ L = [H | T] & (SufL = [H | T] & list(T)
                ∨ suffix_L(T, SufL))

    Logic Description 5.10   suffix_L(L, SufL)

Construction 2
The construction is also possible on the difference between L and SufL (denoted by L\SufL), assuming that SufL is a suffix of L. The structural forms are L\SufL empty and L\SufL non-empty. L\SufL is empty when L = SufL. For L\SufL non-empty, L has the form [H | T] and SufL is a suffix of T with T\SufL smaller than L\SufL (according to the number of elements, for instance). This reasoning has been used, assuming that SufL is a suffix of L! However, the above argument can easily be turned into an algorithm construction. SufL is a suffix of L iff either SufL = L or L = [H | T] and SufL is a suffix of T (that is, suffix(T, SufL)). In the recursive use of suffix, it can be seen that T is smaller than L using the 'proper suffix' well-founded relation. The resulting logic description is given in Logic Description 5.11. Here the choice of L\SufL as the induction parameter has been the basis of the idea of the constructed description. L\SufL is thus a 'false

induction parameter' because the actual induction is performed on L. Logic Descriptions 5.10 and 5.11 are equivalent but constructed differently.

suffix_LSufL(L, SufL) ⇔
    L = SufL & list(SufL)
    ∨ L = [H│T] & suffix_LSufL(T, SufL)

Logic Description 5.11   suffix_LSufL(L, SufL)

EXAMPLE flattree(T, FT)

The next example is the classical problem of determining whether a list of terms is the list of the elements of a binary tree. Let us first introduce the necessary concepts illustrated in Figure 5.3.

> **Definition 5.7** A **tree** is either empty or non-empty. A non-empty tree is composed of three parts:
>
> - a term (called the root element of the tree)
> - two trees (called subtrees): a left one and a right one
>
> An empty tree is represented by the constant void. A non-empty tree is represented by the term tree(E, LT, RT) where E is the root element, LT is the left subtree and RT is the right subtree. The **elements** of a tree are its root element and the elements of its subtrees.

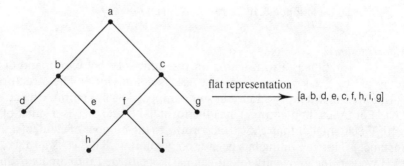

Figure 5.3 Flat representation of a tree.

> **Definition 5.8** The **flat representation** of a tree is the list of all the elements of the tree, corresponding to a prefix traversal.

procedure flattree(T, FT)

Type: T : Tree
FT : List

Relation: FT is the flat representation of T.

Specification 5.12 flattree(T, FT)

Construction 1: *induction on* T

(1) *Choice of an induction parameter* : T

(2) *Choice of a well-founded relation*
$t_1 < t_2$ iff t_1 is a subtree of t_2

(3) *Structural forms of the induction parameter* T
T is either an empty tree (that is, T = void) or a non-empty tree
(that is, T = tree(E, LT, RT)).

(4) *Construction of the structural cases*
(4.1) Suppose T is a tree and FT is a list.
- For T = void, FT must be the empty list.
- For T = tree(E, LT, RT), FT is the concatenation of the flat
representation of LT and RT, preceded by E. Hence the
formula:

flattree(LT, FLT) & flattree(RT, FRT)
& append(FLT, FRT, Tail_FT) & FT = [E | Tail_FT]

Note that LT and FT are smaller than T. See Specification 4.2
for append.
(4.2) *Verification of the domain membership*
No literals have to be added.

The resulting logic description is Logic Description 5.12.

flattree_T(T, FT) ⇔
    T = void & FT = []
  ∨ T = tree(E, LT, RT) & flattree_T(LT, FLT)
                          & flattree_T(RT, FRT)
                          & append(FLT, FRT, Tail_FT)
                          & FT = [E | Tail_FT]

Logic Description 5.12 flattree_T(T, FT)

Construction 2: *induction on* FT

(1) *Choice of an induction parameter*: FT

(2) *Choice of a well-founded relation*
$l_1 < l_2$ iff l_1 has fewer elements than l_2.

(3)   *Structural forms of the induction parameter*

The structural forms are FT empty (that is, FT = []) and non-empty (that is, FT = [E | Tail_FT]).

(4)   *Construction of the structural cases*

(4.1) Suppose T is a tree and FT is a list.
- For FT = [], we immediately obtain T = void.
- For FT = [E | Tail_FT], T must be a non-empty tree of the form tree(E, LT, RT). FT is a flat representation of T iff Tail_FT is decomposable into a prefix Pref and a suffix Suf such that Pref and Suf are the flat representations of the left and right subtrees of T(LT and RT), respectively. We obtain:

append(Pref, Suf, Tail_FT) & flattree(LT, Pref)
& flattree(RT, Suf)

Note that Pref and Suf are smaller than FT.

(4.2) *Verification of the domain membership*
No literal has to be added.

The resulting logic description is Logic Description 5.13.

flattree_FT(T, FT) ⇔
    FT = [] & T = void
    ∨ FT = [E | Tail_FT] & T = tree(E, LT, RT) & append(Pref, Suf, Tail_FT)
                                                    & flattree_FT(LT, Pref)
                                                    & flattree_FT(RT, Suf)

Logic Description 5.13   flattree_FT(T, FT)

Comparison

The definition parts of the two resulting logic descriptions are identical. But here, the construction processes were quite different. In the construction of flattree_T, the flat representation of a tree T was unique, and the construction was straightforward. In flattree_FT, more than one tree could be represented by FT. The necessary and sufficient condition was therefore not obvious to find because we had to be sure to consider all the possible cases. This was done by considering all the prefixes and suffixes of FT. In the construction of flattree_FT, the 'proper suffix' well-founded relation could not be used since a stronger induction hypothesis was needed (Pref is not a proper suffix of FT). It should be noted that the construction of flattree_T is based on an intrinsic approach since the focus is on trees. The construction of flattree_FT turns out to be extrinsic because we tried to decompose FT into two smaller parts reflecting the structure of the other parameter T. What about an intrinsic approach with FT as induction parameter?

EXAMPLE   compress(L, CL), ***induction on*** CL

Two logic descriptions for compress(L, CL) have already been constructed with L as induction parameter. Depending on the choice of an intrinsic or extrinsic well-founded relation, we obtained two logic descriptions (compress_int_L and compress_ext_L). Two other logic descriptions are now constructed with CL as the induction parameter.

Construction with an intrinsic well-founded relation

(1)   *Choice of an induction parameter*: CL

(2)   *Choice of a well-founded relation*
      The intrinsic heuristic guides the choice of a well-founded relation reflecting the structure of a compact list. The 'proper suffix' well-founded relation will be sufficient in this problem.

$$cl_1 < cl_2 \quad \text{iff} \quad cl_1 \text{ is a proper suffix of } cl_2$$

This well-founded relation induces the following idea of solution:

$$[c_1, lg_1, \quad c_2, lg_2, \dots, c_n, lg_n]$$

$$\underbrace{}$$

recursion

(a)   construction of the first max-subsequence

(b)   recursion for the other max-subsequences

(c)   L is the concatenation of the first subsequence and the others

This yields the sequence subproblem (Specification 5.13).

> procedure   sequence(C, Lg, List_C)
>
> *Type*:   C : Character
>   Lg : Positive integer
>   List_C : List of characters
>
> *Relation*:   List_C is a list composed of Lg occurrences of C.

Specification 5.13   sequence(C, Lg, List_C)

(3)   *Structural forms of the induction parameter*
      The structural forms of the compact list of characters CL are CL empty (that is, CL = []) and CL non-empty (that is, CL = [C, Lg | Tail_CL]).

(4)   *Construction of the structural cases*

      (4.1) Suppose that L is a list of characters and CL is a compact list of characters.
      - For CL = [], L = [].
      - For CL = [C, Lg | Tail_CL], we first determine the first max-subsequence:

      sequence(C, Lg, First_seq)

We now have a reduced problem (Tail_CL < CL):

compress(T, Tail_CL)

The necessary and sufficient condition is now that L must be the concatenation of the first sequence (First_Seq) and the others (T).

append (First_Seq, T, L)

(4.2)   *Verification of the domain membership*
L is already verified to be a list of characters since it is the concatenation of First_seq and T which are both lists of characters (because of sequence and compress). Because of the recursive compress, Tail_CL is verified to be a compact list of characters. We also have that Lg is a positive integer and C a character by sequence. It thus remains to verify that the first character of Tail_CL is different from C. This could be done by adding the formula

Tail_CL = [] ∨ (Tail_CL = [C1, Lg1 | TTL] & C ≠ C1)

But, such a verification can be achieved with the following simpler formula:

(∀Y)(Tail_CL ≠ [C | Y])

The resulting logic description is Logic Description 5.14.

```
compress_int_CL( L, CL ) ⇔
    CL = [] & L = []
    ∨ CL = [C, Lg | Tail_CL] & sequence( C, Lg, First_seq )
                             & compress_int_CL( T, Tail_CL )
                             & append( First_seq, T, L )
                             & ( ∀Y )Tail_CL ≠ [C | Y]
```

Logic Description 5.14   compress_int_CL(L, CL)

Construction with an extrinsic well-founded relation

(1)   *Choice of an induction parameter*: CL

(2)   *Choice of a well-founded relation*
Using the extrinsic heuristic, the well-founded relation should reflect the structural form of L (list of characters). If the proper suffix relation is taken, the structure of L is not reflected since the first two elements of CL correspond to a whole subsequence of characters in L. The concept of a character within a subsequence must appear in the well-founded relation. The idea of the following (non-trivial) well-founded relation is to compare the length of the first sequences of two compact lists.

Let $cl_1 = [c_1, lg_1, \ldots, c_n, lg_n]$ $n \geq 0$
$\qquad cl_2 = [c'_1, lg'_1, \ldots, c'_m, lg'_m]$ $m \geq 0$
$cl_1 < cl_2$ iff

- either cl_1 is a proper suffix of cl_2
- or $n = m \geq 1$
  and $c_i = c'_i$, $lg_i = lg'_i$ for $2 \leq i \leq n$
  and $c_1 = c'_1$, $0 < lg_1 < lg'_1$
  (This is well-founded because lg_1 is bounded by 0.)

The chosen well-founded relation suggests the following method of solution:

- recursion for the compact list 'just smaller' than CL
- extend the result of the recursion in order to treat CL

$$[c_1, lg_1, c_2, lg_2, \ldots, c_n, lg_n]$$
$$[c_1, lg_1 - 1, c_2, lg_2, \ldots, c_n, lg_n]$$

recursion

(3) *Structural forms of the induction parameter*
The definition of the well-founded relation induces the following three structural cases:

```
CL = []
CL = [C, 1 | Tail_CL]
CL = [C, Lg | Tail_CL] & greater( Lg, 1 )
```

(4) *Construction of the structural cases*
(4.1) Suppose L is a list of characters and CL is a compact list of characters.
- For CL = [], L = [].
- For CL = [C, 1 | Tail_CL], the relation holds iff the first character of L is C and its tail is the compression of Tail_CL:

$$L = [C | TL] \ \& \ compress(TL, Tail\_CL)$$

- For CL = [C, Lg | Tail_CL] & greater(Lg, 1), the relation holds iff the first character of L is C and its tail is the compression of the compact list 'just smaller' to CL:

$$L = [C | TL] \ \& \ add(Lg1, 1, Lg)$$
$$\& \ compress(TL, [C, Lg1 | Tail\_CL]).$$

(4.2) *Verification of the domain membership*
The verification reduces to ensuring that CL is a compact list of characters because in that case, L will be a list of

characters. Such a verification is accomplished by the recursive literal *compress*, except in the second structural case (that is, when CL = [C, 1 | Tail_CL]) for which it must be verified that C is a character different from the first character of Tail_CL.

The resulting logic description is Logic Description 5.15.

compress_ext_CL(L, CL) ⇔
    CL = [] & L = []
  ∨ CL = [C, 1 | Tail_CL] & L = [C | TL]
                     & compress_ext_CL(TL, Tail_CL)
                     & (∀Y)Tail_CL ≠ [C | Y]
  ∨ CL = [C, Lg | Tail_CL] & greater(Lg, 1) & L = [C | TL]
                     & add(Lg1, 1, Lg)
                     & compress_ext_CL(TL, [C, Lg1 | Tail_CL])

Logic Description 5.15   compress_ext_CL(L, CL)

Comparison

Let us compare these two constructions of compress and the resulting logic descriptions. The induction parameter is CL in both cases. In the intrinsic approach (compress_int_CL), the well-founded relation was found immediately and the construction process was carried out easily. The resulting logic description is quite simple and easy to understand. The construction process based on the extrinsic well-founded relation was not so easy, the discovery of the well-founded relation being the most difficult task. Let us finally observe that compress_int_CL is a 'two loops' logic description while compress_ext_CL is a 'one loop' algorithm. This comparison is illustrated in Figures 5.4 and 5.5. In Figure 5.4, the second parameters of the successive recursive uses of compress_int_CL are given in the right-hand column for CL = [p, 2, d, 3, e, 1]. The second column presents the corresponding successive uses of the first two parameters of the successive uses of sequence (see Exercise 5.21 for a logic description of sequence). In Figure 5.5, the second parameters of the successive recursive uses of compress_ext_CL are also given.

5.7.2 How to choose an induction parameter

The influence of the chosen induction parameter on the construction process and the resulting logic description is now analysed. From the above examples, the possible induction parameters can be classified as follows:

Class 1: Inadequate induction parameter

The given problem cannot be solved (or is at least difficult to solve) by induction on such a parameter, because the structure of the parameter is

compress_int_CL	sequence
[p, 2, d, 3, e, 1]	
	p, 2
	p, 1
	p, 0
[d, 3, e, 1]	
	d, 3
	d, 2
	d, 1
	d, 0
[e, 1]	
	e, 1
	e, 0
[]	

Figure 5.4 Example of recursive uses of compress_int_CL.

not related to the problem. For instance, the first parameter X was shown to be inadequate as an induction parameter in efface(X, L, LEff). The inadequacy can also result from the available primitives on the considered data object. This has already been illustrated with suffix(L, SufL), attempting to use SufL as induction parameter.

Class 2:   Similar induction parameters where the construction process as well as the resulting logic descriptions are almost the same

The similarity is due to the existence of a simple correspondence between the different induction parameters. As a consequence, there will be no major difference between an intrinsic and an extrinsic approach in the choice of a well-founded relation. Two examples are length(L, Lg) for L and Lg; and efface(X, L, LEff) for L and LEff. In such cases, the choice of an induction parameter is not essential in either the construction process or the resulting logic description.

compress_ext_CL
[p, 2, d, 3, e, 1]
[p, 1, d, 3, e, 1]
[d, 3, e, 1]
[d, 2, e, 1]
[d, 1, e, 1]
[e, 1]
[]

Figure 5.5 Example of recursive uses of compress_ext_CL.

Class 3:   Induction parameters with different construction process complexities

In this class, the construction processes are different and their complexities are also different, even if the resulting logic descriptions are sometimes similar. An example is flattree(T, FT). There is no simple correspondence between the structure of a tree and the structure of a list so that the construction processes have different approaches. The difference is more pronounced by the fact that a flat representation of a tree is unique, but a list of integers can be the flat representation of more than one tree. Therefore, with T as induction parameter, it only has to be checked that FT is *the* flat representation of T. On the other hand, with FT as induction parameter, it has to be verified that T is *one of* the possible trees having FT as flat representation. The second construction is therefore more complicated. In this class, the choice of an induction parameter is important even if the resulting logic descriptions are similar since this choice can influence the simplicity of the construction process.

In order to simplify the construction process, the following heuristic can be used for choosing the induction parameter.

> **Functionality heuristic:**   Choose an induction parameter such that, given a ground instance of it, the relation can hold for at most one ground instance of the other parameters.

Class 4:   Different induction parameters

This class covers the induction parameters yielding different construction processes as well as different logic descriptions, but without an *a priori* 'best' choice. An example is compress(L, CL). With L as induction parameter (Logic Descriptions 5.5 and 5.6), it has been possible to define an intrinsic and an extrinsic well-founded relation yielding two different logic descriptions. They are different because of the different structures of L and CL (list of characters and compact list of characters). Therefore, with CL as induction parameter, both an intrinsic and an extrinsic approach are possible (Logic Descriptions 5.14 and 5.15). It is worth noticing the duality of the general structure of these two pairs of logic descriptions:

    'one loop' : compress_int_L,   compress_ext_CL
    'two loops' : compress_ext_L,   compress_int_CL

An intrinsic well-founded relation on one induction parameter yields a logic description and construction process structurally similar to those obtained with an extrinsic well-founded relation on the other parameter.

This observation can be generalized to any problem p(X, Y) where an extrinsic and an intrinsic well-founded relation result in different logic

Table 5.1   Structural similarities in p(X, Y).

	intrinsic wfr	extrinsic wfr
induction on X	*p_int_X*	p_ext_X
induction on Y	p_int_Y	*p_ext_Y*

descriptions for both X and Y as induction parameter. An extrinsic well-founded relation on X reflects the structural form of Y. An intrinsic well-founded relation on Y also reflects the structural form of Y. The construction processes and the resulting logic descriptions will therefore be structurally similar. The same argument holds conversely, as illustrated in Table 5.1.

Generally speaking, there is *a priori* no best induction parameter, nor any superiority of an intrinsic well-founded relation to an extrinsic one and vice versa. This holds if we only consider the construction process and the resulting logic description. However, in Chapter 9, it will be seen that it is easier to derive a correct logic program when the induction parameter is specified as ground in the directionality description. This induces the following heuristic for choosing the induction parameter, which will be justified later.

> **Directionality heuristic:**   Choose an induction parameter which is always ground in the *in* part of the specified directionalities of the procedure.

The above classification could be extended by considering multiple induction parameters. It should also be noticed that the choice of an induction parameter and a well-founded relation can sometimes be the starting point of the idea for a construction process, even if the actual induction parameter has to be reconsidered. This has been illustrated with suffix(L, SufL), using L\SufL as induction parameter.

EXERCISES

5.21 What are the possible induction parameters, their associated construction processes and the resulting logic descriptions for sequence(C, Lg, List_C) (see Specification 5.15)?

5.22 Let member(E, L) hold iff the term E is an element of the list L. What are the possible induction parameters, their associated construction processes and the resulting logic descriptions?

5.23 What are the possible induction parameters for append(L1, L2, LApp) (see Specification 4.2), their associated construction processes and the resulting logic descriptions? Is L2 appropriate?

5.24 Construct a logic description for prefix(L, PrefL) with L as induction parameter. Compare the construction process and the resulting logic description with the result of Exercise 5.12. What about L\PrefL as induction parameter?

5.25 Let permutation(L, LPerm) hold iff the list LPerm is a permutation of the list L. What are the differences between L and LPerm as induction parameters in the construction processes and the resulting logic descriptions?

5.26 Construct a logic description for remove(X, L, LRem) with LRem as induction parameter. Compare the construction process and the resulting logic description with the result of Exercise 5.15.

5.27 Construct a logic description for merge(L1, L2, LM) with LM as induction parameter. Compare the construction process and the resulting logic description with the result of Exercise 5.16.

5.28 Redefine the concept of flat representation of a tree such that the elements of a flat representation are the elements of the tree in an infix order. Reconstruct flattree(T, FT) with T and with FT as induction parameter; compare the construction processes. What about a postfix order?

5.29 Let sublist(L, SubL) hold iff the list SubL is a sublist of the list L. The concept of a sublist is here supposed to be known (for example, [3, 1] is a sublist of [2, 3, 1, 4], but [2, 1] is not). Give three different constructions using L, SubL and L\SubL as induction parameters (with L\SubL to be defined). Are the resulting logic descriptions equivalent?

5.30 Let append3(L1, L2, L3, LApp) hold iff LApp is the concatenation of L1, L2 and L3. The type of L1, L2, L3 and LApp is list. Construct three recursive logic descriptions: one with L1 as induction parameter, another with LApp as induction parameter and a third with the couple (L1, L2) as induction parameter. The last two constructions should not use append as a subproblem. What about other combinations of induction parameters? Compare the construction processes and the resulting logic descriptions.

5.31 Let a **posint tree** be a tree whose elements are positive integers. Let maxtree(T, Max) hold iff Max is the maximum of the elements of T. The type of Max is positive integer, and T is a posint tree. By definition, the maximum of an empty posint tree is 0. Construct a logic description with T as induction parameter.

5.32 Let substitute(X, E, L, LSubst) hold iff the list LSubst is the list L in which all the occurrences of the term X as an element of L have been replaced by the term E. Construct a logic description for all the possible induction parameters. Compare the construction processes and the resulting logic descriptions.

5.8 Generalizing problems

We will now consider what happens if, given an induction parameter and a well-founded relation, it is impossible to reduce the problem to a 'smaller one' that can be solved with a recursive use of the algorithm. In such cases, a subproblem is usually obtained which seems far more complicated than the initial one. Besides the possibility of changing the induction parameter or the well-founded relation, it is proposed here to generalize the given subproblem so that this subproblem and the initial one are both special cases of the general one. The generalization process already exists in computer science (program synthesis from examples, machine learning, automatic theorem proving, and so on) as well as in mathematics. Theorems are sometimes generalized so that there is a stronger induction hypothesis when proving the induction step. Paradoxically, a more general statement may be easier to prove.

Two generalization strategies are proposed. The first one generalizes the structure of a parameter (**structural** generalization). For example, a problem dealing with a term can be generalized into a problem dealing with a *list* of terms. This particular structural generalization is called **tupling** generalization. A second generalization characterizes a general state of a computation in terms of what has already been done and what remains to be done (**computational** generalization). Within this generalization, a distinction can be made between **ascending** and **descending** generalizations.

If the generalization of a problem is sometimes necessary (see Exercise 5.43), it is also useful for efficiency purposes. It will be shown in Part III that logic programs that have been derived from logic descriptions constructed with a generalization are more efficient than logic programs derived from logic descriptions constructed without generalization. This benefit can be seen as the result of loop merging and recursion removal (that is, recursion replaced by iteration).

The following generalization methods are also applicable outside the particular framework for constructing logic descriptions considered here. These generalizations can be also be used in the context of functional or imperative programming, as well as in other approaches to logic program development.

5.8.1   Structural generalization

In order to simplify the presentation, a particular case of structural generalization will be developed: the tupling generalization. The following discussion can easily be extended to other forms of structural generalization. Tupling generalization is first presented through an example, then the underlying principles are presented.

EXAMPLE   flattree(T, FT)

Let us reconsider the flattree(T, FT) problem (Specification 5.12), using a tupling generalization.

(1)   *Choice of an induction parameter* : T

(2)   *Choice of a well-founded relation* : 'is a subtree of'

GEN   Generalization of the induction parameter
    In a tupling generalization on a tree T, a list of trees should be considered. The generalized problem thus consists of flattening a list of trees. The specification of the generalization flattree_tupl(List_T, FT) is given in Specification 5.14.

> procedure   flattree_tupl(List_T, FT)
>
> *Type*:   List_T : *List* of trees
>   FT : List
>
> *Relation*:   FT is the concatenation of the flat representations of the trees from List_T.

Specification 5.14   flattree_tupl(List_T, FT)

(3)   Flattree *as a special case of* flattree_tupl
    Flattree(T, FT) is obviously a particular case of flattree_tupl. Take

    flattree_tupl([T], FT)

GEN-1   Choice of an induction parameter for flattree_tupl
    Since the generalization is done on T, List_T is a good candidate as induction parameter.

GEN-2   Choice of a well-founded relation for flattree_tupl
    The chosen well-founded relation on trees was: $t_1 < t_2$ iff t_1 is a subtree of t_2. A derived well-founded relation over lists of trees could be the following:

Let $lt_2 = [t_1, t_2, \ldots, t_n]$ $n \geq 0$
$lt_1 < lt_2$ iff lt_1 is a proper suffix of lt_2
                    or lt_1 is $[ta_1, ta_2, t_2, \ldots, t_n]$ (with $n > 0$ and ta_1, ta_2
                    subtrees of t_1)

This relation is well-founded because it is a particular case of multiset ordering (Dershowitz and Manna, 1979).

GEN-3   Structural forms of the induction parameter of flattree_tupl
From the well-founded relation, the structural forms are List_T empty, List_T = [void | Tail_T] since the empty tree has no subtrees, and List_T = [tree(E, LT, RT) | Tail_T].

GEN-4   Construction of the structural cases of flattree_tupl
   GEN-4.1   Suppose List_T and FT are in the domain of flattree_tupl (that is, List_T is a list of trees and FT is a list).

   • For List_T = [], FT = [].
   • For List_T = [void | Tail_T], we immediately obtain

        flattree_tupl(Tail_T, FT)

     since the flat representation of the empty tree is the empty list.
   • For List_T = [tree(E, LT, RT) | Tail_T] : FT must have the form [E | Tail_FT], with Tail_FT being the concatenation of the flat representations of LT, RT and the trees of Tail_T. We thus obtain

        FT   =   [E | Tail_FT]   &   flattree_tupl([LT,   RT | Tail_T], Tail_FT)

   GEN-4.2   Verification of the domain membership
   No literal has to be added.

The resulting logic description is Logic Description 5.16.

        flattree(T, FT) ⇔ flattree_tupl([T], FT)
        flattree_tupl(List_T, FT) ⇔
            List_T = [] & FT = []
          ∨ List_T = [void | Tail_T] & flattree_tupl(Tail_T, FT)
          ∨ List_T = [tree(E, LT, RT) | Tail_T] & FT = [E | Tail_FT]
                                    & flattree_tupl([LT, RT | Tail_T], Tail_FT)

Logic Description 5.16   flattree_tupl(List_T, FT)

If the constructed logic description is compared with the one obtained without generalization (Logic Description 5.12), it can be seen that there is at most one recursion here for each case whilst a conjunction of two recursions was necessary in the previous logic description (one for

LT and one for RT). Moreover, the generalization does not need to concatenate lists. The append loop is thus somewhat merged with the recursion. This suggests that a logic program derived from a generalized logic description will be more efficient than a program derived from a non-generalized description.

Tupling generalization: principles

Tupling generalization can be applied to problems with the following form of specification.

> procedure   p(X, Y)
> *Type*:   X : Type_X
>   Y : List
> *Relation*: $\langle$ X, Y $\rangle \in p$.

The construction process proceeds in the following steps.

(1)   *Choice of an induction parameter* : X

(2)   *Choice of a well-founded relation over type_X*

GEN   *Tupling generalization* :
       The specification of a tupling generalization p_tupl of p is schematically presented in Specification 5.15, and illustrated in Figure 5.6 (where $\langle \ \rangle$ denotes concatenation).

> procedure   p_tupl(List_X, Y)
> *Type*:   List_X : List of objects of type_X (say, $[X_1, \ldots, X_n]$)
>   Y : List
> *Relation*:   Y is the concatenation of $Y1, \ldots, Y_n$ where
> $\langle X_i, Y_i \rangle \in p \ (1 \leq i \leq n)$.

Specification 5.15   p_tupl(List_X, Y)

This specification can be generalized by introducing terms between and/or after the Y_i (see Exercise 5.43) or by replacing concatenation by another operation. Both the procedures p and p_tupl can have more than two parameters.

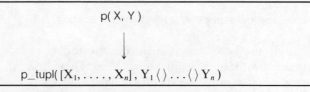

Figure 5.6   Tupling generalization.

(3)   *Initial problem as a particular case of the generalization*
       Obviously, p(X, Y) is a particular case of p_tupl

$$p(X, Y) \Leftrightarrow p\_tupl([X], Y)$$

GEN-1   Choice of an induction parameter for the generalization
       In a tupling generalization, the construction is usually easier to
       perform with List_X as induction parameter. However, the choice
       of Y could also be considered (see Exercise 5.43).

GEN-2   Choice of a well-founded relation for the generalization
       If a well-founded relation is defined over type_X, it is possible to
       extend it to lists of objects of type_X, by means of multiset
       ordering (Dershowitz and Manna, 1979). In a tupling generaliza-
       tion, multiset ordering usually reduces to the following well-
       founded relation.

       Let l_1, l_2 be lists of objects of type_X
       $l_1 < l_2$ iff l_1 can be obtained from l_2

       • by removing at least one element from l_2,

       • and by adding any number (possibly 0) of type_X elements
         which are smaller than one of the removed elements,
         according to the well-founded relation defined on type_X.

GEN-3   Structural forms of the induction parameter of the generalization
       The general idea of the construction process is usually to treat the
       first element of List_X and to use recursion. Two structural forms
       are thus List_X empty and List_X non-empty. However, in the case
       List_X non-empty, one should distinguish the case where the first
       element is minimal (according to the well-founded relation defined
       over type_X). In such a situation, recursion is usually done on the
       tail of List_X. When the first element is not minimal, it can be re-
       placed by some smaller elements in the recursion. Therefore, the
       usual structural forms are:

       List_X = []
       List_X = [X | Tail_X] & minimal(X)
       List_X = [X | Tail_X] & ¬minimal(X)

       where minimal(X) holds iff X is minimal according to the well-
       founded relation defined over type_X.
             In some tupling generalizations, other structural forms have
       to be considered (see Exercise 5.34).

GEN-4   Construction of the structural cases of the generalization

       GEN-4.1 Suppose the parameters are in the domain of p_tupl
       (that is, List_X is a list of type_X objects, and Y is a list).

       •   For List_X = [], obviously Y = [].

- For List_X = [X | Tail_X] & minimal(X).
  The general idea here is to handle X (that is, (∃Head_Y) p(X, Head_Y)). Since X is minimal, this is often trivial. Recursion can then be used for Tail_X. Y is the concatenation of the two partial results. In practice, this concatenation can be done without using append since Head_Y is often a list of fixed length.
- For List_X = [X | Tail_X] & ¬minimal(X).
  The general idea here is to decompose X into smaller elements which can be combined with Tail_X in order to use recursion. In practice, this combination can be done without explicit concatenation (that is, append) since the decomposition of X usually yields a fixed number of elements. The result of the recursion has then to be extended to handle the loss of information between X and its decomposition.

GEN-4.2   Verification of the domain membership
This verification is done by adding some extra literals if necessary.

The above construction schema must of course be adapted for each particular tupling generalization. It can also easily be modified for other forms of structural generalization. For instance, when Y is not a list but a set, a bag, or a tree, the generalization deals with sets of X, bags of X, trees of X, and so on. A composition operator corresponding to the concatenation on lists is also necessary.

5.8.2   Computational generalization

Principles
A second method of generalizing a problem involves the characterization of a general state of a computation. This can appear remote from the ideas of logic but it is close to the ideas of algorithms. This characterization is just a heuristic for finding a 'good' generalization of the problem and it is therefore not necessary to define exactly the meaning of 'general state of computation' in a logic description. Computational generalization can be applied to problems with the following form of specification:

procedure   p(X, Y)
Type: X : Type_X
      Y : Type_Y
Relation: ⟨X, Y⟩ ∈ p.

The construction process proceeds in the following steps.

(1)   *Choice of an induction parameter* : X

(2)   *Choice of a well-founded relation over type_X*
GEN   *Computational generalization*

Using the well-founded relation defined over type_X, it is usually possible to deduce from any type_X object X a finite decreasing sequence

$$X_1 X_2 \ldots X_i X_{i+1} \ldots X_n$$

with $X_1 = X$, $X_{i+1} < X_i$ ($1 \le i < n$), and X_n minimal ($n > 0$). From this decreasing sequence, X could be schematically decomposed as follows:

$$X: e_1 e_2 \ldots e_i e_{i+1} \ldots e_n$$

with X_i as $e_i e_{i+1} \ldots e_n$.

The nature of the e_i depends on the well-founded relation. When X is a list, this decomposition is trivial for the proper suffix relation; when X is an integer k, a decomposition could be $k, k-1, \ldots 2, 1$. An algorithm constructed with X as the induction parameter and the defined well-founded relation will actually go through the structure of X according to the well-founded relation and thus through the above decomposition of X. It should therefore be possible to characterize a general state of computation in terms of what has been done already, and what remains to be done. This can be schematically represented as follows:

X:	$e_1 e_2 \ldots e_i$	$e_{i+1} \ldots e_n$
	Pref_X	Suf_X
	Int_Y	
	already done	to be done

where   Pref_X is $e_1 e_2 \ldots e_i$ ('already done' part of X)
         Suf_X is $e_{i+1} \ldots e_n$ ('to be done' part of X)
         Int_Y is a correct partial result: $\langle Pref\_X, Int\_Y \rangle \in p$

The general form of the specification of a computational generalization p_comp of p is given in Specification 5.16. Figure 5.7 illustrates the computational generalization and its particular cases.

procedure   p_comp(Suf_X, Y, Int_Y, Pref_X)

Type: Pref_X, Suf_X : Type_X
           Y, Int_Y : Type_Y

Restrictions on parameters:
   • $\langle Pref\_X, Int\_Y \rangle \in p$

   • there exists a term X of type_X such that X is Pref_X <> Suf_X (where <> is an appropriate composition operator over type_X)

Relation: $\langle X, Y \rangle \in p$.

Specification 5.16   p_comp(Suf_X, Y, Int_Y, Pref_X)

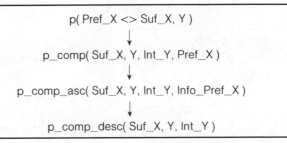

Figure 5.7   Computational generalization.

This generalization is described as computational because it characterizes a general state of computation. This specification could be further generalized by replacing $\langle X, Y \rangle \in p$ by $\langle X, Y \rangle \in p'$, where p' is a generalization of the specified relation p. The hypothesis that Pref_X is of type_X is not necessary, but it simplifies the presentation. In order to be effective, computational generalization requires the functionality heuristic to be fulfilled: for every type_X object X, there exists at most one type_Y object Y such that $\langle X, Y \rangle \in p$. Without this functional dependency, the construction is far more difficult since a partial result Int_Y is not necessarily going in the 'right way' towards the complete result (see Exercise 5.39). This functionality requirement reinforces the functionality heuristic for choosing the induction parameter since such a choice allows computational generalization.

(3) *Initial problem as a special case of the generalization*
    p(X, Y) is a particular case of p_comp if there exist terms $\varnothing_X$ and $\varnothing_Y$ such that

- X is $\varnothing_X$ <> X (left identity)
- $\langle \varnothing_X, \varnothing_Y \rangle \in p$

In that case, we have

$$p(X, Y) \Leftrightarrow p\_comp(X, Y, \varnothing_Y, \varnothing_X)$$

GEN-1   Choice of an induction parameter for the generalization
    In a computational generalization, the construction is usually easier to perform with Suf_X as the induction parameter. However, the choice of Y could also be considered (see Exercise 5.43).

GEN-2   Choice of a well-founded relation for the generalization
    The well-founded relation for the generalization is the well-founded relation defined over type_X.

GEN-3   Structural forms of the induction parameter of the generalization

The structural forms of the induction parameter are obviously Suf_X minimal and Suf_X non-minimal.

GEN-4 *Construction of the structural cases of the generalization*
 GEN-4.1 Suppose the parameters are in the domain of p_comp (that is, Pref_X and Suf_X are type_X objects; Y and Int_Y are type_Y objects; ⟨Pref_X, Int_Y⟩ ∈ *p*; and X is Pref_X <> Suf_X).

- For Suf_X minimal (say ∅′$_X$), Pref_X is X itself. The considered composition operator <> over type_X must thus have the property

  Pref_X <> ∅′$_X$ is Pref_X (right identity)

  By hypothesis, ⟨Pref_X, Int_Y⟩ ∈ *p*. Since Pref_X is X itself and *p* has a functional dependency, p_comp holds iff Y = Int_Y.

- For Suf_X not minimal, the general idea will be to reduce Suf_X to something 'just smaller' and to extend Pref_X and Int_Y accordingly. Recursion can then be used.

GEN-4.2 *Verification of the domain membership*
 Such a verification may appear very difficult since it requires the verification of ⟨Pref_X, Int_Y⟩ ∈ *p*, which is the initial problem we are trying to solve! However, in practice the specification of a computational generalization is simpler, with much simplified restrictions on parameters, as will be seen in the examples.

Ascending versus descending generalization

In a computational generalization, the parameter Pref_X is present to help to extend Int_Y when reducing Suf_X. Usually Pref_X is not in itself necessary, but some key information about it is needed. In some cases, Pref_X can be totally suppressed. A distinction can thus be made between those computational generalizations where Pref_X can be totally suppressed and those where it cannot. The two resulting generalizations will be called ascending and descending, as illustrated in Figure 5.7 and justified below.

Ascending generalization: Some information about Pref_X is needed to construct p_comp.

Descending generalization: No information about Pref_X is needed to construct p_comp.

Inductive reasoning is described as ascending if one proceeds from 'simple' elements to 'more complicated' elements. With it a result is extended to its successor. While in a descending approach, one proceeds from 'more general' elements to 'more particular' ones and a result is reduced to its predecessor. In imperative programming, a reasoning is ascending when it considers prefixes of execution in some way; it is descending if it deals with suffixes of execution. With prefixes of execution, partial results are extended by considering bigger prefixes of execution. The question here is 'what has been done already'. With suffixes of execution, the question is 'what remains to be done'. The problem is reduced to a smaller one by considering shorter suffixes of execution. For instance, inductive assertion (Floyd, 1967) is ascending; Burstall's structural induction (Burstall, 1974) as well as Manna and Waldinger's intermittent assertion (Manna and Waldinger, 1978) can be ascending or descending. Since an ascending generalization requires information about what has been done already, the construction process will reflect an ascending reasoning. Conversely, the construction process of a descending generalization will reflect a descending reasoning because one only considers what remains to be done.

There is no strict boundary between ascending and descending generalization. The less information required about Pref_X, the more descending the generalization is. A pure ascending generalization is p_comp. The principles of ascending and descending generalizations will now be described as particular cases of the above schema.

Ascending generalization: principles

In an ascending generalization, Pref_X is replaced by Info_Pref_X which represents information about Pref_X. The specification schema of an ascending generalization is Specification 5.17.

> procedure   p_asc(Suf_X, Y, Int_Y, Info_Pref_X)
>
> *Type*:   Suf_X : Type_X
>   Y, Int_Y : Type_Y
>   Info_Pref_X : Type_Info_Pref_X
>
> *Restriction on parameters*:   there exist terms X and Pref_X of type_X such that
> - X is Pref_X <> Suf_X
> - $\langle$ Pref_X, Int_Y $\rangle \in p$
> - Info_Pref_X represents information about Pref_X
>
> *Relation*: $\langle$ X, Y $\rangle \in p$.

Specification 5.17   p_asc(Suf_X, Y, Int_Y, Info_Pref_X)

The problem p_asc is ascending since some information about Pref_X is needed. In an ascending generalization, the characterization of Info_Pref_X is the crucial point and it is usually determined when constructing the logic description for the generalization. It is difficult to decide *a priori* what the necessary information about Pref_X is. It may turn out that a descending generalization is actually possible.

In practice, the specification of p_asc can be simplified in various ways. The preconditions can be replaced by an explicit characterization of X in terms of Int_Y and Info_Pref_X. No references are made to Pref_X nor to ⟨Pref_X, Int_Y⟩ ∈ *p*. Such generalizations are almost descending since no explicit reference is made to the part already dealt with. However, they are still called ascending since Info_Pref_X is necessary.

Descending generalization: principles

In a descending generalization, Pref_X as well as Info_Pref_X is suppressed, yielding the following specification.

> procedure   p_desc(Suf_X, Y, Int_Y)
>
> *Type*:   Suf_X : Type_X
>   Y, Int_Y : Type_Y
>
> *Restriction on parameters*: there exist terms X and Pref_X of type_X such that
> - X is Pref_X <> Suf_X
> - ⟨Pref_X, Int_Y⟩ ∈ *p*
>
> *Relation*:   ⟨X, Y⟩ ∈ *p*.

This specification schema can be further simplified. There is no need to assume the existence of X and Pref_X, nor to relate Int_Y with Pref_X. There follows a simplified specification schema of a descending generalization (Specification 5.18). The name Suf_X is now meaningless since X and Pref_X are no longer considered.

> procedure   p_desc(XX, Y, Int_Y)
>
> *Type*:   XX : Type_X
>   Y, Int_Y : Type_Y
>
> *Relation*:   Y is Int_Y ω YY, with ⟨XX, YY⟩ ∈ *p*.
>
> (where ω is an appropriate composition operator over type_Y)
>
> **Specification 5.18**   p_desc(XX, Y, Int_Y)

Specification 5.18 expresses that the partial result Int_Y is extended by YY which is the partial result of what remains to be done (that is XX). Note that the composition operator <> over type_X is replaced here by a composition operator ω over type_Y. In a descending generalization, the following construction steps are also simplified.

(3)   *Initial problem as a particular case of the generalization*
       In a descending generalization, p(X, Y) is a special case of p_desc(XX, Y, Int_Y) if there exists $\varnothing_Y$ such that $Y = \varnothing_Y$ ω Y (left identity).

       In that case, we have:

$$p(X, Y) \Leftrightarrow p\_desc(X, Y, \varnothing_Y)$$

GEN-4   Construction of the structural cases of the generalization

As previously, the induction parameter is XX and the well-founded relation is defined over type_X.

- For XX minimal (say $\varnothing'_X$), there must exist $\varnothing'_Y$ such that $\langle \varnothing'_X, \varnothing'_Y \rangle \in p$. Y is thus Int_Y ω $\varnothing'_Y$. This often reduces to Int_Y since $\varnothing'_Y$ is usually a right identity element.
- For XX not minimal, XX is reduced to something just smaller, and Int_Y is extended accordingly and recursion is used.

In a descending generalization, (Y, Int_Y) can be seen as a representation of YY. Let us denote this by $\langle$Y\Int_Y$\rangle$. Such a representation is well defined if one can describe an operator ω' over type_Y such that:

Y = Int_Y ω YY   implies   YY = Y ω' Int_Y.

The operator ω' is thus an inverse of ω.

The construction of programs with d-lists (Clark and Tärnlund, 1977) is thus a particular case of a descending generalization. When type_Y is list and ω is concatenation, $\langle$L\Int_L$\rangle$ is a d-list representing the difference between the lists L and Int_L, with Int_L a suffix of L. Thus, in this generalization framework, d-lists are not a new data structure, but the result of a generalization. Moreover, d-lists are a particular case of a more general phenomenon. For other operators ω, similar concepts could also be defined. For addition, d-integer $\langle i,j \rangle$ could be defined, with $i > j$, representing the integer $i-j$. For a maximum, d-max $\langle m, n \rangle$ could represent the maximum between the integers m and n; and so on.

Descending generalization: examples

If it is possible to construct a logic description with a descending generalization, it is also possible to construct a logic description for the initial problem directly. A descending generalization means that no information is needed about what has already been done. Therefore, a classical recursive logic description could be constructed without generalization. However, a descending generalization may result in a much more efficient logic program.

EXAMPLE   length(L, Lg)

Let us apply a descending generalization with L as the induction parameter. This problem has already been specified (Specification 5.10) and solved without generalization (Logic Description 5.8).

(1)   *Choice of an induction parameter*: L

(2)   *Choice of a well-founded relation*: 'proper suffix'

GEN   Descending generalization

procedure   length_desc(Suf_L, Lg, Int_Lg)

Type: Suf_L : List
         Lg, Int_Lg : Positive integer

Restriction on parameters: there exist lists L and Pref_L such that

- L is the concatenation of Pref_L and Suf_L
- Int_Lg is the number of elements of Pref_L

Relation: Lg is the number of elements of L.

This specification can be simplified by removing the references to the lists L and Pref_L as well as to the restrictions on the parameters.

procedure   length_desc(LL, Lg, Int_Lg)

Type: LL : List
         Lg, Int_Lg : Positive integer

Relation: Lg is Int_Lg plus the number of elements of LL.

Specification 5.19   length_desc(Suf_L, Lg, Int_Lg)

The operation considered on positive integers is addition. $\langle$Lg\Int_Lg$\rangle$ can thus be seen as representing the length of LL.

(3)   Length *as a particular case of* length_desc
Obviously, Lg is 0 + Lg (left identity). Thus

length(L, Lg) $\Leftrightarrow$ length_desc(L, Lg, 0)

GEN-3   *Structural forms of the induction parameter* LL *of* length_desc
The structural forms of LL are LL empty (that is, LL = [ ]) and LL non-empty (that is, LL = [H | T]).

GEN-4   *Construction of the structural cases of* length_desc
   GEN-4.1   Suppose LL is a list, Lg and Int_Lg are positive integers.

- For LL = [], since 0 is the length of the empty list, Lg must be Int_Lg + 0 which reduces to Int_Lg (right identity). Hence the formula:

   Lg = Int_Lg

- For LL = [H | T], Lg must be Int_Lg + YY, where YY is the length of LL. But YY is 1 + length of T. Lg must thus be Int_Lg + 1 + length of T. Hence the following formula:

   add(Int_Lg, 1, New_Int_Lg)
   & length_desc(T, Lg, New_Int_Lg)

   GEN-4.2   *Verification of the domain membership*
   This reduces to the verification that Lg is a positive integer in the first structural case (pos_int(X) holds iff X is a positive integer).

The resulting logic description is Logic Description 5.17.

length(L, Lg) ⇔ length_desc(L, Lg, 0)
length_desc(LL, Lg, Int_Lg) ⇔
    LL = [] & Lg = Int_Lg & pos_int(Lg)
  ∨ LL = [H | T] & add(Int_Lg, 1, New_Int_Lg)
             & length_desc(T, Lg, New_Int_Lg)

Logic Description 5.17   length_desc(LL, Lg, Int_Lg)

Since a descending generalization is not really necessary to solve the initial problem, why are we interested in it? In Part III, it will be shown that logic programs derived from a descending generalization are often tail-recursive when the logic program derived from the initial problem is not tail-recursive. In such cases, a descending generalization yields a more efficient logic program. The process of describing a generalization is actually quite systematic. In the transformation of logic descriptions, it will be seen that such a generalization can be deduced from a logic description, and that the resulting logic description can be obtained by transformations.

EXAMPLE   flattree(T, FT)

The flattree problem is now well known (Specification 5.12). Three logic descriptions have already been constructed: induction on T (Logic Description 5.12), induction on FT (Logic Description 5.13) and structural generalization (Logic Description 5.16). Two other constructions based on descending generalization are now investigated.

(1)   *Choice of an induction parameter*: T

(2)   *Choice of a well-founded relation*: 'is a subtree of'

GEN   *Descending generalization*
      The general form of a descending generalization of flattree is given in Specification 5.20.

procedure flattree_desc(TT, FT, Int_FT)
Type: TT : Tree
        FT, Int_FT : Lists
Relation: FT is Int_FT ω YY, where YY is the flat representation of TT.

Specification 5.20   flattree_desc(TT, FT, Int_FT)

Depending on the choice of ω (operator on lists), two different generalizations can be obtained.

flattree_desc_1: (Int_FT ω YY) is the concatenation of Int_FT and YY.

flattree_desc_2: (Int_FT ω YY) is the concatenation of YY and Int_FT.

(3)   Flattree *as a particular case of* flattree_desc
Since the empty list is an identity element (left and right) for concatenation, the initial problem is the same particular case in both generalizations.

flattree(T, FT) ⇔ flattree_desc(T, FT, [])

GEN-3   *Structural forms of the induction parameter* of flattree_desc
In both generalizations, the structural forms are TT empty (that is, TT = void) and TT non-empty (that is, TT = tree(E, LT, RT)).

GEN-4a   *Construction of the structural cases of* flattree_desc_1

GEN-4a.1   Suppose TT is a tree, FT and Int_FT are lists.

- For TT = void, since [] is the flat representation of the empty tree, FT must be the concatenation of Int_FT and []. Hence the following formula:

FT = Int_FT

- For TT = tree(E, LT, RT), FT must be the concatenation of Int_FT, [E], LT* and RT*, where LT* and RT* are the flat representations of LT and RT, respectively. This can be decomposed as the concatenation of Int2_FT and RT*, where Int2_FT is the concatenation of Int1_FT and LT*, where Int1_FT is the concatenation of Int_FT and [E]. Hence the formula

append(Int_FT, [E], Int1_FT)
& flattree_desc_1(LT, Int2_FT, Int1_FT)
& flattree_desc_1(RT, FT, Int2_FT)

GEN-4a.2   *Verification of the domain membership*
In the first structural case, it must be verified that FT is a list.

GEN-4b   *Construction of the structural cases of* flattree_desc_2

GEN-4b.1   Suppose TT is a tree, FT and Int_FT are lists.
- For TT = void, since [] is the flat representation of the empty tree, FT must be the concatenation of [] and Int_FT. Hence the following formula:

FT = Int_FT

- For TT = tree(E, LT, RT), FT must be the concatenation of [E], LT*, RT* and Int_FT, where LT* and RT* are the flat representations of LT and RT, respectively. This can be decomposed as the concatenation of [E] and Int2_FT, where Int2_FT is the concatenation of LT* and Int1_FT, where Int1_FT is the concatenation of RT* and Int_FT. Hence the formula

> flattree_desc_2(RT, Int1_FT, Int_FT)
> & flattree_desc_2(LT, Int2_FT, Int1_FT)
> & FT = [E | Int2_FT]

GEN-4b.2　Verification of the domain membership
In the first structural case, it must be verified that FT is a list.

The two resulting logic descriptions are Logic Description 5.18 and Logic Description 5.19.

> flattree(T, FT) ⇔ flattree_desc_1(T, FT, [])
> flattree_desc_1(TT, FT, Int_FT) ⇔
>   TT = void & FT = Int_FT & list(FT)
> ∨ TT = tree(E, LT, RT) & append(Int_FT, [E], Int1_FT)
>   & flattree_desc_1(LT, Int2_FT, Int1_FT)
>   & flattree_desc_1(RT, FT, Int2_FT)

Logic Description 5.18　flattree_desc_1(TT, FT, Int_FT)

> flattree(T, FT) ⇔ flattree_desc_2(T, FT, [])
> flattree_desc_2(TT, FT, Int_FT) ⇔
>   TT = void & FT = Int_FT & list(FT)
> ∨ TT = tree(E, LT, RT) & flattree_desc_2(RT, Int1_FT, Int_FT)
>   & flattree_desc_2(LT, Int2_FT, Int1_FT)
>   & FT = [E | Int2_FT]

Logic Description 5.19　flattree_desc_2(TT, FT, Int_FT)

The major difference between these two logic descriptions is the presence of append in the first and its absence from the second. One can therefore imagine that the logic program derived from the second description will be more efficient. If Logic Description 5.19 is compared with the one obtained with a structural generalization (Logic Description 5.16), it can be seen that a conjunction of recursions is necessary here. Compared with Logic Description 5.12 obtained without generalization, the append 'loop' has been merged with the recursive literals.

Ascending generalization

EXAMPLE　max_seq(L, Max)
Specification 5.21 uses the concept of max-subsequence defined earlier (see Definition 5.5).

> procedure　max_seq(L, Max)
> *Type*:　L : List of characters
>   Max : Positive integer.
> *Relation*:　Max is the maximal length of all the max-subsequences of L.

Specification 5.21　max_seq(L, Max)

With Specification 5.21, we have for instance:

max_seq([y, y, v, v, v, e, s, s], 3)

because the lengths of the max-subsequences are 2, 3, 1 and 2, respectively. The maximum of these lengths is 3.

(1)   *Choice of an induction parameter*
      The induction parameter here is obviously L because it is difficult to imagine an algorithm based on the structural form of Max.

(2)   *Choice of a well-founded relation*
      An intrinsic well-founded relation is the proper suffix relation, which underlines the structure of a list. But L can also be thought of as a representation of the second parameter, or of the relation itself. L can be seen as a sequence of max-subsequences instead of a list of characters. This yields an extrinsic well-founded relation such as the one defined for compress(L, CL). Here, we will only develop a logic description for an intrinsic well-founded relation.

GEN   Ascending generalization
      It is very difficult to construct a recursive description with an intrinsic well-founded relation. From the maximum length of the max-subsequences of the tail of L, it is difficult to deduce the maximum length of the max-subsequences of L itself. Let us generalize it as follows, where the contents of Info_Pref_L will be determined during the construction process.

          procedure   max_seq_asc(Suf_L, Max, Int_Max, Info_Pref_L)

          Type: Suf_L : List of characters
                    Max, Int_Max : Positive integer
                    Info_Pref_L : . . .

          Restriction on parameters: there exist non-empty lists L and Pref_L such that

          •   L is Pref_L <> Suf_L
          •   Int_Max is the maximum length of the max-subsequences of Pref_L
          •   Info_Pref_L represents information about Pref_L

          Relation: Max is the maximum length of the max-subsequences of L.

GEN-1   *Choice of an induction parameter for* max_seq_asc : Suf_L

GEN-2   *Choice of a well-founded relation for* max_seq_asc : 'proper suffix'

GEN-3   Structural forms of the induction parameter of max_seq_asc
Obviously, the structural forms are Suf_L empty (that is, Suf_L = [ ]) and Suf_L non-empty (that is, Suf_ L = [H|T]).

GEN-4   Construction of the structural cases of max_seq_asc

GEN-4.1   Suppose the parameters are in the domain of max_seq_asc:

- For Suf_L = [ ], Pref_L is L and Int_Max is the maximum length of the max-subsequences of L. Hence the following formula:

  Max = Int_Max

- For Suf_L = [H|T], there are two subcases depending on the last character of Pref_L. This last character must be part of the information of Info_Pref_L (say C). It is easier to consider non-empty lists L and Pref_L in the specification.
  case 1: H = C
  In order to modify Int_Max, we need the length of the last max-subsequence of Pref_L (say Lg). Lg is thus also part of Info_Pref_X.

  add(Lg, 1, New_Lg)
  & maximum(Int_Max, New_Lg, New_Int_Max)

We can now use a recursion

  max_seq_asc(T, Max, New_Int_Max, C, New_Lg)

case 2: H ≠ C
In this case, we can immediately perform a recursion with 1 as New_Lg, and H as New_C. Since Pref_L is not empty, Int_Max ≥ 1. Therefore, New_Int_Max is Int_Max. We obtain

  max_seq_asc(T, Max, Int_Max, H, 1)

Maximum(A, B, C) holds iff C is the maximum of A and B (where A, B and C are integers). From the construction process, we have that Info_Pref_L is composed of the last character of Pref_L and the length of the last max-subsequence of Pref_L.

The specification of the generalization can be simplified (Specification 5.22). The preconditions can be partly replaced by a characterization of L in terms of Int_Max and Info_Pref_L.

  procedure   max_seq_asc(Suf_L, Max, Int_Max, C, Lg)
  Type: Suf_L : List of characters
          Max, Int_Max, Lg : Positive integer
          C : Character

Restriction on parameters: Lg ≤ Int_Max.
Let L be the list [C, C, . . . , C | Suf_L] with Lg occurrences of
C before Suf_L.

Relation: Max is the maximum value of Int_Max, and the
maximum length of the max-sequences of L.

Specification 5.22   max_seq_asc(Suf_L, Max, Int_Max, C,
                                        Lg)

This specification is less ascending (and thus more descending)
than the previous one, but they are equivalent.

GEN-4.2   Verification of the domain membership

In the first structural case (Suf_L = []), it should be verified
that Max, Int_Max and Lg are positive integers, C is a character
and Lg ≤ Int_Max. In the second alternative (H ≠ C) of the
second structural case, it should be verified that Lg is a
positive integer, C a character and Lg ≤ Int_Max. This domain
verification is however not explicitly added in Logic Description 5.20.

(3)   Max_seq *as a particular case of* max_seq_asc
Now that Info_Pref_L has been specified, it can be seen that max_seq
is a particular case of the generalization when Lg and Int_Max are 0.
C can be any character (we use 'a' in Logic Description 5.20).

max_seq(L, Max) ⇔ max_seq_asc(L, Max, 0, a, 0)
max_seq_asc(Suf_L, Max, Int_Max, C, Lg) ⇔
     Suf_L = [] & Max = Int_Max
  ∨ Suf_L = [H | T] &
     (H = C & add(Lg, 1, New_Lg)
               & maximum(Int_Max, New_Lg, New_Int_Max)
               & max_seq_asc(T, Max, New_Int_Max, C, New_Lg)
       ∨ H ≠ C & max_seq_asc(T, Max, Int_Max, H, 1))

Logic Description 5.20   max_seq_asc(Suf_L, Max, Int_Max, C,
                                          Lg)

EXERCISES

5.33 Let maxtree(T, Max) be as defined in Exercise 5.31. Construct three
different logic descriptions with T as induction parameter using the
following generalizations:

(a)   tupling generalization

(b)   descending generalization

(c)   tupling + descending generalization.

Compare the resulting logic descriptions.

5.34 Redefine the concept of flat representation of a tree such that the elements of a flat representation are the elements of the tree in an infix order. Reconstruct flattree(T, FT) with T as induction parameter using a tupling generalization. Be sure the induction parameter is smaller in the recursive literals. Reconstruct flattree(T, FT) using a descending generalization. What about a postfix order in both constructions?

5.35 Construct a logic description for palindrome(L) (see Exercise 5.10) using a descending generalization.

5.36 Construct a logic description for sumlist(L, S) (see Exercise 5.13) using a descending generalization.

5.37 Construct a logic description for minlist(L, Min) (see Exercise 5.14) using a descending generalization.

5.38 Construct a logic description for reverse(L, LRev) (see Specification 4.1) using a descending generalization.

*5.39 What is the computational generalization when there is no functional dependency between Pref_X and Int_Y (that is, for some Pref_X, there exists more than one Int_Y such that ⟨Pref_X, Int_Y⟩ ∈ p)?

5.40 Construct a logic description for quicksort(L, SL) (see Exercise 5.19) with L as induction parameter, using a tupling generalization. Be sure the induction parameter is smaller in the recursive literals. Construct another logic description using a descending generalization. Compare the resulting logic descriptions.

5.41 Construct two logic descriptions for factorial(N, FactN) (see Exercise 5.11), with N as the induction parameter using the following generalizations:

(a)   descending using the decomposition N, (N−1), . . . , 2, 1

(b)   ascending using the decomposition 1, 2, . . . , (N−1), N.

5.42 This is a logic programming version of Dijkstra's Dutch flag problem.

- A **coloured object** X is either red (denoted red(X)), white (denoted white(X)) or blue (denoted blue(X)).

- A list of coloured objects is a **Dutch flag list** iff all the red objects precede the white objects, and all the white objects precede the blue objects.

- Let dutchflag(L, RWB) hold iff RWB is a permutation of L, and RWB is a dutch flag list preserving the relative order between objects of the same colour. The type of L and RWB is list of coloured objects.

(a) Construct a logic description for dutchflag with L as the induction parameter, using the idea of splitting L into three lists: a list of the red objects, a list of the white objects and a list of the blue objects (for example, split(L, Red, White, Blue)).

(b) Specify and construct a descending generalization of split. (*Hint:* the intermediate result is composed of three lists: Int_Red, Int_White and Int_Blue).

(c) Show that dutchflag is a particular case of split_desc.

(d) Show that Int_Blue is actually not needed in the particular case of the dutchflag problem.

(e) Compare the logic descriptions of dutchflag obtained with and without the generalization of split. (*Hint:* Three 'loops' have been merged into a single one).

5.43 Suppose we want to represent ground terms by **simple lists** (that is lists whose elements are not lists) without losing information. Such a representation is called a **flat representation** and is defined recursively as follows:

- The flat representation of a term t which is not a list is the simple list [t].

- The flat representation of a list $[e_1, \ldots, e_n]$ is the simple list obtained by concatenating [p], $e^*_1, \ldots, e^*_n$ and [q] where p and q are two given constants and e^*_i is the flat representation of e_i.

   The constants p and q 'represent' the beginning and the end of a list, respectively. It is not assumed that p and q do not occur in the term so that two different terms can have the same flat representation. Some examples are:

terms	flat representations
3	[3]
[]	[p, q]
[1, 2]	[p, 1, 2, q]
[1, [2]]	[p, 1, p, 2, q, q]
[1, p, 2]	[p, 1, p, 2, q]
[tree(1, nil, nil)]	[p, tree(1, nil, nil), q]

- Let flat(Term, SList) hold iff SList is the flat representation of Term. The type of Term is term, and SList is a simple list.

(a)   First try to construct a logic description for flat by induction and without any form of generalization.

(b)   Construct a logic description using a tupling generalization on T (*Hint:* Consider a generalization of the form flat_tupl([t_1, ..., t_n], t^*_1 <> ... <> t^*_n <> [q])). From this construction, do a descending generalization.

(c)   Construct a logic description using a descending generalization followed by a tupling generalization (*Hint:* Consider a resulting generalization of the form flat_gen([t_1, ..., t_n], t^*_1 <> ... <> t^*_n <> Int_SL, Int_SL)).

(d)   What about SL as an induction parameter?

5.44   Show that the Prolog translation of Definite Clause Grammar uses a particular case of descending generalization (Specification 5.18) (*Hint:* p_gen(L, Suf_L) holds iff L is Pref_L <> Suf_L with Pref_L $\in p$).

5.9   Induction versus decomposition and iteration through the universal quantifier

Besides the proposed construction process based on induction, other construction techniques are also applicable. Here are two other construction methods.

- Decompose the problem into simpler ones, or show that the considered problem is a particular case of an already solved problem. The resulting logic description is thus not recursive.
- Use universal quantifiers instead of recursion.

The first approach is directly related to the top down methodology as well as reusability. The second approach is sometimes referred to as 'iteration through negation' since the derived logic program performs an iteration by means of negation as failure and backtracking. These two techniques will not be developed but rather illustrated on simple examples and compared with an inductive approach.

The first example is append3(L1, L2, L3, LApp) (Specification 5.23). Two logic descriptions are given. The first one (Logic Description 5.21) decomposes the problem into simpler ones (that is, append) and is not recursive. The iterative behaviour of append3 is performed in the append literals. The second logic description (Logic Description 5.22) is built by induction on the couple (L1, L2). It does not use append as a subproblem. Logic Description 5.21 is certainly more elegant, easier to construct and easier to understand than the recursive one. In order to be complete, a comparison should also be made at the logic program level.

procedure   append3(L1, L2, L3, LApp)

Type: L1, L2, L3, LApp : List

Relation: LApp is the concatenation of L1, L2 and L3.

Specification 5.23   append3(L1, L2, L3, LApp)

append3(L1, L2, L3, LApp) ⇔ append(L1, L2, L1_2)
& append(L1_2, L3, LApp)

Logic Description 5.21   append3(L1, L2, L3, LApp)

The second example is between(Inf, Sup, I) (Specification 5.24). A first logic description is constructed by reducing between to two comparisons and is thus not recursive. less_eq is considered as a primitive logic description (less_eq(A, B) holds iff $A \leq B$ with A and B integers). The procedure between can also be constructed by induction on (Sup-Inf) ≥ 0.

append3(L1, L2, L3, LApp) ⇔
    L1 = [] & L2 = [] & LApp = L3 & list(LApp)
∨ L1 = [] & L2 = [H | T] & LApp = [H | TApp]
                    & append3(L1, T, L3, TApp)
∨ L1 = [H | T] & LApp = [H | TApp] & append3(T, L2, L3, TApp)

Logic Description 5.22   append3(L1, L2, L3, LApp)

procedure   between(Inf, Sup, I)

Type: Inf, Sup, I : Integer

Relation: Inf $\leq$ I $\leq$ Sup.

Specification 5.24   between(Inf, Sup, I)

between(Inf, Sup, I) ⇔ less_eq(Inf, I) & less_eq(I, Sup)

Logic Description 5.23   between(Inf, Sup, I)

for Inf > Sup : false;
for Inf = Sup : I = Inf;
for Inf < Sup : Inf $\leq$ I $\leq$ Sup iff I = Inf or Inf + 1 $\leq$ I $\leq$ Sup.

The resulting logic description is Logic Description 5.24 where a straightforward simplification has been made (less(A, B) holds iff $A < B$ with A and B integers). The non-recursive logic description is of course simpler and easier to understand, and it actually reflects the specification. However, at the logic program level, the recursive logic description will turn out to have certain advantages.

$$between(\ Inf, Sup, I\ ) \Leftrightarrow less\_eq(Inf, Sup\ )\ \&\ I = Inf$$
$$\lor\ less(\ Inf, Sup\ )\ \&\ add(\ Inf, 1, Inf1\ )$$
$$\&\ between(\ Inf1, Sup, I\ )$$

Logic Description 5.24   between(Inf, Sup, I)

Induction versus decomposition can also be illustrated with the classical member(E, L) problem (Specification 5.25). It can be solved by means of a recursive logic description (see Exercise 5.22), however it is possible to reduce it to a particular case of append. The resulting logic description is then Logic Description 5.25. The iteration is performed here on the append literal.

procedure   member(E, L)

Type: L : List
          E : Term

Relation: E is an element of L.

Specification 5.25   member(E, L)

member(E, L) $\Leftrightarrow$ append(Before_E, [E | After_E], L)

Logic Description 5.25   member(E, L)

Iteration through a universal quantifier is illustrated on the minlist(L, Min) example (Specification 5.26). It is based on the observation that Min is the minimum of the elements of L iff Min is a member of L and Min is less than or equal to all the elements of L. The resulting logic description is Logic Description 5.26. For a recursive logic description, see Exercise 5.14.

procedure   minlist(L, Min)

Type: L : Non-empty list of positive integers
          Min : Positive integer

Relation: Min is the minimum of the elements of L.

Specification 5.26   minlist(L, Min)

minlist(L, Min) $\Leftrightarrow$
        member(Min, L) & ($\forall E$) (member(E, L) $\Rightarrow$ less_eq(Min, E))

Logic Description 5.26   minlist(L, Min)

Logic Description 5.26 is certainly very clear. It is however not clear how far problems can be solved naturally with universal quantifiers, their possible uses being somewhat restricted by the target logic programming language (for example, Prolog). It is usually restricted to special cases of quantification over implication.

Universal quantifiers have actually already been used within the proposed construction method (Logic Description 5.14 and 5.15). Let us illustrate their use on the simple example of verifying that a list L has at most two elements (Specification 5.27). Logic Description 5.27 uses universal quantifiers while Logic Description 5.28 does not. The former tests that L has 0, 1 or 2 elements, while in the latter, E1 and E2 are implicitly existentially quantified. Note that in Logic Description 5.27 atmost2 is (incorrectly) true when L is not a list.

procedure   atmost2(L)

Type: L : List

Relation: L has at most 2 elements.

Specification 5.27   atmost2(L)

atmost2(L) ⇔ (∀E1 ∀E2 ∀E3 ∀T) ¬L = [E1, E2, E3 | T]

Logic Description 5.27   atmost2(L)

atmost2(L) ⇔ L = [] ∨ L = [E1] ∨ L = [E1, E2]

Logic Description 5.28   atmost2(L)

EXERCISES

5.45   Let last(X, L) hold iff X is the last element of the list L. Construct two logic descriptions; the first by induction on L and the second by considering last as a special case of another well-known problem.

5.46   Let adjacent(X, Y, L) hold iff the element X is adjacent to the element Y in the list L. Construct two logic descriptions; the first by induction on L and the second by considering last as a special case of another well-known problem.

5.47   Construct a logic description for prefix(L, PrefL) (see Exercise 5.12) by considering it as a special case of another well-known problem.

5.48   Construct a logic description for suffix(L, SuffL) (see Specification 5.11) by considering it as a special case of another well-known problem.

5.49   Construct a logic description for palindrome(L) (see Exercise 5.10) by considering it as a special case of another well-known problem.

5.50   Construct a logic description for maxtree(T, Max) (see Exercise 5.31) using a universal quantifier approach.

5.51   • Let sets be represented by lists (without duplicates).

• Let union(S1, S2, SUni) hold iff the set SUni is the union of the sets S1 and S2.

• Let intersection(S1, S2, SInter) hold iff the set SInter is the intersection of the sets S1 and S2.

Construct logic descriptions for union and intersection using a universal quantifier approach (*Hint*: use member as the only subproblem).

5.10   Towards a computer-aided approach

Although the construction of a logic description is basically a human task, this does not imply that a computer-aided approach is useless. On the contrary, such an approach would allow the user to concentrate on the creative aspects alone while the computer takes care of the burdensome details. Moreover, the user can be guided within a methodology. The computer is just seen as a useful tool which can facilitate the construction of a logic description. We concentrate here on what could be useful and formalizable information about the construction of logic descriptions.

Two kinds of information can be distinguished. The first kind deals with object knowledge about the construction of a logic description. This covers, for example, information about types, structural forms of types, well-founded relations, transformation rules, properties of primitives, and so on. Such information does not describe how to construct logic descriptions, it merely constitutes the basic blocks for this construction. Within object knowledge, general information, containing information about the construction of any logic description, can be distinguished from specific information about the logic description under construction.

Heuristic knowledge constitutes the second kind of information. It describes how to use object knowledge to achieve the construction of a logic description. It is basically a formalization of heuristics or processes. This information is also sometimes called meta-knowledge because it is knowledge about the object knowledge.

The above distinctions are familar in knowledge-based systems, which separate knowledge relative to the application domain (here the construction of logic descriptions) from knowledge relative to a particular problem in this domain, and from knowledge relative to the typical forms of reasoning in the application domain (heuristics). In the literature, these knowledge components form what is ambitiously called a knowledge base. Let us now describe some possible general object knowledge and heuristic knowledge for the construction of logic descriptions.

Object knowledge

The general part of the object knowledge should contain information about the construction process. The method presented here for constructing logic descriptions is based on structural induction, the basic blocks of this construction being types, well-founded relations and structural forms. Therefore, object knowledge could take the form of a catalogue of well-founded relations and structural forms for types. Example 5.3 presents some possible instances.

EXAMPLE 5.3

    Type : Integer
      Well-founded relation : 'less than'
        Structural forms
          basis : X = 0
          general : X ≠ 0

    Type : List
      Well-founded relation : 'is a proper suffix'
        Structural forms
          basis : X = []
          general : (∃H ∃T) X = [H|T]
      Well-founded relation : 'has a shorter length'
        Structural forms
          basis : length(X, 0)
          general : (∃N) length(X, N) & N ≠ 0

    Type : Tree
      Well-founded relation : 'is a subtree of'
        Structural forms
          basis : X = void
          general : (∃E ∃Left ∃Right) X = tree(E, Left, Right)

    Type : Finite set
      Well-founded relation : 'is a proper subset of'
        Structural forms
          basis : empty(X)
          general : ¬empty(X)

Such a knowledge description does not require a formal definition either of types or of well-founded relations. The description of well-founded relations is intended to help the user in the construction and verification of logic descriptions. The logical description of the structural forms has to be formalized. This is not a restriction because it has to be done in the construction of the logic description. This object knowledge is well adapted for abstract data types. The structural forms do not have to describe the representation of the types, they may be expressed in terms of operations defined on these types. Such a catalogue could also contain more than one well-founded relation per type, so that the user could choose the one best-suited to his or her problem, or alternatively define a new one.

Heuristic knowledge

The heuristics for constructing logic descriptions are very rich, but no general recipe can handle the whole process of construction. This reflects the very creative aspect of this task. However, an attempt could be made to formalize heuristics in order to help the user when constructing his or her logic description. Let us thus describe some possible automation in the proposed construction process. Using the object knowledge, a computer system should be able to propose induction parameters, well-founded relations and the associated structural forms. In an intrinsic approach, the proposed well-founded relations would reflect the structural form of the induction parameter. The choice of an extrinsic well-founded relation is more difficult to automate since it should reflect the structural form of another parameter, or of the relation itself. For the construction of the structural cases, interactive syntactical analysers could also recognize recursion and point out to the user that the chosen well-founded relation must hold between the induction parameter of the logic description and the actual parameter of the recursion. The system could also verify the domain membership and add the literals necessary to realize this verification.

A major aid in the construction process could be to propose logic description schemata as well as specification schemata for possible generalizations. Specification schemata have been proposed in Section 5.8 for tupling generalization (Specification 5.15), ascending generalization (Specification 5.17) and descending generalization (Specification 5.18). Logic Description 5.29 which follows describes a possible schema for a logic description constructed by induction on X. Logic Description 5.30 is a schema for a tupling generalization. Logic Descriptions 5.31 and 5.32 are schemata for descending and ascending generalizations. These schemata are derived from the presentation of the construction method, with and without generalization.

$$
\begin{aligned}
p(X, Y) \Leftrightarrow\ &\text{minimal}(X) \ \&\ \text{directly\_solve}(X, Y) \\
\vee\ &\neg\text{minimal}(X) \ \&\ \text{decompose}(X, \text{FirstPart\_X}, \text{Rem\_X}) \\
&\&\ \text{process}(\text{FirstPart\_X}, \text{Part\_Y}) \\
&\&\ p(\text{Rem\_X}, \text{Rem\_Y}) \\
&\&\ \text{compose}(\text{Part\_Y}, \text{Rem\_Y}, Y)
\end{aligned}
$$

Logic Description 5.29   Schema with X as induction parameter

In these schemata, the literals minimal and decompose could be automatically specified and generated from the well-founded relation. The
other subproblems should be specified, constructed and simplified in
each particular case. The append literal can often be replaced by a unification since the length of the first list is usually fixed.

p(X, Y) ⇔ p_tupl([X], Y)
p_tupl(List_X, Y) ⇔
    List_X = [] & Y = []
  ∨ List_X = [X | Tail_X] & minimal(X)
        & directly_solve(X, Head_Y)
        & p_tupl(Tail_X, Tail_Y)
        & append (Head_Y, Tail_Y, Y)
  ∨ List_X = [X | Tail_X] & ¬minimal(X)
        & decompose(X, List_Smaller_X)
        & append(List_Smaller_X, Tail_X, New_List_X)
        & p_tupl(New_List_X, Part_Y)
        & compose(X, Part_Y, Y)

Logic Description 5.30   Schema for a tupling generalization

p(X, Y) ⇔ p_desc(X, Y, $\varnothing_Y$)
p_desc(XX, Y, Int_Y) ⇔
    minimal(XX) & extend_Int_min(XX, Int_Y, Y)
  ∨ ¬minimal(XX) & decompose(XX, FirstPart_XX, Rem_XX)
            & extend_Int(FirstPart_XX, Int_Y, New_Int_Y)
            & p_desc(Rem_XX, Y, New_Int_Y)

Logic Description 5.31   Schema for a descending generalization

p(X, Y) ⇔ p_asc(X, Y, $\varnothing_Y$, $\varnothing_X$)
p_asc(Suf_X, Y, Int_Y, Info_Pref_X) ⇔
    minimal(Suf_X) & Y = Int_Y
  ∨ ¬minimal(Suf_X)
        & decompose(Suf_X, FirstPart_Suf_X, Rem_Suf_X)
        & extend_Int(FirstPart_Suf_X, Info_Pref_X,
                            Int_Y, New_Int_Y)
        & extend_Info(FirstPart_Suf_X, Info_Pref_X,
                            New_Info_Pref_X)
        & p_asc(Rem_Suf_X, Y, New_Int_Y, New_Info_Pref_X)

Logic Description 5.32   Schema for an ascending generalization

*5.11 Background

In 1968, Dijkstra introduced the idea of a constructive approach to the
problem of program correctness (Dijkstra, 1968). This problem is usually

tackled as follows: 'Given a specification and given an algorithm, prove that the algorithm meets the given specification'. But Dijkstra tackled the problem from the other side: 'Given a specification, how do we construct, from the given specification, an algorithm meeting it?'. The work presented in this book is particularly inspired by this latter approach.

Structural induction construction

The construction and correctness proof of programs by a structural induction technique is due to Burstall (1969, 1974). Similar proof methods had already been used in Knuth (1968, Section 2.3.1). It is now a major technique for functional program construction and verification (Turner, 1982; Stoy, 1982). However, structural induction can be used successfully for procedural programming languages (Burstall, 1974; Manna and Waldinger, 1978). Techniques of imperative program construction and verification are discussed and compared in Le Charlier's thesis (Le Charlier, 1985).

Structural induction in logic program construction has already been seen in Clark and Tärnlund's paper (Clark and Tärnlund, 1977). The construction of an axiomatic definition of a relation is performed by case analysis on the structural form of a parameter. However, the concept of directionality is already present in the construction. The parameter chosen for the case analysis is considered as an input parameter. The correctness of the logic program is thus established when this parameter is ground. The definition of a well-founded relation and the inductive aspect of the construction are also implicit.

The induction principle presented in this book is more general than that which is usually called generalized induction (Burstall, 1969) or complete induction (Manna *et al.*, 1973; Clark and Tärnlund, 1977), where (E, <) has to be well-ordered (that is, well-founded and transitive). Well-founded sets are also called Noetherian sets; and well-ordered sets are sometimes called (confusingly) well-founded (see, for example, Manna (1974)). Our definition of well-founded sets is taken from Schoenfield (1967) and Boyer and Moore (1979).

The distinction between ascending and descending correctness proofs originates from imperative programming, where it was introduced by Leroy (1978) and developed by Le Charlier (1985). The ascending concept can be related to bottom-up computation (Berry, 1976), and dynamic programming (Dreyfus and Law, 1977).

In this book a method for logic description construction has been proposed, and it has been shown that the logic descriptions obtained are correct by construction. In Smith (1985), a general schema is presented for functional programs using a divide and conquer strategy. Construction strategies are described, and the generic correctness of the resulting functional programs is also proven. This program schema and the construction strategies are particular cases of the general form of logic descriptions, and of the construction methodology.

Here induction has been compared with the use of the universal quantifier. Kowalski (1983) claims that universal quantifiers are more natural than recursion. A precise class of possible uses of the universal quantifier is given in Dayantis (1987).

The FOLON research project at the University of Namur is a first attempt at a computer-aided approach for logic program development (Deville and Burnay, 1989). The approach is related to program development systems. Good surveys can be found in Partsch and Steinbrüggen (1983), Biermann *et al.* (1984), IEEE (1985) and Goldberg (1986).

Generalization

The concept of generalization is not new in computer science. For instance, generalization can be used for synthesizing programs from examples (Summers, 1977, Biermann and Krishnaswamy, 1976; Biermann, 1978; Smith, 1984). Generalization is also used in the process of elaborating an invariant from a postcondition (Gries, 1981). The concept of generalization within the logic framework, independent of any programming concern (Genesereth and Nilsson, 1987) will now be presented.

Let G and F be formulae, and T a set of formulae. G generalizes F in T iff

- $T \cup \{G\} \vDash F$
- $T \cup \{F\} \nvDash \neg G$ (consistency).

The presentation of computational generalization is based on a 'general state of computation'. Such a generalization can also be described in four different ways. Firstly, it can be seen as a generalization of a function between parameters. For instance, a generalization of factorial(N, FactN) can be seen as a generalization of the function N!. Secondly, it can be seen as a generalization of a definition or of a subformula, as mentioned in Chapter 6. Thirdly, computational generalization can be deduced from the trace of an execution of the initial algorithm (using some appropriate procedural semantics). Finally, in the imperative framework, computational generalization can be seen as the generalization of an invariant.

Generalization is the opposite of particularization. In a generalization approach, the initial problem is first generalized, and the generalized problem is then particularized to the initial one. Although not developed here, an opposite approach can be taken for solving certain problems.

The initial problem (for example, dealing with graphs) is first particularized (for example, graphs without cycle), and then the particularized algorithm is generalized to solve the initial problem. This amounts to first strengthening the hypothesis and then progressively relaxing it up to the initial problem.

SUMMARY

- A well-founded relation is a relation with no infinite decreasing sequences.

- The construction of a logic description can be performed in four steps:
  (i)   choice of an induction parameter,
  (ii)   choice of a well-founded relation,
  (iii)   structural forms of the induction parameter,
  (iv)   construction of the structural cases.

- Logic descriptions obtained with the construction method are correct by construction.

- The choice of a well-founded relation can be guided by the intrinsic or the extrinsic heuristic.

   Intrinsic heuristic: choose a well-founded relation reflecting the structural form of the induction parameter(s).

   Extrinsic heuristic: choose a well-founded relation reflecting the structural form of some other parameter(s), or reflecting the structural form of the relation itself.

- The choice of an induction parameter can be guided by the functionality heuristic and by the directionality heuristic.

   Functionality heuristic: choose an induction parameter such that, given a ground instance of it, the relation can hold for at most one ground instance of the other parameters.

   Directionality heuristic: choose an induction parameter which is always ground in the *in* part of the specified directionalities of the procedure.

- Structural and computational generalization are two strategies for generalizing problems

   In a **structural generalization**, the structure of a parameter is generalized. In the particular case of **tupling generalization**, an object is generalized into a list of objects.

In a **computational generalization**, the state of computation is generalized. In an **ascending generalization**, some information about the 'already visited' part of the induction parameter is necessary. In a **descending generalization**, no information about the 'already visited' part of the induction parameter is necessary.

6

Transformation of logic descriptions

PREVIEW   A logic description is not the same as a logic program: the program has to be derived from the description. However, it can be said that logic descriptions composed of a disjunction of conjunctions of literals yield logic programs almost directly, although it is often difficult to estimate whether the derived program will be efficient or not. Part of this efficiency is related to recursive and iterative (or tail-recursive) logic programs. A transformational approach attempts to increase the efficiency of the derived logic program by means of transformations. Such transformations can be made at the logic program level or at the logic description level. The transformations considered here will only deal with logic, without any procedural aspects, and will therefore be easier to carry out while preserving correctness.

Once a correct logic description has been constructed, it can be transformed. Transformations can be made by means of a transformation system that ensures correctness. This approach has many advantages:

- it concentrates the truly creative effort on the construction of the logic description;
- the form and complexity of this first version are less important than the correctness;
- the transformation of a correct logic description into another is easier than the construction of a second one from scratch;
- it is easier to optimize a correct algorithm than to correct an optimized algorithm;
- finally, the initial logic description is often simpler and easier to understand than its transformed version. Therefore, the initial logic description and its construction process are basic information to be found in the documentation.

169

In this chapter we first present a transformation system for logic descriptions. This is then used in different ways to transform logic descriptions previously obtained. The relationship between transformations and certain construction techniques will also be shown.

6.1   A transformation system

The proposed transformation system basically has three classes of inference rules. The first class defines new logic descriptions, the second infers logical consequences from previous steps, and the third uses properties of the specifications of certain logic descriptions.

In the transformation process, we will use formulae which are no longer restricted to the form of logic descriptions: the left-hand side can be any formula rather than just an atomic formula. Therefore, the formulae handled here will be closed formulae of the form

$$\forall(A \Leftrightarrow B)$$

where A and B are formulae. This will be abbreviated as

$$A \Leftrightarrow B$$

In order to avoid confusion, existential quantifiers will be explicit in B during the transformation process. The inference rules will now be described.

(1)   *Auxiliary definition*
Introduce a logic description LD(p) such that p does not occur in any previous step of the transformation process.

(2)   *Logic inference*
(2.1)   *Instantiation*
From   A $\Leftrightarrow$ Def_A,
Infer   A & C $\Leftrightarrow$ C & Def_A,
where the free variables of C are free variables of A.

(2.2)   *Unfolding*
From   E $\Leftrightarrow$ Def_E   and   F $\Leftrightarrow$ Def_F,
where a subformula F′ in Def_E is an instance of F
(F′ = Fθ)
Infer   E $\Leftrightarrow$ New_Def_E
where New_Def_E is Def_E with F′ replaced by Def_Fθ.

(2.3)   *Folding*
From   E $\Leftrightarrow$ Def_E   and   F $\Leftrightarrow$ Def_F,
where a subformula Def_F′ in Def_E is an instance of

Def_F (Def_F' = Def_Fθ)
Infer   E ⇔ New_Def_E
where New_Def_E is Def_E with Def_F' replaced by Fθ.

(2.4) *Use of the usual logic inferences*

(3)   *Use of the properties of the specifications*

Rules 2.1–2.3 are particular cases of 2.4. They are made distinct because they are often used in transformations. These inference rules are similar to those introduced by Burstall and Darlington (1977) for developing recursive equations although here, of course, it is logic descriptions that are being dealt with rather than recursive equations. It is worth noticing that folding and unfolding are similar from a logical point of view, but, when applied to logic descriptions, their use will be very different. It could be shown that each transformation rule preserves the correctness of the logic descriptions involved (see Exercise 6.1).

Rules of class (3) refer to properties deduced from a specification or from the associated concepts which can be used to infer an equivalence. Some examples are presented below:

EXAMPLE 6.1

From the specification of append (Specification 4.2), we have that:

(∃AB) (append(list_a, list_b, AB)
             & append(AB, list_c, list_abc))

can be replaced, in a logic description, by

(∃BC) (append(list_b, list_c, BC)
             & append(list_a, BC, list_abc))

where list_a, list_b, list_c, list_abc are lists, while preserving the correctness of the logic description. This expresses a consequence of the associativity of the append relation. Similarly, append([], X, Y) can be replaced by X = Y & list(X).

From the specification of syntactical equality (Specification 5.1), we have that:

- (∃X) (X = t & Exp) is logically equivalent to (∃X) (X = t & Exp {X/t}), or simply Exp {X/t}, where t is a term (not containing X) and Exp is a conjunction of literals.

- (∃X) (X = t1 & X = t2) is false if there are no ground instances of t1 and t2 (say t1* and t2*) such that t1* = t2*, where t1 and t2 are terms.

- (∃X) X = t is always true, where t is a term not containing X.

Depending on the inference rules involved in the transformation process, three families of transformations will be presented. In the first one (known as transformation by simplification), only inference rules (2.4) and (3) will be used. In the second family, inference rule (1) will not be used. Such transformations will be called isotopic because they do not introduce new predicates. In the third family, all the inference rules will be used, yielding transformations with auxiliary definitions.

EXERCISE_____

6.1 Show that the inference rules 2.1, 2.2 and 2.3 infer H-logical consequences.

6.2 Transformations by simplification

The proposed transformation system can be used to simplify logic descriptions by means of inference rules 2.4 and 3. This is illustrated with the logic description of efface(X, L, LEff), obtained using an induction on LEff (Logic Description 5.7).

$$\text{efface(X, L, LEff)} \Leftrightarrow (\exists \text{ H, T, TEff)} \tag{1}$$
$$(\quad \text{Leff} = [\,] \,\&\, L = [X]$$
$$\lor \text{Leff} = [H \,|\, \text{TEff}] \,\&\, (\quad L = [X, H \,|\, \text{TEff}] \,\&\, \text{list(TEff)}$$
$$\lor H \neq X \,\&\, \text{efface(X, T, TEff)} \,\&\, L = [H \,|\, T]\,)\,)$$

Existential quantifiers are here explicitly put all along the transformation process. The objective of this transformation is to derive the logic description obtained with L as the induction parameter (Logic Description 5.4). The first transformation tries to obtain a conjunction for each structural case of L.

Distribute & over ∨

$$\text{efface(X, L, LEff)} \Leftrightarrow (\exists \text{ H, T, TEff)} \tag{2}$$
$$(\quad \text{LEff} = [\,] \,\&\, L = [X]$$
$$\lor \text{LEff} = [H \,|\, \text{TEff}] \,\&\, L = [X \,|\, \text{TEff}] \,\&\, \text{list(TEff)}$$
$$\lor \text{LEff} = [H \,|\, \text{TEff}] \,\&\, H \neq X \,\&\, \text{efface(X, T, TEff)} \,\&\, L = [H \,|\, T]\,)$$

Properties of =

$$\text{efface(X, L, LEff)} \Leftrightarrow (\exists \text{ H, T, TEff)} \tag{3}$$
$$(\quad \text{LEff} = [\,] \,\&\, L = [X \,|\, \text{LEff}]$$
$$\lor \text{LEff} = [H \,|\, \text{TEff}] \,\&\, L = [X \,|\, \text{LEff}] \,\&\, \text{list(TEff)}$$
$$\lor \text{LEff} = [H \,|\, \text{TEff}] \,\&\, H \neq X \,\&\, \text{efface(X, T, TEff)} \,\&\, L = [H \,|\, T]\,)$$

Factoring

$$efface(X, L, LEff) \Leftrightarrow (\exists H, T, TEff) \tag{4}$$
$$(\quad LEff = [] \vee LEff = [H \,|\, TEff] \,\&\, list(TEff)) \,\&\, L = [X \,|\, LEff]$$
$$\vee LEff = [H \,|\, TEff] \,\&\, H \neq X \,\&\, efface(X, T, TEff) \,\&\, L = [H \,|\, T])$$

Properties of lists

$$efface(X, L, LEff) \Leftrightarrow (\exists H, T, TEff) \tag{5}$$
$$(\quad L = [X \,|\, LEff] \,\&\, list(LEff)$$
$$\vee LEff = [H \,|\, TEff] \,\&\, H \neq X \,\&\, efface(X, T, TEff) \,\&\, L = [H \,|\, T])$$

The two subcases $L = [H \,|\, T] \,\&\, H = X$, and $L = [H \,|\, T] \,\&\, H \neq X$ appearing in the target logic description are now put forward.

Properties of =

$$efface(X, L, LEff) \Leftrightarrow (\exists H, T, TEff) \tag{6}$$
$$(\quad L = [H \,|\, T] \,\&\, H = X \,\&\, LEff = T \,\&\, list(LEff)$$
$$\vee L = [H \,|\, T] \,\&\, H \neq X \,\&\, efface(X, T, TEff) \,\&\, LEff = [H \,|\, TEff])$$

Finally, the case $L = []$ is added and a factorization is performed.

Factoring and standard logic inferences

$$efface(X, L, LEff) \Leftrightarrow (\exists H, T, TEff) \tag{7}$$
$$(\quad L = [] \,\&\, false$$
$$\vee L = [H \,|\, T] \,\&\, (\quad H = X \,\&\, LEff = T \,\&\, list(T)$$
$$\vee H \neq X \,\&\, efface(X, T, TEff) \,\&\, LEff = [H \,|\, TEff]))$$

EXERCISE

6.2   Transform Logic Description 5.10 (suffix_L) into Logic Description 5.11 (suffix_LSufL).

6.3   Isotopic transformations

An isotopic transformation is one that does not use inference rule 1 which introduces new logic descriptions. It is illustrated on the non-recursive logic description member(E, L) obtained by decomposition (Logic Description 5.25).

$$member(E, L) \Leftrightarrow (\exists \text{ Before, After }) \text{ append}(\text{Before}, [E \,|\, After], L) \tag{1}$$
$$append(L1, L2, LApp) \Leftrightarrow (\exists H, T, TApp) \tag{2}$$
$$(\quad L1 = [] \,\&\, LApp = L2 \,\&\, list(LApp)$$
$$\vee L1 = [H \,|\, T] \,\&\, LApp = [H \,|\, TApp] \,\&\, append(T, L2, TApp))$$

The objective here is to obtain a recursive logic description for member. The strategy will be to unfold the append literal, to rearrange the resulting literals and finally to fold in order to obtain a recursive logic description. When unfolding, variables are usually renamed in order to facilitate the transformation.

Unfold append *with (2)*

$$\text{member}(E, L) \Leftrightarrow (\exists \text{ Before, After}) \tag{3}$$
$$(\exists H\_Before, T\_Before, T)$$
$$(\quad Before = [] \ \& \ L = [E \mid After] \ \& \ list(L)$$
$$\vee \ Before = [H\_Before \mid T\_Before] \ \& \ L = [H\_Before \mid T]$$
$$\& \ append(T\_Before, [E \mid After], T))$$

Property of = and distribution of quantifiers

$$\text{member}(E, L) \Leftrightarrow \tag{4}$$
$$(\exists \ After) (L = [E \mid After] \ \& \ list(L))$$
$$\vee (\exists \ H\_Before, T) (L = [H\_Before \mid T]$$
$$\& (\exists \ After, T\_Before) \ append(T\_Before, [E \mid After], T))$$

Fold with (1)

$$\text{member}(E, L) \Leftrightarrow \tag{5}$$
$$(\exists \ After) (L = [E \mid After] \ \& \ list(L))$$
$$\vee (\exists \ H\_Before, T) (L = [H\_Before \mid T] \ \& \ member (E, T))$$

Distribution of quantifiers and variable renaming

$$\text{member}(E, L) \Leftrightarrow (\exists H, T) \tag{6}$$
$$(L = [E \mid T] \ \& \ list(L)$$
$$\vee L = [H \mid T] \ \& \ member(E, T))$$

The resulting logic description (6) is similar to the one obtained by induction on L (Exercise 5.22).

Our interest in transformations by simplification and transformations without auxiliary definition is twofold. Firstly, the equivalence of logic descriptions constructed using different methods can be shown: for example, logic descriptions constructed using different induction parameters, or those obtained by decomposition (non-recursive and recursive ones). Secondly, such transformations can be used to derive new logic descriptions. This approach is particularly interesting when the initial description has been constructed easily, but yields an inefficient derived logic program.

EXERCISES

6.3   Transform Logic Description 5.21 (append3 by decomposition) into Logic Description 5.22 (append3 by induction).

6.4   In Exercises 5.45–5.49, transform the logic descriptions constructed without induction into the logic descriptions obtained with induction.

6.4   Transformations with auxiliary definitions

Transformations are more powerful if definition rule 1 is used. Such an auxiliary definition is sometimes called a **Eureka** because it must be found by the user and contain the 'essence' of the induced transformation. These transformations are now illustrated by two examples. The relation between the choice of a definition and the generalization process is also dealt with. Finally we describe how to choose a 'good' definition and which inference rules to use.

EXAMPLE   reverse(L, LRev)

The first example is the logic description reverse(L, LRev) (Logic Description 4.1).

$$\text{reverse}(L, LRev) \Leftrightarrow (\exists H, T, TRev) \tag{1}$$
$$(\quad L = [] \;\&\; LRev = []$$
$$\vee L = [H\,|\,T] \;\&\; \text{reverse}(T, TRev) \;\&\; \text{append}(TRev, [H], LRev))$$

The Eureka will now be presented without justification. This choice will be studied later.

Task A   Eureka

Auxiliary definition (Eureka)

$$\text{reverse\_def}(L, LRev, LInt) \Leftrightarrow (\exists X) \tag{2}$$
$$(\text{reverse}(L, X) \;\&\; \text{append}(X, LInt, LRev))$$

Task B   reverse *as a special case of* reverse_def

To achieve this goal, the instantiation rule is used with LInt = [], and the identity property of [] for the append relation is applied.

Instantiate (2)

$$\text{reverse\_def}(L, LRev, LInt) \;\&\; LInt = [] \Leftrightarrow LInt = [] \;\&\; (\exists X) \tag{B1}$$
$$(\text{reverse}(L, X) \;\&\; \text{append}(X, LInt, LRev))$$

Properties of = and append *(right identity element)*

$$\text{reverse\_def(L, LRev, LInt) \& LInt} = [] \Leftrightarrow (\exists X) \tag{B2}$$
$$(\text{ LInt} = [] \text{ \& reverse(L, X) \& X} = \text{LRev \& list(X))}$$

Properties of = and type of reverse

$$\text{reverse\_def(L, LRev, LInt) \& LInt} = [] \Leftrightarrow \text{reverse(L, LRev)} \tag{B3}$$

Rewrite (B3)

$$\text{reverse(L, LRev)} \Leftrightarrow \text{LInt} = [] \text{ \& reverse\_def(L, LRev, LInt)} \tag{B4}$$

Task C   *Recursive logic description for* reverse_def

The objective is to obtain a recursive logic description for reverse_def, without the occurrence of reverse. The strategy is to obtain an instance of the right-hand side of the definition of reverse_def followed by folding, thus yielding a recursive use of reverse_def.

Unfold reverse *with (1)*

$$\text{reverse\_def(L, LRev, LInt)} \Leftrightarrow (\exists X) \tag{C1}$$
$$((\exists H, T, TRev)(\quad L = [] \text{ \& X} = []$$
$$\lor L = [H \mid T] \text{ \& reverse(T, TRev)}$$
$$\text{\& append(TRev, [H], X))}$$
$$\text{\& append(X, LInt, LRev))}$$

Distribute & *over* ∨ *and properties of =*

$$\text{reverse\_def(L, LRev, LInt)} \Leftrightarrow (\exists X, H, T, TRev) \tag{C2}$$
$$(\quad L = [] \text{ \& append([], LInt, LRev)}$$
$$\lor L = [H \mid T] \text{ \& reverse(T, TRev) \& append(TRev, [H], X)}$$
$$\text{\& append(X, LInt, LRev))}$$

Properties of append *(associativity and left identity)*

$$\text{reverse\_def(L, LRev, LInt)} \Leftrightarrow (\exists Y, H, T, TRev) \tag{C3}$$
$$(\quad L = [] \text{ \& LRev} = \text{LInt \& list(LRev)}$$
$$\lor L = [H \mid T] \text{ \& reverse(T, TRev) \& append([H], LInt, Y)}$$
$$\text{\& append(TRev, Y, LRev))}$$

Properties of append

$$\text{reverse\_def(L, LRev, LInt)} \Leftrightarrow (\exists Y, H, T, TRev) \tag{C4}$$
$$(\quad L = [] \text{ \& LRev} = \text{LInt \& list(LRev)}$$
$$\lor L = [H \mid T] \text{ \& reverse(T, TRev) \& Y} = [H \mid LInt]$$
$$\text{\& append(TRev, Y, LRev))}$$

Distribution of existential quantifiers

> reverse_def(L, LRev, LInt) ⇔ (∃Y, H, T)   **(C5)**
> (L = [] & LRev = LInt & list(LRev)
> ∨ L = [H|T] & Y = [H|LInt]
>   & (∃TRev) (reverse(T, TRev)
>   & append(TRev, Y, LRev)))

Fold with (2)

> reverse_def(L, LRev, LInt) ⇔ (∃Y, H, T)   **(C6)**
> (L = [] & LRev = LInt & list(LRev)
> ∨ L = [H|T] & Y = [H|LInt] & reverse_def(T, LRev, Y))

The logic description for reverse is the composition of (B4) and (C6).

6.4.1   The principles of transformations with auxiliary definitions

Transformations with auxiliary definitions versus generalization

It is worth comparing the Eureka, as well as the derived logic description for reverse_def, with a descending generalization of the initial problem (Specification 6.1).

> procedure   reverse_desc(L, LRev, LInt)
> *Type*:   L, LRev, LInt : List
> *Relation*:   LRev is the concatenation of the reverse of L, and LInt.

Specification 6.1   reverse_desc(L, LRev, LInt)

Constructing a logic description for this generalization using L as the induction parameter yields the same logic description as (C6). Let us compare the generalization approach with the transformation one. The superiority of the latter has already been suggested, but which approach is the easier? When generalizing problems, a generalization has to be found and a logic description explicitly constructed for it. With a transformational approach, the Eureka and adequate transformation rules must be found. At first sight, the latter may appear more difficult. However, if one can define heuristics to find Eurekas as well as some general strategies of transformation, a transformational approach can be easier, especially if some automated tools are supporting the transformations.

The Eureka

How was the definition (Eureka) found? The answer is twofold. Firstly, one can see it as a logic description for the generalized problem, but in terms of reverse and without induction. Secondly one can also see it as a definition for the following literals appearing in the logic description of reverse:

> reverse(T, TRev) & append(TRev, [H], LRev)

where the parameter [H] is generalized to a variable, and TRev does not appear as an argument of reverse_def because it is 'local' to these literals (that is, it only appears there).

Transformation rules

The choice of inference rules is guided by two objectives. First, we want reverse to be expressed in terms of reverse_def. Secondly, reverse_def is transformed in order to be recursive.

In order to achieve the first objective (Task B), the instantiation rule is used with the generalized parameter (LInt) and the identity element of the append relation (LInt = []). The result is obtained by the identity property of append. For the second objective, reverse is unfolded. The identity property of append is used to suppress one append literal. The associativity property of append is then applied in order to allow folding.

Transformation strategy

From the above example, a general heuristic can be defined for finding the Eureka p_def from a logic description LD(p), as well as for applying the inference rules.

Task A   Find an auxiliary definition

(1)   In the definition part of LD(p), find a subformula of the form

$$(\exists Y)(p(t) \& q(s))$$

such that q has two properties corresponding to the existence of a (left and right) identity element and associativity.

(2)   Define a new logic description LD(p_def)

$$p\_def(x) \Leftrightarrow (\exists Y)(p(t') \& q(s'))$$

such that:

- p(t') & q(s') is a generalized form of p(t) & q(s) where non-variable parameters are replaced by variables.
- x is the tuple of variables appearing in t' and s', except Y.

Task B   p as a special case of p_def

(1)   Instantiate the definition with $z = n$ where z are variables, from the formal parameter x, of p_def that do not appear in p(t), and n is the identity element of q.

(2)   Properties of =. Try to obtain an instance of q where the identity property can be applied.

(3)   Property of q: existence of an identity element. Simplify the resulting logic description.

(4)   Rewrite the preceding result by reversing its left- and right-hand sides.

Task C   Recursive definition of p_def

(1)   Unfold p in the auxiliary definition.

(2)   Rearrange the literals.

(3)   Property of q: associativity and existence of an identity element.

(4)   Fold (repeatedly if necessary).

A similarity can be seen between the description of the heuristic and the general construction schema of a descending generalization (Specification 5.18).

EXAMPLE   compress(L, CL)

In this example, the logic description compress(L, CL) constructed with L as the induction parameter, using an extrinsic well-founded relation, is transformed. This example illustrates another interesting aspect of logic description transformation: loop combinations. The general idea of such transformations is to interweave independent parts which have been kept apart for reasons of clarity. The three logic descriptions involved are now presented: compress_ext_L (Logic Description 5.6), first_max_seq (given here without construction), and length (Logic Description 5.8).

$$
\begin{aligned}
&\text{compress\_ext\_L(L, CL)} \Leftrightarrow (\exists C, T, F\_Seq, Suf\_L, Lg, Tail\_CL) \qquad \textbf{(1)}\\
&\quad (\quad L = [] \ \& \ CL = []\\
&\quad \lor L = [C\,|\,T] \ \& \ \text{first\_max\_seq(L, F\_Seq, Suf\_L)}\\
&\qquad\qquad\qquad \& \ \text{length(F\_Seq, Lg)}\\
&\qquad\qquad\qquad \& \ CL = [C, Lg\,|\,Tail\_CL]\\
&\qquad\qquad\qquad \& \ \text{compress\_ext\_L(Suf\_L, Tail\_CL))}
\end{aligned}
$$

$$
\begin{aligned}
&\text{first\_max\_seq(L, F\_Seq, Suf\_L)} \Leftrightarrow (\exists C1, C2, T, TF\_Seq) \qquad \textbf{(2)}\\
&\quad (\quad L = [C1] \ \& \ F\_Seq = [C1] \ \& \ Suf\_L = [] \ \& \ \text{char(C1)}\\
&\quad \lor L = [C1, C2\,|\,T] \ \& \ (\quad C1 \neq C2 \ \& \ F\_Seq = [C1] \ \& \ Suf\_L = [C2\,|\,T]\\
&\qquad\qquad\qquad\qquad\qquad\qquad \& \ \text{list\_char(L)}\\
&\qquad\qquad\qquad \lor C1 = C2 \ \& \ F\_Seq = [C1\,|\,TF\_Seq]\\
&\qquad\qquad\qquad\qquad\qquad\quad \& \ \text{first\_max\_seq([C2\,|\,T], TF\_Seq,}\\
&\qquad\qquad\qquad\qquad\qquad\qquad \text{Suf\_L))}
\end{aligned}
$$

$$
\begin{aligned}
&\text{length(L, Lg)} \Leftrightarrow (\exists H, T, Lg\_T) \qquad \textbf{(3)}\\
&\quad (\quad L = [] \ \& \ Lg = 0\\
&\quad \lor L = [H\,|\,T] \ \& \ \text{length(T, Lg\_T)} \ \& \ \text{add(Lg\_T, 1, Lg))}
\end{aligned}
$$

Task A   Finding the Eureka

We use the heuristics defined above, but without any recursive literal. A possible subformula is:

$$(\exists F\_Seq) (\text{first\_max\_seq}(L, F\_Seq, Suf\_L) \& \text{length}(F\_Seq, Lg))$$

The variable F_Seq is local to these literals. The Eureka is therefore:

lg_first_max_seq(L, Lg, Suf_L) ⇔ (∃ X) **(4)**
(first_max_seq(L, X, Suf_L) & length(X, Lg))

Task B   lg_first_max_seq *in* compress

The above definition can be used for simplifying the definition part of the compress logic description.

Fold (1) with (4)

compress_ext_L(L, CL) ⇔ (∃ C, T, F_Seq, Suf_L, Lg, Tail_CL)   **(B1)**
(L = [] & CL = []
    ∨ L = [C | T] & lg_first_max_seq(L, Lg, Suf_L)
        & CL = [C, Lg | Tail_CL]
        & compress_ext_L(Suf_L, Tail_CL))

Task C   *Recursive logic description for* lg_first_max_seq

This task is performed by unfolding the definition part of lg_first_max_seq, simplifying and then folding so as to obtain a recursion while getting rid of the length and first_max_seq literals.

Unfold (4) with (2) and (3), distribute & over ∨

lg_first_max_seq(L, Lg, Suf_L) ⇔ (∃ X) (∃ C1, C2, T, TX)   **(C1)**
(L = [C1] & X = [C1] & Suf_L = [] & char(C1)
        & (∃H, T', Lg_TX) (X = [H | T'] & length_L(T', Lg_TX)
                                & add(Lg_TX, 1, Lg))
    ∨ L = [C1, C2 | T] & C1 ≠ C2 & X = [C1] & Suf_L = [C2 | T]
                                & list_char(L)
        & (∃H, T', Lg_TX) (X = [H | T'] & length_L (T', Lg_TX)
                                & add(Lg_TX, 1, Lg))
    ∨ L = [C1, C2 | T] & C1 = C2 & X = [C1 | TX]
                                & first_max_seq([C2 | T], TX, Suf_L)
        & (∃H, T', Lg_TX) (X = [H | T'] & length_L(T', Lg_TX)
                                & add(Lg_TX, 1, Lg))
    ∨ L = [C1] & X = [C1] & . . . & X = []
    ∨ L = [C1, C2 | T] & C1 ≠ C2 & X = [C1] & . . . & X = [] & . . .
    ∨ L = [C1, C2 | T] & C1 = C2 & X = [C1 | TX] & . . . & X = [] & . . .)

Properties of =, length, *addition and simplification and distribution of quantifiers*

lg_first_max_seq(L, Lg, Suf_L) ⇔ (∃ C1, C2, T, Lg_TX)   **(C2)**
(L = [C1] & Suf_L = [] & Lg = 1 & char(C1)
    ∨ L = [C1, C2 | T] & C1 ≠ C2 & Suf_L = [C2 | T] & Lg = 1
                                & list_char(L)
∨ L = [C1, C2 | T] & C1 = C2
        & (∃TX) (first_max_seq ([C2 | T], TX, Suf_L)
                                & length_L(TX, Lg_TX))
        & add(Lg_TX, 1, Lg))

Fold with (4)

lg_first_max_seq(L, Lg, Suf_L) ⇔ (∃ C1, C2, T, Lg_TX)   **(C3)**
   (L = [C1] & Suf_L = [] & Lg = 1 & char(C1)
    ∨ L = [C1, C2 | T] & C1 ≠ C2 & Suf_L = [C2 | T] & Lg = 1
                                            & list_char(L)
    ∨ L = [C1, C2 | T] & C1 = C2
                    & lg_first_max_seq([C2 | T], Lg_TX, Suf_L)
                    & add(Lg_TX, 1, Lg))

The procedure lg_first_max_seq is easily specified. The compress description can also be constructed directly with this subproblem. However, from a reusability point of view, the initial description can use the length subproblem which could be part of a library of logic descriptions. Moreover, the initial description is easier to understand since the concepts of max-sequence and length are not interlinked in a single subproblem. A logic program derived from the transformed logic description will be more efficient because two 'loops' are merged into one. In other words, the first max-subsequence will be inspected only once instead of twice.

The lg_first_max_seq logic description could be further transformed since the following subproblem appears:

(∃ Lg_TX) (lg_first_max_seq([C2 | T], Lg_TX, Suf_L)
               & add(Lg_TX, 1, Lg))

Note that Lg_TX is local to these literals and addition has an identity element and an associativity property. The Eureka is obtained by generalizing [C2 | T] to L, and the constant 1 to Int_Lg. Hence the following definition:

lg_first_max_seq_def(L, Lg, Suf_L, Int_Lg) ⇔ (∃ X)
   (lg_first_max_seq(L, X, Suf_L) & add(X, Int_Lg, Lg))

This transformation is not presented here (see Exercise 6.5).

In the above, only one sort of auxiliary definition has been considered, but transformations cannot be restricted solely to this form of definition.

EXERCISES

6.5   Complete the transformation of lg_first_max_seq.

6.6   Transform Logic Description 5.12 (flattree) using a definition. Compare the transformation and the resulting logic description with flattree_desc_2 (Logic Description 5.19).

6.7   Transform the logic description of factorial(N, FactN) (see Exercise 5.11) constructed by induction without generalization. Use an auxiliary definition.

6.8   Transform the logic description of sumlist(L, S)(see Exercise 5.13) constructed by induction without generalization. Use an auxiliary definition.

6.9   Transform the logic description of minlist(L, Min) (see Exercise 5.14) constructed by induction without generalization. Use an auxiliary definition.

6.10 Transform the logic description of quicksort(L, LSorted) (see Exercise 5.19) constructed by induction without generalization. Use an auxiliary definition. (*Hint*: fold twice).

6.11 Transform the logic description of maxtree(T, Max) (see Exercise 5.31) constructed by induction without generalization. Use an auxiliary definition.

---

*6.5   Background

The transformation rules presented in this chapter are based on the work of Burstall and Darlington (1975, 1977). Similar transformation principles have also been proposed by Manna and Waldinger (1977).

Most of the transformations with auxiliary definitions presented here are based on the associativity of an operation. These transformations could also be obtained in Burstall and Darlington's system if a functional language were used instead of a logical one. The same kind of transformations are performed by Arsac and Kodratoff (1982), but on imperative programs. Le Charlier (1985) proposes functional program transformations based on a property which generalizes associativity. In Wand (1980), an alternative to generalization is presented; an extra argument is introduced or a function is extended to deal with a list of inputs. The use of continuations (which are data structures representing the future course of a computation) is also proposed. Similar techniques are presented in Bird (1984).

The application of Burstall and Darlington's transformation techniques to the problem of deriving a Horn clause program from a first-order specification was first investigated in Clark and Sickel (1977) (see also Clark, 1979; Clark and Darlington, 1980). Since most of their first-order specifications have the form of logic descriptions, such derivations can be seen as algorithm or program transformations. In Clark (1981), a new family of transformations is introduced. They correspond somewhat to an ascending generalization of a problem.

In Hogger (1981, 1984), methods are presented for deriving programs from a specification. Given that Hogger's specification has the same form as the logic descriptions presented here, such a derivation can be seen as a transformation. Given a logic specification of a relation p whose form is $p(x) \Leftrightarrow Def$ (where Def is any first-order formula), Hogger tries to obtain a set of Horn clauses. One of his techniques is successively to replace subformulae of the definition part by logically equivalent subformulae. This could also be done with the isotopic transformation system considered here. Another of his techniques is to simulate the execution of a goal. From this quasi-computation, a set of Horn clauses is derived.

More recently, Sato and Tamaki (1983, 1984a, 1986) defined fold/unfold transformations for logic programs. Their transformations preserve the equivalence of programs as defined by the least Herbrand model. However, heuristics are not explicitly described, and the transformations are restricted to definite programs. In Debray (1984), an application of Sato and Tamaki's transformations is explored in order to optimize a class of almost tail-recursive logic programs. These transformations use the associativity properties of predicates. Since transformations are made at the logic program level (Prolog programs), the procedural semantics must be considered in the transformation process. This complicates the transformations. The associativity property is also exploited extensively in Brough and Hogger (1987) in order to propose generic transformations. The relationship with difference structures is also discussed. In Kanamori and Fujita (1984), Sato and Tamaki's Prolog program transformation is used to merge computational induction schemes into more simple ones. This technique is also used in Seki and Furukawa (1987) for a class of generate and test logic programs, and in Kanamori and Horiuchi (1987) for the derivation of logic programs. Logic program transformations are also considered in Azibi and Kodratoff (1986). Other transformations are presented in Dayantis (1987) which transform logic descriptions with universal quantifiers into Prolog programs.

Another approach is taken by the UPMAIL group of Uppsala. Data structures are formalized and a first-order definition of a relation is given. The form of these definitions is similar to that given here for logic descriptions. They are supposed to be 'intuitively' correct and to give the specification of a relation. From this definition, Horn clauses are derived by means of a natural deduction system. See for instance Hansson and Tärnlund (1979), Hansson (1980), Tärnlund (1981) and Eriksson (1984). Program derivation is also assisted by a derivation editor (Eriksson and Johansson, 1981, 1982; Eriksson *et al.*, 1983). Mapping between data structures is also defined, so that different programs can be obtained depending on the chosen data structure. Similarly, Nakagawa (1985) uses intermediate list representations to transform tree manipulation programs. Johansson (1984, 1985, 1986) uses symmetry and transitivity properties to shorten the derivation of a logic program.

SUMMARY

- Transformations preserve the correctness of logic descriptions.
- Transformations can simplify logic descriptions.
- Transformations can show the equivalence between logic descriptions.
- Given a logic description constructed with an induction on one parameter, it is possible to transform it into another logic description, as if it had been constructed with an induction on another parameter.
- Given a logic description constructed without induction, it is possible to transform it into another logic description, as if it had been constructed by induction on one of its parameters.
- A transformation with an auxiliary definition can yield a logic description as if it had been constructed with a descending generalization. Moreover, the specification of the general problem is also a specification for the auxiliary definition.
- Definitions can be made from literals such that one is a recursion and another has two properties corresponding to the existence of an identity element and associativity. They must also have a local variable which is existentially quantified.
- It can be easier to find a Eureka and perform transformations with this auxiliary definition than to find the corresponding descending generalization and construct its logic description, especially if the transformation is supported by some automated tool.
- A transformation with an auxiliary definition can interweave independent parts and perform the equivalent of 'loop combinations'.

PART III

Logic Programs

Once a logic description has been constructed, it should then be turned into an executable logic program. This is the final step in the development of a logic program. At this level, the procedural semantics of the chosen logic programming language will be considered; thus application conditions (such as directionality) and side-effects described in the specification will be dealt with. In this book, Prolog is chosen as the target logic programming language, but most of the results can easily be adapted to particular Prolog dialects or other logic programming languages.

Chapter 7 introduces logic programs and describes the principles of SLDNF-resolution, a model of the procedural semantics. Chapter 8 handles the problem of correctness, answering the question: 'What does it mean for a logic program to be correct with respect to its specification?'. Instead of considering the declarative semantics as in Chapter 4 (correctness of a logic description), the definition of correctness here relates the results of an execution to the specification. The key chapter (Chapter 9) deals with the derivation of a logic program from a logic description. It will be shown that a straightforward syntactical translation of a correct logic description yields an 'almost correct' logic program. The tasks still outstanding to achieve correctness will be clearly set out and methods such as dataflow analysis and abstract interpretation will be proposed. In order to increase their efficiency, logic programs can also be transformed by means of control introduction and transformation rules, as described in Chapter 10. The techniques presented in these chapters can also be applied successfully in other methodological approaches to logic program construction.

Belvédère, M. C. Escher (1958). Collection Haags Gemeentemuseum, The Hague. © 1989 M. C. Escher Heirs/Cordon Art, Baarn, Holland

7

Procedural semantics of a logic program

PREVIEW   This chapter introduces the procedural semantics of logic programming, that is, the execution mechanism of Prolog programs. The procedural semantics is well known to Prolog programmers, although its precise modelling may appear somewhat technical. Programs with negations are treated directly, using the usual 'negation as failure' inference rule. The terminology is presented first, followed by a description of SLDNF-resolution. Finally, the basic soundness property of SLDNF-resolution is stated, and completeness is discussed briefly. The following definitions are partly based on Lloyd (1987), where a more complete description can be found.

7.1   Logic programs

To begin with, logic procedures and logic programs will be defined precisely.

Definition 7.1   A **program clause** is a closed formula of the form

$$\forall(\, p(\, t_1, \ldots, t_n) \Leftarrow L_1 \,\&\, \ldots \,\&\, L_m \,)$$

where $p(\, t_1, \ldots, t_n)$ is an atom and L_i are literals ($m \geq 0$). Such a program clause is represented as

$$A \leftarrow L_1, \ldots, L_m$$

where the negative literals $\neg B$ are denoted by not(B) (the same metavariable L_i is however still used). When $m = 0$, the program clause

$$p(t_1, \ldots, t_n) \leftarrow$$

represents the formula $\forall(\, p(\, t_1, \ldots, t_n\,)\,)$. In the above program clause, $p(\, t_1, \ldots, t_n\,)$ is the **head** and $L_1 \& \ldots \& L_m$ is the **body**.

Definition 7.2   A **logic procedure** LP(p) (with arity n) is a sequence of program clauses $C_1, \ldots, C_k$ ($k > 0$), each head having the same predicate symbol p (with arity n). Such a logic procedure represents the closed formula

$$C_1 \& \ldots \& C_k$$

By extension, the built-in procedures of a particular logic programming language are also called logic procedures.

Definition 7.3   A **logic program** P is a finite set of logic procedures { LP(p_1), $\ldots$, LP(p_k)} ($k > 0$). Such a logic program represents the closed formula

$$LP(\, p_1\,) \& \ldots \& LP(\, p_k\,)$$

Logic procedures deal with sequences of program clauses (and not sets) because the order is important from a procedural point of view. The order of the procedures is, however, irrelevant. Program clauses with different variables as arguments in their heads are of special interest in the derivation of a logic program from a logic description. Such program clauses will be called **pure** (they are also known as **normalized** clauses).

Definition 7.4   A **pure program clause** is a program clause of the form

$$p(\, X_1, \ldots, X_n) \leftarrow L_1, \ldots, L_m$$

where X_i are distinct variables ($n \geq 0$).

Definition 7.5   A **pure logic procedure** is a logic procedure composed of pure program clauses. A **pure logic program** is a logic program composed of pure logic procedures.

EXAMPLE 7.1

```
efface( X, [X | T], T ) ←
efface( X, [H | T], [H | TEff] ) ← not( X = H ), efface( X, T, TEff)
   is a logic procedure.
```

efface(X, L, LEff) ← L = [H | T], H = X, LEff = T
efface(X, L, LEff) ← L = [H | T], LEff = [H | TEff], not(H = X),
                                efface(X, T, TEff)

is a pure logic procedure.

Definition 7.6   A **goal** is a closed formula of the form

$$\neg \exists (L_1 \ \& \ \ldots \ \& \ L_m)$$

where L_i are literals ($m \geq 0$). Such a formula is represented as

$$\leftarrow L_1, \ldots, L_m$$

where the negative literals $\neg B$ are denoted by not(B). When $m = 0$, the goal is called the **empty goal** and is denoted by □. It represents the formula false.

EXAMPLE 7.2

← efface(X, L, [1]), L = [1, 2]   is a goal.

Since the target logic programming language is Prolog, it is necessary to define what a Prolog program is.

Definition 7.7   A **(pure) Prolog procedure** is a (pure) logic procedure possibly augmented with Prolog control information (such as cuts, represented by !).

Definition 7.8   A **(pure) Prolog program** is a set of (pure) Prolog procedures.

EXERCISE_____

7.1   Show that clauses with at least one positive literal (that is, formulae of the form $\forall (A_1 \vee \ldots \vee A_k \vee \neg B_1 \vee \neg B_m)$ with A_i, B_i atoms and $k > 0$, $m \geq 0$) can be represented by different program clauses (with different heads) which are logically equivalent.

7.2   SLDNF-resolution

7.2.1   Unification

The concepts of substitution and instance were introduced in Chapter 2. Now unifiers will be presented. But first some useful notation is introduced and the composition of substitutions is defined.

Definition 7.9 Let E be an expression. **VARS(E)** is the set of variables occurring in E.

Definition 7.10 Let θ be a substitution $\{V_1/t_1, \ldots, V_n/t_n\}$.

$$\mathbf{dom}(\theta) = \{V_1, \ldots V_n\}$$
$$\mathbf{vcod}(\theta) = \text{VARS}(\{t_1, \ldots, t_n\}).$$

The terminology dom stands for 'domain', and vcod for 'variables of the codomain'.

Definition 7.11 The substitution given by the empty set is the **identity substitution** and is denoted by ε.

Definition 7.12 A **simple expression** is either a term or a quantifier-free formula.

The following concept of a variant is used during the computation process to rename variables.

Definition 7.13 Let E and F be simple expressions. F is a **variant** of E iff $F = E\theta$, where:

- $\theta = \{X_1/Y_1, \ldots, X_n/Y_n\}$ and Y_i are distinct variables (θ renames variables)
- $(\text{VARS}(E)\backslash\text{dom}(\theta)) \cap \{Y_1, \ldots, Y_n\} = \varnothing$ (the new names Y_i are different from the non-renamed variables of E, that is $(\text{VARS}(E) \backslash \text{dom}(\theta))$.

EXAMPLE 7.3

p(Y, a) ← q(X), r(f(W))

is a variant of

p(X, a) ← q(Y), r(f(W))   (for example, $\theta = \{X/Y, Y/X\}$)

But

p(X, a) ← q(Y), r(f(X))

is not a variant of the first program clause.

If F is a variant of E, then E is a variant of F (see Exercise 7.2). It may thus be said that E and F are variants.

Definition 7.14 Let θ and σ be substitutions. The **composition** of θ and σ is the substitution γ such that for any expression E, $E\gamma = (E\theta)\sigma$.

The following definition provides an algorithm with which to compute the composition of substitutions.

Definition 7.15 Let $\theta = \{X_1/t_1, \ldots, X_n/t_n\}$ and $\sigma = \{Y_1/s_1, \ldots, Y_m/s_m\}$. The substitution denoted $\theta\sigma$ is the substitution

$$\{X_1/t_1\sigma, \ldots, X_n/t_n\sigma, Y_1/s_1, \ldots, Y_m/s_m\}$$

where

- the elements $X_i/t_i\sigma$ with $X_i = t_i\sigma$ are suppressed ($1 \leq i \leq n$), and
- the elements Y_j/s_j with $Y_j \in \{X_1, \ldots, X_n\}$ are suppressed ($1 \leq j \leq m$).

Property 7.1

Let θ and σ be substitutions. $\theta\sigma$ is the unique composition of θ and σ.

Proof
See Exercise 7.3   ∎

EXAMPLE 7.4
$\theta = \{X/f(Y), Y/Z\}$
$\sigma = \{X/a, Y/b, Z/Y\}$
$\theta\sigma = \{X/f(b), Z/Y\}$
$\sigma\theta = \{X/a, Y/b\}$

The composition operator is not commutative and can be simplified when the substitutions considered have some simple properties (see Exercise 7.5).

Definition 7.16 Let E and F be simple expressions. A substitution θ is a **unifier** of E and F iff $E\theta = F\theta$. E and F are then **unifiable**. A unifier θ is called a **most general unifier (mgu)** of E and F iff for any unifier σ of E and F, there exists a substitution γ such that $\sigma = \theta\gamma$. It can be shown that an mgu exists for two unifiable simple expressions.

The computation of unifiers and mgus is a central task within the procedural semantics of logic programming and thus in Prolog. This nontrivial task is performed using what is known as a **unification algorithm**. Unification algorithms will not be discussed here, but references will be given in Section 7.4. Notice that, from the definition of a unifier, the two terms X and f(X) are not unifiable, as demonstrated in Example 7.5. This is often referred to as the **occur check**, that is, if t_1 is a variable and t_2 is a term, then t_1 and t_2 are not unifiable when t_1 occurs in t_2. The occur check is not available in most Prolog systems for efficiency reasons. Such an omission can cause logical difficulties, as already described in Section 1.2.4, that ought to be solved.

EXAMPLE 7.5

  p(X, a) and p(f(Y), Z) are unifiable,
    {X/f(b), Y/b, Z/a} is a unifier and {X/f(Y), Z/a} is an mgu.

  p(X, a) and p(f(Y), b) are not unifiable.

  p(X, X) and p(Y, f(Y)) are not unifiable.

EXERCISES_____

7.2   Show that if F is a variant of E, then E is a variant of F.

7.3   Prove Property 7.1.

7.4   Let θ, σ, γ be substitutions. Prove the following:

   (a) $\theta\varepsilon = \varepsilon\theta = \theta$ (left and right identity)

   (b) $(\theta\sigma)\gamma = \theta(\sigma\gamma)$ (associativity)

7.5   Let $\theta = \{X_i/t_i\}$ and $\sigma = \{Y_i/s_i\}$ be substitutions. Show that $\theta\sigma = \{X_i/t_i\sigma, Y_i/s_i\}$ if dom(θ) $\cap$ vcod(σ) $= \varnothing$, and dom(θ) $\cap$ dom(σ) $= \varnothing$.

*7.6   A substitution θ is **idempotent** iff $\theta\theta = \theta$. Give an example of a non-idempotent substitution. Prove that a substitution θ is idempotent iff dom(θ) $\cap$ vcod(θ) $= \varnothing$.

*7.7   Let θ, σ be idempotent substitutions. Show that $\theta\sigma$ is not always idempotent. Prove that $\theta\sigma$ is idempotent if dom(θ) $\cap$ vcod(σ) $= \varnothing$.

*7.8   Let θ be a unifier of E and F. Show that θ is an idempotent mgu iff for any unifier σ of E and F, $\sigma = \theta\sigma$.

**7.9   Let θ be an idempotent mgu of E and F. Prove the following:

   (a)   vcod(θ) $\subseteq$ VARS({E, F}) (that is, θ does not introduce new variables).

(b)   dom(θ) $\subseteq$ VARS({E, F}) (that is, θ only instantiates variables of E and F).

Give counter-examples when θ is not idempotent.

**7.10 Let $\theta 1$, $\theta 2$ and σ be mgus of E and F, with $\theta 1$ and $\theta 2$ idempotent, but σ non-idempotent.
Show that idempotent mgus are 'similar', that is:

- dom($\theta 1$) $\cup$ vcod($\theta 1$) = dom($\theta 2$) $\cup$ vcod($\theta 2$)
- $|$ dom($\theta 1$)$|$ = $|$ dom($\theta 2$)$|$
- $|$ vcod($\theta 1$)$|$ = $|$ vcod($\theta 2$)$|$

Show that idempotent mgus are the 'shortest', that is:

- $|$ dom($\theta 1$)$|$ < $|$ dom(σ)$|$

(where $|$ S $|$ denotes the number of elements of the set S).

7.2.2 SLDNF-tree

The following definitions characterize the procedural behaviour of logic programs. The procedural model, called SLDNF-resolution, is based on SLD-resolution. **SLDNF-resolution** is SLD-resolution augmented with the negation as failure rule handling negative literals in the body of the program clauses. The general idea of negation as failure is to replace the execution of not(p) by the execution of p. If it succeeds then not(p) fails, and if it fails then not(p) succeeds. The following concept of an SLDNF-tree characterizes the computation space of a program for a given goal.

Definition 7.17 Let A be an atom and P be a program. An **applicable program clause** of P for A is (a variant of) a program clause in P such that A and the head of the program clause are unifiable.

Definition 7.18 A **computation rule** R is a function from the set of goals to the set of literals such that the value of the function for a goal is a literal of this goal called the **selected** literal in the goal.

Definition 7.19 Let P be a program, G be a goal and R be a computation rule. An **SLDNF-tree** for P $\cup$ {G} via R is a tree satisfying the following conditions:

(1)   Each node of the tree is a goal.
(2)   A substitution is attached to each arc.
(3)   The root node is G.

(4)   Nodes which are the empty goal have no children. These nodes are called **success nodes**. The branch from the root G to a success node is called a **success branch**.

(5)   Let $\leftarrow L_1, \ldots, L_k, \ldots, L_n$, be a node G′ in the tree ($n \geq 1$), and L_k be the literal selected by the computation rule R.

    (a)   If L_k is a positive literal:

        (i)   This node has one descendant for each applicable program clause (variant) $A \leftarrow B_1, \ldots, B_r$ in P.

        (ii)   The substitution attached to the arc is θ, an mgu of L_k and A.

        (iii)   The descendant node is

$$\leftarrow (L_1, \ldots, L_{k-1}, B_1, \ldots, B_r, L_{k+1}, \ldots, L_n) \theta$$

If the node G′ has no descendant, it is called a **failure node** and the branch from the root to G′ is called a **failure branch**.

    (b)   If L_k is a negative literal $\mathsf{not}(A_k)$, then either:

        (i)   There exists a finitely failed SLDNF-tree for $P \cup \{\leftarrow A_k\}$ via R. In such a case, the unique descendant node is

$$\leftarrow L_1, \ldots, L_{k-1}, L_{k+1}, \ldots, L_n$$

and the substitution attached to the arc is the empty substitution ε.

        (ii)   Or there exists a success branch in an SLDNF-tree for $P \cup \{\leftarrow A_k\}$ via R. In such a case, there are no descendant nodes for G′. The node G′ is again called a **failure node** and the branch from the root to G′ is again a **failure branch**.

        (iii)   Otherwise, the unique descendant node is G′ itself, and the attached substitution is the empty substitution ε (thus yielding an infinite branch).

Definition 7.20   A **finitely failed** SLDNF-tree is an SLDNF-tree for which every branch is a failure branch.

These definitions need to be considered further. Variants of program clauses are used to ensure that the applicable program clauses contain no variables which have already appeared in the branch from the root up to the considered node. Such a renaming simplifies the SLDNF-tree and the composition of substitutions (see Exercise 7.5). The renaming can be achieved, for example, by using a subscript i to indicate variables of the program clause used at a node of level i in the tree.

A **leaf node** of an SLDNF-tree can be the empty goal, or a non-empty goal such that the selected literal is positive and does not unify with the head of the program clauses of P, or a non-empty goal such that the selected literal is negative (not(A_k)) and the SLDNF-tree for $P \cup \{\leftarrow A_k\}$ has a success branch.

Condition (5b) (that is, that the selected literal is negative) actually yields a recursive definition of an SLDNF-tree. From a purely mathematical point of view, this definition is unsatisfactory since it could lead to a circular definition, although this can be avoided by introducing intermediate concepts and definitions including the depths of the trees (Lloyd, 1987). The resulting definitions are, however, somewhat artificial. Condition (5b) of the above definition is not ambiguous since the three subconditions are mutually exclusive, as shown below.

SLDNF-trees for $P \cup \{G\}$ via R may vary with regard to the order of the descendants of the nodes, the chosen variants of program clauses, and the considered mgus. However, two different SLDNF-trees for $P \cup \{G\}$ via R are isomorphic in the sense that each branch of the first tree has a corresponding branch in the second one and vice versa. Thus, there are the same number of infinite branches, failure branches and success branches. The three subcases of 5b are thus exclusive and the third subcase (iii) is applicable when an SLDNF-tree for $P \cup \{G\}$ via R has no success branch but has an infinite branch. The definition of a unique descendant in this last subcase (iii), which is G' itself, can be seen as a coding trick, reporting the behaviour of $P \cup \{\leftarrow A_k\}$ (that is, neither success nor failure). Such a definition allows the association of an SLDNF-tree via R to every $P \cup \{G\}$.

SLD-trees are particular cases of SLDNF-trees, for which the goals and the program clauses do not contain any negative literals. Condition (5b) of the definition is then useless. In the definition of an SLDNF-tree given here, the computation rule will always select the same literals in different nodes with the same goal. The concept of a computation rule could be generalized such that the selection of a literal considers not only the goal but also information from other parts of the SLDNF-tree or from the program.

A success branch characterizes a possible solution for the goal, known as computed answer substitution.

Definition 7.21   A **computed answer substitution** θ for $P \cup \{G\}$ via R is a substitution obtained by restricting the composition $\theta_1\theta_1 \ldots \theta_m$ to the variables of G, where $\theta_1, \theta_2, \ldots, \theta_m$ are the substitutions attached to the arcs of a success branch of an SLDNF-tree for $P \cup \{G\}$ via R.

The isomorphism between two different SLDNF-trees for $P \cup \{G\}$ via R can be further taken. If θ is a computed answer substitution related to a success branch of the first tree, and σ is a computed answer substitution related to the corresponding success branch in the second tree, then $G\theta$ and $G\sigma$ are variants. It is therefore possible to discuss *the* SLDNF-tree for $P \cup \{G\}$ via R.

EXAMPLE 7.6

P : efface(X, [X | T], T) ←   (1)
    efface(X, [H | T], [H | TEff] ← not(X = H), efface(X, T, TEff)   (2)
G : ← efface(2, [1, 2, 3], LEff)
SLDNF-tree for $P \cup \{G\}$, see Figure 7.1.

(a)   ← efface(2, [1, 2, 3], LEff)

(2) |θ₁ = {X1/2, H1/1, T1/[2, 3],
                                    LEff/[1 | TEff1] }

                    ← (not(X1 = H1), efface(X1, T1, TEff1))θ₁
(b)   ← not(2 = 1), efface(2, [2, 3], TEff1)

                             | θ₂ = {}

(c)   ← efface(2, [2, 3], TEff1)

(1) | θ₃ = {X/2, T3/[3], TEff1/[3]}

(d)   □

Figure 7.1   SLDNF-tree for $P \cup \{\text{←efface}(2, [1, 2, 3], \text{LEff})\}$.

In Figure 7.1, the computation rule is supposed to select the first literal in a goal. For the (a) node, there is only one applicable clause (clause (2)). For node (c), there is only one applicable clause (clause (1)). Since $P \cup \{\text{←}2 = 1\}$ has a finitely failed SLDNF-tree ($=$ is supposed to be a primitive), the (b) node has a descendant. This SLDNF-tree is finite and has a single success branch. The computed answer substitution corresponding to the branch is the substitution

$$\theta_1\theta_2\theta_3 = \{X1/2, H1/1, T1/[2, 3], LEff/[1, 3], X3/2, T3/[3], TEff1/[3]\}$$

restricted to the variables of G; that is { LEff/[1, 3] }.

7.2.3   SLDNF-refutation procedure

Given a program P and a goal G, the associated SLDNF-tree depends on the computation rule. The construction of such a tree and thus the search for computed answer substitutions depends on the adopted search strategy. A search strategy determines the order in which the nodes of a tree are visited (for example, depth-first and from left to right). The computation rule together with the search rule are the two components of an execution mechanism based on SLDNF-resolution.

> **Definition 7.22**   A **search rule** is a strategy for searching SLDNF-trees.

> **Definition 7.23**   An **SLDNF-refutation procedure** is specified by a computation rule together with a search rule.

Standard Prolog's SLDNF-refutation procedure can now be defined.

> **Definition 7.24   Prolog's computation rule** selects the leftmost literal in every goal. **Prolog's search rule** is a depth-first search rule that searches the subtrees of a node according to the order (in the program) of the applicable program clauses for the selected literal.

As introduced already in Chapter 2, the result of a computation can be seen as a sequence of computed answer substitutions.

> **Definition 7.25**   Given an SLDNF-refutation procedure with a computation rule R, let P be a program and G be a goal. The **sequence of answer substitutions** for $P \cup \{G\}$ is the sequence of computed answer substitutions associated with the success branches whose success nodes are eventually reached, according to the search rule, in the SLDNF-tree for $P \cup \{G\}$ via R. We will say that the execution of G **computes** this sequence of answer substitutions.

Which SLDNF-refutation procedure is used in a sequence of answer substitutions will be determined by the context. When Prolog programs are considered, it is implicitly assumed that the Prolog SLDNF-refutation procedure is used.

EXAMPLE 7.7

```
append( [], L, L ) ←
append( [H|T], L2, [H|TApp] ) ← append( T, L2, TApp )
```

Using Prolog's refutation procedure for the program in Example 7.7, the sequence of answer substitutions for $P \cup \{\leftarrow append(L1, [], LApp)\}$ is the infinite sequence $\theta_1, \ldots, \theta_i, \ldots$, where

$\theta_1 = \{L1/[], LApp/[]\}$
$\theta_2 = \{L1/[H1], LApp/[H1]\}$
$\theta_3 = \{L1/[H1,H2], LApp/[H1,H2]\}$
$\vdots \quad \vdots$

EXAMPLE 7.8

$$p(f(X)) \leftarrow p(X)$$
$$p(a) \leftarrow$$

Using Prolog's refutation procedure for the program in Example 7.8, the sequence of answer substitutions for $P \cup \{\leftarrow p(X)\}$ is empty since the success branches are never reached according to Prolog's search rule.

The concepts of safety and linearity are now introduced. Informally, a computation rule will be safe for $P \cup \{G\}$ if it selects negative literals which are ground. Safety will be necessary for soundness. A computation rule will be linear for $P \cup \{G\}$ when it finishes the evaluation of one literal before selecting another one (note that this use of 'linear' should not be confused with linear resolution).

Definition 7.26 A computation rule R is **safe** for $P \cup \{G\}$ iff, in the SLDNF-tree for $P \cup \{G\}$ via R, when a negative literal $not(A_k)$ is selected by R in some node, A_k is ground and R is safe for $P \cup \{\leftarrow A_k\}$. When R is not safe for $P \cup \{G\}$, G is referred as a **floundering goal**.

Definition 7.27 A computation rule R is **linear** for $P \cup \{G\}$ iff the following condition holds. Let G_1 be a goal $\leftarrow L_1, \ldots, L_k, \ldots, L_n$ in the SLDNF-tree of $P \cup \{G\}$ via R, and L_k be the literal selected by R.

If L_k is a positive literal, then none of the L_i ($i \neq k$) will be selected by R until a goal G_2 is achieved, G_2 having the form

$$\leftarrow (L_1, \ldots, L_{k-1}, L_{k+1}, \ldots, L_n)\theta_1 \ldots \theta_h$$

where $\theta_1 \ldots \theta_h$ are the mgus in the SLDNF-tree from G_1 to G_2.

If L_k is a negative literal $not(B)$, then R is linear for $P \cup \{\leftarrow B\}$.

EXAMPLE 7.9

- Prolog's computation rule is always linear.
- Using the program of Example 7.6, Prolog's computation rule is safe for

$$P \cup \{\leftarrow \text{efface(} 2, [1, 2, 3], \text{LEff })\}$$

but it is not safe for

$$P \cup \{\leftarrow \text{efface(} X, [1, 2, 3], \text{LEff })\}$$

since the negative literal not($X = 1$) will be selected while being not ground.

7.2.4   Control information

A distinction has been made between logic programs and Prolog programs since Prolog programs may contain control information. Prolog's cut is certainly a major control primitive, whose procedural semantics is worth defining. The following presentation is based on Sterling & Shapiro (1986).

A cut affects the search in SLDNF-trees by dynamically pruning subtrees. A precise, concise, but somewhat obscure definition of the procedural effect of a cut is the following:

> 'The goal succeeds and commits Prolog to all the choices made since the parent goal was unified with the head of the clause the cut occurs in.'

This definition can be clarified by the following three points:

(A)   A cut prunes the search in all the program clauses below it in the procedure.

(B)   A cut prunes the search of alternative success nodes (and thus alternative solutions) to the literals appearing to its left in the program clause. Therefore, a program clause ending with a cut will produce at most one solution.

(C)   A cut does not affect the search for success nodes for the literals appearing on its right.

EXAMPLE 7.10

```
a ← b( X ), c
b( 1 ) ← d( Y )
b( 2 ) ← e( Y ), !, f( Z )
b( 3 ) ← g( Y )
c ←
d( 1 ) ←                f( 1 ) ←
d( 2 ) ←                f( 2 ) ←
e( 1 ) ←                g( 1 ) ←
e( 2 ) ←                g( 2 ) ←
```

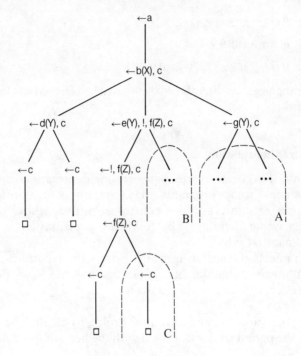

Figure 7.2   Effect of a cut.

Figure 7.2 gives the SLDNF-tree for $P \cup \{\leftarrow a\}$ using the Prolog program of Example 7.10. Subtree (A) illustrates point (A). This subtree will not be searched, preventing two success nodes from being visited. Subtree (B) illustrates point (B). The literal $e(Y)$ can succeed only once, its alternative solutions will not be searched. Subtree (C) illustrates point (C). After the selection of a cut, the subtree below is normally searched.

7.3   A basic result: soundness

Completed logic programs

It could be thought surprising that logic descriptions use equivalences (that is, $\Leftrightarrow$) while program clauses use implications (that is, $\leftarrow$). Although the procedural semantics manipulates logic programs, the relationship between logic and the procedural semantics concerns completed logic programs, that is, roughly speaking, logic programs where implications are replaced by equivalences, thus yielding logic descriptions. For the purpose of logic program development considered here, the definition of completed logic programs can be restricted to pure logic programs.

Definition 7.28
Let:

$$p(X_1, \ldots, X_n) \leftarrow E_1$$
$$p(X_1, \ldots, X_n) \leftarrow E_2$$
$$\vdots \qquad \qquad \vdots$$
$$p(X_1, \ldots, X_n) \leftarrow E_k$$

be a pure logic procedure LP(p).
The **completed definition** of the pure procedure LP(p) is the logic description

$$p(X_1, \ldots, X_n) \Leftrightarrow E_1 \vee E_2 \vee \ldots \vee E_k$$

where the symbols not and ',' in the E_i are replaced by $\neg$ and &, respectively.

This definition also extends when the E_i are formulae instead of conjunctions of literals. The completion of a program P contains the completed definition of all its procedures. In order to be precise, one should also consider the primitive procedures, as well as occurrences of procedure names without corresponding procedures in P.

Definition 7.29   Let P be a pure logic program. The **completion of P**, denoted **comp(P)**, is the set composed of one logic description per procedure name p occurring in P, defined as follows:

- If there is a logic procedure LP(p) in P,
  then the completed definition of LP(p) is in comp(P).
- If p is the name of a primitive procedure (for instance, =),
  then the primitive logic description LP(p) is in comp(p).
- Otherwise, comp(p) contains the logic description

$$p(X_1, \ldots, X_n) \Leftrightarrow \text{false}$$

The last case in Definition 7.29 (that is, when there is no logic procedure for p in P, and p is not a primitive) is a natural extension of Definition 7.28 when $k = 0$. When p is the name of a primitive procedure, remember that the existence of a correct logic description is always assumed.

**Differences from Clark's definition of completion

There are three minor differences between the above definition of completion and Clark's definition (Clark, 1978; Lloyd, 1987). Firstly, the concept of completed definition is only defined here for *pure* logic procedures, although Clark's completion process always begins by 'purifying' clause headings. Secondly, the identity theory is not explicitly added in the completion. In the (unusual) case where the equality symbol does not occur in a pure program P, there is no need to add the identity theory since the above definition does not introduce any equality symbols. Finally, $=$ is not considered as the only primitive of the langauge.

Soundness of SLDNF-resolution

The following soundness property states that the result of a computation (that is, a sequence of answer substitutions) is logically correct (that is, an H-logical consequence) with respect to the completion of the program.

Property 7.2   Soundness of SLDNF-resolution

Given an SLDNF-refutation procedure, let:

- P be a pure logic program
- $\leftarrow L_1, \ldots, L_k$ be a goal G
- *Subst* be the sequence of answer substitutions for $P \cup \{G\}$.

If the computation rule is safe for $P \cup \{G\}$
then:

(i) $\forall \theta \in \textit{Subst} : \text{comp}(P) \models_H \forall((L_1 \& \ldots \& L_k)\theta)$.

(ii)   if the SLDNF-tree for $P \cup \{G\}$ is finitely failed,
        then $\text{comp}(P) \models_H \neg \exists (L_1 \& \ldots \& L_k)$.

**Proof
This result is a consequence of Clark's result (Clark, 1978; Lloyd, 1987), since $S \models_H F$ implies $S \models F$ for any S and F, and the identity theory is an H-logical consequence of $LD(=)$ (see Exercise 5.4). This soundness result assumes full unification with the occur check: ∎

Completeness of SLDNF-resolution

A second important property of SLDNF-resolution would be its completeness (that is, every logically correct solution is computed, or is at least somewhere in the SLDNF-tree). Such a result does not hold. Let us however present the concept of completeness with the following two definitions. A distinction is made here between weak and strong completeness, depending on whether the computed answer substitutions or the sequence of answer substitutions is considered. The differences lies in the computed answer substitutions that are never reached, according to the search rule.

Definition 7.30   Weak completeness
Given an SLDNF-refutation procedure, let:

- P be an everywhere defined pure logic program, and
- $\leftarrow L_1, \ldots, L_k$ be a goal G

P is **weakly complete** for G iff

(i)   If comp(P) $\vDash_H \forall((L_1 \& \ldots \& L_k) \sigma)$ for some σ
       then there exists a computed answer substitution θ for
       $P \cup \{G\}$ such that $\sigma = \theta\gamma$ for some γ.

(ii)   If comp(P) $\vDash_H \neg\exists(L_1 \& \ldots \& L_k)$
       then the SLDNF-tree for $P \cup \{G\}$ is finitely failed.

Definition 7.31   Strong completeness
Given an SLDNF-refutation procedure, let:

- P be a pure logic program,
- $\leftarrow L_1, \ldots, L_k$ be a goal G, and
- *Subst* be the sequence of answer substitutions for $P \cup \{G\}$.

P is **strongly complete** for G iff

(i)   If comp(P) $\vDash_H \forall((L_1 \& \ldots \& L_k)\sigma)$
       then there exists $\theta \in \textit{Subst} : \sigma = \theta\gamma$ for some γ.

(ii)   If comp(P) $\vDash_H \neg\exists(L_1 \& \ldots \& L_k)$
       then the SLDNF-tree for $P \cup \{G\}$ is finitely failed.

Note that strong completeness implies weak completeness, and that (ii) is actually redundant with (i) (see Exercise 7.12).

EXERCISES

7.11   Find an example of a program P and a goal G such that, for $P \cup \{G\}$, Prolog's computation rule is not safe and soundness is not respected.

*7.12   Show that in the soundness and completeness requirements, (ii) can be deduced from (i), and (i) can be restricted to the case $k = 1$. (*Hint*: add extra program clauses to P.)

*7.4   Background

SLDNF-resolution

The procedural model known as SLDNF-resolution is based on SLD-resolution (Kowalski, 1974; Apt and Van Emden, 1982) augmented with the 'negation as failure' rule (Clark, 1978) handling negative literals in the body of the program clauses. SLD-resolution stands for SL-resolution for definite clauses (that is, program clauses without negation in their body). The name LUSH-resolution has also been used (Hill, 1974). SL-resolution stands for Linear resolution with Selected function (Kowalski and Kuehner, 1971). They are all based on the resolution inference rule due to Robinson (1965). For a discussion on the origin of SLD, see Ringwood (1988).

SLDNF-resolution is not the only possible model of the procedural behaviour of Prolog. A totally different approach is taken in Prolog II, for which Colmerauer proposes a theoretical model based on rewriting trees rather than on logic (Colmerauer, 1985; Giannesini *et al.*, 1986). All connections with logic have actually been severed in this theoretical model. A broader description of SLD-resolution, SLDNF-resolution and their properties can be found in Lloyd (1987).

The first unification algorithm had already appeared in Herbrand (1930). It is however in Robinson (1965) that a systematic treatment of unification was first proposed. Other classical unification algorithms are presented in Paterson and Wegman (1978) and Martelli and Montanari (1982). Theoretical developments of unification can be found in Huet (1976), Eder (1985) and Lassez *et al.* (1988). A survey, as well as further references, are given in Knight (1989).

Completeness of SLDNF-resolution

Various ways of introducing negative information in a logic program have been investigated. The two major ways are the closed world assumption (CWA) (Reiter, 1978) and Clark's completed database theory (CDT) (Clark, 1978) which are compared and analysed in Shepherdson (1984, 1985, 1988).

The semantics presented here is based on Clark's definition of completed programs and the negation as failure inference rule (Clark, 1978). In that paper, the soundness of the negation as failure rule is proven under the assumption of a safe computation rule. The completeness of negation as failure is a difficult issue. It is worth briefly discussing the difficulty of such a requirement.

For definite programs (that is, programs without negation), there is a completeness result independent of the computation rule. It is therefore sufficient to consider a single SLDNF-tree. In the negation as failure inference rule, only one SLDNF-tree is searched for a failure proof. But this is not always sufficient since some computation rules may yield finitely failed SLDNF-trees, while others yield infinite SLDNF-trees. Completeness is also a difficult requirement because, for some programs (for example, Example 1.7), every computation rule yields infinite SLDNF-trees, while a finitely failed SLDNF-tree should be obtained. This shows that completeness cannot be achieved without any restrictions.

For definite programs, negation as failure is complete (Jaffar *et al.*, 1983). Completeness is also achieved for hierarchical programs (that is, without recursion) (Clark, 1978). This is, however, restrictive. More general completeness theorems have been stated, for example, for 'structured' programs (Barbuti and Martelli, 1986). Completeness results are discussed in Shepherdson (1988).

A safe computation rule

The requirement of a safe computation rule is essential for soundness. A simple way of obtaining such a rule is to delay the execution of the negative literals until they are ground (Dahl, 1980). This is implemented in MU-Prolog (Naish, 1985a). The advantage of the delay-until-ground computation rule is that soundness is ensured. The literals do not have to be permuted in different ways for the different directionalities in order to obtain a safe computation rule. However, it must be verified that, for the specified directionalities, there will be no floundering branches (that is, every negative literal must eventually become ground). Such a floundering property is, in general, undecidable. Moreover, the programmer does not know *a priori* in which order the subgoals will be executed. This could be problematic if some of the procedures have side-effects.

The definition of a safe computation rule is quite restrictive: only the ground negative literals can be selected. This definition is actually stronger than is strictly necessary for soundness. Possible extensions are as follows. In the append example (Example 7.7), the goal $\leftarrow$append([X], [2], [2]) fails. We therefore have ($\forall$X)¬append([X], [2], [2]) which implies ($\exists$X)¬append([X], [2], [2]). In this case, the goal $\leftarrow$not(append([X], [2], [2]) (that is, $\leftarrow$($\exists$X)¬append([X], [2], [2])) will succeed correctly. The safe computation rule can therefore be extended as follows: if the SLDNF-tree with root $\leftarrow$p(t) finitely fails, then the goal $\leftarrow$not(p(t)) succeeds even if t is not ground.

Using the same procedure, the goal $\leftarrow$append([X], [], [X]) succeeds with ε as answer substitution. Therefore, ($\forall$X)append([X], [], [X]) is true and, hence, ($\exists$X)¬append([X], [], [X]) is false. In this case, the goal $\leftarrow$not(append([X], [], [X])) correctly fails. A further extension of the computation rule is: if the goal $\leftarrow$p(t) succeeds with an empty answer substitution, then the goal $\leftarrow$not(p(t)) fails, even if t is not ground. These extensions have already been described in Clark (1978). Their integration with a delay mechanism is presented in Naish (1985b).

SUMMARY

- SLDNF-resolution is a model of the procedural behaviour of a logic program.
- An SLDNF-tree characterizes the computation space of a program for a given goal.
- The computation of a program for a given goal yields a sequence of answer substitutions.
- A computation rule is safe if the selected negative literals are ground.
- The cut affects the search by dynamically pruning subtrees.
- SLDNF-resolution is sound. The result of a computation is logically correct with respect to the completion of the program.

8

Correctness
of a logic program

PREVIEW   The definition of correctness criteria for logic programs is a particularly important task. It determines what the user can expect from the execution of a program, with regard to its specification. Since the execution of a logic program for a given goal yields a sequence of answer substitutions, the correctness definition characterizes this sequence of answer substitutions relatively to the specified relation. The correctness definition also deals with types, directionality and side-effects. A logic program will be correct when all its logic procedures are correct. As for logic descriptions, the correctness of a logic procedure should be independent of the logic procedures for its subproblems. The construction of a correct procedure should therefore involve only the specification of its subproblems, and not the explicit construction of correct procedures for them.

   Before presenting the correctness definition (Section 8.2), correctness criteria will be introduced (Section 8.1). They include the concepts of partial correctness and completeness for sequences of answer substitutions. The correctness definitions are then justified (Section 8.3) and some properties proved (Section 8.4). Because correctness is related to specifications, the reader is therefore referred to Section 2.2 where the general form of a specification is presented and the role of each part of it is defined (see Table 2.1 on p. 47 for a summary).

8.1   Correctness criteria

Before presenting the correctness criteria, some notation for describing the set of solutions for a given goal and the set of candidate solutions induced by a substitution for a given goal is introduced.

Definition 8.1   Let p be the relation described in the specification of p, t be an n-tuple of terms, θ be a substitution and *Subst* be a sequence of substitutions.

$$\mathbf{Sol}(\leftarrow p(\mathbf{t})) = \{s \mid s \text{ is a ground instance of } \mathbf{t},$$
$$s \text{ is in the domain of p, and}$$
$$s \in p \qquad\qquad\qquad \}$$

$$\mathbf{Cand\text{-}Sol}(\theta; \leftarrow p(\mathbf{t})) = \{s \mid s \text{ is a ground instance of } \mathbf{t}\theta,$$
$$\text{and } s \text{ is in the domain of p} \}$$

$$\mathbf{Cand\text{-}Sol}(\textit{Subst}; \leftarrow p(\mathbf{t})) = \bigcup_{\theta \in \textit{Subst}} \mathbf{Cand\text{-}Sol}(\theta; \leftarrow p(\mathbf{t}))$$

These definitions are illustrated in Example 8.1 on the classical append problem.

EXAMPLE 8.1

Let G be the goal $\leftarrow$ append([1], L2, LApp)

Let θ_1 = {L2/[H | T], LApp/[1,H | T]}
  θ_2 = {LApp/[1 | L2]}
  θ_3 = {LApp/[H | L2]}
  θ_4 = {L2/bill, LApp/[1 | bill]}

Sol(G) = {⟨[1], l, [1 | l]⟩ | l is a ground list}

Cand-Sol(θ_1; G) = {⟨[1], [h | t], [1, h | t]⟩ | h is a ground term
                          and t is a ground list}

Cand-Sol(θ_2; G) = {⟨[1], l, [1 | l]⟩ | l is a ground list}

Cand-Sol(θ_3; G) = {⟨[1], l, [h | l]⟩ | h is a ground term
                          and l is a ground list}

Cand-Sol(θ_4; G) = {⟨[1], bill, [1 | bill]⟩ | bill is a ground list}
             = { }   (since the term bill is not a list)

These definitions are now extended to goals.

Definition 8.2   Let $\leftarrow L_1, \ldots, L_k$ be a goal G, with L_i either $q_i(\mathbf{t}_i)$ or not($q_i(\mathbf{t}_i)$).

$$\mathbf{Sol}(\text{ G }) = \{\langle s_1, \ldots, s_k \rangle \mid \langle s_1, \ldots, s_k \rangle \text{ is a ground instance of}$$
$$\langle \mathbf{t}_1, \ldots, \mathbf{t}_k \rangle,$$
$$s_i \text{ in the domain of } q_i,$$
$$s_i \in q_i \text{ if } L_i \text{ is a positive literal, and}$$
$$s_i \notin q_i \text{ if } L_i \text{ is a negative literal}\}$$

$$\text{Cand-Sol}(\ \theta;\ G\ ) = \{\langle s_1, \ldots, s_k\rangle \,|\, \langle s_1, \ldots, s_k\rangle \quad \text{ground} \quad \text{in-}$$
$$\text{stance of } \langle t_1, \ldots, t_k\rangle\theta, \text{ and}$$
$$s_i \text{ in the domain of } q_i\}$$

The idea behind the correctness criteria is to relate the sets of candidate solutions Cand-Sol(θ_i; G), that is, the solutions induced by the computations, to the set of solutions Sol(G). It is to be expected that the sets of candidate solutions form a partition of the set of solutions, as illustrated in Figure 8.1 (here illustrated with a finite number of answer substitutions). The concept of partition includes four conditions:

(1)   Each set of candidate solutions is included in the set of solutions.
(2)   The set of solutions is covered by the sets of candidate solutions.
(3)   The sets of candidate solutions are not empty.
(4)   The sets of candidate solutions are disjoint.

Let us now develop the correctness criteria.

8.1.1   Partial correctness

Partial correctness is represented by condition (1) for partitions, that is, each set of candidate solutions is included in the set of solutions. It thus expresses that a sequence of substitutions yields correct solutions, that is, all the candidate solutions are correct solutions.

> **Definition 8.3**   Let *Subst* be a sequence of substitutions. *Subst* is **partially correct** for p(t) (w.r.t. the specification of p) iff

Solutions

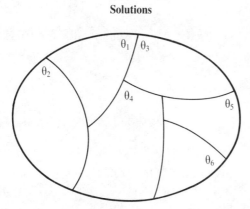

Figure 8.1   Solutions partitioned by candidate solutions.

$$\text{Cand-Sol}(\textit{Subst}; \leftarrow p(\mathbf{t})) \subseteq \text{Sol}(\leftarrow p(\mathbf{t}))$$

This can also be expressed in a more intuitive form:

$$\forall \theta \in \textit{Subst} : \text{if } \mathbf{s} \text{ is a ground instance of } \mathbf{t}\theta, \text{ and} \\ \mathbf{s} \text{ is in the domain of } p, \\ \text{then } \mathbf{s} \in p$$

In Example 8.1, substitutions $\theta_1, \theta_2, \theta_4$, are partially correct, however, θ_3 is not. Note that a substitution θ can be partially correct even if some instances of $\mathbf{t}\theta$ are not in the domain of p. Such instances are not considered in the sets of candidate solutions, as otherwise a substitution such as θ_2 in Example 8.1 would not be partially correct even though it reflects an intuitively correct result.

8.1.2   Completeness

Completeness is represented by condition (2) for partitions, that is, the set of solutions is covered by the sets of candidate solutions. It thus expresses that every solution is covered by some substitution in the sequence of answer substitutions.

> **Definition 8.4**   Let *Subst* be a sequence of substitutions. *Subst* is **complete** for p(t) (w.r.t. the specification of p) iff
>
> $$\text{Cand-Sol}(\textit{Subst}; \leftarrow p(\mathbf{t})) \supseteq \text{Sol}(\leftarrow p(\mathbf{t}))$$

This can also be expressed in a more intuitive form:

$$\forall \mathbf{s} \in \text{Sol}(\leftarrow p(\mathbf{t})), \quad \exists \theta \in \textit{Subst} : \mathbf{s} \text{ is a ground instance} \\ \text{of } \mathbf{t}\theta$$

In Example 8.1, the sequences of answer substitutions composed of θ_2 or θ_3 are complete.

8.1.3   Termination

The termination of the execution of a goal can be characterized in terms of SLDNF-trees.

> **Definition 8.5**   Given an SLDNF-refutation procedure, we say that $P \cup \{\leftarrow p(\mathbf{t})\}$ **terminates** iff the SLDNF-tree for $P \cup \{\leftarrow p(\mathbf{t})\}$ is finite.

If $P \cup \{ \leftarrow p(\mathbf{t})\}$ terminates, the computed sequence of answer substitutions is finite. But if the sequence of answer substitutions is finite, the SLDNF-tree for $P \cup \{ \leftarrow p(\mathbf{t})\}$ is not necessarily finite (infinite SLDNF-tree with a finite number of success branches).

8.1.4 Minimality

The intuitive idea behind minimality is that a sequence of answer substitutions should not contain useless information, and should be as small as possible. Minimality is represented by conditions (3) and (4) for partitions: the sets of candidate solutions are disjoint and not empty. It also includes a minimal coverage requirement. Before defining minimality more precisely, it will be illustrated on the append problem for the same goal as in Example 8.1.

- Consider the following goal G and sequence of answer substitutions *Subst*:

  $\leftarrow$ append([1], L2, LApp)
    $\theta_1 = \{$ L2/bill, LApp/[1 | bill] $\}$
    $\theta_2 = \{$ LApp/[1 | L2] $\}$

Subst is partially correct and complete for this goal, but θ_1 does not respect the type of the parameters. The set of candidate solutions induced by θ_1 is thus empty (Cand-Sol(θ_1; G) = $\varnothing$), and therefore the term L2θ_1 is not compatible with the domain of append (L2θ_1 is not a list). This situation should be avoided in 'correct' sequences of substitutions; a substitution should at least cover a correct solution. This characterizes the postcondition aspect of types and can thus be seen as type or domain consistency.

- Consider the following goal G and sequence of answer substitutions *Subst*:

  $\leftarrow$ append([1], L2, LApp)
    $\theta_1 = \{$ L2/[] , LApp/[1] $\}$
    $\theta_2 = \{$ LApp/[1 | L2] $\}$

Subst is partially correct and complete for this goal; θ_1 and θ_2 respect the type of the parameters (the sets of candidate solutions are not empty). But there is some redundancy between θ_1 and θ_2: Cand-Sol(θ_1; G) $\cap$ Cand-Sol(θ_2; G) $\neq \varnothing$ (for example, $\langle$[1], [ ], [1]$\rangle$ belongs to the intersection). Some solutions are thus covered twice, which could cause some trouble if this goal were inside a clause and followed by other literals. Redundancy should usually be avoided in 'correct' sequences of answer substitutions.

- Consider the following goal G and sequence of answer substitutions *Subst*:

$$\leftarrow \text{append}([1], \text{L2}, \text{LApp})$$
$$\theta_1 = \{ \text{L2/[]}, \text{LApp/[1]} \}$$
$$\theta_2 = \{ \text{L2/[E1]}, \text{LApp/[1, E1]} \}$$
$$\theta_3 = \{ \text{L2/[E1, E2]}, \text{LApp/[1, E1, E2]} \}$$
$$\vdots \qquad \vdots$$

Subst is partially correct and complete for this goal. All the θ_i respect the type of the parameters (Cand-Sol(θ_i; G) $\neq \varnothing$) and there is no redundancy (Cand-Sol(θ_i; G) $\cap$ Cand-Sol(θ_j; G) $= \varnothing$ for $i \neq j$). However, the same criteria could be achieved with a *finite* sequence of substitutions, such as:

$$\theta_1 = \{ \text{L2/[]}, \text{LApp/[1]} \}$$
$$\theta_2 = \{ \text{L2/[H|T]}, \text{LApp/[1, H|T]} \}$$

This sequence of substitutions is preferable to *Subst* because infinite sequences of answer substitutions are difficult to handle and compose.

Definition 8.6   Let *Subst* be a sequence of answer substitutions. *Subst* is said to be **minimal** for p(t) (w.r.t. the specification of p) iff the following conditions hold:

Domain compatibility
$$\forall \theta \in Subst : \text{t}\theta \text{ compatible with the domain of p}$$
$$(\text{Cand-Sol}(\theta; \leftarrow \text{p}(\text{t})) \neq \varnothing).$$

Non-redundancy
$$\forall \theta_i, \theta_j \in Subst : \text{Cand-Sol}(\theta_i; \leftarrow \text{p}(\text{t})) \cap \text{Cand-Sol}(\theta_j;$$
$$\leftarrow \text{p}(\text{t})) = \varnothing \quad (\text{for } i \neq j).$$

Minimal coverage
If there exists a finite, partially correct and complete sequence of answer substitutions for p(t), then *Subst* is finite.

Stronger conditions could be required for minimality in this definition. For example, the condition for minimal coverage could be replaced by:

If there exists a finite, partially correct and complete sequence of answer substitutions for p(t) of length *lg'*, then *Subst* is finite and has a length $lg \leq lg'$.

However, the first definition is preferred because, in practice, the second is often useless and difficult to establish.

For some procedures, minimality can be too strong or inadequate. For the member(X, L) procedure (see Specification 5.25), it could be desirable that the goal $\leftarrow$ member(a, [a, b, a]) or $\leftarrow$ member(X, [a, b, a]) succeeds twice (which is redundant according to minimality).

EXERCISES

8.1   Show that the sequence of answer substitutions composed of the empty substitution ε is always complete.

8.2   Give an example of a partially correct, complete and minimal sequence of answer substitutions for each of the goals ← append (L1, [1], LApp) and ← append(L1, [], LApp).

8.2   Definition of correctness

8.2.1   Correctness in a set of logic procedures

The idea of correctness criteria is to establish some equivalence between the relation described in the specification and the sequences of answer substitutions, as well as to state that the other postconditions (directionality, type and side-effects) are satisfied. Correctness is, however, restricted to actual parameters respecting the preconditions of the procedure.

> **Definition 8.7**   An n-tuple **t respects the preconditions** (of the specification) of p iff

- **t** is compatible with the domain of p,
- **t** satisfies the *in* part of a directionality of p, and
- the environment preconditions are fulfilled.

> **Definition 8.8**   Given an SLDNF-refutation procedure let:

- P be a logic program containing LP(p).

LP(p) is **correct in P** w.r.t. its specification iff for any n-tuple **t** the following condition holds. If **t** respects the preconditions of p, where the satisfied directionality is in($m_1, \ldots, m_n$): out($M_1, \ldots, M_n$) $\langle Min-Max \rangle$, and *Subst* is the sequence of answer substitutions for $P \cup \{\leftarrow p(\, t\,)\}$, then:

- *Subst* is partially correct, complete and minimal for p(**t**)
- If *Subst* is finite, then $P \cup \{\leftarrow p(\, \mathbf{t}\,)\}$ terminates
- $\forall \theta \in Subst$: $\mathbf{t}\theta$ satisfies out($M_1, \ldots, M_n$)
- *Subst* satisfies the multiplicity $\langle Min-Max \rangle$
- any side-effects described in the specification are fulfilled by the execution of p(**t**).

This definition of correctness can be applied to Prolog procedures if the SLDNF-refutation procedure is the Prolog one. Moreover, the control primitives introduced in the Prolog procedures can influence the search in the SLDNF-tree and therefore the sequence of answer substitutions.

8.2.2   Correctness of a logic procedure (in a set of specifications)

When defining the correctness of a logic procedure, it should be possible for this to be discussed independently of the logic procedures associated with its subproblems. Only the specification of these subproblems should be involved, thus leading to the abstraction principle.

Definition 8.9   Given an SLDNF-refutation procedure, let:

- LP(p) be a logic procedure
- $q_1, \ldots, q_n$ be all the procedure names appearing in LP(p) and distinct from p
- $Spec_1, \ldots, Spec_n$ be the specifications of $q_1, \ldots, q_n$.

LP(p) is **correct** w.r.t. its specification (in $\{Spec_1, \ldots, Spec_n\}$) iff for any logic program P such that

- LP(q_j) is correct in P w.r.t. its specification $Spec_j$ ($1 \leq j \leq n$), and
- P contains no occurrence of p

LP(p) is correct in $P \cup \{LP(p)\}$ w.r.t. its specification.

In the above definition, the logic program P represents a correct implementation of the subproblems involved in LP(p). As for logic descriptions, such a set cannot contain any occurrence of p. Otherwise, the introduction of LP(p) in P could destroy the correctness of others. Thus the correctness of mutually recursive logic procedures must be established simultaneously. The following definition expresses the correctness criterion for k mutually recursive logic procedures.

Definition 8.10   Given an SLDNF-refutation procedure, let:

- LP(p_1), ..., LP(p_k) be logic procedures
- $q_1, \ldots, q_n$ be all the procedure names appearing in LP(p_1), ..., LP(p_k) and distinct from $p_1, \ldots, p_k$,
- $Spec_1, \ldots, Spec_n$ be the specifications of $q_1, \ldots, q_n$.

LP(p_1), ..., LP(p_k) are **correct** w.r.t. their specifications (in {$Spec_1$, ..., $Spec_n$}) iff for any logic program P such that

- LP(q_j) is correct in P w.r.t. its specification $Spec_j$ ($1 \leq j \leq n$), and
- P contains no occurrence of p_1, ..., p_k

LP(p_i) is correct in $P \cup$ {LP(p_1), ..., LP(p_k)} w.r.t. its specification ($1 \leq i \leq k$)

Definition 8.9 is thus a particular case of Definition 8.10 (that is $k = 1$) for non-recursive or simply recursive logic procedures. The above definitions can also be applied to Prolog procedures.

8.3 Justification

Given the procedural semantics of a logic programming language, it is natural that the correctness definition characterizes the sequence of answer substitutions. The correctness definition in a set of logic procedures refers to what has already been introduced in Section 2.2 (general form of a specification). Let us analyse the role of each part of a specification (summarized in Table 2.1 on p. 47) in the correctness criteria.

Types

Types act as preconditions: at least one ground instance of t must respect the specified types (that is, t is compatible with the domain of p). Compatibility with the domain of p also covers the possible 'restrictions of parameters'. Types also act as postconditions: at least one ground instance of $t\theta$ must belong to the specified type, for $\theta \in Subst$ (that is $t\theta$ is compatible with the domain of p). This postcondition aspect is dealt with through the minimality of *Subst* (domain compatibility).

Relation

For each t, the relation described in the specification induces a set of correct solutions. Partial correctness ensures that the substitutions of *Subst* yield correct solutions. Completeness ensures that every correct solution is covered by some substitution of *Subst*. The minimality requirement includes the absence of redundancy and the minimal coverage requirements. This could be excessive for some problems and could thus be relaxed for such procedures, provided it is explicitly stated in their specifications.

Directionality

The correctness definition deals clearly with the precondition and postcondition aspects of the directionalities.

Multiplicity

The requirement that *Subst* satisfies the multiplicity ⟨*Min–Max*⟩ should be related to the termination criterion. Thus, for Max finite or *, termination is ensured. Termination cannot always be required since the sequence of answer substitutions can be infinite.

Environment preconditions and the description of side-effects

This part of the specification is also included in the correctness definition. Reasoning about procedures with side-effects is simplified when the number of answer substitutions is finite. It is then possible to state when the side-effects must be considered (which is no later than after visiting the last success node). This could however be inappropriate for procedures requiring side-effects and an infinite number of answer substitutions.

8.4   Properties

In this section, properties of correct logic procedures are stated and proven. Unless explicitly stated otherwise, no assumption about the SLDNF-refutation procedure will be made.

As an immediate consequence of our definition of correctness, negation as failure is complete for correct logic procedures.

Property 8.1   Negation as failure
Let:

- P be a logic program
- LP(p) be correct in P
- p be the relation described in the specification of p.
- t be ground with respect to the preconditions of p.

Then $t \notin p$ iff $P \cup \{\leftarrow p(\, t\,)\}$ has a finitely failed SLDNF-tree.

*Proof
Let *Subst* be the sequence of answer substitutions for $P \cup \{\leftarrow p(\, t\,)\}$. Since LP(p) is correct in P, either *Subst* contains only the empty substitution (and therefore by soundness $t \in p$), or *Subst* is empty (and therefore by completeness $t \notin p$). In both cases, the SLDNF-tree is finite (termination). Thus if $t \in p$, the SLDNF-tree is finite and has a success branch. If $t \notin p$, the SLDNF-tree is finite and has no success branches (finitely failed SLDNF-tree).   ∎

As for logic descriptions, the concept of correctness of logic procedures must be monotonic. When a logic procedure is correct in a set

P, it must remain correct in extensions of P. The following property states sufficient conditions for obtaining monotonicity of correctness.

Property 8.2   Monotonicity of correctness

Let:

- P be a logic program
- $P' = P \cup \{LP(r)\}$.

If:

- LP(p) is correct in P w.r.t. its specification, and
- P contains no occurrences of r

then LP(p) is correct in P' w.r.t. its specification.

*Proof

Because P contains no occurrences of r, any SLDNF-tree for $P \cup \{\leftarrow p(t)\}$ (with **t** any n-tuple of terms) will be the same as the SLDNF-tree for $P' \cup \{\leftarrow p(t)\}$. Hence the result.   ∎

The next property states a result about the composition of correct procedures. Informally, the property expresses that, for a goal composed of several literals, every computed answer substitution covers correct solutions (partial correctness aspect) and every correct solution is covered by one and only one computed answer substitution (completeness aspect). It does not state the actual completeness criterion since some of the computed answer substitutions could never be reached according to the search strategy. This property requires a safe and linear computation rule.

Property 8.3   Composition of correct procedures

Let:

- P be a logic program
- $\leftarrow L_1 \ldots, L_k$ be a goal G with L_i either $q_i(t_i)$ or not($q_i(t_i)$), where all the q_i are correct in P ($k > 0$).

If:

- the computation rule is safe and linear for $P \cup \{G\}$, and
- the preconditions for $q_i(t_i)$ are respected when the literals L_i are selected in the SLDNF-tree for $P \cup \{G\}$

then, we have:

- partial correctness, that is:
  For every θ computed answer substitution for $P \cup \{G\}$
  if $\langle s_1, \ldots, s_k \rangle$ is a ground instance of $\langle t_1, \ldots, t_k \rangle \theta$ and s_i is in the domain of q_i
  then $\langle s_1, \ldots, s_k \rangle \in Sol(\,G\,)$.

- completeness and non-redundancy, that is:
  For every $\langle s_1, \ldots, s_k \rangle \in Sol(\,G\,)$,
  there exists exactly one computed answer substitution θ for $P \cup \{G\}$
  such that $\langle s_1, \ldots, s_k \rangle$ is a ground instance of $\langle t_1, \ldots, t_k \rangle \theta$.

Before proving this property, a technical lemma will be presented. This states that every partial computed answer substitution can always be extended to cover a solution. For example, if $\langle s_1, \ldots, s_k \rangle$ is a ground instance of $\langle t_1, \ldots, t_k \rangle$, and if θ is a partial computed answer substitution such that s_1 is a ground instance of $t_1 \theta$, then $\langle s_1, \ldots, s_k \rangle$ is a ground instance $\langle t_1, \ldots, t_k \rangle \theta$. However, some technical restrictions on θ are necessary.

*Lemma 8.1

Let:

- s_1, s_2, t_1, t_2 be terms
- θ be a substitution such that:
  - $dom(\,\theta\,) \subseteq VARS(\,t_1\,)$ (*)
  - all the variables appearing in θ but not in t_1 do not appear in t_2 (**)

If:

(1) $\langle s_1, s_2 \rangle$ is a ground instance of $\langle t_1, t_2 \rangle$, and

(2) s_1 is a ground instance of $t_1 \theta$

then $\langle s_1, s_2 \rangle$ is a ground instance of $\langle t_1, t_2 \rangle \theta$.

*Proof of Lemma 8.1

Condition (**) expresses that the new variables introduced by θ are brand-new variables. It implies that

$$VARS(\,t_1 \theta\,) \cap (\,VARS(\,t_2\,) \backslash VARS(\,t_1\,)\,) = \varnothing$$

By (1), there exists a substitution δ such that

(3) $\langle s_1, s_2 \rangle = \langle t_1, t_2 \rangle \delta$

By (2), there exists a substitution β such that

(4) $s_1 = t_1\theta\beta$

By (**), β can be chosen such that

$$\text{dom}(\beta) \cap (VARS(t_2) \backslash VARS(t_1)) = \varnothing$$

For $x \in VARS(t_1)$, we have:

- $(x\theta\beta)\delta = x\theta\beta$ (since $t_1\theta\beta = s_1$ is ground)
- $x\theta\beta = x\delta$ (by (4) and (3))

Hence

(5) $x\theta\beta\delta = x\delta$

For $x \in (VARS(t_2) \backslash VARS(t_1))$, we have:

- $x\theta = x$ (by (*))
- $x\beta = x$ (by (4) and the choice of β)

Hence

(6) $x\theta\beta\delta = x\delta$

From (5) and (6), we thus have:

(7)   for $x \in (VARS(t_1) \cup VARS(t_2))$: $x\theta\beta\delta = x\delta$

By (3) and (7), we obtain:

$$\langle s_1, s_2 \rangle = \langle t_1, t_2 \rangle \delta = t_1, t_2 \rangle\theta\beta\delta$$

Hence our lemma: $\langle s_1, s_2 \rangle$ is a ground instance of $\langle t_1, t_2 \rangle\theta$.   ∎

Proof of Property 8.3

The completeness and non-redundancy result is proven by induction on k (for partial correctness, see Exercise 8.3).

For $k = 1$

If L_1 is a positive literal $q(t)$, the result is an immediate consequence of the correctness of LP(q) (completeness and non-redundancy).

    If L_1 is a negative literal $not(q(t))$, since the computation rule is safe for $P \cup \{G\}$, t is ground, and by hypothesis t is in the domain of q since the preconditions of q are respected. For Sol(G) not empty, we have $t \notin q$ and the derivation tree for $P \cup \{\leftarrow q(t)\}$ finitely fails (Property 8.1). Therefore, ε (empty substitution) is the only computed answer substitution for $P \cup \{\leftarrow not(q(t))\}$ since LP(q) is correct. Hence the result.

For k > 1

Since the computation rule is linear, without loss of generality, it can be assumed that the literals of G are selected from left to right.

Let G′ be the goal $\leftarrow L_1, \ldots, L_{k-1}$

Any computed answer substitution for $P \cup \{G\}$ can be decomposed as $\theta = \theta_1\theta_2$, where:

- θ_1 is a computed answer substitution for $P \cup \{G'\}$, and
- θ_2 is a computed answer substitution for $P \cup \{\leftarrow L_k\theta_1\}$

Let $\langle s_1, \ldots, s_k \rangle \in \text{Sol}(G)$. From the definition of Sol(G) and Sol(G′), we have:

(1) $\langle s_1, \ldots, s_k \rangle$ is a ground instance of $\langle t_1, \ldots, t_k \rangle$ and $\langle s_1, \ldots, s_{k-1} \rangle \in \text{Sol}(G')$

By the induction hypothesis, there exists one and only one computed answer substitution θ_1 for $P \cup \{G'\}$ such that:

(2) $\langle s_1, \ldots, s_{k-1} \rangle$ is a ground instance of $\langle t_1, \ldots, t_{k-1} \rangle\theta_1$

From the definition of SLDNF-resolution, we have dom(θ_1) ⊆ VARS ($\{t_1, \ldots, t_{k-1}\}$), and all the variables appearing in θ_1 but not in G′ are brand-new variables (and thus do not appear in t_k). Applying Lemma 8.1 to (1) and (2), we obtain:

(3) $\langle s_1, \ldots, s_k \rangle$ is a ground instance of $\langle t_1, \ldots, t_k \rangle\theta_1$

If L_k is a positive literal $q_k(\ t_k\ )$, by the correctness of LP(q_k), there exists one and only one computed answer substitution θ_2 for $P \cup \{\leftarrow q_k$ ($t_k\theta_1$)} such that s_k is a ground instance of $t_k\theta_1\theta_2$.

If L_k is a negative literal not(q(t)), since the computation rule is safe for $P \cup \{G\}$, t is ground, and by hypothesis t is in the domain of q since the preconditions of q are respected. For Sol(G) not empty, we have $t \notin q$ and the derivation tree for $P \cup \{\leftarrow q(\ t\ )\}$ finitely fails (Property 8.1). Therefore, ε (empty substitution) is the only computed answer substitution for $P \cup \{\leftarrow$ not(q(t))} since LP(q) is correct. Hence the result.

In both cases, we have:

(4) s_k is a ground instance of $t_k\theta_1\theta_2$

From the definition of SLDNF-resolution, we also have dom(θ_2) ⊆ VARS(t_k), and all the variables appearing in θ_2 but not in L_k are brand-new variables (and thus do not appear in $\langle t_1, \ldots, t_{k-1} \rangle \theta_1$). Applying Lemma 8.1 to (3) and (4), we obtain:

$\langle s_1, \ldots, s_k \rangle$ is a ground instance of $\langle t_1, \ldots, t_k \rangle \theta_1 \theta_2$

Hence the result, since θ_1 and θ_2 are unique.   ∎

In Property 8.3, the safety and linearity hypothesis could be restricted to the top goal G instead of being applied over the whole SLDNF-tree. It should be noted that in Property 8.3, domain compatibility (that is, that every substitution covers at least one solution) is not ensured. More formally, the following criterion:

$$\forall \theta \in Subst : \text{Cand-Sol}(\, \theta; \text{G}\,) \neq \varnothing$$

or, equally,

$$\forall \theta \in Subst : \exists \langle s_1, \ldots, s_k \rangle \text{ ground instance of } \langle t_1, \ldots, t_k \rangle \theta$$
$$\text{such that } s_i \text{ in the domain of } q_i$$

is not fulfilled. A simple counter-example is the goal

← append([], L2, LApp), L2 = bill

using the Prolog SLDNF-refutation procedure. After the execution of the first literal, the substitution $\theta = \{L2/bill, LApp/bill\}$ is obtained, thus leading to domain incompatibility. This could induce incorrect results if these literals were in the body of a program clause. Domain incompatibility usually occurs when a variable is used in different places with different types. In this example, L2 is used in the first literal as a parameter of type *list*, and in the second literal as a parameter of type *term*.

EXERCISE

*8.3   Prove the partial correctness case in Property 8.3.

*8.5   Background

In Section 4.5, correctness definitions based on the declarative semantics were presented. They represent most of the proposed correctness definitions in the logic programming literature.

An interesting feature of Hogger's work is that two levels of correctness are introduced (Hogger, 1981, 1984). The first deals with the declarative semantics and has thus already been presented. The second deals with the procedural semantics.

Let:

- P be a definite logic program
- S be a first-order specification of P
- G be a definite goal $\leftarrow p(\,t\,)$.

Total correctness
The pair $(\,P, G\,)$ is totally correct w.r.t. S
iff $\forall \theta : S \vDash p(\,t\theta\,)$ $\Leftrightarrow$ $P \vdash p(\,t\theta\,)$ where θ is a substitution
Termination
The pair $(\,P, G\,)$ terminates
iff the execution of G with program P terminates

These definitions are actually refined by the introduction of a control component. If the two levels of correctness are combined, total correctness can be expressed as:

$$S \vDash p(\,t\theta\,)   \text{iff}   P \vDash p(\,t\theta\,)   \text{iff}   P \vdash p(\,t\theta\,)$$

This can be seen as the basis of a methodological approach for logic program construction, and this approach is of course very close to the underlying principles of the methodology proposed in this book.

The above procedural correctness criteria have, however, some limitations. The relation $P \vdash p(\,t\theta\,)$ does not imply that $P \cup \{\leftarrow p(\,t\,)\}$ eventually produces θ (or a more general substitution) as a computed answer substitution. This implication only holds when the inference system is complete and termination is satisfied. When the sequence of computed answer substitutions is infinite, termination is meaningless and should be replaced by some fairness condition expressing that every correct substitution will eventually be produced (or will be an instance of some substitution that is eventually produced) by $P \cup \{\leftarrow p(\,t\,)\}$. Note that Hogger's correctness definition does not prevent redundancy between different computed answer substitutions.

SUMMARY

- Correctness requires the actual parameters of a procedure to respect the preconditions of that procedure (domain, directionality and environment).
- The sequence of answer substitutions computed by a correct procedure for a given goal respecting the preconditions is:
  – **partially correct**: all the solutions induced by these substitutions are correct

    – **complete**: every correct solution is covered
    – **minimal**: that is domain compatibility, non-redundancy and minimal
    coverage.

- Termination is required if the sequence of answer substitutions is finite.

- A correct program remains correct when new procedures are introduced.

9

Derivation
of a logic program

PREVIEW   In this chapter, we handle the derivation of a correct Prolog
procedure from a correct logic description. In order to obtain a correct Prolog
procedure, the logic description is first translated into a pure logic procedure
by means of a straightforward syntactical translation (Section 9.2). It is shown
that partial correctness and completeness are already achieved (Section 9.3).
The remaining correctness criteria to be verified are also clearly stated. Roughly
speaking, these criteria will be fulfilled by rearranging the clauses of the
procedure, and by rearranging the literals in these clauses. In Sections 9.4–9.10,
techniques for analysing and solving the possible problems in achieving
correctness are presented. These techniques could equally well be applied
outside our methodological approach.

9.1   Primitive logic procedures

In Chapter 5, the concept of primitive logic descriptions was introduced.
Such descriptions do not have to be constructed because their existence
and correctness is assumed. It was also pointed out that whether logic
descriptions are also primitives actually depends on the target logic
programming language. For each primitive logic description there will be
a corresponding primitive logic procedure which is a built-in procedure
of the programming language. It is sometimes useful to define small
interfaces between primitive logic descriptions and primitive procedures
so as to get rid of the syntactical peculiarities of the target language and

225

therefore to be more language independent (for example, the use of add(A, B, AplusB) as an interface to the built-in X is Expr).

Derivation of LP(=)

Although syntactical equality (see Specification 5.1) is usually considered as a primitive procedure, a logic description has been constructed. Let us now investigate how this logic description can be turned into a logic procedure. LD(=) has the form of three axiom schemata (Logic Description 5.1) named Eq1, Eq2 and Eq3. Eq1 formalizes when $t_1 = t_2$ should hold, while Eq2 and Eq3 formalize when $t_1 \neq t_2$ should hold. It was also shown that Eq1′ is an alternative for formalizing when $t_1 = t_2$ should hold (Logic Description 5.2).

$$\forall(f(X_1, \ldots, X_n) = f(Y_1, \ldots, Y_n) \Leftarrow X_1 = Y_1 \& \ldots \& X_n = Y_n)$$
for each function f ($n \geq 0$).   **(Eq1)**

$$(\forall X)(X = X).$$ **(Eq1′)**

The essence of the passage from a logic description (p $\Leftrightarrow$ Def_p) to a program is to consider the 'if part' of the predicate definition. This amounts to considering only when p should hold (that is, p $\Leftarrow$ Def_p) and eliminating the definition of when ¬p should hold (that is, ¬p $\Leftarrow$ ¬Def_p, or equivalently p $\Rightarrow$ Def_p). Applying this idea to the derivation of LP(=) we obtain two different logic procedures depending upon the chosen LD(=): Logic Description 5.2 with {Eq1′, Eq2, Eq3} or Logic Description 5.1 with {Eq1, Eq2, Eq3}.

In the first case, Eq1′ is the formalization of when $t_1 = t_2$ should hold. This yields Procedure 9.1. It is the classical Prolog (re)definition of syntactical equality. The syntactical equality is achieved here through unification and is type independent.

X = X ←

Procedure 9.1   T1 = T2

In the second case, Eq1 is the formalization of when $t_1 = t_2$ should hold. It is more problematic since this axiom schema would yield an infinite number of program clauses, which is not implementable as such. This can be overcome only by restricting the syntactical equality to a finite number of functors (with a fixed arity), which can be achieved by defining the syntactical equality for each type. Procedure 9.2 illustrates the syntactical equality for integers (where the integer n is represented as $s^n(0)$), and lists of integers. Subscripts are used to underline the type aspects in this syntactical equality. Such an approach can be compared with Turbo Prolog's equality where all the objects have to be typed and explicit equality procedures must be defined by the programmer for non-primitive types. Thus in this language, syntactical equality cannot be considered as a primitive as soon as new types (or new functors) are used.

$0 =_{int} 0 \leftarrow$
$s(X) =_{int} s(Y) \leftarrow X =_{int} Y$
$[] =_{list} [] \leftarrow$
$[H1 \mid T1] =_{list} [H2 \mid T2] \leftarrow H1 =_{int} H2, T1 =_{list} T2$

Procedure 9.2 $T1 = T2$

EXERCISES

*9.1   What is the difference between Procedure 9.2 and its four program clauses in which $=$ is not subscripted?

*9.2   What are the advantages of Turbo Prolog's approach to equality? (*Hint:* is unification needed in a computation?) What are the disadvantages?

9.2   Syntactical translation

The objective is to translate a logic description into a pure logic procedure (that is, with only variables in the heads of the clauses) by means of syntactic transformations. Given a set of logic descriptions S, the completion of the obtained pure logic program P (that is, comp(P)) should be logically equivalent to S. General derivation rules are now presented for the syntactical translation of any logic description. When the definition part of a logic description only handles disjunctions and conjunctions of literals, the syntactical translation is straightforward.

9.2.1   Translation rules

Initial translation
Replace the logic description A $\Leftrightarrow$ Def_A
by A $\Leftarrow$ Def_A

Intermediate translation
These transformations rules are based on classical equivalences in first-order logic (except for transformation (1)) and are a simple extension of the transformations presented in Lloyd and Topor (1984) and Lloyd (1987). In the following rules, the symbols *Goals* and *MoreGoals* denote a conjunction of formulae.

(a)   Replace A $\Leftarrow$ *Goals* & (V $\vee$ W) & *MoreGoals*
        by   A $\Leftarrow$ *Goals* & V & *MoreGoals*
                A $\Leftarrow$ *Goals* & W & *MoreGoals*

(b)   Replace A $\Leftarrow$ *Goals* & $\neg$(V $\vee$ W) & *MoreGoals*
        by   A $\Leftarrow$ *Goals* & $\neg$V & $\neg$W & *MoreGoals*

(c)   Replace A $\Leftarrow$ *Goals* & $\neg$(V & W) & *MoreGoals*
        by   A $\Leftarrow$ *Goals* & $\neg$V & *MoreGoals*
                A $\Leftarrow$ *Goals* & $\neg$W & *MoreGoals*

(d)   Replace A $\Leftarrow$ *Goals* & (V $\Rightarrow$ W) & *MoreGoals*
        by   A $\Leftarrow$ *Goals* & $\neg$V & *MoreGoals*
                A $\Leftarrow$ *Goals* & W & *MoreGoals*

(e)   Replace A $\Leftarrow$ *Goals* & $\neg$(V $\Rightarrow$ W) & *MoreGoals*
        by   A $\Leftarrow$ *Goals* & V & $\neg$W & *MoreGoals*

(f)   Replace A $\Leftarrow$ *Goals* & (V $\Leftrightarrow$ W) & *MoreGoals*
        by   A $\Leftarrow$ *Goals* & V & W & *MoreGoals*
                A $\Leftarrow$ *Goals* & $\neg$V & $\neg$W & *MoreGoals*

(g)   Replace A $\Leftarrow$ *Goals* & $\neg$(V $\Leftrightarrow$ W) & *MoreGoals*
        by   A $\Leftarrow$ *Goals* & $\neg$V & W & *MoreGoals*
                A $\Leftarrow$ *Goals* & V & $\neg$W & *MoreGoals*

(h)   Replace A $\Leftarrow$ *Goals* & $\neg\neg$W & *MoreGoals*
        by   A $\Leftarrow$ *Goals* & W & *MoreGoals*

(i)   Replace A $\Leftarrow$ *Goals* & ($\forall X_1 \ldots \forall X_k$)W & *MoreGoals*
        by   A $\Leftarrow$ *Goals* & $\neg$($\exists X_1 \ldots \exists X_k$)$\neg$W & *MoreGoals*

(j)   Replace A $\Leftarrow$ *Goals* & $\neg$($\forall X_1 \ldots \forall X_k$)W & *MoreGoals*
        by   A $\Leftarrow$ *Goals* & ($\exists X_1 \ldots \exists X_k$)$\neg$W & *MoreGoals*

(k)   Replace A $\Leftarrow$ *Goals* & ($\exists X_1 \ldots \exists X_k$)W & *MoreGoals*
        by   A $\Leftarrow$ *Goals* & W & *MoreGoals*
        where $X_1, \ldots, X_k$ do not occur free outside W (otherwise rename
                the variables).

(l)   Replace A $\Leftarrow$ *Goals* & $\neg$($\exists X_1 \ldots \exists X_k$)W & *MoreGoals*
        by   A $\Leftarrow$ *Goals* & $\neg$r($Y_1, \ldots, Y_n$) & *MoreGoals*

        r($Y_1, \ldots, Y_n$) $\Leftarrow$ ($\exists X_1 \ldots \exists X_k$)W
        where $Y_1, \ldots, Y_n$ are all the free variables occurring in ($\exists X_1 \ldots$
                $\exists X_k$)W and r is a new predicate.

Final translation

Replace A $\Leftarrow$ W_1 & $\ldots$ & W_i & $\ldots$ & W_m
by   A $\leftarrow$ $W'_1, \ldots, W'_i, \ldots, W'_m$
where W_j are literals ($1 \leq j \leq m$)
        W'_j is W_j if W_j is a positive literal
        W'_j is not(B) if W_j is a negative literal $\neg$B.

The syntactical translation of a logic description consists of applying the initial transformation, the intermediate translation and then the final translation. The result is a logic procedure. The intermediate translation rules should be applied continuously, in any order. The translation process may yield more than one logic procedure (because of rule (1)). From a logical point of view, the various transformations for negations could be handled by a general transformation generalizing (1). However, the above transformation rules will overcome the limitations of the negation as failure rule to a certain extent by reducing the number of negative literals.

The syntactical translation is defined for non-primitive logic descriptions. Let us extend the transformation to primitive logic descriptions as follows: given a primitive logic description LD(p), its syntactical translation is the built-in logic procedure LP(p).

Example 9.1 presents the syntactical translation of Logic Description 5.26.

EXAMPLE 9.1

minlist(L, Min) $\Leftrightarrow$ ($\forall$X) (member(X, L) $\Rightarrow$ less_eq(Min, X))

Initial translation

minlist(L, Min) $\Leftarrow$ ($\forall$X) (member(X, L) $\Rightarrow$ less_eq(Min, X))

By (i)

minlist(L, Min) $\Leftarrow$ $\neg$($\exists$X) $\neg$(member(X, L) $\Rightarrow$ less_eq(Min, X))

By (l)

minlist(L, Min) $\Leftarrow$ $\neg$r(L, Min)
r(L, Min) $\Leftarrow$ ($\exists$X) $\neg$(member(X, L) $\Rightarrow$ less_eq(Min, X))

By (k)

minlist(L, Min) $\Leftarrow$ $\neg$r(L, Min)
r(L, Min) $\Leftarrow$ $\neg$(member(X, L) $\Rightarrow$ less_eq(Min, X))

By (e)

minlist(L, Min) $\Leftarrow$ $\neg$r(L, Min)
r(L, Min) $\Leftarrow$ member(X, L) & $\neg$less_eq(Min, X))

Final translation

minlist(L, Min) $\leftarrow$ not(r(L, Min))
r(L, Min) $\leftarrow$ member(X, L), not(less_eq(Min, X))

Another interesting example is the syntactical translation of Logic Description 5.27 given in Example 9.2.

EXAMPLE 9.2

atmost2(L) $\Leftrightarrow$ ($\forall$E1$\forall$E2$\forall$E3$\forall$T) $\neg$L = [E1, E2, E3 | T]

Initial translation

atmost2(L) $\Leftarrow$ ($\forall$E1$\forall$E2$\forall$E3$\forall$T) $\neg$L = [E1, E2, E3 | T]

By (i)

atmost2(L) ⇐ ¬(∃E1∃E2∃E3∃T) ¬¬L = [E1, E2, E3 | T]

By (l)

atmost2(L) ⇐ ¬r(L)
r(L) ⇐ (∃E1∃E2∃E3∃T) ¬¬L = [E1, E2, E3 | T]

By (k)

atmost2(L) ⇐ ¬r(L)
r(L) ⇐ ¬¬L = [E1, E2, E3 | T]

By (h)

atmost2(L) ⇐ ¬r(L)
r(L) ⇐ L = [E1, E2, E3 | T]

Final translation

atmost2(L) ← not(r(L))
r(L) ← L = [E1, E2, E3 | T]

EXERCISES

9.3   What are the disadvantages of replacing rule (f) by the following rule?

> Replace   A ⇐ *Goals* & (V ⇔ W) & *MoreGoals*
> by   A ⇐ *Goals* & (V ⇒ W) & (V ⇐ W) & *MoreGoals*

9.4   Perform the syntactical translation of Logic Descriptions 5.14 (compress_int_CL) and 5.6 (compress_ext_L).

9.5   Perform the syntactical translation of the two logic decriptions constructed in Exercise 5.51 (union and intersection).

9.6   Perform the syntactical translation of the logic description

$$p(X) ⇔ (∃Y)q(X, Y) \& (∃Y)r(X, Y)$$

9.2.2   Properties of syntactical translation

The first property expresses that the translation process terminates and yields a set of pure logic procedures.

Property 9.1

The process of continually applying the translation rules to a given logic description terminates within a finite number of steps with a set of pure logic procedures.

Proof

Straightforward extension of Lloyd and Topor (1984) and Lloyd (1987). ∎

The second property states the logical equivalence of the formula A $\Leftarrow$ W and its resulting form after applying one of the intermediate transformation rules (a) to (k).

Property 9.2

Let S be a set of logic formulae of the form p($X_1, \ldots, X_n$) $\Leftarrow$ W, and S' be a set resulting from a single transformation (a) or (b) or ... or (k) applied to S. S and S' are H-equivalent, and comp(S) and comp(S') are H-equivalent as well.

Proof
See Exercises 9.7 and 9.8.   ■

Property 9.2 is now extended to the global translation process. Since new predicates are added by rule (l), the relationship will not be a logical equivalence any more.

Property 9.3

Let

- S be a set of logic descriptions
- P be a logic program syntactically translated from S
- F be a closed formula containing only predicates which appear in S.

Then

$$\text{Comp}(P) \models_H F \text{ iff } S \models_H F.$$

Proof
Straightforward extension of Lloyd and Topor (1984) and Lloyd (1987).   ■

The last property combines the soundness property of SLDNF-resolution (Property 7.2) and the previous property. Here it will be known as **extended soundness**.

Property 9.4   *Extended soundness*
Given an SLDNF-refutation procedure
Let

- S be a set of logic descriptions
- P be a logic program syntactically translated from S

- ← $L_1, \ldots, L_k$ be a goal G containing only predicates which appear in S
- *Subst* be the sequence of answer substitutions for $P \cup \{G\}$.

If the computation rule is safe for $P \cup \{G\}$
then

$$\forall \theta \in Subst : S \vDash_H \forall ((L_1 \& \ldots \& L_k) \theta).$$

Proof
From the soundness of SLDNF-resolution (Property 7.2) and Property 9.3, this result is straightforward.   ∎

EXERCISES_____

9.7   Prove Property 9.2 for the derivation rules (f) and (j).

9.8   Prove Property 9.2 for the derivation rule (k). Show that renaming can be necessary. (*Hint*: take the example of Exercise 9.6.)

_____

9.3   Towards correctness

Given a logic description LD(p), the syntactical translation yields a logic procedure LP(p), or more correctly a set of logic procedures, since new intermediate procedures can be introduced by transformation rule (l). In practice, most of the logic descriptions constructed by induction yield a unique logic procedure since universal quantifiers are rarely used. This section analyses whether the obtained logic procedures are correct, assuming the correctness of the logic descriptions. First, the correctness criteria already satisfied will be described (that is, partial correctness and completeness), and then the remaining criteria to be verified in order to achieve correctness will be clarified. This presentation is independent of the chosen SLDNF-refutation procedure and thus independent of the target language. The following sections will present methods for verifying these correctness criteria for Prolog's refutation procedure. Mutually recursive logic descriptions will not be explicitly considered here, but the following discussion can easily be extended to deal with such descriptions.

9.3.1   Correctness criteria already satisfied

Given a correct logic description, it is shown that at the logic program level, partial correctness and completeness are both achieved. The following theorems ensure these two major criteria. However, a hypothesis has to be stipulated. It basically supposes that in the body of the program clauses, if an answer substitution is computed, then it covers at least one correct solution of each literal. This is not always the case, as explained after Proper 8.3 (composition of correct procedures: partial correctness). For instance, in the program clause

$$p(X) \leftarrow \text{append}([ ], L2, LApp), L2 = \text{bill}$$

the variable L2 appears in two literals. After the execution of append, L2 is still a variable. After the execution of L2 = bill, the variable L2 is instantiated by something that is incompatible with the domain of append, which is logically incorrect. This is not prevented by the correctness of append. Such a problem did not occur at the logic description level since type checking was explicitly included in the correctness criteria of a logic description. At the logic program level, type checking is weakened to the existence of a ground instance of the correct type after the execution of the literal. When such a problem occurs, the partial correctness of the syntactically translated procedure cannot be fulfilled, nor can completeness if this problem occurs through a negative literal. The following definition states precisely the hypothesis which must be satisfied in order to avoid such problems.

Definition 9.1
Let

- $LD(p)$ be a logic description
- $LP(p)$, $LP(r_1)$, . . . , $LP(r_s)$ be procedures syntactically translated from $LD(p)$ (where $LP(r_i)$ are procedures introduced by the transformation process)
- P be a logic program
- t be an n-tuple of terms whose variables do not occur in $LP(p)$.

$LP(p)$ is **domain consistent** for $p(t)$ in P iff

(1)   For any program clause $p(x) \leftarrow L_1, \ldots, L_k$ of $LP(p)$ (with L_i either $q_i(t_i)$ or not($q_i(t_i)$)), let θ be a computed answer substitution for $P \cup \{\leftarrow x = t, L_1, \ldots, L_k\}$. If s is a ground instance of $t\theta$, and s is in the domain of p, then there exists $\langle s_1, \ldots, s_k \rangle$ such that

$\langle s, s_1, \ldots, s_k \rangle$ is a ground instance of $\langle t, t_1, \ldots, t_k \rangle\theta$
and s_i is in the domain of q_i.

(2)   For any ground literal of the form not($r_j(\mathbf{u})$) selected in the SLDNF-tree for $P \cup \{\leftarrow p(\mathbf{t})\}$, let $r_j(\mathbf{y}) \leftarrow L_1, \ldots, L_k$ be the corresponding program clause (with L_i either $q_i(\mathbf{t}_i)$ or not($q_i(\mathbf{t}_i)$)), and let θ be a computed answer substitution for $P \cup \{\leftarrow \mathbf{y} = \mathbf{u}, L_1, \ldots, L_k\}$. Then there exists $\langle s_1, \ldots, s_k \rangle$ such that

$\langle s_1, \ldots, s_k \rangle$ is a ground instance of $\langle t_1, \ldots, t_k \rangle \theta$
and s_i is in the domain of q_i.

The second part of the definition is only needed when the syntactical translation introduces new intermediate procedures (denoted $LP(r_i)$). This part is also a special case of the first one since the type of the parameters of the intermediate procedures r_j can be assumed to be *term* (the most general type), and $\mathbf{u}$ is required to be ground when the computation rule is safe. This definition can be seen as an extension of the domain preconditions attached to the subproblems, as well as the domain postconditions (that is, minimality: domain compatibility). Instead of requiring the existence of a ground instance in the domain of q before and after the execution of q, it is required that any further instantiations of the variables occurring in the procedure call remain compatible with the domain of q (see also Exercises 9.9 and 9.10).

The partial correctness and completeness properties are both achieved for a goal p(t), where t is *any* term; that is not necessarily ground and not necessarily respecting the preconditions of p. It is however required that the subproblems of p are correctly implemented and that their preconditions are satisfied when they are selected within the execution of p(t). Such a requirement will be easier to establish when t is restricted to satisfy the preconditions of p.

Theorem 9.1   *Partial correctness*

Given an SLDNF-refutation procedure, let

- LD(p) be a correct logic description
- $LP(p), LP(r_1), \ldots, LP(r_s)$ be procedures syntactically translated from LD(p),
- P be a logic program containing $LP(p), LP(r_1), \ldots, LP(r_s)$, where the subproblems of LD(p) are correct, and
- t be an *n*-tuple of terms.

If

- the computation rule is safe and linear for $\leftarrow p(\mathbf{t})$,
- LP(p) is domain consistent for p(t) in P, and

- for any subproblem $q_i(\mathbf{u}_i)$ appearing in LD(p), the preconditions of q_i are satisfied, when $q_i(\mathbf{u}_i)$ is selected in the SLDNF-tree for $P \cup \{\leftarrow p(\mathbf{t})\}$,

then the sequence *Subst* of answer substitution for $P \cup \{\leftarrow p(\mathbf{t})\}$, p(t) is partially correct for p(t).

*Proof

The following proof of partial correctness is actually slightly stronger. We prove the following:

> For any computed answer substitution θ for $P \cup \{\leftarrow p(\mathbf{t})\}$
> if **s** is a ground instance of tθ and **s** is in the domain of P,
> then $\mathbf{s} \in p$
> where *p* is the relation described in the specification of P.

Let us first suppose that the syntactical translation of LP(p) does not produce intermediate procedures LP(r_j), and that LD(p) is not recursive. Since the computation rule is linear, a left to right selection rule will be assumed.

Let θ be a computed answer substitution for $P \cup \{\leftarrow p(\mathbf{t})\}$, and s be a ground instance of tθ with **s** in the domain of p. By definition of SLDNF-resolution, θ is a substitution obtained by restricting some substitution β' to the variables of **t**, where β' is a computed answer substitution for

$$P \cup \{\leftarrow (L_1, \ldots, L_k)\{x/t\}\}$$

for some program clause $p(\mathbf{x}) \leftarrow L_1, \ldots, L_k$ of LP(p) (with L_i either $q_i(\mathbf{t}_i)$ or not($q_i(\mathbf{t}_i)$)). By a property of equality (assuming LP(=) is correct in P and t contains no variables occurring in this program clause), θ is also obtained from β, the computed answer substitution for

$$P \cup \{\leftarrow \{x = t, L_1 \ldots, L_k\}$$

Since LP(p) is domain consistent for p(t) in P, there exists $\langle s_1, \ldots, s_k\rangle$ such that

> $\langle s, s_1, \ldots, s_k\rangle$ is a ground instance of $\langle t, t_1, \ldots, t_k\rangle\beta$
> and s_i is in the domain of q_i.

Since the literal x = t appears in the above goal, we also have

> $\langle s, s, s_1, \ldots, s_k\rangle$ is a ground instance of $\langle x, t, t_1, \ldots, t_k\rangle\beta$

Applying Property 8.3 (composition of correct procedures: partial correctness), the above statement can be refined as follows:

There exists $\langle s_1, \ldots, s_k \rangle$ such that

    (a) $s_i \in q_i$ and s_i is in the domain of q_i if L_i is a positive literal

    (b) $s_i \notin q_i$ and s_i is in the domain of q_i if L_i is a negative literal

    (c) $\langle s, s, s_1, \ldots, s_k \rangle$ is a ground instance of $\langle x, t, t_1, \ldots, t_k \rangle \beta$

Observe that (b) and (c) obviously imply

    (b') $s_i \notin q_i$ *or* s_i *is not* in the domain of q_i if L_i is a negative literal

    (c') $\langle s, s, s_1, \ldots, s_k \rangle$ is a ground instance of $\langle x, s, t_1, \ldots, t_k \rangle$

Let S be a set of logic descriptions containing LD(p) such that the logic descriptions associated to the subproblems of LD(p) are correct in $S \setminus \{LD(p)\}$, and there is no occurrence of p in $S \setminus \{LD(p)\}$. Due to (a), (b') and (c'), Property 4.5 (existence of a witness) can be applied: $S \vDash_H \exists$ ($x = s \,\&\, L_1 \,\&\, \ldots \,\&\, L_k$). Using a property of equality (assuming LD(=) is correct in S), we also have $S \vDash_H \exists$ ($L_1 \,\&\, \ldots \,\&\, L_k$)$\{x/s\}$. Hence $S \vDash_H$ p(s). Finally, since s is in the domain of p and by correctness of LD(p) in S, we get $s \in p$.

    For recursive LD(p), a simple induction can be done on the number of literals p selected for the computed answer substitution θ. When intermediate procedures LP(r_j) are generated through the syntactical translation, the proof is a (technical) extension of the above one.

    When recursion through negation occurs (via not(p(a)), say), then the goal $\leftarrow$ p(a) cannot fail for $a \in p$, which is a completeness requirement. Theorems 9.1 and 9.2 should actually be proved simultaneously. Hence the necessity to have the same hypothesis in both theorems.   ■

    The following completeness theorem does not state that *Subst* is complete, but that every correct solution is covered by some computed answer substitution. This was called weak completeness in Section 7.3. As in Property 8.3 (composition of correct procedures: completeness), the difference lies in the fact that certain computed answer substitutions could be never reached according to the search rule.

Theorem 9.2   Completeness
Given an SLDNF-refutation procedure, let

- LD(p) be a correct logic description
- LP(p), LP(r_1), $\ldots$, LP(r_s) be procedures syntactically translated from LD(p)
- P be a logic program containing LP(p), LP(r_1), $\ldots$, LP(r_s), where the subproblems of LD(p) are correct
- t be an *n*-tuple.

If

- the computation rule is safe and linear for $\leftarrow p(\,t\,)$
- $LP(\,p\,)$ is domain consistent for $p(\,t\,)$ in P
- for any subproblem $q_i(\,u_i\,)$ appearing in $LD(\,p\,)$, the preconditions of q_i are satisfied when $q_i(\,u_i\,)$ is selected in the SLDNF-tree for $P \cup \{\leftarrow p(\,t\,)\}$

then $\forall s \in \text{Sol}(\leftarrow p(\,t\,))$, $\exists \theta$ computed answer substitution for $P \cup \{\leftarrow p(\,t\,)\}$ such that s is a ground instance of $t\theta$.

*Proof

Let us first suppose that the syntactical translation of $LP(\,p\,)$ does not produce intermediate procedures $LP(\,r_j\,)$. Since the computation rule is linear, a left to right selection rule will be assumed. Let S be a set of logic descriptions containing $LD(\,p\,)$ such that the subproblems of $LD(\,p\,)$ are correct in $S \backslash \{LD(\,p\,)\}$, and there is no occurrence of p in $S \backslash \{LD(\,p\,)\}$.

Let $s \in \text{Sol}(\leftarrow p(\,t\,))$. By correctness of $LD(\,p\,)$, we have

$$S \vDash_H p(\,s\,)$$

Hence, for some clause $p(\,x\,) \leftarrow L_1, \ldots, L_k$ in $LP(\,p\,)$,

$$S \vDash_H \exists(\,L_1 \& \ldots \& L_k\,)\,\{x/s\}$$

By a property of equality (assuming $LD(=)$ is correct in S), this can also be expressed as

$$S \vDash_H \exists(\,x = s \& L_1 \& \ldots \& L_k\,)$$

Using Property 4.5 (existence of a witness), we get

(1)   There exists $\langle s_1, \ldots, s_k \rangle$ such that

         (a) $s_i \in q_i$ and s_i is in the domain of q_i if L_i is a positive literal $q_i(\,t_i\,)$

         (b) $s_i \notin q_i$ or s_i is not in the domain of q_i if L_i is a negative literal $\text{not}(\,q_i(\,t_i\,)\,)$

         (c) $\langle s, s, s_1, \ldots, s_k \rangle$ is a ground instance of $\langle x, s, t_1, \ldots, t_k \rangle$

Since s is a ground instance of t, assuming the variables of t do not occur in $LP(\,p\,)$ (which can be obtained by some variable renaming in $LP(\,p\,)$), (c) can be replaced by

         (c′) $\langle s, s, s_1, \ldots, s_k \rangle$ ground instance of $\langle x, t, t_1, \ldots, t_k \rangle$

Two cases are now distinguished, depending on whether the considered clause is recursive or not.

Non-recursive clause

Any computed answer substitution for $P \cup \{\leftarrow p(\, t\,)\}$ by this clause is equivalent to a computed answer substitution for $P \cup \{\leftarrow x = t, L_1, \ldots, L_k\}$, where the substitution is restricted to the variables of t (assuming $LP(\, = \,)$ is correct in P).

Let us first show that (b) can be replaced by

(b′) $s_i \notin q_i$ *and* s_i *is in the domain of* q_i *if* L_i *is a negative literal* $\neg q_i(\, t_i\,)$

Suppose that (1) holds with (a), (b) and (c′), but not with (a), (b′) and (c′). For some $1 \leq f \leq k$, s_f is thus not in the domain of q_f. Take f such that $not(\, q_i(\, t_f\,)\,)$ is the first negative literal selected in the clause, with s_f not in the domain of q_f. Applying Property 8.3 (Composition of correct procedures: completeness) for the goal $P \cup \{\leftarrow x = t, L_1, \ldots, L_{f-1}\}$, we get a computed answer substitution δ such that

$$\langle s, s, s_1, \ldots, s_{f-1}\rangle \text{ is a ground instance of } \langle x, t, t_1, \ldots, t_{f-1}\rangle\delta$$

Hence, by Lemma 8.1,

$$\langle s, s, s_1, \ldots, s_{f-1}, s_f\rangle \text{ is a ground instance of } \langle x, t, t_1, \ldots, t_{f-1}, t_f\rangle\delta$$

The selected literal L_f will thus have the form $not(q_f(\, t_f\delta\,))$. Since the computation rule is safe for $P \cup \{\leftarrow p(\, t\,)\}$, $t_f\delta$ is ground and is thus s_f. Since the preconditions are satisfied when the literals are selected, $t_f\delta$ is thus compatible with the domain of q_f. Hence s_f is in the domain of q_f. Contradiction. The verification of the preconditions thus ensures the domain membership. Statement (b) can then be replaced by (b′) in (1).

From (1) ((a), (b′) and (c′)), Property 8.3 (composition of correct procedures: completeness) can be applied to the goal $\leftarrow x = t, L_1, \ldots, L_k$. Thus there exists a computed answer substitution β for $P \cup \{\leftarrow x = t, L_1, \ldots, L_k\}$ such that

$$\langle s, s, s_1, \ldots, s_k\rangle \text{ ground instance of } \langle x, t, t_1, \ldots, t_k\rangle\beta$$

By restricting β to the variables of t, we obtain a computed answer substitution θ for $P \cup \{\leftarrow p(\, t\,)\}$ such that s is a ground instance of $t\theta$.

Recursive clause

For a recursive clause, induction must be used. The induction hypothesis can be stated as follows:

Let t' be an n-tuple with a safe and linear computation rule for $P \cup \{\leftarrow p(t')\}$, such that the preconditions of the $q_i(t_i)$ are satisfied when selected. For all s' belonging to the set of solutions for $p(t')$ such that $s' < s$ (according to some well-founded relation $<$); there exists θ' computed answer substitution for $P \cup \{\leftarrow p(t')\}$, such that s' is a ground instance of $t'\theta'$.

Since $LD(p)$ is correct, if a literal L_f in the considered clauses is a recursive use of p, then (1) will hold for some s_f smaller than s according to some well-founded relation. The proof is then a simple extension of the non-recursive case where the induction hypothesis has to be used in the proof of (b') and in the proof of the existence of β.

When intermediate procedures $LP(r_j)$ are generated through the syntactical translation, the proof is a (technical) extension of the above one. However it is required that $LP(p)$ is domain consistent for $p(t)$ in P. This ensures the partial correctness of the body of the intermediate procedures $LP(r_j)$, which is necessary to obtain completeness for the negative literals $not(r_j)$.

When recursion through negation occurs (via $not(p(a))$, say), then the goal $\leftarrow p(a)$ cannot succeed for $a \notin p$, which is a partial correctness requirement. Theorems 9.1 and 9.2 should actually be proved simultaneously. Hence the necessity to have the same hypothesis in both theorems.   ■

EXERCISES

*9.9 In Theorems 9.1 and 9.2, why is t not required to respect the preconditions of p?

*9.10 In Theorems 9.1 and 9.2, the following hypotheses are made:

(i) $LP(p)$ is domain consistent for $p(t)$ in P

(ii) For any subproblem $q_i(u_i)$ appearing in $LD(p)$, the domain preconditions of q_i are satisfied when $q_i(u_i)$ is selected in the SLDNF-tree for $P \cup \{\leftarrow p(t)\}$.

Find examples showing that (i) does not imply (ii), and (ii) does not imply (i). (*Hint*: What about failure branches?)

*9.11 Find an example of procedure $LP(p)$ and goal $\leftarrow p(t)$ such that $LP(p)$ is domain consistent for $p(t)$, but the first minimality criterion (domain compatibility) is not satisfied.

9.3.2   Criteria to be verified

Given a correct logic description $LD(p)$ and its syntactical translation $LP(p)$, what needs to be verified in order for $LP(p)$ to be correct?

Theorems 9.1 and 9.2 ensure the two major correctness criteria of partial correctness and completeness. We will now examine what remains to be verified.

Given an SLDNF-refutation procedure, let

- LD(p) be a correct logic description
- LP(p) be a procedure syntactically translated from LD(p)
- P be a program where all the subproblems of LD(p) are correct
- t be an *n*-tuple of terms respecting the preconditions of p
- *Subst* be the sequence of answer substitutions for $P \cup \{\leftarrow p(\ t\ )\}$.

Hypotheses to be fulfilled

In Theorems 9.1 and 9.2, the following hypotheses have to be fulfilled:

(1)   The computation rule is safe and linear for $P \cup \{\leftarrow p(\ t\ )\}$.

(2)   LP(p) is domain consistent for p(t) in P.

(3)   For any subproblem $q_i(\ \mathbf{u}\ )$ appearing in LD(p), the preconditions of q_i are satisfied when q_i is selected in the SLDNF-tree for $P \cup \{\leftarrow p(\ t\ )\}$. That is

   (3.1) domain compatibility

   (3.2) directionality (*in* part)

   (3.3) environment preconditions

Completeness

Theorem 9.2 (completeness) shows that every correct solution is covered by some computed answer substitution. In order for *Subst* to be complete, it is sufficient to show that

(4)   Every computed answer substitution for $P \cup \{\leftarrow p(\ t\ )\}$ belongs to *Subst*.

Others

From the definition of correctness, the following correctness criteria also have to be verified:

(5)   *Subst* minimal:

   (5.1) domain compatibility

   (5.2) no redundancy

   (5.3) minimal coverage

(6)   If *Subst* is finite, then $P \cup \{\leftarrow p(\ t\ )\}$ terminates.

(7) $\forall\ \theta \in Subst$, $t\theta$ satisfies the *out* part of the directionality.

(8)   *Subst* satisfies the multiplicity.

(9)   Side-effects fulfillment.

Here, the verification only has to be carried out for **t** respecting the preconditions of p, which is sufficient to obtain correctness. What about the intermediate logic procedures introduced during the syntactical translation of LP(p) from LD(p)? They have no specification and assuming or proving their correctness is meaningless. The above criteria actually also refer to these intermediate logic procedures. In criteria (2) and (3) for instance, reference is made to the subproblems of LD(p), thus appearing in LP(p) or in some intermediate procedure. In what follows, these intermediate procedures will be implicitly present in the notation LP(p).

The following sections present techniques for verifying the above criteria for Prolog's refutation procedure. These techniques are also useful independently of the methodological framework proposed here. Roughly speaking, the above criteria could be fulfilled by rearranging the clauses of the procedure, by rearranging the literals in the clauses and by adding literals in certain clauses. It can already be seen that Prolog's computation rule is linear and that criterion (1) is thus partly verified. We should not forget the occur check problem exposed in Section 1.2.4. Criteria will be dealt with by considering these topics:

Section 9.4	Safe computation rule	(Criterion (1))
Section 9.5	Directionality	(Criteria (3.2) and (7))
Section 9.6	Types	(Criteria (2), (3.1) and (5.1))
Section 9.7	Searching SLDNF-trees	(Criteria (4) and (6))
Section 9.8	Minimality and multiplicity	(Criteria (5.2), (5.3) and (8))
Section 9.9	Side-effects	(Criteria (3.3) and (9))
Section 9.10	Occur check	

All the above criteria may appear cumbersome to verify but, in practice, very few things have to be verified and most of these can be verified systematically and automatically.

9.4   The safe computation rule

Prolog's computation rule (that is, selection of the leftmost literal) is not always safe. The problem of verifying that the computation rule is safe for $P \cup \{\leftarrow p(t)\}$ amounts to verifying that the negative literals in LP(p) are ground when selected. The selection of other negative literals (that is outside LP(p)) need not be considered since the subproblems in LP(p) are assumed to be correct. The verification that the negative literals in LP(p) are ground when selected is equivalent to the requirement of a ground directionality for these literals. There is no logical meaning behind this because not(A) is a representation of ¬A, where A is an atom. But in Prolog, the syntax of atoms and terms are almost the same. not can therefore be considered as a pseudo-procedure with the directionality

in(ground) : out(ground)   ⟨0–1⟩

If this directionality is respected when using this pseudo-procedure (representing the logical negation), this literal will be ground when selected.

The verification of the safe computation rule can thus be included in the verification of the preconditions of the subproblems, including the pseudo-procedure not.

9.5   Directionality

The problem of directionality verification for a procedure LP(p) is as follows. For each program clause of the procedure, a permutation of the literals must be found such that the directionality preconditions of these literals are respected for Prolog's selection rule. For a positive literal q(t), this amounts to verifying that, when selected, the parameters t of q satisfy the *in* part of a directionality of q. For a negative literal not(q(t)), this amounts to verifying that when selected, the parameters of q are ground (safe computation rule) and satisfy the *in* part of a directionality of q. Finally, for each specified *in* part of the directionality of p, the corresponding *out* part must be satisfied after the execution of the last subproblem. When these conditions hold for each program clause of a logic procedure, we say that this logic procedure is correct w.r.t. its directionality. The multiplicity part will be analysed separately. This raises the following queries: firstly, given a program clause, how can it be determined whether it is correct w.r.t. a given directionality; secondly, how can a correct permutation be found and how can different permutations be chosen; finally, what can be done when no correct permutation can be found?

9.5.1   Intermediate procedures and generalization

The verification of a directionality assumes the existence of a specified directionality for each subproblem. However, intermediate procedures introduced during the syntactical translation do not have a specification and thus have no specified directionality. The absence of directionality (and multiplicity) for such intermediate procedures is not problematic since they are used only once and via a negative literal. Because the computation rule has to be safe, the implicit directionality is thus in(ground, . . . , ground) : out(ground, . . . , ground)

Its associated multiplicity is $\langle 0-1 \rangle$.

A similar problem arises for procedures derived from a logic description constructed by generalization. In the specification of the generalized problem, the directionality part has not been considered at the logic description level. Suppose that LD(p(X, Y)) is constructed by generalization, and let

in(m_X, m_Y) : out(M_X, M_Y) $\langle I-J \rangle$

be a directionality of p. Let us derive the associated directionality for the generalization.

If LD(p) is constructed by means of a tupling generalization (see schema in Logic Description 5.30), then the derived logic procedure will have the form

p(X, Y) ← p_tupl([X] , Y)

The associated directionality of p_tupl will be the same as for p, except that *var* is replaced by *ngv* in m_X and M_X.

If LD(p) is constructed by means of a descending or ascending generalization (see schemata in Logic Descriptions 5.31 and 5.32), the derived logic procedure will have the form

p(X, Y) ← p_desc(X , Y, $\varnothing_Y$)

or

p(X, Y) ← p_asc(X , Y, $\varnothing_Y$, $\varnothing_X$)

Since $\varnothing_X$ and $\varnothing_Y$ are ground terms, the associated directionalities of p_asc and p_desc will be respectively

in(m_X, m_Y, ground) : out(M_X, M_Y, ground)

and

in(m_X, m_Y, ground, ground) : out(M_X, M_Y, ground, ground)

In all the above cases, the associated multiplicity will be the same $\langle I-J \rangle$. These directionalities do not prevent the generalized problem from being correct also for others directionalities.

Table 9.1   Directionalities of syntactical equality LP(=).

in(ground, ground)	:	out(ground, ground)	$\langle 0-1 \rangle$
in(ground, ngv)	:	out(ground, ground)	$\langle 0-1 \rangle$
in(ground, var)	:	out(ground, ground)	$\langle 1-1 \rangle$
in(ngv, ground)	:	out(ground, ground)	$\langle 0-1 \rangle$
in(ngv, ngv)	:	out(novar, novar)	$\langle 0-1 \rangle$
in(ngv, var)	:	out(ngv, ngv)	$\langle 0-1 \rangle$
in(var, ground)	:	out(ground, ground)	$\langle 1-1 \rangle$
in(var, ngv)	:	out(ngv, ngv)	$\langle 0-1 \rangle$
in(var, var)	:	out(var, var)	$\langle 1-1 \rangle$

9.5.2   Primitive procedures

Primitive procedures are built-in procedures of the programming language and thus have a predefined directionality. In order to be more language independent, it is sometimes useful to use some interfaces. An example is the procedure add (Specification 5.7) and the widespread built-in is (Specification 2.1). If the directionality of add were

in(ground, any, ground) : out (ground, ground, ground) $\langle 0-1 \rangle$

then a small interface could be

add(X, Y, XplusY) ← Y is XplusY − X

Syntactical equality LP(=) is the major primitive. It is worth stating its directionality precisely. Let t_1 and t_2 be two terms. When t_1 is a variable, the unification of t_1 and t_2 yields two terms of the same form as t_2. When t_1 is ground, the unification yields two ground terms. When t_1 and t_2 are ngv terms, the unification can give two ground terms (for example, f(1, X) = f(Y, 2)), or two ngv terms (for example, f(1, X) = f(1, Y)). The resulting directionalities (and multiplicities) are given in Table 9.1. These directionalities should be combined when dealing with the forms *noground*, *gv*, *novar*, or *any*. For the *in* part in(any, ngv) for instance, the corresponding *out* part will be out(novar, novar). It is obtained by combining the *out* parts out(ground, ground), out(novar, novar) and out(ngv, ngv), corresponding to the in parts in(ground, ngv), in(ngv, ngv), and in(var, ngv) respectively.

EXERCISES

9.12   In the following directionality of LP(=), why is the multiplicity $\langle 0-1 \rangle$ and not $\langle 1-1 \rangle$?

in(ngv, var) : out(ngv, ngv) $\langle 0-1 \rangle$

9.13 What is the corresponding *out* part of in(noground, gv) for LP(=)?

9.5.3 General framework of abstract interpretation

The verification of directionalities can be performed through flow analysis or abstract interpretation of the program clauses, using information from the specification of the subproblems. Flow analysis is a method for proving or discovering properties of the running behaviour of a program, without actually running it, but by analysing it statically. This static analysis can be seen as a computation of the program in some abstract domain, hence the name of abstract interpretation. Abstract interpretation is introduced here, but adapted to the context of the proposed methodology for logic program derivation from logic descriptions. Abstract interpretation is much simplified in this context since information will be taken from the specification of the subproblems rather than from their abstract interpretation. We are thus dealing with abstract verification rather than abstract interpretation. References to further reading on abstract interpretations are given in Section 9.11.

Let us first characterize the actual behaviour of a goal of the form $\leftarrow p(x)\theta$ for a family of θ, using the pure program clause $p(x) \leftarrow L_1, \ldots L_s$ in a program P.

$$p(x) \leftarrow \Theta_0 \, L_1 \ldots \Theta_{i-1} \, L_i \, \Theta_i \ldots L_s \, \Theta_s$$

where

- Θ_0 is some given set of substitutions θ with $\mathrm{dom}(\theta) = \{ x \}$
- $\Theta_i = \{ \theta\sigma \mid \theta \in \Theta_0$ and σ is a computed answer substitution for $P \cup \{ \leftarrow (L_1 \ldots L_i)\theta \} \}$ $(i \geq 1)$

The set Θ_i characterizes the partial result of the computation. From the definition of SLDNF-resolution and Prolog's refutation procedure, we also have

$$\Theta_i = \{ \theta \sigma \mid \theta \in \Theta_{i-1} \text{ and } \sigma \text{ is a computed answer substitution for } P \cup \{ \leftarrow L_i \theta \} \}$$

The above formulation can be used for stating that the program clause is correct w.r.t. some preconditions and postconditions. Let pre(p) and post(p) denote some preconditions and postconditions for LP(p).

Given $\Theta_0 = \{ \theta \mid \mathrm{dom}(\theta) = \{ x \}$ and $x\theta$ respects pre(p)}, then post(p) is verified iff

(1) $\forall \theta \in \Theta_s$, $x\theta$ respects post(p)

The verification that some preconditions pre(q_i) are satisfied when the subproblem q_i is selected in the program clause can be characterized as

(2)   For each literal L_i of the program clause with L_i either $q_i(\mathbf{u})$ or not($q_i(\mathbf{u})$) ($i \geq 1$),

$\forall \theta \in \Theta_{i-1}$, $\mathbf{u}\theta$ respects pre(q_i)

Such a verification can only be obtained by executing the program. In abstract interpretation, the execution is performed in some (finite) abstract domain and the sets Θ_i are approximated by larger sets Θ'_i ($\Theta_i \subseteq \Theta'_i$). If criteria (1) and (2) are fulfilled with the approximated sets Θ'_i, then these criteria are fulfilled by the actual sets Θ_i (soundness aspect). However, the converse does not necessarily hold (completeness aspect). The precision of the abstract interpretation depends on the quality of the approximated sets Θ'_i.

In the case of directionality verification, the abstract domain is the set {var, ground, ngv}. Instead of computing the value of the variables (that is, substitutions), abstract interpretation will here only determine the form of the variables at the various places in the program clause. The approximated sets Θ'_i are thus formed of all the substitutions where the variables are bound to a term with the computed form. Directionality verification can now be described precisely.

Definition 9.2
Let C be a program clause $p(X_1, \ldots, X_n) \leftarrow L_1, \ldots, L_s$ with variables $X_1, \ldots, X_n, X_{n+1}, \ldots, X_{n+m}$.
A **directionality context** α for C is a set of the form

$$\{(X_1, N_1), \ldots, (X_n, N_n), (X_{n+1}, N_{n+1}), \ldots, (X_{n+m}, N_{n+m})\}$$

where N_i is a non-empty subset of {ground, var, ngv}.
This directionality context α represents the set of substitutions Θ, with $\theta \in \Theta$ iff

- dom(θ) $\subseteq \{ X_1, \ldots, X_{n+m}\}$

- if $X_i/t_i \in \theta$, then t_i has one of the forms of N_i, otherwise $var \in N_i$ ($1 \leq i \leq m + n$).

Given a directionality

in($m_1, \ldots, m_n$) : out($M_1, \ldots, M_n$)

every Θ_i will be represented by a directionality context α_i. The computation of the α_i is performed simultaneously with the directionality verification as follows:

- $\alpha_0 = \{(X_1, m_1), \ldots, (X_n, m_n), (X_{n+1}, \{ \text{var} \}), \ldots, (X_{n+m}, \{ \text{var} \}) \}$
- Let L_i be a literal ($q_i(t_1, \ldots, t_k)$ or not($q_i(t_1, \ldots, t_k)$)) of the program clause.
  - Given α_{i-1}, determine the form ($f_1, \ldots, f_k$) of $t_1, \ldots, t_k$ in α_i.
  - If L_i is a negative literal, verify that all the f_i are ground (safe computation rule).
  - Verify that ($f_1, \ldots, f_k$) satisfies the *in* part of a directionality of q.
  - Determine α_i from α_{i-1} and the *out* part corresponding to the *in* part of the above involved directionality of q.
- Verify that the form of $X_1, \ldots, X_n$ in α_s satisfies out($M_1, \ldots, M_n$).

This verification of directionality can fail in two ways; either when the directionality of a subproblem is not respected (including the pseudo-directionality for not), or when the *out* part of the given directionality is not satisfied after the last literal L_s. Since abstract interpretation is an approximation of the actual execution, the above verification process can fail for a program clause which is actually correct for the analysed directionality (see example below). The simplicity of this verification process implies that in some cases, it may incorrectly succeed (see Exercise 9.14).

9.5.4   Examples of directionality verification

Directionality verification is illustrated on the efface procedure (Specification 1.1). Procedure 9.3 is the syntactical translation of Logic Description 5.4 (where an obvious simplification has been made). The literals have been permuted for the purpose of the example.

```
efface( X, L, LEff ) ← L = [H | T], H = X, LEff = T, list( T )
efface( X, L, LEff ) ← L = [H | T], LEff = [H | TEff],
                       efface( X, T, TEff ), not( H = X )
```

Procedure 9.3   efface(X, L, LEff)

In the following directionality verification, the notation $m_i t_i M_i$ is used for describing the form of the term t_i before (m_i) and after (M_i) the selection of a literal p(..., t_i, ...). When t_i is neither a ground nor a variable term (say f(..., Y, ...)), the notation f(..., m_Y Y M_Y, ...) is used for describing the form of the variable Y before (m_Y) and after (M_Y) the selection of a literal p(..., t_i, ...). This is a convenient way of representing the directionality contexts as well as the form of the parameters.

For the first specified directionality (that is in(any, ground, any) : out(ground, ground, ground)), the analysis is the following for the first program clause:

> efface(*any* X **ground**, *ground* L **ground**, *any* LEff **ground**) ←
>   *ground* L **ground** = *ngv* [*var* H *ground*| *var* T *ground*] *ground*
>   *ground* H *ground* = *any* X **ground**
>   *any* LEff *ground* = *ground* T *ground*
>   list(*ground* T **ground**)

The bold symbols in the body show the final form of the formal parameters. They should agree with the *out* part of the directionality (bold symbols in the head of the clause). A similar dataflow analysis would show that this clause is also correct w.r.t. the second specified directionality (that is, in(ground, any, ground) : out(ground, ground, ground)). The directionality of list is assumed to be in(ground) : out(ground).

For the second program clause, we have

> efface(*any* X **ground**, *ground* L **ground**, *any* LEff **ground**) ←
>   *ground* L **ground** = *ngv* [*var* H *ground*| *var* T *ground*] *ground*
>   *any* LEff **novar** = *ngv* [*ground* H *ground*| *var* TEff *any*] *novar*
>   efface(*any* X *ground*, *ground* T *ground*, *any* TEff *ground*)
>   not (*ground* H *ground* = *ground* X **ground**)

Here, it seems that LEff is *novar* after its last occurrence while it should be *ground* in order to respect the *out* part of the directionality. But LEff is actually *ground* after the execution of the last literal because TEff becomes *ground* after the third literal. This example illustrates that the verification process can fail in a program clause which is correct w.r.t. the directionality. In such a case, extra knowledge should be used for proving the correctness w.r.t. the directionality. Directionality verification could also be made more precise by adding information about variable sharing in the directionality contexts. The above permutation is also correct w.r.t. the second directionality of efface. Procedure 9.3 is thus correct w.r.t. its directionality. Note that in this directionality verification, an implicit induction is made since in the body of the program clause, recursion is assumed to yield parameters with the correct form.

9.14 Given the directionality context {(L, any), (H, ground), (T, var)}, determine the directionality context after the selection of the literal L=[H | T].

Analysis of directionality

Some more technical aspects of the directionality verification process are developed below.

(1)   Given a directionality context α, determine the form f of a parameter t in α. It is assumed that the form of all the variables occurring in t is described in α. If Y is a variable occurring in t, m_Y will denote its form in α (that is, Y, m_Y) $\in \alpha$). A simple analysis of t can determine its syntactical form and the following cases are straightforward.

- If t is a ground term, then the form of t in α is $f = \{$ ground $\}$.
- If t is a variable Y, then $f = m_Y$.
- If t is neither ground nor a variable, three cases should be distinguished.
    - if for each variable Y occurring in t, $m_Y = \{$ ground $\}$, then $f = \{$ ground $\}$.
    - if for some variable Y occurring in t, ground $\notin m_Y$, then $f = \{$ ngv $\}$.
    - otherwise, $f = \{$ ground,ngv $\}$.

(2)   Given the form ($f_1, \ldots, f_k$) with $f_i \subseteq \{$ ground,var,ngv $\}$, and given a set of directionalities D, determine whether ($f_1, \ldots, f_k$) satisfies the *in* part of some directionality in D, and determine the corresponding *out* form ($F_1, \ldots, F_k$).

(2.1)   All the f_i are singletons. This problem has been solved in Section 2.2.3 (directionality: coverage and compatibility of directionalities). The resulting F_i are non-empty, assuming the directionalities in D are not incompatible.

(2.2)   Some f_i are non-singletons. The problem is here more complex since ($f_1, \ldots, f_k$) may satisfy none of the *in* parts of the directionalities, but any parameter satisfying ($f_1, \ldots, f_k$) can satisfy some of these directionalities. This is illustrated in Example 9.3. The strategy for determining the F_i is to consider separately every possible ($f'_1, \ldots, f'_k$) with f'_j being a singleton included in f_j. Each of these forms should satisfy some *in* part of the directionalities in D. Otherwise $(f_1, \ldots, f_k)$ does not satisfy these directionalities. For each $(f'_1, \ldots, f'_k)$, the corresponding *out* form $(F'_1, \ldots, F'_k)$ can be determined as in 2.1 since the f'_j are singletons. In the *out* form $(F_1, \ldots, F_k)$ of $(f_1, \ldots, f_k)$, each F_i is the union of the various F'_i obtained with all the possible $(f'_1, \ldots, f'_k)$. As in 2.1 the resulting F_i are non-empty assuming the directionalities are not incompatible.

EXAMPLE 9.3

in(ground, var) : out(ground, ground)
in(ngv, var) : out(ngv, ngv)

The form (novar, var) (that is ({ ground, ngv }, { var })) satisfies none of these two *in* parts. Parameters satisfying (novar, var) have either the form (ground, var) or the form (ngv, var). They both satisfy the *in* part of one of these two directionalities. The two resulting forms are (ground, ground) and (ngv, ngv). The *out* form corresponding to (novar, var) is then (novar, novar).

(3)   Given a variable Y occurring in a term t, and given the form $F \subseteq \{$ ground,var,ngv $\}$ of t in some directionality context α, determine the form M_Y of Y in α.

Since Y occurs in t, t is either the variable Y or is neither a ground nor a variable term.

- If t is the variable Y, then $M_Y = F$.
- If t is neither ground nor a variable, then F may contain only ground or ngv.
    - If $F = \{$ ground $\}$, then $M_Y = \{$ ground $\}$.
    - If $F = \{$ ngv $\}$ or $F = \{$ ground, ngv $\}$, then $M_Y = \{$ ground, var, ngv $\}$. In this case, since t can be ngv, its variables may have the form ground, ngv or even var. However, they cannot be all ground. The form M_Y could further be refined by considering simultaneously all the variables occurring in t (see Exercise 9.16).

The above characterization of M_Y can be used in the directionality verification for computing the directionality context α_i from α_{i-1} and from the form $(F_1, \ldots, F_k)$ of the parameters in the literal L$_i$ after its execution.

Let $(Y, m_Y) \in \alpha_{i-1}$. The form of Y in α_i is given according to the three following cases.

- If Y does not occur in L$_i$, then $(Y, m_Y) \in \alpha_i$.

This simple case is actually incorrect since some sharing between variables could exist (see Exercise 9.15).

- If Y occurs in a single parameter t in L_i, then $(Y, M'_Y) \in \alpha_i$, where $M'_Y = $ minimal(m_Y, M_Y) with M_Y determined as in (3) above (see Definition 2.12 for minimal).

  The set M'_Y is not empty assuming that the directionalities are not incompatible.

- If Y occurs in more than one parameter in L_i, then $(Y, M''_Y) \in \alpha_i$,

  where M''_Y is the intersection of the M'_Y computed as in the previous case.

Here, the set M''_Y could be empty (see Exercise 9.17). This signifies that no computed answer substitution exists for $L_1, \ldots, L_i$. It could be a symptom of some possible directionality or type errors in subproblems.

What about recursion in the directionality verification process? If a literal L_i is a recursion, can we assume that LP(p) is correct w.r.t. the analysed directionality? Yes, indeed. The directionality verification can be performed for all the program clauses of the procedure. An induction can be done on the number of recursions in a successful derivation in an SLDNF-tree for $P \cup \{ \leftarrow p(t)\}$. This number is finite for each computed answer substitution. The base case of the induction considers the correctness of the program clauses without recursion w.r.t. the analysed directionality. For the other clauses, when a recursive literal L_j is selected, the number of recursions in a successful derivation of this literal is less than for the literal p(t). By the induction hypothesis, the analysed directionality can be used for L_j. In practice, this induction schema will be implicit.

EXERCISES_____

*9.15 Perform the directionality verification for the program clause

$$p(X) \leftarrow q(X, H), H = a$$

for the directionalities in(var) : out(ground) and in(var): out(ngv), assuming the directionality of q is in (var, var): out(ngv,var). What is the actual form of X after the execution of p(X) if q is implemented by

$$q(X, H) \leftarrow X = [H]$$

*9.16   Given the directionality context {(X, ground), (Y, var)}, determine the directionality context after the execution of the literal
p(f(X, Y)), where the directionality of p is in(ngv) : out(ngv). In
an actual execution of the literal p(f(X,Y)), is it possible to get Y
ground? Modify the directionality analysis process in order to get a
more precise directionality context when this case occurs.

*9.17   Given the directionality context {(X, var)}, determine the form of
X after the execution of the literal p(X, X) where the directionality
of p is in(var, var) : out(novar, ground). Analyse the same problem, but for the following directionality of p : in(var, var) :
out(ngv, ground).

9.5.5   Finding a permutation

Up to now, only the problem of verifying the correctness of a given
procedure w.r.t. a given directionality has been considered. But one
actually has to *find* a permutation which satisfies *all* the specified
directionalities. Moreover, if more than one permutation yields a correct
logic procedure w.r.t. its directionality, which one should we choose? The
following strategy can be proposed: choose the correct permutation yielding the more efficient Prolog procedure. In order to find correct
permutations, try first the permutations which give efficiency. The
concept of efficiency will be introduced in Chapter 10, when pure Prolog
procedures will be transformed into more efficient ones.

EXERCISES

9.18   Find a correct permutation for the procedure compress_int_CL (see
Exercise 9.4) for the directionality

in(var, ground) : out(ground, ground)

The directionality of sequence is given as

in(any, any, ground) : out(ground, ground, ground)
in(any, ground, ground) : out(ground, ground, ground)

The directionality of append is given as

in(ground, ground, any) : out(ground, ground, ground)
in(any, any, ground) : out(ground, ground, ground)

Find also a permutation for compress_int_CL for the directionality

in(ground, var) : out(ground, ground)

9.19 Find a permutation for the procedure length (syntactically translated from Logic Description 5.8) which is correct for the three following directionalities:

> in(ground, any) : out(ground, ground)
> in(any, ground) : out(novar, ground)
> in(any, any) : out(novar, ground)

The directionality of add is given as

> in(ground, ground, any) : out(ground, ground, ground)
> in(any, ground, ground) : out(ground, ground, ground)

9.20 Syntactically translate each logic description of the between(Inf, Sup, I) problem (Logic Descriptions 5.23 and 5.24) into a logic procedure, and determine the necessary directionality of the subproblems if the procedure between has to be correct for the directionality

> in(ground, ground, var) : out(ground, ground, ground)

9.21 Find a permutation and a directionality such that the procedures union and intersection obtained in Exercise 9.5 are correct.

9.5.6 Solving the problems

In the efface example, it was possible to find a permutation of the literals such that the procedure was correct w.r.t. its directionality. This is not always possible, however, and the reasons for this will now be analysed and some solutions proposed. The following cases are not necessarily disjoint.

Case 1 For a program clause of the procedure, no permutation satisfies the *out* part of a specified directionality.
In such a case, the *out* part must be reconsidered (modification of the directionality in the specification). An alternative is to reconsider the directionality of some subproblems.

Case 2 There is no appropriate directionality for one of the procedures used in a clause.
A first solution is to extend the subproblem in order to handle this particular directionality. If this is not possible, a new procedure can be constructed for this subproblem, but with a directionality restricted to the particular required directionality.

When a parameter is not sufficiently instantiated in a subproblem, a solution consists of introducing a new literal before the considered subproblem in order to further instantiate this parameter. The introduced procedure should not modify the logical contents of the procedure, but should act as a term generator (see Exercise 9.21). Finally, one could also redesign the logic description. It may turn out to be easier to derive a correct procedure from a recursive logic description (see Exercise 9.19 assuming the directionality in(ground, ground) : out(ground, ground) for the subproblem less_eq).

Case 3 Each of the directionalities is satisfied by some (distinct) permutations of the literals, but no single permutation satisfies all these directionalities.

This case often arises in practice. A simple solution consists of duplicating the program clauses of the procedure and permuting the literals differently in each version so that every directionality will be covered by one of the versions. One must then enforce the execution of the appropriate version of the procedure according to the directionality. This can be achieved in two ways. First, control procedures ground(X), var(X) or ngv(X) could be added for some of the parameters. These procedures determine whether X is *ground, var* or *ngv*, respectively. They should be placed as guards in front of the literals in the body of the clauses. These control procedures are not necessarily all built-in, but they can be easily implemented with the built-in primitives offered by the programming language. These procedures have no logical meaning, but remember that we are here only concerned with the procedural aspects. Let us take the following example.

$$p(X, Y) \leftarrow L1, L2 \quad \text{is correct w.r.t. in(var, ground) : out(ground, ground)}$$
$$p(X, Y) \leftarrow L2, L1 \quad \text{is correct w.r.t. in(ground, var) : out(ground, ground)}$$

and the procedure p has to be correct w.r.t. both directionalities. With this approach, we obtain

$$p(X, Y) \leftarrow var(X), L1, L2$$
$$p(X, Y) \leftarrow var(Y), L2, L1$$

No literal ground(. . .) has been added in the first program clause, nor in the second because what is added is sufficient to discriminate between the two specified directionalities.

The other solution for enforcing the execution of the appropriate version consists of giving different names to each version. When using this procedure, the choice of the correct procedure name could be determined statically by the abstract interpretation. This solution does not introduce any overhead for selecting the appropriate version. However, a static choice is not always possible. The two solutions could then be combined.

Case 4 It is impossible to have a safe computation rule (that is, floundering).

This means that there is no permutation of the literals of a clause such that a negative literal not(q(...)) is ground when selected. A first solution consists of restricting the possible directionality in order to get a safe computation rule. Next, the logic description may be redesigned without this negative literal. A special logic description can be built for the directionalities raising problems.

There are two more general solutions to this problem. First, one can construct a procedure not_q(...) for the necessary non-ground directionalities. One has to specify it, to construct a logic description and to derive a logic procedure (its specification is the same as the one of q, except that the specified relation is the complement of the relation described in the specification of q). It is not always possible to construct such a procedure for not_q because the same problem (unsafe computation rule) could also arise. A second solution consists of generalizing the procedure q by adding an extra parameter with domain { yes, no }. Literals q(...) and not(q(...)) correspond to q_gen(... , yes) and q_gen(... , no), respectively. This is similar to the previous solution but here, both procedures (q and not_q) are gathered within one specification and one logic procedure. An interesting example is presented by Hogger (1984, p. 93).

The safety problem can also sometimes be reduced to a single inequality when the following conditions are satisfied. All but one (say X) of the parameters of the negative literal not(q(...)) are ground. The procedure q must act as a total function from the ground parameters to the other ones. In that case, not(q(... , X)) can be replaced by q(... , Y), not(X=Y) (Naish, 1985b). This does not solve the safety problem because not(X=Y) is not ground and cannot be ground even by permuting literals. Nevertheless, this transformation is interesting for logic programming languages with built-in inequality (for example, Prolog II) or with delayed negation (for example, MU-Prolog).

EXERCISES

9.22 Suppose that the procedure add(A, B, AplusB) (Specification 5.7) is needed with the directionality in(var, var, ground), but the only available directionality for add is

> in(ground, any, ground) : out(ground, ground, ground)

Solve this problem by the construction of a generator procedure int(A). This procedure should be constructed as usual: specification, logic description and logic procedure (Type of A: Term; relation: A is an integer; directionality: in(var) : out(ground)).

(*Hint*: use a generalization int_gen(A, N) with type A, N: Integer; relation: $|A| \geq N$; directionality: in(var, ground) : out(ground, ground).)

9.23 Combine the two versions of compress_int_CL obtained in Exercise 9.18.

9.6   Types

As introduced at the end of Section 9.3, the verification of types, or more generally of domains, for a procedure LP(p) is threefold. First, LP(p) must be domain consistent (Definition 9.1). Second, when a subproblem q is selected, its parameters must be compatible with the domain of q (Definition 2.8). Third, for any θ belonging to the sequence of answer substitutions for a goal $\leftarrow$ p(t), the set of candidate solutions for tθ cannot be empty (Definition 8.1). When the 'restriction on parameters' part in the specification is empty, domain verification reduces to type checking. In practice, these verifications usually reduce to the verification of the type preconditions of each subproblem and to the verification that any further instantiation of a variable remains compatible with the type of the parameters where it occurs previously. The framework of abstract interpretation is also suitable for performing this analysis. It should be combined with the directionality information during the type analysis and vice versa. Techniques taken from type inference systems could also be appropriate. References for further reading are given in Section 9.11.

When a problem is detected, extra literals could be added to restrict the type of a parameter to the correct type. Remember that when constructing a logic description, the type of the formal parameters is verified. Some extra type checking formulae were sometimes added in order to perform such a verification (Step 4.2 of the general construction process: verification of the domain membership). In practice, the type checking formulae introduced at the logic description level deal with most of the type problems that could arise at the logic program level. Most of the procedures derived from correct logic descriptions do not have any type problems at all.

It is now shown that type checking formulae introduced at the logic description level can often be removed at the logic program level and we will illustrate this with the logic description compress(L, CL) (Logic Description 5.14). Procedure 9.4 presents its syntactical translation, with a permutation of the literals which is correct w.r.t. the directionality in(var, ground) : out(ground, ground). Procedure 9.5 is correct w.r.t. the directionality in(ground ,var) : out(ground, ground). The directionality of the subproblems is specified in Exercise 9.18. The name of the procedure has been suffixed for purposes of distinction. In both procedures, there is no type problem. However, in compress_v_g, CL is known to be a ground compact list of characters before the execution of the procedure. By definition of a compact list of characters, the two characters in the first two couples of CL are distinct (see Definition 5.4). The type checking literal not(r(C, Tail_CL)) is useless since it will always succeed (with the empty substitution). It has thus been suppressed without affecting the correctness of compress_v_g.

> compress_v_g(L, CL) ← CL = [], L = []
> compress_v_g(L, CL) ← CL = [C, Lg | Tail_CL],
>   sequence(C, Lg, First_seq),
>   compress_v_g(T, Tail_CL),
>   append(First_seq, T, L)

Procedure 9.4   compress_v_g(L, CL)

> compress_g_v(L, CL) ← CL = [], L = []
> compress_g_v(L, CL) ← CL = [C, Lg | Tail_CL],
>   append(First_seq, T, L),
>   sequence(C, Lg, First_seq),
>   compress_v_g(T, Tail_CL),
>   not(r (C, Tail_CL))
> r(C, L) ← L = [C | Y]

Procedure 9.5   compress_g_v(L, CL)

In compress_g_v, however, CL is a variable before the execution of the procedure. The type checking literal is necessary here to force CL to be a compact list. Without it, the goal

> ← compress_g_v([a, a, b], CL)

could give the answer substitution

> θ = { CL / [a, 1, a, 1, b, 1] }

In the above example, the type checking literals introduced at the logic description level can be suppressed when the induction parameter CL is ground. More generally, type checking literals introduced at the logic description level can usually be suppressed when the chosen induction parameter is ground. The other parameters are somehow 'constructed' according to the structural form of the induction parameter. However, when the induction parameter is not ground, it is constructed via literals determining its structural form and such literals may yield terms of different types. The type checking literals introduced can then be useful. This argues for the directionality heuristics of choosing the induction parameter when constructing a logic description since the resulting logic procedure is usually simpler.

In some problems, other literals than the type checking ones introduced at the logic description level can sometimes be suppressed because they always succeed with the empty substitution (see Exercises 9.25 and 9.27).

EXERCISES

9.24 Perform a type analysis of the procedure efface(X, L, LEff) (Procedure 9.3) for the directionality in(any, ground, any) : out(ground, ground, ground). Remove the unnecessary type checking literals.

9.25 This is the same exercise as 9.19, but from Logic Description 5.9. The directionality of greater(X, Y) is in(ground, ground) : out(ground, ground). In the resulting procedure, which literals could be suppressed?

9.26 This is the same exercise as 9.25, but length should only be correct for the directionality in(any, ground) : out(novar, ground), and the last literal of the recursive clause must be length. Perform a type analysis and solve the possible problems by adding extra type checking literals.

9.27 Construct a recursive logic description for less_eq(X, Y) (Type: X, Y Integer; relation: $X \leq Y$) by induction on X–Y, using less(A, B) and add(A, B, AplusB) as subproblems. Syntactically translate it into a logic procedure and find a permutation of the literals which is correct for the directionality

> in(ground, var) : out(ground, ground)

The directionality of less is given as

> in(ground, ground) : out(ground, ground)

The directionality of add is given as

> in(ground, ground, any) : out(ground, ground, ground)

Perform a type analysis and suppress the useless literals.

9.7 Searching SLDNF-trees

This section deals with two aspects of correctness related to the search in SLDNF-trees: the termination requirement when the sequence of answer substitutions is finite and the completeness of sequences of answer substitutions. It has been shown that completeness is achieved when every computed answer substitution belongs to the sequence of answer substitutions. In other words, any computed answer substitution of the SLDNF-tree must *eventually* be reached, according to Prolog's search rule. Two cases are distinguished, depending on whether the sequence of answer substitutions can be infinite or not. This information is usually obtained from the specification (multiplicity). For each specified directionality, it is thus known if the sequence of answer substitutions can be infinite or not. The analysis of SLDNF-trees can be achieved easily thanks to the multiplicity information attached to the directionality of the involved subproblems. This illustrates the usefulness of the multiplicity information within specifications.

9.7.1   Finite sequences of answer substitutions

Here, the SLDNF-tree must be finite to fit the termination criterion, and because it is finite, every computed answer substitution will be reached and completeness will be achieved. In order for the SLDNF-tree to be finite, the SLDNF-tree for each literal in each program clause of the procedure has to be finite. This should be verified for a goal respecting the preconditions of the procedure under analysis. Information about the size of the SLDNF-tree of the subproblems can be found in the multiplicity attached to the directionality of the subproblems. When a subproblem is selected, it must fit one of its specified directionalities. One can thus use the multiplicity information attached to this directionality. If in every program clause of the procedure the upper bound to the number of answer substitutions of every subproblem is finite, then the overall SLDNF-tree is finite. However, since multiplicity indicates upper bounds, one can have an infinite upper bound for a subproblem which actually has a finite SLDNF-tree. The above analysis can be carried out during the directionality analysis.

Three cases will be analysed below, depending on the existence of infinite SLDNF-trees for subproblems, and depending on whether the procedure is recursive or not. These cases cover the problems that could occur when the sequence of answer substitutions must be finite.

No recursion and finite SLDNF-trees for all the subproblems

In this case, termination and completeness are trivially satisfied.

No recursion and infinite SLDNF-trees for some subproblems

Since the number of answer substitutions is finite, termination is not achieved. Two solutions can be given. First, literals can be permuted in order to suppress the infinite SLDNF-tree (see Exercise 9.29). Second, a cut could be added at the end of the program clauses of the procedures.

This is only correct if the number of solutions is not only finite but also at most equal to one (Exercise 9.28).

Recursive procedure

Given that the sequence of answer substitutions is finite, all the subproblems (except the recursion) must have a finite SLDNF-tree. If this is not the case, permuting the literals may achieve the objective. For recursive literals, an induction proof is necessary. It has to be shown that for any parameters respecting the preconditions, the parameters of the recursive literals are smaller according to some well-founded relation. For minimal elements of this well-founded relation, the SLDNF-tree must be finite. Induction cannot be performed on variables since a well-founded relation would be impossible to define. The easiest way is to choose a parameter which is ground according to the *in* part of each specified directionality. If it is not possible, different termination proofs must be carried out. The corresponding parameter in the recursive literal also has to be ground when being selected.

Termination proof is illustrated on the compress(L, CL) problem (Procedure 9.4 for the directionality in(var, ground) : out(ground, ground), and Procedure 9.5 for the directionality in(ground, var) : out(ground, ground)). In both directionalities, the number of answer substitutions is finite. The SLDNF-trees must thus be finite. For compress_v_g, one could show that the SLDNF-trees for sequence and append are both finite and that Tail_CL is ground when the recursive literal is selected.

For CL empty, the first clause yields a finite SLDNF-tree and the second one a finitely failed one. The global SLDNF-tree is therefore finite. For CL non-empty, obviously we have Tail_CL<CL when the recursive literal is selected. Termination is therefore proven.

The compress procedures were actually derived from a logic description constructed with CL as induction parameter (Logic Description 5.14). By construction, we know that at least one program clause has no recursion and that Tail_CL is smaller than CL (according to a well-founded relation) when both are ground. In this case, a termination proof can therefore be reduced to showing that CL is ground when the recursive literal is selected, and all the literals (except the recursive one) have a finite SLDNF-tree.

In compress_g_v, the previous proof of termination cannot be used any more since CL is not ground. However, L is ground. It could be shown that T is ground when the recursive literal is selected, and the SLDNF-trees for the subproblems are all finite. Since L was not the induction parameter of the logic description construction, we do not know *a priori* that T is smaller than L according to some well-founded relation; it has to be proven explicitly. In this example, an obvious well-founded relation is the 'proper suffix' one. From the specification of append and the directionality analysis, it is only known that before the selection of the recursive literal, L is the concatenation of the list First_seq and T, all three being ground. However, one cannot prove that First_seq is not empty. The list T can be the same list as L and T is therefore not necessarily smaller than L. A solution could be to add a literal which is logically redundant with the compress logic description. It could restrict First_seq to non-empty lists. Let us add the literal

First_seq = [H | Tail_FS]

before the second literal of the last clause. This literal is logically redundant because Lg > 0 and sequence(C, Lg, First_seq) implies First_seq not empty. With this literal, T is still ground before the selection of the recursive literal, but T is now a proper suffix of L. The resulting procedure is given in Procedure 9.6.

Generally speaking, if the induction parameter chosen during the logic description construction is not ground, termination is not necessarily achieved. An independent proof has to be made. Extra literals must sometimes be added in order to force termination. Such literals have to be logically redundant in the logic description. However, when the induction parameter is ground, termination is almost immediately proven. This reduces to the verification that it is ground when the recursive literal is selected.

```
compress_g_v( L, CL ) ← CL = [], L = []
compress_g_v( L, CL ) ← CL = [C, Lg | Tail_CL],
                        First_seq = [H | Tail_FS],
                        append( First_seq, T, L ),
                        sequence( C, Lg, First_seq ),
                        compress_v_g( T, Tail_CL )
                        not( r( C, Tail_CL ) )
r( C, L ) ← L = [C | Y]
```

Procedure 9.6   compress_g_v(L, CL)

This example illustrates another interesting aspect of logic program development. The above compress_g_v procedure (with the termination literal) is not efficient at all for its directionality. Let n be the length of the ground list L, and $f(n)$ the maximum number of computed answer substitutions for all the append literals selected in the SLDNF-tree of compress.

$$f(0) = 0$$

$$f(n) = n + \sum_{0 \le i < n} f(i) \quad (n > 1)$$

The append literal of the second clause can give n computed answer substitutions, hence the second equation. The closed form of these equations is:

$$f(n) = 2^n - 1$$

Since the induction parameter CL of the logic description is not ground, CL is guessed and then verified rather than constructed or verified deterministically.

Generally speaking, let X be the induction parameter of a logic description. When X is ground in the *in* part of the directionality, the derived logic procedure is usually more efficient than (and certainly as efficient as) a logic procedure derived from a logic description constructed with another induction parameter.

The arguments developed above (termination proof and efficiency) support the directionality heuristic for choosing an induction parameter when constructing a logic description.

9.7.2   Infinite sequence of answer substitutions

For an infinite sequence of answer substitutions, termination is meaningless since the SLDNF-tree has to be infinite. However, in order to obtain completeness, each computed answer substitution has to be reached eventually. It can easily be seen that in this case, one and only one literal has to yield an infinite SLDNF-tree. If two subproblems (in the same program clause) yield infinite SLDNF-trees, the search will never resume in the first one, according to Prolog's search strategy. If these subproblems are in two different program clauses, the second SLDNF-tree will never be reached. If there is a unique literal with an infinite SLDNF-tree which is not in the last program clause of the procedure, the SLDNF-trees associated with the following program clauses will never be searched. In this case, completeness is achieved only if these SLDNF-trees are finitely failed.

When the sequence of answer substitutions can be infinite, a sufficient criterion for completeness is the following: *one literal at most can induce an infinite SLDNF-tree, and this literal is in the last clause.* In order to achieve this criterion, sometimes one has to permute program clauses and literals but if problems are detected, such as infinite SLDNF-trees for more than one literal, permuting literals may suppress some of these infinite SLDNF-trees. However, a practical solution is to redesign the logic description. One could also modify Prolog's search rule for this specific procedure in order to search all the infinite SLDNF-trees. This is theoretically possible since the number of nodes in an infinite SLDNF-tree is enumerable. This amounts to programming a breadth-first search.

EXERCISES_____

9.28 Consider the following versions of the procedure derived from Logic Description 5.21.

(i) append3(L1, L2, L3, LApp) ← append(L1, L2, L1_2),
                              append(L1_2, L3, LApp)

(ii) append3(L1, L2, L3, LApp) ← append(L1_2, L3, LApp),
                              append(L1, L2, L1_2)

Assume the following directionality and multiplicity for append

in(ground, ground, any) : out(ground, ground, ground)   ⟨0–1⟩
in(any, any, ground) : out(ground, ground, ground)   ⟨0–*⟩
in(any, any, any) : out(any, any, any)   ⟨0–∞⟩

Analyse the SLDNF-trees of append3 version (i) and (ii) for the directionality

in(ground, ground, ground, any) : out(ground, ground, ground, ground)   ⟨0–1⟩

Try to solve the possible problems.

9.29 This is the same exercise as Exercise 9.28, but for the directionality

in(any, any, any, ground) : out(ground, ground, ground, ground)   ⟨0–*⟩

9.30 This is the same exercise as Exercise 9.28, but for the directionality

in(var, var, ground, var) : out(any, any, ground, any)   ⟨∞–∞⟩

Note the importance of the finite coverage requirement in the correctness definition (of append(L1, L2, L1_2) in version (ii)).

9.31 Take the result of Exercise 9.20 (between(Inf, Sup, I)) and analyse the SLDNF-tree for the two given directionalities of between. Specify first the associated multiplicity as well as the multiplicity to associate with the directionality of less_eq.

_____

9.8   Minimality and multiplicity

The first criterion of minimality (domain compatibility) has been analysed in Section 9.6. Two criteria still have to be checked. First, a solution cannot be covered by more than one computed answer substitution (no redundancy). Second, if the solutions can be covered by a finite sequence of answer substitutions, then the sequence of computed answer substitutions must be finite. In order to achieve correctness, a logic procedure also has to satisfy the specified multiplicity (attached to each specified directionality).

Multiplicity verification

A multiplicity attached to a directionality can be not respected in two ways. First, the minimum number of computed answer substitutions may be less than *Min*. In this case, the *Min* value has to be changed in the specification (assuming all the other correctness criteria are fulfilled). Second, the maximum number of computed answer substitutions may be greater than *Max*. Here, either the *Max* part should be modified, or the logic procedure itself. It depends on whether it is theoretically possible to cover all the solutions with a sequence of answer substitutions of length *lg* with $lg \leq Max$. For instance, when the solutions cannot be covered by a finite sequence of answer substitutions, then *Max* must be infinite. This aspect is related to the finite coverage criterion of minimality. Note finally that a modification of the specified multiplicity could influence the analyses made in the previous section.

Redundancy

Redundancy could be produced by different clauses or within the same clause. However, redundancy within the same clause is impossible. This would imply redundant computed answer substitution for its literals, which is impossible if the subproblems are correct (Property 8.3).

Redundancy from different clauses is not impossible. At the logic description level, a ground instance of the parameters can be deduced from different parts of the logic description. For recursive descriptions, this case usually occurs when all the chosen structural forms of the induction parameter are not mutually exclusive. Non-redundancy can be proven by using either the declarative semantics or the procedural one. Let B1 and B2 be the bodies of two program clauses of a procedure LP(p(x)), and **t** be a ground *n*-tuple respecting the preconditions of p. Using the declarative semantics, it should be shown that B1$\{x/t\}$ implies ¬B2$\{x/t\}$. Using the procedural semantics, it should be shown that the goal ← (B1,B2)$\{x/t\}$ finitely fails.

If redundancy is detected, one has to add literals in the non-mutually exclusive clauses to make them mutually exclusive, but without destroying the other correctness criteria (completeness in particular).

Minimal coverage

Minimal coverage can be verified as follows. First determine all the patterns of the parameters where a finite sequence of answer substitutions covering all the solutions exists. Then if completeness is already achieved, verify that termination occurs for each of these patterns. When the multiplicity parts of the directionalities are correct, the determination of such patterns reduces to the patterns respecting the *in* part of directionalities whose attached multiplicity has an infinite upper bound.

The determination of patterns with solutions covered by finite sequences of answer substitutions can be made separately for each specified directionality. A possible way is to construct a set of test data for the parameters, representing all their possible forms and values (not only *ground*, *var* or *ngv*, but also the different possible values of *ground* and *ngv* parameters). Since all the possible cases are usually infinite, one has to detect classes within this set of possible values, and pick a witness from each class. This is a well-known technique in software engineering for testing programs (see for example, Howden and Miller (1978)). Finally, it just has to be determined which of these test data have solutions covered by a finite sequence of answer substitutions.

This analysis is illustrated on the append example (see Procedure 9.7) for the directionality

in(var, ground, var) : out(novar, ground, novar)   ⟨∞−∞⟩

append(L1, L2, LApp) ← L1 = [], LApp = L2
append(L1, L2, LApp) ← L1 = [H|T],
                          LApp = [H|TApp], append(T, L2, TApp)

Procedure 9.7   append(L1, L2, LApp)

The only possible form for L1 and LApp is var. For L2, ground values have to be considered. Let us take

(1)   L2 = []
(2)   L2 = [a]
(3)   L2 = [a, b, c, d]

These three cases are representative of the possible forms of a ground list. Since the procedure does not analyse the form of the elements of the lists, the values of the elements of the list in the test data are not important.

For (2) and (3), the solutions cannot be covered by a finite sequence of answer substitutions. However, if L2 has the first form, all the solutions are covered by the substitution

{L1 / LApp}

But the sequence of answer substitutions for such a goal is infinite with Procedure 9.7. Minimality is therefore not achieved. A solution could be to add a new clause for this particular case.

append(L1, L2, LApp) ← L2 = [], LApp = L1

But now, redundancy appears. The simplest way to suppress this redundancy is to make the program clauses mutually exclusive by adding the literal L2 = [H2|T2] in the other program clauses. The resulting procedure is given in Procedure 9.8.

> append(L1, L2, LApp) ← L2 = [], LApp = L1
> append(L1, L2, LApp) ← L2 = [H2|T2], L1 = [], LApp = L1
> append(L1, L2, LApp) ← L2 = [H2|T2], L1 = [H|T],
>   LApp = [H|TApp], append(T, L2, TApp)

Procedure 9.8   append(L1, L2, LApp)

9.9   Side-effects

Two different families of procedures with side-effects will now be considered. In the first one, the relation determined by the procedure is the central part of the specification. Side-effects are added to this relation. A classical example is a logic procedure which prints some of its results. The second family covers procedures whose specifications are basically a description of side-effects. Typical examples are input/output procedures.

Before considering procedures with side-effects, one also has to consider procedures without side-effects. Two things must be verified. First, none of the procedures used as subproblems can have side-effects otherwise the procedure itself would have side-effects. Second, the environment conditions must be satisfied before the selection of the literals. This second aspect also holds for procedures with side-effects.

For procedures of the first family, the side-effects issue is just one aspect of their correctness and therefore, the proposed methodological framework can be applied. The resulting logic procedures then have to be modified in order to achieve the desired side-effects. Side-effects can be performed via procedures which are already in the logic procedure. If this is not the case, extra literals should be added in order to perform the desired side-effects. This must be done with perfect knowledge of the computation rule and search strategy.

For procedures of the second family, the overall methodology is not always applicable and the concept of logic description can be meaningless to them. Prolog programs must then be directly constructed, regardless of any logic aspect. Here, Prolog is used as a language to perform sequential actions. The computation rule and search strategy is thus essential.

A major difficulty for Prolog procedures with side-effects is backtracking. Without side-effects, a procedure can backtrack in a first clause and finally succeed in another one. But usually the backtracking in side-effects procedures cannot undo the side-effects previously obtained and therefore, without special care, unexpected side-effects can occur.

　We will now illustrate that the intermediate level of logic description can sometimes be useful for problems with side-effects. Suppose we want to print all the solutions of a given procedure p(X). The specification of the procedure called print_all_p is given in Specification 9.1. It has no parameters, the relation part is empty, meaning that it is always true. Its multiplicity describes that it always succeeds once.

> procedure　print_all_p
>
> *Relation*:　true.
>
> *Application conditions*:
> in( ) : out( ) ⟨1–1⟩
>
> *Side-effects*:
> All the solutions of p(X) are printed on the Current Output Stream.
>
> **Specification 9.1**　print_all_p

Even with this trivial relational aspect, it is still possible to construct some logic description. The definition part of Logic Description 9.1 is always true, but reflects the intuitive idea of the solution of the problem. Here the subproblem print(X) is supposed to be always true.

> print_all_p ⇔ ∀X(p(X) ⇒ print(X))
>
> **Logic Description 9.1**　print_all_p

The derivation of a logic procedure yields Procedure 9.9, which is perfectly correct. The procedure print(X) could be replaced by some more eleborate pretty-printing procedure.

> print_all_p ← not(r)
> r ← p(X), not(print(X))
>
> **Procedure 9.9**　print_all_p

The above construction prevents the programming tricks often referred to as 'failure driven loops', yielding Procedure 9.10 as a solution of the above problem.

> print_all_p ← p(X), print(X), fail
> print_all_p ←
>
> **Procedure 9.10**　print_all_p

9.10　Occur check

For reasons of efficiency, most Prolog implementations use a unification algorithm without occur check but this can lead to unsoundness (see

Section 1.2.4). The built-in procedure LP(=) is thus incorrect in such cases. For instance, the goal

    ← append([1], L, L)

will succeed for the classical append procedure (Procedure 9.7). This append procedure is thus not correct with respect to its specification. There are basically two solutions to this problem. First, one could add preconditions to the specification of append so that such goals are not permitted. This solution is not very elegant since it complicates specifications. A second solution consists of statically detecting the unifications that could make trouble and adding an explicit occur check test after these unifications (loopfree, say), or replacing the literal t1=t2 by unify(t1, t2), where unify is a procedure implementing the unification with occur check. Some Prolog implementations offer unify as an alternative built-in to LP(=) without occur check. This second solution is certainly more appropriate than adding preconditions.

The detection of unifications that could raise problems can certainly be achieved within the framework of abstract interpretation. This analysis is much simplified by the fact that at this level, only *pure* logic procedures are considered (that is, different variables in the head of the program clauses). Occur check problems can then only arise for literals of the form t1 = t2. From the forms of t1 and t2 before the selection of this literal, it is possible to state necessary conditions such that the occur check is useful. For t1 *var*, t2 *ngv*; t1 *ngv*, t2 *ngv*; and t1 *ngv*, t2 *var*, the occur check can be necessary. For all the other basic cases, the occur check is useless. This could be further refined by noting that the occur check is also useless when t1 contains only distinct variables not occurring in t2 (or conversely) and not occurring in the preceding literals nor in the head of the considered program clause. Type information could also be taken into account to refine this analysis.

For the append procedure (Procedure 9.7), the above analysis detects that two unifications could raise problems for the directionality

    in(var, any, any) : out(novar, any, any)

In Procedure 9.11 the literals involved have been replaced by a unification with occur check.

    append(L1, L2, LApp) ← L1 = [], unify(LApp, L2)
    append(L1, L2, LApp) ← L1 = [H | T], unify(LApp, [H | TApp]),
                append(T, L2, TApp)

Procedure 9.11   append(L1, L2, LApp)

EXERCISE

9.32 Find examples showing that Procedure 9.7 is incorrect for the directionality in(var, any, any), assuming that LP(=) does not make the occur check. Show that the two unify literals in Procedure 9.11 are necessary for this directionality.

*9.11   Background

Syntactical translation

The syntactical translation of a pure logic program from a logic description is an adaptation of transformation rules presented in Lloyd and Topor (1984) and Lloyd (1987), where these rules are used for transforming extended goals and extended programs (that is, where the body of the clause is an arbitrary formula) into goals and programs.

The translation rules are specially designed to reduce the number of negative literals in the transformation process. The most interesting rules are the ones which transform universally quantified formulae using a double negation technique (rules (i) and (l) in Section 9.2.1). This particular technique is also described in examples in Clark (1978) and Kowalski (1979, 1985). A similar double transformation technique is presented by Sato and Tamaki (1984b). Finally, these two transformation rules are built-ins in MU-Prolog. for the inequality primitive (Naish, 1985b, 1986).

Negation and constraint logic programming

The necessity of a safe computation rule for the soundness property has already been underlined. But what can be done if safety cannot be achieved? A first solution deals with finite domains. Let us suppose that X has a type whose domain is $\{e_1, \ldots, e_n\}$ in the goal $\leftarrow$ not(p(X, a)). If one of the SLDNF-trees for the goals $\leftarrow$ p(e_i, a) ($1 \le i \le n$) is finitely failed, then $\leftarrow$ not(p(X, a)) should succeed since ($\exists X$)$\neg$p(X, a) is true. If every SLDNF-tree has a success branch, then $\leftarrow$ not(p(X, a)) should fail since ($\forall X$)p(X, a) is true. This extension is not supported in standard Prolog, but could be used when constructing the logic procedure not_p(X, Y) as described in Section 9.5.

A different approach to the negation problem is taken in Prolog II where inequality is built-in (Colmerauer, 1984). The unification process is extended to systems of equations and inequations. The inequation literals do not need to be ground to be selected (that is, safety is not required). They form constraints to be respected by the computation. The specification of t1 $\ne$ t2 (actually denoted by diff(t1, t2)) is that the terms t1 and t2 will always represent two different trees (the trees are the terms in Prolog II) (Giannesini *et al.*, 1986). The forthcoming Prolog III will support more elaborated constraints (Colmerauer, 1987, 1989).

The combination of the constraint concept and finite domain in the context of logic programming is investigated by Van Hentenryck and Dincbas (1986, 1987) and Van Hentenryck (1989). The proposed extensions of Prolog are shown to lead to substantial improvements of efficiency for constraint satisfaction problems. These extensions are implemented in CHIP, a constraint logic programming language (Dincbas *et al.*, 1988). Constraint logic programming is also investigated by Jaffar and Lassez (1987), Jaffar and Michaylov (1987) and Lassez (1987).

Program analysis

Discussions on completeness and termination in Prolog are presented by Elcock (1983) and Vasak and Potter (1985). The solution proposed consists of adding control annotations written in first-order logic. These annotations are used to generate runtime environments within which it is possible to exclude infinite computations. This is further developed in Vasak's thesis (Vasak, 1986) where UNSW-Prolog is described. A theoretical characterization of termination for logic programs is also developed by Vasak and Potter (1986). The set of terminating queries can be constructed in a bottom-up manner. Means are given for representing such termination sets. A method for proving termination properties is presented by Baudinet (1988). Reasoning is carried out on functional equations associated with the program. A discussion on types is presented by Naish (1987), where the concept of a 'type correct program' is defined. Types are also discussed by Horiuchi and Kanamori (1987).

The theory of abstract interpretation has been introduced by Cousot and Cousot (1977). The reader is referred to Hecht (1977) and Abramski and Hankin (1987) for more development and further references on flow analysis and abstract interpretation of computer programs. The framework of abstract interpretation has been applied in logic programming for analysing programs (Mellish, 1986, 1987), (Bruynooghe *et al.*, 1987), (Mannila and Ukkonen, 1987), (Jones and Sondergaard, 1987), (Bruynooghe and Janssens, 1988), (Warren and Debray, 1988), (Waem, 1988) and (Marriott and Sondergaard, 1988). Analysis and generation of modes (that is directionalities) are described by Mellish (1981, 1986, 1987), Reddy (1984), and Debray and Warren (1986b). Bellia *et al.* (1983) also proposed a dataflow analysis in the form of a dependency graph for annotated clauses.

Abstract interpretation has also been used for occur check detection (Sondergaard, 1986). The occur check problem is investigated by Plaisted (1984). A preprocessor is presented for identifying which program clauses may cause problems because of the lack of occur check. Checking literals are then added in these program clauses. Deransart and Maluszynski (1985) related logic programs and attribute grammars. This result allows the definition of a class of logic programs which can be executed without occur check. This investigation is further developed by Maluszynski and Komorowski (1985). In Prolog II, the lack of occur check is an essential feature for the language. For example, the execution of X = f(X) results in a tree with root f and with itself as subtree (these trees are called rational trees). A logical reconstruction of Prolog II has been proposed by Van Emden and Lloyd (1984).

Our example print_all_p is taken from Bundy (1988) where logical extensions of Horn clauses are investigated. Such extensions are also investigated by Warren (1981).

SUMMARY

- The derivation of a correct logic procedure from a correct logic description is carried out in two steps: a syntactical translation and the verification of certain criteria.

- Given a correct logic description, a straightforward syntactical translation yields a logic procedure satisfying the two major criteria of partial correctness and completeness.

- The remaining correctness criteria are fulfilled by:
    - rearranging the literals in the program clauses,
    - rearranging the program clauses,
    - adding certain literals (usually to perform the side-effects).

- The choice of a permutation of the literals and the clauses results from an analysis of directionalities, types and SLDNF-trees.

- When the induction parameter has the directionality *ground*, the derivation process is greatly simplified:
    - type problems are mostly non-existent,
    - termination proofs are immediate,
    - the derived logic procedure is more efficient than if derived from a logic description constructed with a non-ground induction parameter.

- Multidirectionality is usually difficult to achieve.

10

Transformation
of logic programs

PREVIEW   In Chapter 9, we were not concerned about the efficiency of the logic procedures. Even though a first level of optimization was achieved by the transformation of logic descriptions, most of the logic procedures derived did not resemble the procedures a Prolog programmer would write. In particular, the heads of the derived program clauses were not instantiated (that is, we obtained pure logic procedures) and their bodies did not contain cuts. But now that correct pure logic procedures have been derived, optimization can take place. Let us restate the maxim 'It is easier to optimize a correct program than to correct an optimized program'. Optimization is carried out by means of transformations based on the operational semantics of Prolog, and a suitable introduction of control. Such optimized procedures are far more difficult to understand because the logical aspects are destroyed but this is not a problem because the resulting procedures are obtained by systematic (and automatic) transformations. It is therefore sufficient to understand the initial pure logic procedure. The non-optimized correct version can of course also be executed if certain tests or debugging need to be performed. The usefulness of such optimizations could be doubted and it could be argued that the gain would be insignificant compared with the progress of the technology. We believe, however, that if the optimization techniques can be automated and included in a logic programming environment in a way that is transparent to the user, then these optimizations will be worthwhile.

   In all subsequent transformation rules, it will be supposed that the initial logic procedures are correct w.r.t. their specifications (given the Prolog refutation procedure). The transformation rules are intended to preserve the correctness of the logic procedures. The conditions given for applying the transformation rules are sufficient but not always necessary. These conditions were chosen for their simplicity. The concepts of efficiency and complexity are introduced first (Section 10.1). Then the transformation rules are presented (Section 10.2). An

273

efficiency comparison is made in Section 10.3 and Section 10.4 analyses transformation strategies.

The transformations presented in this chapter are independent of the methodological framework. They can thus be applied successfully to any Prolog program. The only assumption is that, initially, the program under transformation contains pure program clauses. This can easily be obtained by replacing unification within the head by equalities at the beginning of the body. After transformation, the resulting program will be more efficient than the initial one.

10.1   Complexity

The concept of efficiency is closely related to the concept of complexity and complexity can be dealt with at either the logic description or the logic program level. Efficiency and complexity were not introduced at the logic description level since this level only handles the declarative semantics without any procedural concerns. It is however possible to discuss the complexity aspects of logic descriptions thanks to the following property.

Property 10.1
Let

- S be a set of logic descriptions
- P be a syntactical derivation of S
- G be a goal (containing only predicates appearing in S).

The number of success branches as well as the length of these success branches are identical in every SLDNF-tree for $P \cup \{G\}$ via R, where R is a safe computation rule for $P \cup \{G\}$.

Proof
From Lloyd (1987), Theorem 10.3, by noting that in the switching lemma (Lemma 9.1), the length of the derivation does not change. This result also has to be extended to include the selection of ground negative literals. ■

Property 10.1 can be seen as expressing a complexity property of logic description itself. Such a complexity measure will be illustrated on the reverse problem (Specification 4.1). Procedure 10.1 is a syntactical translation of Logic Description 4.1 to which the procedure append has been added for the purpose of the analysis. Procedure 10.2 is a syntactical translation of the logic description obtained by transforming LD (reverse) or by generalizing it (Specification 6.1). Both procedures are correct for the directionality

in(ground, var) : out(ground, ground)

using Prolog's refutation procedure. There is thus a unique success branch for a goal of the form ← reverse($[e_1, \ldots, e_n]$, LRev) where the e_i are ground terms. Using Property 10.1, the length of the success branch of these two procedures is independent of the computation rule. This measure can thus be seen as a complexity measure of the corresponding logic descriptions. The following complexity analysis is based on Mignon (1988).

reverse(L, LRev) ← L = [], LRev = []
reverse(L, LRev) ← L = [H|T], reverse(T, TRev),
                                    append(TRev, [H], LRev)
append(L1, L2, LApp) ← L1 = [], LApp = L2
append(L1, L2, LApp) ← L1 = [H|T], LApp = [H|TApp],
                                    append(T, L2, TApp)

Procedure 10.1   reverse(L, LRev)

reverse(L, LRev) ← reverse_desc(L, LRev, [])
reverse_desc(L, LRev, LInt) ← L = [ ], LRev = LInt
reverse_desc(L, LRev, LInt) ← L = [H | T], Y = [H | LInt],
                                    reverse_desc(T, LRev, Y)

Procedure 10.2   reverse_desc(L, LRev, LInt)

Let us first determine the complexity of append for a goal of the form ←append($[e_1, \ldots, e_n]$, [f], TApp) where e_i and f are ground terms. Cpl–app(n) will denote the length of the unique success branch (that is, the number of nodes) for the above goal (n is thus the length of the first list).

Cpl–app(0) = 4
Cpl–app(i) = 3 + Cpl–app($i - 1$)   (for $i > 0$)

Hence Cpl-app(n) is linear (that is, O(n) in the usual complexity notation).

The complexity of reverse via append can now be expressed using Cpl–app. Cpl–rev–1(n) will denote the length of the unique success branch for a goal of the form ← reverse($[e_1, \ldots, e_n]$, LRev) where the e_i are ground terms.

Cpl–rev–1(0) = 3
Cpl–rev–1(i) = 2 + Cpl–rev–1($i - 1$) + Cpl–app($i - 1$)   (for $i > 0$)

Hence Cpl–rev–1(n) is quadratic (that is, O(n^2)).

For reverse via reverse_desc, Cpl–rev–desc(n) will denote the length of the unique success branch for a goal of the form ← reverse _desc($[e_1, \ldots, e_n]$, LRev, $[f_1, \ldots, f_m]$). Cpl–rev–2 will denote the length of the unique success branch for a goal of form ← reverse($[e_1, \ldots, e_n]$, LRev) where the e_i are ground terms.

Cpl–rev–2(n) = Cpl–rev–desc(n)
Cpl–rev–desc(0) = 4
Cpl–rev–desc(i) = 3 + Cpl–rev–desc($i-1$)   (for $i > 0$)

Hence Cpl–rev–2(n) is linear (that is, O(n)).

The complexities Cpl–rev–1(n) and Cpl–rev–2(n) can be seen as a characterization of the complexities of the corresponding logic descriptions. This example illustrates the efficiency increase obtained by transforming logic descriptions or by generalizing a problem.

Measuring the length of the success branches is not a very precise characterization of the efficiency of a procedure (see Exercise 10.1). The number of visited nodes and the time complexity or the space complexity should also be considered. If the choice of a computation rule does not influence either the number or the length of the success branches, it does influence the size of the SLDNF-trees. Since Prolog's computation rule is fixed, the choice of a permutation of the literals within the program clauses influences the SLDNF-trees. The number of nodes visited depends not only on the computation rule, but also on the search strategy. Since Prolog's search rule is fixed, the choice of a permutation of the program clauses of a procedure influences the number of nodes visited. The number of nodes visited can also be modified by the introduction of control information. The following transformation rules are intended to reduce the number of nodes visited (and the space complexity) and thus to increase the efficiency of the procedures.

EXERCISE

10.1   Consider the two following informal descriptions of the classical sort(L, LS) procedures:

Naïve sort   Guess a permutation of L and test whether this permutation is a sorted list.

Insertion sort   Sort the tail of L and insert the head of L in the right place.

Show that in both procedures, the length of the success branch for a goal ← sort([e₁, . . . , eₙ], LS) is quadratic with respect to *n*. What about the number of nodes visited using Prolog's refutation procedure?

10.2   Transformation rules

Transformations fall into different classes, depending on their foundations. Transformation rules can also be divided into two categories. Rules of the first category transform whole logic procedures into logic procedures. Rules of the second category transform one program clause into another, independent of the other program clauses of the procedure. The category of each transformation rule will be explicitly specified (procedure or clause), as will whether the transformation only applies to pure procedures or pure program clauses.

10.2.1   Definitions

The following definitions characterize literals in terms of the length of their sequence of answer substitutions.

> **Definition 10.1**
> A literal $p(t_1, \ldots, t_n)$ is **deterministic** iff the sequence of answer substitutions for this literal has *at most one* computed answer substitution.
>
> A literal $p(t_1, \ldots, t_n)$ is **fully deterministic** iff the sequence of answer substitutions for this literal has *one and only one* answer substitution.
>
> A literal $p(t_1, \ldots, t_n)$ is **infinite** iff the sequence of answer substitutions for this literal is infinite.
>
> A literal $p(t_1, \ldots, t_n)$ is **incompatible** with the literal $q(s_1, \ldots, s_m)$ iff the sequence of answer substitutions for $q(s_1, \ldots, s_m)$ is empty when the sequence of answer substitutions for $p(t_1, \ldots, t_n)$ is not empty.

In order to be precise, the above definitions should be relative to some program P. This is, however, not necessary in this context because such characteristics of literals are usually determined from the specifications of their procedures. For instance, the multiplicity part of a specification can be used to detect (fully) deterministic and infinite literals. The incompatibility relation is symmetric. It can therefore be said that $p(t_1, \ldots, t_n)$ and $q(s_1, \ldots, s_m)$ are incompatible. For example,

L = [] and L = [H | T] are incompatible when L is ground but not neces-
sarily when L is not ground. In what follows, a cut will be considered as a
literal which is of course fully deterministic. These definitions can be
generalized for sequences of literals. A sufficient condition for a sequence
of literals to be (fully) deterministic is that all the literals are (fully)
deterministic.

The symbols P, Q and C will be used to denote positive literals and
the boldface letters **S** and **T** to denote sequences of literals. In a
transformation schema, the transformed version of a Prolog program
clause or procedure will be separated from the initial version by a
horizontal line, as in

$$\frac{P \leftarrow S}{P \leftarrow S'}$$

As usual, **x** and **y** will denote n-tuples of variables, and **s** and **t** will denote
n-tuples of terms.

EXERCISES

10.2 For which directionalities is the literal t1 = t2 (a) deterministic
and (b) fully deterministic? (t1 and t2 are terms.)

10.3 For what forms of the variables are the literals L = [] and L = [H | T]
incompatible?

10.2.2   Transformations based on equivalent SLDNF-trees

The first transformation (10.1) is based on the assumption that two
identical sequences of literals exist in two different program clauses of a
procedure. In this case, any SLDNF-tree of this procedure will contain
two equivalent subtrees. This can be avoided by using the following
transformation.

Transformation 10.1   (Pure procedure)

$$\frac{\begin{array}{l} p(\,x\,) \leftarrow T, S_1 \\ p(\,x\,) \leftarrow T, S_2 \end{array}}{\begin{array}{l} p(\,x\,) \leftarrow T, p1(\,y\,) \\ p1(\,y\,) \leftarrow S_1 \\ p1(\,y\,) \leftarrow S_2 \end{array}}$$

where

- **y** is the *n*-tuple of all the variables occurring in S_1 and S_2,
- p has no side-effects,
- T, S_1, S_2 contain no cuts, and
- p is not infinite.

This transformation modifies the order of answer substitutions. If p were infinite, completeness could be lost (for instance, when S_2 is infinite but S_1 is neither deterministic nor infinite). The third condition ensures that no answer substitution will be added or suppressed by the transformation.

The second transformation (10.2) is based on the negation as failure inference rule. Given a ground negative literal not(C), negation as failure builds an SLDNF-tree for the goal C. If C occurs in another program clause of the procedure, its SLDNF-tree is redundant because of the one built after the selection of not(C). The suppresssion of one of them would gain efficiency.

Transformation 10.2 (Pure procedure)

$$p(x) \leftarrow C, S_1$$
$$p(x) \leftarrow not(C), S_2$$

$$p(x) \leftarrow C, !, S_1$$
$$p(x) \leftarrow S_2$$

where C has no side-effects.

From the correctness of p and C, C will be ground before its selection (safe computation rule) and is deterministic. For any literal p(t) respecting the preconditions of p, the initial procedure C either succeeds or fails. If it succeeds, then S_1 is executed. By backtracking, C cannot succeed again and not(C) will fail. If C fails initially, then not(C) succeeds and S_2 is executed. By backtracking, not(C) cannot succeed again. The same scenario occurs in the transformed procedure. If C succeeds, then S_1 is executed. Because of the cut, no backtracking occurs in C, and S_2 is not executed. If C fails, then S_2 is executed. The difference between these two procedures is that there is no backtracking through C and the useless execution of not(C) is avoided. However, C cannot have side-effects.

Using a similar argument, the following transformation can also be stated.

Transformation 10.3   (Pure procedure)

$$p(x) \leftarrow not(C), S_1$$
$$p(x) \leftarrow C, S_2$$

$$\overline{}$$

$$p(x) \leftarrow not(C), !, S_1$$
$$p(x) \leftarrow S_2$$

where C has no side-effects.

Transformation 10.2 can also be generalized as follows:

Transformation 10.4   (Pure procedure)

$$p(x) \leftarrow T, C, S_1$$
$$p(x) \leftarrow T, not(C), S_2$$

$$\overline{}$$

$$p(x) \leftarrow T, C, !, S_1$$
$$p(x) \leftarrow T, S_2$$

where

- T and C have no side-effects, and
- T is deterministic.

The justification of this transformation is almost the same as for Transformation 10.2. The difference is that, here, some literals can appear before C. The literals **T** must be deterministic because, otherwise, some of its answer substitutions could satisfy C and others not(C). Moreover, if more than one answer substitution of **T** satisfies C, then the introduction of a cut prevents these alternatives and can destroy completeness.

Let us apply this transformation to the efface procedure (Procedure 9.3) for the directionality

in(ground, ground, var) : out(ground, ground, ground) $\langle 0-1 \rangle$

efface(X, L, LEff) ← L   = [H|T], H = X, LEff = T
efface(X, L, LEff) ← L   = [H|T], not(H = X),
                           LEff = [H|TEff], efface(X, T, TEff)

efface(X, L, LEff) ← L   = [H|T], H = X, !, LEff = T
efface(X, L, LEff) ← L   = [H|T], efface(X, T, TEff), LEff = [H|TEff]

Transformation 10.4 can be applied because L = [H|T] is deterministic. By the correctness of the procedure for this directionality, H = X will be ground. Therefore, if it succeeds, not(H = X) will fail and vice versa.

When applying the transformation rules, the directionality information in the specification can be used to determine whether or not some literal within the procedure is deterministic.

Transformation 10.3 can also be generalized by considering two incompatible literals:

Transformation 10.5 (Pure procedure)

$$p(x) \leftarrow C_1, S_1$$
$$p(x) \leftarrow C_2, S_2$$

$$p(x) \leftarrow C_1, !, S_1$$
$$p(x) \leftarrow C_2, S_2$$

where

- C_1 is deterministic,
- C_1 and C_2 have no side-effects,
- C_1 and C_2 are incompatible.

The correctness of this transformation is based on the following argument. If C_1 succeeds, backtracking through C_1 is useless because this literal is deterministic. Backtracking to the second program clause is also useless because C_2 will fail (incompatibility). If C_1 fails, the execution of the two procedures is identical. The benefit in efficiency here is the non-construction of a finitely failed SLDNF-tree for C_2 when C_1 succeeds.

A classical application is the append procedure (Procedure 9.7).

```
append( L1, L2, LEff ) ← L1 = [], L2 = LEff
append( L1, L2, LEff ) ← L1 = [H|T], append( T, L2, TEff ), LEff = [H|T]

append( L1, L2, LEff ) ← L1 = [], !, L2 = LEff
append( L1, L2, LEff ) ← L1 = [H|T], append( T, L2, TEff ), LEff = [H|T].
```

But the transformation is valid only if the directionality of append specifies that L1 is ground. In this case, L1 = [] and L1 = [H|T] are incompatible. Otherwise, they are not incompatible and completeness is lost.

The above transformation is particularly useful when the logic description is constructed by structural induction. In this case, the C_i determining the structural forms of the induction parameter will often be incompatible when this parameter is ground. Transformation 10.5 also can be extended for a set of incompatible literals, giving:

Transformation 10.6   (Pure procedure)

$$p(x) \leftarrow C_1, S_1$$
$$p(x) \leftarrow C_2, S_2$$
$$\vdots \qquad \vdots$$
$$p(x) \leftarrow C_{n-1}, S_{n-1}$$
$$p(x) \leftarrow C_n, S_n$$

$$p(x) \leftarrow C_1, !, S_1$$
$$p(x) \leftarrow C_2, !, S_2$$
$$\vdots \qquad \vdots$$
$$p(x) \leftarrow C_{n-1}, !, S_{n-1}$$
$$p(x) \leftarrow C_n, S_n$$

where

- C_i are deterministic
- C_i have no side-effects
- C_i are incompatible with C_j ($i \neq j$).

The justification of these tranformations is similar to that of Transformation 10.5. We could also extend for the case in which the C_i are sequences of literals, as the efficiency increase can be worthwhile. When C_i succeeds, the finitely failed SLDNF-trees for $C_{i+1}, \ldots, C_n$ are not constructed.

The last transformation rule of this section is a variant of Transformation 10.6, in which C_n is the conjunction of the negations of the C_i.

Transformation 10.7   (Pure procedure)

$$p(x) \leftarrow C_1, S_1$$
$$p(x) \leftarrow C_2, S_2$$
$$\vdots \qquad \vdots$$
$$p(x) \leftarrow C_{n-1}, S_{n-1}$$
$$p(x) \leftarrow \text{not}(C_1), \text{not}(C_2), \ldots, \text{not}(C_{n-1}), S_n$$

$$p(x) \leftarrow C_1, !, S_1$$
$$p(x) \leftarrow C_2, !, S_2$$
$$\vdots \qquad \vdots$$
$$p(x) \leftarrow C_{n-1}, !, S_{n-1}$$
$$p(x) \leftarrow S_n$$

where

- C_i have no side-effects
- C_i are incompatible with C_j ($i \neq j$).

It is not necessary to require the C_i to be deterministic because this property is derived from the correctness of p and the C_i (see Exercise 10.4). All the C_i appear negatively in the last program clause and the computation rule is safe. Therefore, because the C_i are correct, they must be deterministic. We also have that every C_i is incompatible with the conjunction of negations of the last program clause. Transformation 10.6 can then be applied. But here, the conjunction of the negative literals can be removed because it will only be executed when $C_1, C_2, \ldots, C_{n-1}$ fail and it will therefore succeed (with an empty substitution).

The increase in efficiency is twofold. If C_i succeeds, none of the finitely failed SLDNF-trees for $C_{i+1}, \ldots, C_n$ will be constructed. When all the C_i fail, none of these finitely failed SLDNF-trees will be reconstructed in the last program clause.

EXERCISE

10.4 In Transformation 10.7, why are the literals C_i not required to be deterministic?

10.2.3 Transformations based on computation and search rules

In this family, a distinction is made between three possible transformations. The first reorders the program clauses, the second reorders the literals in a program clause and the third avoids useless backtracking in deterministic procedures. All of them try to minimize the size of the SLDNF-trees or the search in such trees, given the computation and search rules of Prolog.

A logic procedure can be correct for various permutations of its program clauses. It is therefore worth trying to put them in an 'efficient order'. One possibility is to order the program clauses from the most general to the most specific. By 'more general', is meant program clauses that are more likely than others to give answer substitutions. This statistical measure can be refined by balancing it with a time factor associated with each program clause. Such a complexity measure is difficult to estimate and is very dependent on the actual form of the parameters of the procedure.

A program clause of a logic procedure can be correct for more than one permutation of the literals. Which one should be chosen? Here, one of the few theoretical results concerning the size of SLDNF-trees can be used (Naish, 1985b). This result states that if the subgoals that match only one program clause are put first, then the SLDNF-tree is minimal, provided it is not a finitely failed one. A heuristic could therefore be to order the literals with respect to the number of matching program clauses. If the SLDNF-tree is known to be finitely failed, another heuristic consists of putting the ground literals first because they fail more often than the others. These heuristics have some drawbacks. Given that it is impossible to know *a priori* whether a procedure will fail or succeed, they are conflicting and a compromise is necessary. It is sometimes better to choose a permutation to the literals such that other transformation rules could be applied which would result in a far more efficient procedure.

Finally, useful heuristics can be stated for deterministic procedures. In this case, a permutation of the literals should, if possible, be chosen such that any prefix of the subgoals is also deterministic. This is illustrated for the reverse procedure (Procedure 9.10).

A permutation of the literals of the second program clause could be:

$$\text{reverse(L, LRev)} \leftarrow \text{L} = [\text{H} \,|\, \text{T}], \text{reverse(T, TRev)},$$
$$\text{append (TRev, [H], LRev)}.$$

The directionality in(ground, var) : out(ground, ground) makes the procedure deterministic, as is every prefix of the body of the program clauses. But the second permutation:

$$\text{reverse(L, LRev)} \leftarrow \text{L} = [\text{H} \,|\, \text{T}], \text{append(TRev, [H], LRev)},$$
$$\text{reverse(T, TRev)}$$

does not fit the above heuristic. It is not efficient at all because append is not deterministic in this case. It will guess the form of TRev which will then be tested by reverse(T, TRev). If it is not a good guess, another one will be made, and so on.

When a literal is deterministic, the search in its SLDNF-tree can be reduced by avoiding backtracking as illustrated in the following two transformation rules.

Transformation 10.8   (Procedure)

$$p(\, s_1 \,) \leftarrow S_1$$
$$\vdots \qquad \vdots$$
$$p(\, s_n \,) \leftarrow S_{n1}, S_{n2}$$
$$\overline{p(\, s_1 \,) \leftarrow S_1}$$
$$\vdots \qquad \vdots$$
$$p(\, s_n \,) \leftarrow S_{n1}, !, S_{n2}$$

where

- S_{n1} has no side-effects, and
- S_{n1} is deterministic.

The correctness of this tranformation is obvious given that the cut is inserted in the last program clause. Here, the part of the search in the SLDNF-tree of S_{nl} after its only computed answer substitution is avoided.

Transformation 10.9   (Clause)

$$\frac{p(\ s\ ) \leftarrow S_1\ !, S_2, S_3}{p(\ s\ ) \leftarrow S_1\ !, S_2,\ !, S_3}$$

where

- S_2 is deterministic, and
- S_2 has no side-effects.

The correctness of this rule comes from the existence of a cut in the program clause. Therefore, the addition of a cut to its right only affects the literals between the two cuts. The efficiency increase is the same as for Transformation 10.8.

10.2.4 Transformations based on partial evaluation

The goal of partial evaluation is to transform programs into more efficient ones. This is usually done at the expense of the generality of the resulting program. Restrictions are introduced by fixing a top level goal with fixed values for some parameters. Partial evaluation consists of opening (that is, unfolding) the literals, evaluating the built-in procedures that can be evaluated, and making other improvements.

Apart from the execution of certain equality literals (which will be studied in the next section), almost none of the built-in procedures can be evaluated. Therefore, in this case, partial evaluation is restricted to the opening of certain literals in the program clauses of a procedure. This is actually very close to the unfold transformation of logic descriptions.

Transformation 10.10   (Procedure)

$$\frac{
\begin{array}{l}
p(\ s_1\ ) \leftarrow S_1 \\
\quad \vdots \qquad \vdots \\
p(\ s_i\ ) \leftarrow S_{i1}, q(\ t_i\ ), S_{i2} \\
\quad \vdots \qquad \vdots \\
p(\ s_n\ ) \leftarrow S_n \\
q(\ t\ ) \leftarrow T
\end{array}
}{
\begin{array}{l}
p(\ s_1\ ) \leftarrow S_1 \\
p(\ s_i\ ) \leftarrow S_{i1}, t = t_i, T, S_{i2} \\
\quad \vdots \qquad \vdots \\
p(\ s_n\ ) \leftarrow S_n \\
q(\ t\ ) \leftarrow T
\end{array}
}$$

where

- there is no common variable between t, T and s_i, t_i, S_{i1}, S_{i2}, and
- T contains no cuts.

The correctness of this transformation is obvious because the unification of $q(t_i)$ and $q(t)$ is equivalent to $t = t_i$. A small increase in efficiency is obtained since no search has to be made to find the procedure LP(q). This transformation transfers the procedure call from run-time computation to 'compile time'. It is however particularly interesting when T principally contains equalities that will be suppressed by means of transformation rules based on equality substitutions (see next section). This transformation rule is not very general, being restricted here to procedures with a single program clause and without cut. More sophisticated rules could handle more general cases but their utility could be doubted. First of all, multiple program clauses require disjunctions to open them. The resulting procedure will contain two different forms of disjunction (in the program clauses and from one program clause to another). Next, the combination of disjunctions and cuts is at least problematic and is often solved by introducing other definitions of the cut (such as the soft cut). Finally, such a transformed program would be far more complex without there being a sharp increase in its efficiency. It is actually possible to obtain a less efficient program because the clause indexing could be lost for the opened literals.

Since the above transformation rule is particularly well-adapted when T is a short sequence of literals with equalities, it can be used for most procedures implementing simple operations on abstract data types. The inverse of partial evaluation, that is folding, is not considered here. Folding is particularly interesting for transforming logic descriptions. At this logic program level, folding could be used to reduce the depth of nesting in recursions.

10.2.5   Transformations based on equality substitutions

The reader may wonder why the heads of program clauses only contain variables (that is, pure program clauses). This is contrary to the habits of a Prolog programmer who tries to instantiate the heads as much as possible. This can be dangerous when building a logic description or logic procedure. Firstly, the correctness of a logic procedure may depend on the order of the subgoals. Instantiating a head amounts to assuming that a procedure is correct when the equality subgoals are put first. This is not always the case as already illustrated in Procedures 1.2 and 1.4 in Chapter 1. Secondly, if the head of a procedure has already been instantiated, most of the preceding transformation rules cannot be applied.

Some transformations that propagate an equality forward in a program clause will be analysed first.

Transformation 10.11 (Clause)

$$p(\,s\,) \leftarrow S_1, Y = t, S_2$$
$$\overline{p(\,s\,) \leftarrow S_1, Y = t, S_2\,\{Y/t\}}$$

This transformation rule is often called **forward substitution**. If $Y = t$ succeeds, then Y is bound by t. Therefore, any occurrence of Y in S_2 can be replaced by t. This is a very procedural argument. From a logical point of view, the transformed procedure is logically equivalent to the initial one, given LD(=). A similar argument could logically support the substitution of any occurrence of Y in S_1 by t (**backward substitution**). But in general, this is procedurally incorrect since it could modify the form of the parameters in S_1 containing Y. The required directionality for sub-problems in S_1 could thus be modified and the resulting program clause become incorrect. Using Transformation 10.11, the transformed version is no more efficient than the initial one but, combined with the two following transformations, the literal $Y = t$ may be suppressed, thus reducing the number of unifications.

The second transformation is a special case of the previous one, when S_1 is empty.

Transformation 10.12 (Clause)

$$p(\,s\,) \leftarrow Y = t, S$$
$$\overline{p(\,s\{Y/t\}\,) \leftarrow Y = t, S\,\{Y/t\}}$$

The difference between this transformation and the previous one is that Y is substituted by t in the body as well as in the head of the program clause. This is perfectly correct from a logical and a procedural point of view. Note that it is the only transformation which further instantiates the head of a program clause. It can thus transform a pure program clause into a non-pure version. Removing the literal is not always possible since the variable Y could occur in t. The suppression of this possibility is dealt with by the next transformation rule.

Transformation 10.13 (Clause)

$$p(\,s\,) \leftarrow S_1, Y = t, S_2$$
$$\overline{p(\,s\,) \leftarrow S_1, S_2}$$

where Y does not occur in s, S_1, S_2 and t.

The procedural explanation of this transformation is as follows. If Y does not occur elsewhere in the program clause, the subgoal Y = t will always succeed provided Y does not occur in t. Moreover, the resulting binding for Y will never be used in the computation. These transformation rules can of course also be applied when we have t = Y instead of Y = t (symmetry of equality).

The three previous tranformations can help to get rid of equality literals at the beginning of the body of a program clause. In order to instantiate the head of a program clause as much as possible, permutations of the literals of this program clause should be chosen which make the clause correct and have as many equality literals as possible at its beginning.

The application of the following transformation rule allows an equality substitution in the head of a program clause when the equality literal comes after a cut.

Transformation 10.14   (Clause)

$$\frac{p(\,s\,) \leftarrow S_1, !, q(\,t\,), S_2}{p(\,s\,) \leftarrow S_1, q(\,t\,), !, S_2}$$

where

- q has no side-effects and
- q(t) is fully deterministic.

Because q(t) is fully deterministic, it will succeed only once. The only difference between these two versions is that in the second one, no (useless) backtracking will occur in q(t). One must therefore impose q to have no side-effects because otherwise side-effects might be brought about during the backtracking in q(t). This transformation is especially useful when q is a fully deterministic unification.

These transformation rules will now be illustrated on the efface procedure (Procedure 9.3), for the directionality

in(ground, ground, var) : out(ground, ground, ground).

efface(X, L, LEff) ← L = [H | T], H = X, !, LEff = T
efface(X, L, LEff) ← L = [H | T], LEff = [H | TEff], efface(X, T, TEff)

By Transformations 10.11, 10.12, 10.13

efface(H, [H | T], LEff) ← !, LEff = T
efface(X, [H | T], [H | TEff]) ← efface(X, T, TEff)

By Transformation 10.14   (LEff = T is fully deterministic because LEff is *var*)

> efface(H, [H | T], LEff) ← LEff = T, !
> efface(X, [H | T], [H | TEff]) ← efface(X, T, TEff)

By Transformations 10.11, 10.12, 10.13

> efface(H, [H | T], T)← !
> efface(X, [H | T], [H | TEff]) ← efface(X, T, TEff)

This procedure is correct for the given directionality. But its correctness depends in particular on the fact that LEff is *var* in the directionality. If it were *any*, Transformation 10.14 would no longer hold and the final procedure would be incorrect as illustrated in Chapter 1. For example, the goal

> ← efface(1, [1, 2, 1], [1, 2])

would succeed while $[1, 2]$ is not the list $[1, 2, 1]$ without the first occurrence of 1!

This example can also illustrate the fact that the order of the literals is important, even for the equality literal. With the following program clause

> test ← efface(1, [1, 2, 1], LEff),LEff = [1, 2]   **(1)**

where the efface procedure is the procedure obtained immediately above by transformation, the goal ← test will fail. But if the literals are permuted, that is

> test ← LEff = [1, 2], efface(1, [1, 2 1], LEff)   **(2)**

the goal ← test will succeed. This is because the permutation of the literals causes the directionality of efface to be no longer satisfied. This example also shows that, in general, backward substitution does not preserve correctness. In (1), the substitution {LEff/[1, 2]} cannot be performed backwards because that would give the program clause

> test ← efface(1, [1, 2, 1], [1, 2])   **(3)**

which like (2), does not respect the directionality of efface.

10.2.6   Transformations based on tail recursion

The increase in efficiency from recursive to tail recursive Prolog procedures is comparable to the increase in efficiency from recursive to iterative Pascal programs. Recursion is known to be space and time consuming because of the management of a stack. In a tail recursive procedure, the recursive literal is the last literal of the last program clause. Therefore a stack is sometimes useless because there is nothing left to do after this recursive literal so that the information put on the stack will never be used. It is only 'sometimes useless' because if the subgoals before the recursive literal have multiple solutions, this information is necessary for the backtracking process. Although this technical explanation is not strictly necessary, it can help in the understanding of the definition of tail recursion and of why tail recursive procedures are more efficient.

> **Definition 10.2**   A logic procedure LP(p) is **tail recursive** iff it has one and only one recursive subgoal and its last program clause has the form
>
> $$p(s) \leftarrow S, p(t)$$
>
> where S is deterministic. When the last program clause of a procedure has this form but the procedure has more than one recursive subgoal, the procedure is said to be **semi-tail recursive**.

The tail recursion definition could be generalized in cases where the recursive program clause is not the last one. The behaviour of a tail recursive procedure can be implemented as an iterative one. From a practical point of view, some Prolog systems are not always able to recognize that S is deterministic. The simplest way to make it recognizable is to apply Transformation 10.8 which will insert a cut after S.

Transformations for obtaining tail recursive procedures when no correct permutation yields tail recursion will not be presented at this logic program level. Such transformations are at the logic description level. Transformations of logic descriptions with definitions give logic descriptions from which a tail recursive procedure can be derived. But it is usually impossible to derive a tail recursive logic procedure from the initial logic description. For example, the procedure derived from the reverse logic description (Logic Description 4.1) cannot be tail recursive. If the recursive literal is put at the end of the last program clause, the preceding subgoal is not deterministic. But the logic procedure derived from its transformed logic description is tail recursive (Procedure 10.2).

10.2.7   Transformations based on Prolog implementation techniques

This section presents some transformations of Prolog procedures based on well-known Prolog implementation techniques. This means that these optimizations are independent of SLDNF-resolution principles. Tail recursion is one of these techniques, but it is independent of logic programming implementation techniques. Two major techniques are considered here: anonymous variables and program clause indexing. The second of these can be useful because the efficiency increase can be tremendous for some logic procedures. Moreover, these optimizations are implemented by almost all Prolog systems.

When a variable appears only once in a program clause, its binding is not important during the computation process and therefore it does not have to be memorized. In most versions of Prolog, there is a special character (usually the symbol _) for such variables, and variables denoted by this character are called **anonymous**. Two anonymous variables in the same program clause are considered as two distinct variables. The Prolog system handles the anonymous variables differently from the other ones. Unification is much simplified when it involves anonymous variables and this yields some increase in efficiency. The following transformation introduces anonymous variables in a program clause.

Transformation 10.15   (Clause)

$$\frac{p(\,s\,) \leftarrow S}{p(\,s\{Y/\_\}\,) \leftarrow S\{Y/\_\}}$$

where Y occurs only once in s or in S (but not in both).

The second implementation technique is the indexing of program clauses. This notion will be explained with the following example.

$$p(\,a, X\,) \leftarrow S_1$$
$$p(\,b, X\,) \leftarrow S_2$$
$$p(\,c, X\,) \leftarrow S_3$$
$$p(\,d, X\,) \leftarrow S_4$$

Without indexing, given the goal $\leftarrow p(\,c, 1\,)$, the Prolog interpreter tries to unify $p(\,c, 1\,)$ and $p(\,a, X\,)$. Because it fails, it then tries to unify $p(\,c, 1\,)$ and $p(\,b, X\,), \ldots$ Finally, it successfully unifies $p(\,c, 1\,)$ and $p(\,c, X\,)$ and executes S_3. With an indexing of the first parameter, the interpreter immediately tries to unify $p(\,c, 1\,)$ and $p(\,c, X\,)$ because the latter is the first program clause which has a constant c as the first parameter of its head. Therefore, provided the indexed parameter in the goal is a constant, the indexing technique will only consider those program clauses which have the same constant (or a variable) in the indexed position of the head. The list of potentially unifiable program clauses is found by a hash-code technique in a time that does not depend on the number of program clauses in the procedure. The increase in efficiency from non-indexed to indexed procedures is comparable to that from sequential access to direct access.

Indexing is particularly interesting when the number of program clauses is important and one of the parameters has different constant values in most of the heads of the program clauses. In fact, indexing is carried out on the principal functor of the parameter so that neither ground nor variable terms can be used as indexed parameters.

Because logic procedures are required to be as efficient as possible, this indexing ability should be used. In some Prolog systems, the indexed parameter can be chosen so that no change of the procedures is required, but it is more common for the indexing to be carried out on the principal functor of the first parameter. Therefore, it is sometimes worth permuting the parameters of a procedure in order to use indexing efficiently. Such a transformation requires a modification of the specification, namely a permutation of the parameters.

10.2.8   Transformations based on global parameters

In Section 5.2, two ways of representing data structures were described: terms and relations. Up to now, only term representation has been used. This section shows how a relational representation of an abstract data type can be achieved while preserving the correctness of a logic program. This representation is suitable when the same data structure is used throughout computation and can therefore be seen as a global data structure.

The problem with a relational representation is that it cannot be modified without modifying the formulae (usually called a theory). Therefore, if a theory has to be changed, meta-level extensions of first-order logic should be explored. A first meta-level expression could be

demo(Theo, Form)

which holds when the formula Form is provable from the first-order theory Theo. Modifications of a theory can be described with

add_to(Theo, Ax, New_Theo)

which holds when New_Theo is the first-order theory obtained by adding the axiom Ax to the theory Theo.

drop_from(Theo, Ax, New _Theo)

holds when Ax is an axiom of the first-order theory Theo and New_Theo is the theory Theo without the axiom Ax.

When a relational representation is chosen for a data structure, it is possible to describe actions performed on this structure, but with a meta-level description instead of a first-order one. Two problems need to be solved. Firstly, how can this meta-level description be represented in Prolog, and secondly how can such a relational representation be mixed with a first-order logic program? The second problem can be solved by transforming the derived logic procedure; as for the first one, the built-in procedures assert and retract of the Prolog language could be used. These two aspects are illustrated with the relational representation and exploitation of an Association-list (see Section 5.2).

Given a correct logic program P which uses the association-list ($\langle c, 15 \rangle$, $\langle f, 2 \rangle$, $\langle a, 8 \rangle$), it should be transformed into a program P′ such that

demo(P, G) iff demo(P′ ∪ Ax_AL, G)

where Ax_AL are the axioms representing the relational description of the given association-list.

This transformation is only possible if P uses only one association-list (this could be overcome by assigning a specific name to each association-list). Consequently, the directionality of every procedure with an association-list as parameter (besides the primitive operations on association-lists) must have the directionality in(ground) : out(ground) for this parameter. This transformation is safe because it does not affect the correctness of P. In the transformation process, a relational representation must be chosen for the association-list. For the above example, Ax_AL will be:

```
assoc_list(c, 15 ) ←
assoc_list(f, 2 ) ←
assoc_list(a, 8 ) ←
```

To transform the program, all parameters of type association-list are suppressed in every program clause. Given that the program only uses one association-list, it can be seen as a global parameter for all the procedures.

Next the primitive operations on the association-list data structure are implemented. These are meta-level procedures because they modify the theory, and they will correspond to the assoc, add_elem and drop_elem procedures (Specifications 5.2 to 5.4). The access to a couple $\langle e, v \rangle$ of the association-list will be achieved by implementing assoc(Ax_L, e,v). A couple $\langle e, v \rangle$ can be added by implementing add_elem (Ax_L, e,v, New_Ax_L). Similarly, a couple $\langle e, v \rangle$ can be subtracted by implementing drop_elem(Ax_L, e,v, New_Ax_L). Given that here the theory is the program itself and that the relational representation is part of it, there is no need for the Ax_L parameter. Prolog procedures implementing the primitive operations assoc, add_elem and drop_elem are given in Procedure 10.3, using the classical Prolog primitives assert and retract.

assoc(Elem, Value) ← assoc_list(Elem, Value)

drop_elem(Elem, Value) ← assoc_list(Elem, Value),
                                      retract(assoc_list(Elem, Value))

add_elem(Elem, Value) ← not(p(Elem)),
                                      assert(assoc_list (Elem, Value))

p(Elem) ← assoc_list(Elem, X)

Procedure 10.3   assoc, drop_elem and add_elem

What is gained with such a transformation? If the association-list is large and does not require too many modifications, but is often consulted, then the efficiency gain can be substantial, especially if indexing is available for the assoc_list relation. It is a direct access based on contents instead of a sequential search access.

What is lost? It is often claimed that the use of assert and retract in logic programming should be avoided because it is dangerous (from a correctness point of view) and can lead to tricky programs. This statement is not incorrect if the words 'logic programming' mean the construction of a correct logic description and procedure from a given specification. In this case, a correct logic procedure has already been built. It is simply tranformed while preserving its correctness. Moreover, the use of assert and retract is carefully restricted and this transformation can be performed at the very end of the optimization process.

Transformations based on global parameters can also successfully be applied to handling files. At the logic description level, a file could be considered as a data structure with primitives (that is, an abstract data type). At the logic program level, transformations based on global parameters could be made to remove such data structures from the program clauses, and transform the operations on this data to file operations.

10.3   Efficiency comparison: an example

The efficiency of various versions of the efface problem (Specification 1.1, Logic Description 5.4) will now be compared. This comparison is intended to show the influence of the directionality on the efficiency of the final logic procedure. Procedures 10.4–10.8 correspond to different directionalities and are intended to be as efficient as possible. These procedures include the various versions presented in Chapter 1.

in(ground, ground, var) : out(ground, ground, ground)
efface_1(H, [H | T], T) ← !
efface_1(X, [H | T], [H | TEff]) ← efface_1(X, T, TEff)

Procedure 10.4   efface_1(X, L, LEff)

```
in( ground, ground, any ) : out( ground, ground, ground )
efface_2( H, [H|T], LEff ) ← !, LEff = T
efface_2( X, [H|T], [H|TEff] ) ← efface_2( X, T, TEff )
```

Procedure 10.5   efface_2(X, L, LEff)


```
in( ground, any, ground ) : out( ground, ground, ground )
efface_3( H, [H|T], T ) ←
efface_3( X, [H|T], [H|TEff] ) ← not( X = H ), efface_3( X, T, TEff )
```

Procedure 10.6   efface_3(X, L, LEff)


```
in( ground, any, ground ) : out( ground, ground, ground )
in( any, ground, any ) : out( ground, ground, ground )
efface_4( H, [H|T], T ) ←
efface_4( X, [H|T], [H|TEff] ) ← efface_4( X, T, TEff ), not( X = H )
```

Procedure 10.7   efface_4(X, L, LEff)


```
in( ground, ground, any ) : out( ground, ground, ground)
efface_0( X, L, LEff] ) ← L = [H|T], X = H, LEff = T
efface_0( X, L, LEff] ) ← L = [H|T], efface_0( X, T, TEff ),
                         not( X = H ), LEff = [H|TEff]
```

Procedure 10.8   efface_0(X, L, LEff)

The same procedure as efface_2 is also obtained if *any* is replaced by *ground* or by *ngv* in its directionality. The same procedure as efface_3 is also obtained if *any* is replaced by *var* or by *ngv* in its directionality. Procedure efface_4 is the most general one. For other directionalities, the negation in the second program clause could not be ground and therefore the computation rule would be not safe. Procedure efface_0 is the untransformed pure logic procedure, which is also correct when *ground* is replaced by *any* for the first parameter.

Table 10.1 shows the relative execution times of these five procedures for certain test data. Each relative execution time corresponds to the search in the whole SLDNF-tree. These measurements were carried out on a VAX-750, with the C-Prolog interpreter, but they are quite independent of the machine and the interpreter.

The results show that the optimization of efface_0 increases its efficiency by up to a factor of 8 (efface_2), and illustrate that Transformation 10.2 (negation replaced by a cut) is very effective (efface_1 and efface_2). The difference between tail recursive and non-tail recursive procedures is mostly seen between efface_3 and efface_4 on their last common test data (relative execution time 3 to 6). Note also that the most

Table 10.1 Efficiency comparison efface(X, L, LEff).

Test data				Relative execution times				
X	L	LEff	Answer	efface_0	efface_1	efface_2	efface_3	efface_4
2	[1, 2, 3, 2, 4]	[1, 3, 2, 4]	Yes	8	–	1	2	2
2	[1, 2, 3, 2, 4]	[1, 2, 3, 4]	No	8	–	1	3	3
2	[1, 2, 3, 2, 4]	LEff	LEff = [1, 3, 2, 4]	8	1	1	–	4
0	[1, 2, 3, 2, 4]	LEff	No	5	2	2	–	2
X	[1, 2, 3, 2, 4]	[1, 3, 2, 4]	X = 2	14	–	–	–	3
X	[1, 2, 3, 2, 4]	[1, 2, 3, 4]	No	14	–	–	–	3
2	L	[1, 3, 2, 4]	L = [2, 1, 3, 2, 4] L = [1, 2, 3, 2, 4] L = [1, 3, 2, 2, 4]	–	–	–	3	6
X	[1, 2, 3, 2, 4]	LEff	X = 1 LEff = [2, 3, 2, 4] X = 2 LEff = [1, 3, 2, 4] X = 3 LEff = [1, 2, 2, 4] X = 4 LEff = [1, 2, 3, 2]	14	–	–	–	10

specific versions (correct for the fewest directionalities) are the most efficient ones (efface_1 and efface_3).

This example demonstrates that the transformation rules presented produce final logic procedures as efficiently as if they had been directly written in Prolog by a good Prolog programmer. It can also be seen that the differences between a pure logic procedure and its transformation may be very important from an efficiency point of view. Finally, we see that the more specific the directionality of a procedure is, the greater its efficiency.

10.4   Choice of a permutation and transformation strategy

Choice of a permutation

In Chapter 9, correct pure Prolog procedures were derived from correct logic descriptions. However, such procedures can be correct for different permutations of the program clauses and of the literals. Now that the concept of efficiency has been introduced, heuristics can be given for choosing between different correct permutations. Such heuristics could be included within the automation of the derivation of logic procedures from logic descriptions in order to find correct permutations leading to efficient procedures. The following criteria are presented in decreasing order of importance and are not exclusive:

(1)   *Choose (semi) tail recursive permutations.*
      Tail recursive permutations should be preferred since the increase in efficiency is very important. When such permutations do not exist for a recursive procedure, the transformation of the corresponding logic description should be investigated.

(2)   *Choose permutations of literals with the longest deterministic prefix.*
      This choice prevents useless computed answer substitutions by prefixes of the literals. Multiple answer substitutions are only generated by the suffix corresponding to this longest deterministic prefix. The efficiency gain can be substantial, but not as much as with (1).

(3)   *Choose permutations such that Transformations 10.1–10.7 can be applied.*
      The gain here is more substantial if the SLDNF-trees involved are large.

(4)   *Choose permutations of the literals such that the equality literals are at the beginning.*
With such permutations, transformations based on equality substitutions can be applied to instantiate the head of the program clause and suppress these equality literals.

Transformation strategy

Rules for logic program transformation were presented separately. In the transformation of a logic procedure, there is often more than one possible sequence of transformations, resulting in different logic procedures. The combination of transformation rules is first guided by the above heuristics for choosing permutations since these two aspects are closely related. Given the relative gain in efficiency of each transformation rule, their combination can be guided by the following relative order of use.

(1)   Transformation 10.1, if the execution of the equivalent literals of two program clauses is time consuming (suppression of the equivalent literals in one program clause).

(2)   Transformations 10.2–10.7 (negation replaced by a cut in the preceding program clause).

(3)   Transformation 10.8 to make tail recursion explicit.

(4)   Transformations 10.8 and 10.9 (introduction of cuts).

(5)   Transformation 10.10 (partial evaluation).

(6)   Transformations 10.11–10.14 (equality substitutions).

(7)   Transformation 10.15 (introduction of anonymous variables).

Transformations based on program clause indexing and global parameters should be performed separately; those based on global parameters should be done before any other transformations; while those based on clause indexing should be done at the very end of the transformation process.

Note finally that the whole transformation process as well as the heuristics it involves could easily be automated.

EXERCISES

10.5   Transform reverse(L, LRev) and reverse_desc(L, LRev, LInt) (Procedures 10.1 and 10.2), for the respective directionalities

> in(ground, var) : out(ground, ground)
> in(ground, var, ground) : out(ground, ground, ground)

Try to make them tail recursive.

10.6 From the three logic descriptions for quicksort(L, LS) constructed
in Exercises 5.19 and 5.40, derive correct logic procedures for the
directionality

in(ground, var) : out(ground, ground)

Transform the resulting procedures and compare their efficiency.

---

*10.5   Background

Control information

The deduction process can be controlled in various ways. According to
Gallaire and Lasserre (1982), two types of control decisions can be
distinguished: those made during the forward execution process and
those made during the backtracking process. The possible ways of
expressing control can also be categorized as follows: pragmatic control,
explicit control incorporated in the program, and explicit control
separated from the program. Pragmatic control consists of tailoring the
program according to the fixed strategy of the interpreter. Explicit
control incorporated in the program can have the form of specific
primitives enabling the control of certain aspects of the derivation
process (for example, the cut, or the use of annotations as described in IC-
Prolog (Clark and McCabe, 1979), or the freeze primitive of Prolog II
(Giannesini *et al.*, 1986)). Explicit control separated from the program is
often expressed in the form of metarules, so called because they express
knowledge about the program itself (Davis, 1980). Examples are the wait
declarations in MU-Prolog (Naish, 1985c). Explicit control separated
from the program requires the design of a language expressing the
metarules as well as an interpreter for handling them. Such a language is
proposed in Gallaire and Lassere (1982). The Metalog programming
language allows the description of metarules, as described in Dincbas
(1980) and Dincbas and Le Pape (1984). Explicit control is also proposed
in the context of constraint satisfaction problems (Van Hentenryck,
1989), where the approach taken is based on consistency techniques and
combines finite domain and the constraint concepts. The proposed
inference rules, such as forward checking, are shown to lead to substantial
improvements in efficiency.

Transformations

More information on tail recursion and clause indexing can be found in
Warren (1979, 1980). The theoretical foundations of transformations
based on global parameters can be found in Bowen and Kowalski (1982)
and Bowen and Weinberg (1985). Static transformations of logic

programs, which modify the programs without concern for efficiency, are proposed in Stepankova and Stepanek (1984). In the literature, most of the static program transformations for increasing efficiency deal with partial evaluation and equality substitutions. The idea of partial evaluation is actually already present in the S-m-n theorem (Kleene, 1952). It is not restricted to logic programs; and may also be used for procedural as well as functional program optimization (Wegbreit, 1976; Scheifler, 1977; Loveman, 1977; Kahn, 1982). Similar to partial evaluation is the specialization of programs which restricts a given program to only a subset of possible input data. A specialization procedure is presented in Chang and Lee (1973) where the procedural program is first transformed in a clausal form. A first application of partial evaluation to logic programs was proposed by Komorowski (1982). In Bruynooghe (1983), the necessity of partial evaluation is underlined for operations on abstract data types. A Prolog meta-interpreter for partial evaluation is described in Venken (1984). Partial evaluation is also presented in Takeuchi and Furukawa (1985), O'Keefe (1985), Sawamura and Take-shima (1985), Sawamura *et al.* (1985), and Lloyd and Shepherdson (1987). Further references can be found in Bjorner *et al.* (1987).

The concept of a qualified answer and its application to transformation is presented in Vasey (1986). Its compile-time use corresponds to the technique of partial evaluation and can be used for program specialization, query optimization and transformation. Naughton (1986) suggested a method for statically detecting redundant subgoals. Sufficient conditions for the functionality of Prolog procedures are given in Debray and Warren (1986a), together with an algorithm for detecting such functionalities. A framework for proving the correctness of a transformation rule can be found in Debray and Mishra (1988). Functional dependencies are also presented in Nakamura (1986). Exhaustive search programs can be transformed into deterministic ones (Ueda, 1986b), by transforming the procedures used in a bagof literal so that an exhaustive search is replaced by a deterministic one (giving a list of answer substitutions). Bruynooghe *et al.* (1989) compiled control information into Prolog programs by means of a set of transformation rules. Meta-level programming is investigated in Hill and Lloyd (1988), where further references can also be found.

SUMMARY

- The transformation of Prolog programs increases their efficiency while preserving their correctness.
- The transformation rules are based on the procedural semantics of Prolog, and on a suitable introduction of control information.

- Transformation rules are intended:
  - to suppress useless execution or backtracking;
  - to introduce cuts;
  - to perform partial evaluation;
  - to instantiate the heads of program clauses as much as possible, and suppress the equality literals in their bodies;
  - to obtain tail recursive procedures; and
  - to introduce anonymous variables, clause indexing, and relational representation of data structures.
- Directionalities influence the efficiency of procedures. The most specific procedures (that is, correct for the fewest directionalities) are usually the most efficient ones.

Day and night, M. C. Escher (1938). Collection Haags Gemeentemuseum, The Hague. © 1989 M. C. Escher Heirs/Cordon Art, Baarn, Holland

11
Conclusion

PREVIEW   In this chapter, the methodology proposed is evaluated. Future developments for logic programming are then investigated.

11.1   Evaluation of the methodology

Logic program development can be decomposed into three steps: the elaboration of a specification, the construction of a logic description and the derivation of a logic program. One of the interesting features of this decomposition is that it covers the whole construction process, from informal specifications to efficient Prolog programs. The resulting logic programs have the full power of the Prolog language (that is, multidirectionality, ngv terms, multiple and infinite solutions, negation as failure, control information, side-effects, and so on). We do not claim that this approach is universal, but it is well adapted for most classes of problems.

Documentation

The application of a methodology when developing a program does not prevent errors from being made, as illustrated in Gerhart and Yelowitz (1976). Therefore, the programmer should pay particular attention to the difficult task of program development and the programs constructed should be carefully tested. The use of a methodology is a good guide not only for the programmer, but also for all those who will try to understand the constructed programs. Hence, all the intermediate steps and, especially, the design decisions should be documented. For tutorial purposes, the examples presented have been developed in detail. In practice,

303

the documentation of the construction process should contain everything necessary for its comprehension. This will be illustrated with an example documentation of the now well-known efface problem.

EXAMPLE 11.1

Specification

procedure   efface(X, L, LEff)

Type: X : Term
          L, LEff : List.

Relation: X is an element of L and LEff is the list L without the first occurrence of X in L.

Application conditions:
in(ground, ground, any) : out(ground, ground, ground)   ⟨0–1⟩

Logic description

Induction parameter: L

Well-founded relation: proper suffix

efface(X, L, LEff) ⇔ L = [] & false
$\lor$L = [H | T] & (H = X & LEff = T & list(T)
$\lor$H ≠ X & LEff = [H | TEff]
& efface(X, T, TEff))

Logic procedure

efface(X, L, LEff) ← L = [H | T], X = H, LEff = T
efface(X, L, LEff) ← L = [H | T], not(X = H),
LEff = [H | TEff], efface(X, T, TEff)

Prolog code

efface(H, [H | T], LEff) ← !, LEff = T
efface(X, [H | T], [H | TEff]) ← efface(X, T, TEff)

In the above example, the indication of the induction parameter and the well-founded relation is sufficient for the construction of the logic description to be understood. The correct logic procedure derived from the logic description is also stated. The Prolog code is the transformed logic procedure. It could be argued that the logic description and the logic procedure are redundant information. It is the case here because the form of the constructed logic description is almost a disjunction of conjunctions, and because the order of the literals in the program clauses corresponds to their order in the logic description. For a more complex problem, however, the constructed logic description (as well as its possible transformed version) could be helpful.

The need for a specification should again be emphasized, making explicit the types of the parameters, the computed relation and the directionalities for which the procedure can be used correctly. The need for specifications is independent of the methodological framework. This is also the case of the non-optimized version of the Prolog code. Such a version should not contain control information, in order to facilitate its comprehension. The form of a pure logic procedure is especially adapted for this purpose.

Extensions

The different steps in the development of a logic program could be extended in various ways. At the logic description level, the form of the logic description could be extended to higher-order logic, or it could mix the functional and logical formalisms. Other construction techniques as well as heuristics could be developed. The addition of a formalization of data structures and properties of logic descriptions would extend the transformation of logic descriptions. The construction and transformation processes could also be partly automated.

At the logic program level, constructs outside the logical schema of program clauses could be handled (for example, setof, bagof, call, and so on). They can be useful in solving certain types of problems (Sterling and Shapiro, 1986). Most of the derivation process could be automated. The logic program level is especially adapted here for the Prolog language. It would be interesting to analyse the influence of the available control primitives on the derivation process and on the resulting logic programs. Finally, the development of parallel logic programs could be investigated.

11.2   A future for logic programming

The future of logic programming depends on the future of Prolog which is now a major programming language, already in use for developing software. Here we propose future developments for Prolog in order for it to remain a successful programming language and, hence, for logic programming to become a major programming paradigm.

SLDNF-resolution is a suitable framework for the procedural semantics. Negation as failure is a good compromise between expressiveness and efficiency. In spite of its intrinsic incompleteness, it is an appropriate solution to the negation problem because of its simplicity and efficiency. This does not exclude the use of other negation techniques adapted to particular classes of problems. Prolog's computation rule is simple and effective. It allows unsophisticated reasoning in the execution process. Such simplicity is also obtained with linear computation rules while non-linear computation rules are more difficult to handle. The concept of directionality, for example, becomes much more complicated. Prolog's depth-first search strategy is also simple and efficient. It has the advantage of being easy to understand, easy to use and particularly effective. All that has been said does not deny the utility of defining specific computation rules or search strategies. This can be particularly useful if they can be attached to certain literals within clauses, or to certain procedures (for example, delayed evaluation of literals, breadth-first search, and so on). The lack of occur check is problematic since it complicates the construction process. A correct built-in unification should at least be available.

Prolog has a major control primitive: the cut. It is especially useful when optimizing programs. Other control primitives could be interesting. For instance, the head of a program clause could be annotated

$$p(\ ground\ \mathsf{X}\ ) \leftarrow \ldots$$

This would tell the interpreter or compiler that this program clause could only be used if the parameter of the procedure call is ground. This would be particularly appropriate for a dynamic selection of the correct program clauses for different directionalities (see Section 9.5). A similar control primitive is available in IC-Prolog (Clark and McCabe, 1979).

Extensions of Prolog

We believe that extensions of the Prolog language should be investigated, but only for specific application domains. A typical example is the domain of constraint satisfaction problems, covering problems such as the *N*-queens problem, graph colouring, scheduling, and travelling salesman problems. References to constraint logic programming have already been given in Section 9.11, but note, in particular, Van Hentenryck (1989), which is one of the few books on constraint logic programming. It proposes the theoretical and practical framework of an extended Prolog for solving such problems.

Parallel logic programming

Parallelism has not been investigated as a part of the methodological approach put forward in this book. The development of parallel logic programs will briefly be considered here.

It is usual to make a distinction between two approaches to parallelism in logic programming. In the first approach, Horn clause programs, or Prolog programs, are executed in parallel. The aim of the approach is to solve symbolic applications efficiently. The second approach is based on the concept of a guard. In a guarded logic language, each program clause has a guard consisting of a conjunction of atoms. When a goal ← p(t) is executed, the guards of each applicable clause are executed in parallel. As soon as the guard of one clause succeeds, the execution proceeds with the body of that clause. All the other clauses are discarded. The principle of guards excludes multiple solutions and leads to incompleteness since the possible solutions of the discarded clauses are not considered. Guarded logic languages, however, turn out to be effective and particularly adapted to system programming. The major guarded logic languages are Parlog, Concurrent Prolog and GHC. More references on these languages and on parallel logic programming can be found in Takeuchi and Furukawa (1986), Ueda (1986a), Shapiro (1987) and Gregory (1987).

If a logic framework is used for developing parallel logic programs, then a general schema could be as follows: elaboration of a specification, construction of a logic description and derivation of a parallel logic program. There is no doubt that specifications should contain information other than for sequential Prolog programs. Most of the techniques for constructing a logic description will also be applicable in the context of parallel logic programming. However, if the target language is a guarded logic language, it is possible that some concepts similar to the guards could be included (logically) at the logic description level. For instance, some notion of exclusive formulae could be adequate for deriving guards. The major task of the derivation step consists here of adding suitable control information telling the interpreter how to handle the parallel execution correctly and efficiently.

The definition of and experimentation with a methodological framework for developing parallel logic programs is a challenging and crucial issue, especially if such parallel languages are expected to be used by non-specialists. Conlon (1989) or Jacquet (1989), for example, is a first step in that direction.

Logic programming environment

It can be difficult to develop large Prolog programs with the current lack of Prolog programming environments. Such environments should include modules, intelligent compilers and debuggers, relational database interfaces, graphics and window interfaces, and so on. However, a programming environment should also be an environment supporting the *development* of logic programs. The methodology proposed in this book could serve as a basis for such an environment for logic program development. This could include an integrated set of automated tools supporting the various steps of the methodology. We believe that the future of Prolog depends on the availability of environments for logic program development.

Appendix

A.1   Table of specifications

A.2   Table of logic descriptions

A.3 Table of procedures

Procedure number	Name	Page number
1.1	efface	3
1.2	efface	3
1.3	efface	3
1.4	efface	19
1.5	efface	20
9.1	=	226
9.2	=	227
9.3	efface	247
9.4	compress_v_g	257
9.5	compress_g_v	257
9.6	compress_g_v	261
9.7	append	265
9.8	append	266
9.9	print_all_p	267
9.10	print_all_p	267
9.11	append	268
10.1	reverse	275
10.2	reverse_desc	275
10.3	assoc, drop_elem, add_elem	294
10.4	efface_1	294
10.5	efface_2	295
10.6	efface_3	295
10.7	efface_4	295
10.8	efface_0	295

A.4 Table of problems

Problem	Specification number	Page number	Logic description number	Page number	Procedure number	Page number
=	5.1	94	5.1	96	9.1	226
			5.2	96	9.2	227
add	5.7	115				
add_elem	5.3	98			10.3	294
append	4.2	85			9.7	265
					9.8	266
					9.11	268
append3	5.23	157	5.21–5.22	157		
assoc	5.2	98			10.3	294
assoc_list	5.5	99	5.3	99		
atmost2	5.27	159	5.27–5.28	159		
between	5.24	157	5.23–5.24	157–8		
char	5.8	115	5.5	115		
compress	5.6	113	5.6	117		
			5.14	128		
			5.15	130		
drop_elem	5.4	98	5.4	106	9.4–9.5	257
					9.6	261
					10.3	294
efface	1.1	17	5.7	122	1.1–1.3	3
					1.4–1.5	19–20
					9.3	247
					10.4–10.8	294–5

Bibliography

Abramski, S. and Hankin, C. eds. (1987). *Abstract Interpretation of Declarative Languages*. Chichester: Ellis Horwood

Abrial, J.R. (1980). *The Specification Language Z: Syntax and Semantics*. Programming Research Group, Oxford University

Ait-Kaci H. and Nasr R. (1986a). Logic and Inheritance. *Principles of Programming Languages*, pp. 219–28

Ait-Kaci H. and Nasr R. (1986b). A Logic Programming Language with Built-in Inheritance. *Journal of Logic Programming*, 3(3), 185–215

Apt, K.R. and Van Emden, M.H. (1982). Contribution to the Theory of Logic Programming. *JACM*, 29(3), 841–62

Apt, K.R., Blair, A.H. and Walker, A. (1988). Towards a Theory of Declarative Knowledge. In Minker (1988), pp. 89–148

Arsac, J., Kodratoff, Y. (1982). Some Techniques for Recursion Removal from Recursive Functions. *ACM Trans. on Prog. Lang. and Syst.*, 4(2), 295–322

Azibi, N. and Kodratoff, Y. (1986). *Méthode de transformation de programmes de Burstall-Darlington appliquée à la programmation logique*. Rapport de Recherche 268, Université de Paris-Sud, LRI

Balogh, K. (1978). On an Interactive Program Verifier for Prolog Programs. *Coloquia Mathematica Societatis Jàmos Bolgai 26, Mathematical Logic in Computer Science*, Salgòtarjàn, Hungary, pp. 111–142

Balzer, R., Goldman, N. and Wile, D. (1978). Informality in Program Specifications. *IEEE Trans. on Soft. Eng.*, SE-4(2), 94–103

Balzer, R., Cheatham, T.E. and Green, C. (1983). Software Technology in the 1990's. *IEEE Trans. on Computers*, C-16(11), 39–45

Barbuti, R. and Martelli, M. (1986). Completeness of the SLDNF-Resolution for a Class of Logic Programs. In *Proc. 3rd Int. Logic Programming Conference* (London, July), New York: Springer-Verlag, pp. 600–14

Barstow, D. (1987). Artificial Intelligence and Software Engineering. In *Proc. Int. Conf. on Soft. Eng.*, Monterey, pp. 200–11

Baudinet, M. (1988). *Proving Termination Properties of Prolog Programs: A Semantic Approach*. Report STAN-CS-88-1202, Stanford University, CA

Bellia, M., Levi, G. and Martelli, M. (1983). On Compiling Prolog Programs on Demand Driven Architectures. In *Proc. Logic Programming Workshop 83* (Albufeira, Portugal, June), Lisbon: University of Lisbon, pp. 518–35

Berry, G. (1976). Bottom-Up Computation of Recursive Programs. *Revue Française d'Automatique, Informatique et Recherche Opérationnelle*, 10(3), 47–82

Berzins, V. and Gray, M. (1985). Analysis and Design in MSG.84: Formalizing Functional Specification. *IEEE Trans. on Soft. Eng.*, SE-11(8), 657–70

315

Biermann, A.W. (1978). The Inference of Regular LISP Programs from Examples. *IEEE Trans. on Syst., Man and Cyb.*, **SMC-8**(8), 585–600

Biermann, A.W. and Krishnaswamy, R. (1976). Constructing Programs from Example Computations. *IEEE Trans. on Soft Eng.*, **SE-2**(3), 141–53

Biermann, A.W. Guiho, G. and Kodratoff, Y. eds. (1984). *Automatic Program Construction Techniques*. New York: MacMillan Publishing Company

Bird, R.S. (1984). The Promotion and Accumulation Strategies in Transformational Programming. *ACM Trans. on Prog. Lang. and Syst.*, **6**(4), 487–504

Bjorner, D. *et al.*, eds. (1987). *Workshop on Partial Evaluation and Mixed Computation*. Gl. Avernaes, Denmark

Boehm, B.M., (1976). Software Engineering. *IEEE Trans. on Soft. Eng.*, **SE-25**(12), 1226–41

Boehm, B.M. (1981). *Software Engineering Economics*. Englewood Cliffs, NJ: Prentice Hall

Bowen, K.A. and Kowalski, R.A. (1982). Amalgamating Language and Meta-language in Logic Programming. In Clark (1982), pp. 153–72

Bowen, K.A. and Weinberg, T. (1985). A Meta-Level Extension of Prolog. In *Proc. Symp. on Logic Programming* (Boston, MA, July), Silver Spring MD: IEEE Computer Society Press, pp. 48–53

Boyer, R.S. and Moore, J.S. (1979) *A Computational Logic*. New York: Academic Press

Bratko, I. (1986). *Prolog Programming for Artificial Intelligence*. Wokingham: Addison-Wesley

Brough, D.R. and Hogger, C.J. (1987). Compiling Associativity into Logic Programs. *Journal of Logic Programming*, **4**(4), 345–59

Bruynooghe, M. (1978). Intelligent Backtracking for an Interpreter of Horn Clause Logic Programs. *Mathematical Logic in Computer Science*, Hungary **25**, 215–58

Bruynooghe, M. (1982) Adding Redundacy to Obtain More Reliable and More Readable Prolog Programs. In *Proc. 1st Int. Logic Programming Conf.*, Marseille, pp. 129–133

Bruynooghe, M. (1983). Some Reflexions on Implementation Issues of Prolog. *Logic Programming Workshop* (Albufeira, Portugal, June), Lisbon: University of Lisbon, pp. 1–6

Bruynooghe, M. and Janssens, G. (1988). An Instance of Abstract Interpretation Integrating Type and Mode Inferencing. In *Proc. 5th Int. Conf. and Symp. on Logic Programming* (Seattle, August), Cambridge, MA: MIT Press, pp. 669–83

Bruynooghe, M. *et al.* (1987). Abstract Interpretation: The Global Optimization of Prolog Programs. In *Proc. Int. Symp. on Logic Programming* (San Francisco, September), Silver Spring MD: IEEE Computer Society Press, pp. 192–204

Bruynooghe, M., De Schreye, D. and Krekels, B. (1986). Compiling Control. *Journal of Logic Programming*, **6**(2), 135–62

Bundy, A. (1988). A Broader Interpretation of Logic in Logic Programming. In *Proc. 5th Int. Conf. and Symp. on Logic Programming* (Seattle, August), Cambridge, MA: MIT Press, pp. 1624–48

Burstall, R.M. (1969). Proving Properties of Programs by Structural Induction. *The Computer Journal*, **72**, 41–8

Burstall, R.M. (1974). Program Proving as Hand Simulation with a Little Induction. *IFIP 74*, North Holland, pp. 308–12

Burstall, R.M. and Darlington J. (1975). Some Transformations for Developing Recursive Programs. In *Proc. Int. Conf. on Reliable Software*, Los Angeles, pp. 465–72

Burstall, R.M. and Darlington, J. (1977). A Transformation System for Developing Recursive Programs. *JACM*, **24**(1), 44–67

Burstall, R.M. and Goguen, J.A. (1980). The Semantics of CLEAR, a Specification Language. In *Proc. of Advance Course on Abstract Software Specification* LNCS 86, Berlin: Springer-Verlag

Chang, C.L. and Lee, R.C.T. (1973). *Symbolic Logic and Mechanical Theorem Proving*. New York/London: Academic Press

Chomicki, J. and Minsky, N.H. (1985). Towards a Programming Environment for Large Prolog Programs. In *Proc. Symp. on Logic Programming* (Boston, MA, July), Silver Spring MD: IEEE Computer Society Press, pp. 230–45

Clark, K.L. (1978). Negation as Failure. In Gallaire and Minker (1978), pp. 293–322

Clark, K.L. (1979). *Predicate Logic as a Computational Formalism*. Research Report 79/59, Imperial College of Science and Technology, University of London

Clark, K.L. (1981). *The Synthesis and Verification of Logic Programs*. Research Report DOC 81/36, Imperial College of Science and Technology, University of London, September 1981. (Revised version of a document which first appeared in June 1977)

Clark, K.L. ed. (1982). *Logic Programming*. New York: Academic Press

Clark, K.L. and Darlington, J. (1980). Algorithm Classification through Synthesis. *The Computer Journal*, **23**(1), 61–5

Clark, K.L. and McCabe, F.G. (1979). The Control Facilities of IC-Prolog. In Michie (1979), pp. 122–2.

Clark, K.L. and Sickel, S. (1977). Predicate Logic: A Calculus for Deriving Programs. In *Proc. IJCAI-77*, pp. 419–20

Clark, K. and Tärnlund, S.A. (1977). A First-Order Theory of Data and Programs. In *Proc. IFIP Congress*, Toronto, pp. 939–44

Clocksin, W.F. and Mellish, C.S. (1984). *Programming in Prolog*. 2nd edn. Berlin: Springer-Verlag

Colmerauer, A. (1984). Equations and Inequations on Finite and Infinite Trees. In *Proc. Int. Conf. on Fifth Generation Computer Systems* (Tokyo, November), H. Aido (Ed.), Amsterdam: Elsevier/North Holland, pp. 85–99.

Colmerauer, A. (1985). Prolog in 10 Figures. CACM, **28**(12), 1296–1324.

Colmerauer, A. (1987). Opening the Prolog III Universe. *BYTE Magazine* **12**(9). (Special issue on logic programming.)

Colmerauer, A. (1989). Une Introduction à Prolog III. In *Journée de Synthèse AFECT, Etat de l'Art et Perspectives en Programmation Logique*, INRIA, 1989, pp. 129–55

Colmerauer, A., Kanoui, H., Roussel, P. and Pasero, R. (1973). *Un Système de Communication Homme-Machine en Français*. Groupe de Recherche en I.A., Université d'Aix-Marseille

Conlon, T. (1989). *Programming in Parlog.* Wokingham: Addison-Wesley

Cousot, P. and Cousot, R. (1977). Abstract Interpretation: A Unified Lattice Model for Static Analysis of Programs by Construction of Approxima- tions of Fixpoints. *Principles of Programming Languages*, pp. 238–52.

Dahl, V. (1980). Two Solutions to the Negation Problem. *Logic Programming Workshop 80* (Dreceben, Hungary), Tärnlund (Ed.), pp. 61–72

Darlington, J. ed. (1982). *Functional Programming and its Application.* Cam- bridge: Cambridge University Press

Davis, R. (1980). Meta Rules: Reasoning about Control. *Artificial Intelligence*, **15**(3), 179–222

Dayantis, G. (1987). Logic Program Derivation for a Class of First-Order Logic Relations. In *Proc. IJCAI-87* (Milan, August), pp. 9–14

Debray, S.K. (1984). Optimizing Almost-Tail-Recursive Prolog Programs. *ACM Principles of Functional Languages*, pp. 204–19

Debray, S.K. and Mishra, P. (1988). Denotational and Operational Semantics for Prolog. *Journal of Logic Programming*, **5**(1), 61–91

Debray, S.K. and Warren, D.S. (1986a). Detection and Optimisation of Func- tional Computations in Prolog. In *Proc. 3rd Int. Conf. on Logic Program- ming*, (London, July), New York: Springer-Verlag, pp. 490–504

Debray, S.K. and Warren, D.S: (1986b) Automatic Mode Inference for Prolog Programs. In *Proc. Symp. on Logic Programming* (Salt Lake City, September), Silver Spring, MD: IEEE Computer Society Press, pp. 78–88

Degroot, D. and Lindstrom, G. eds. (1985). *Logic Programming Function, Relation, and Equation.* Englewood Cliffs, NJ: Prentice Hall

Dembinski, P. and Maluszynski, J. (1985). AND-Parallelism with Intelligent Back tracking for Annotated Logic Programs. In *Proc. Int. Symp. on Logic Programming* (Boston, MA, July), Silver Spring, MD: IEEE Computer Society Press, pp. 29–38

Deransart, P. and Maluszynski, J. (1985). Relating Logic Programs and Attribute Grammars. *Journal of Logic Programming*, **2**(2), 119–55

Deremer, F. and Kron, H. (1975). Programming-in-the-Large versus Program- ming-in-the-Small. In *Proc. Int. Conf. on Reliable Software*, Los Angeles, pp. 114–21

Dershowitz, N. and Manna, Z. (1979). Proving Termination with Multiset Orderings. *CACM*, **22**(8), 465–75

Deville, Y. (1986). Some Aspects of Logic Program Construction. *MS Thesis*, Syracuse University, June 1986

Deville, Y. (1987). A Methodology for Logic Program Construction. *PhD Thesis*, Institut d'Informatique, University of Namur, February 1987

Deville, Y. (1988). *Generalized Herbrand Interpretations.* R.P. 88/21, Institut d'Informatique, University of Namur

Deville, Y. and Burnay, J. (1989). Generalization and Program Schemata: A Step Toward Computer-Aided Program Construction. In *Proc. of the North American Conf. on Logic Programming* (Cleveland, October), Cambridge, MA: MIT Press, pp. 409–25

Dijkstra, E.W. (1968). A Constructive Approach to the Problem of Program Correctness. *BIT* 8, pp. 174–86

Dijkstra, E.W. (1970). *Program Inversion.* Berlin: Springer-Verlag

Dijkstra, E.W. (1975). Guarded Commands, Nondeterminacy and Formal Derivation of Programs. *CACM*, **18**(8), 453–57

Dijkstra, E.W. (1976). *A Discipline of Programming*. Hemel Hempstead: Prentice Hall

Dincbas, M. (1980). The Metalog Problem-Solving System, an Informal Presentation. *Logic Programming Workshop 80* (Dreceben, Hungary), Tärnlund (Ed.), pp. 80–91

Dincbas, M. and Le Pape, J-P. (1984). Metacontrol of Logic Programming in METALOG. In *Proc. Int. Conf. on Fifth Generation Comp. Syst.* (Tokyo, November), H. Aido (Ed.), Amsterdam: Elsevier/North Holland, pp. 361–70

Dincbas, M. *et al.* (1988). The Constraint Logic Programming Language CHIP. In *Proc. Int. Conf. on Fifth Gen. Comp. Syst.*, (Tokyo, Japan)

Drabent, W. and Maluszynski, J. (1987). Inductive Assertion Method for Logic Programs. In *Proc. TAPSOFT '87*, **2**, LNCS 250, Springer-Verlag, pp. 167–81

Dreyfus, S.E. and Law, A.M. (1977). *The Art and Theory of Dynamic Programming*. Mathematics in Science and Engineering, Vol. 130. New York: Academic Press

Ebbinghaus, H.D., Flum, J. and Thomas, W. (1984). *Mathematical Logic*. Berlin: Springer-Verlag

Eder, E. (1985). Properties of Substitutions and Unifications. *Journal of Symbolic Computation*, **1**(1), 31–46

Elcock, E.W. (1983). The Pragmatic of Prolog: Some Comments. In *Logic Programming Workshop 83* (Albufeira, Portugal, June), Lisbon: University of Lisbon, pp. 94–106

Eriksson, A. and Johansson, A.-L. (1981). *NATDED, a Derivation Editor*. UPMAIL Technical Report No. 3, October 1981

Eriksson, A. and Johansson, A-L. (1982). *Computer-Based Synthesis of Logic Programs*. UPMAIL Technical Report No. 12, August 1982

Eriksson, A., Johansson, A-L. and Tarnlund, S-A. (1983). *Towards a Derivation Editor*. UPMAIL Technical Report No. 11, November 1983

Eriksson, L.-H. (1984). *Synthesis of a Unification Algorithm in Logic Programming Calculus*. UPMAIL Technical Report No. 22B, June 1984

Fairley, R.E. (1985). *Software Engineering Concepts*. New York: McGraw-Hill

Feather, M.S. (1983). Specification and Transformation: Automated Implementation. In *Proc. of the Program Transformation and Programming Environments Workshop*, München, Germany, September 1983

Feuer, A. (1983). Building Libraries in Prolog. In *Proc. IJCAI-83*, pp. 550–2

Floyd, R.W. (1967). Assigning Meanings to Programs. In *Proc. Symp. on Applied Math.*, **19**, *Math. Aspect in Comp. Sc.*, Providence, Rhode Island, American Society, pp. 19–32

Foster, J. M. and Elcock (1989). ABSYS1: An Incremental Compiler for Assertions – An Introduction. In *Machine Intelligence 4*, Michie D. (Ed.), Edinburgh: Edinburgh University Press

Furukawa, K. and Nakajima, R. (1983). *Modularization and Abstraction in Logic Programming*. ICOT Research Center, Technical Report TR-022, August 1983

Gabbay, D.M. and Sergot, M.J. (1984). *Negation as Inconsistency*. Imperial College, Technical Report DOC 84/7, February 1984

Gallaire, H. and Lasserre, C. (1982). Meta-Level Control for Logic Programs. In Clark (1982), pp. 173–88

Gallaire, H. and Minker, J. eds (1978). *Logic and Databases*. New York: Plenum Press

Gang, Y. and Zhiliang, X. (1986). An Efficient Type System for Prolog. *IFIP 86*, pp. 355–9

Gehani, N. and McGettrick, A., eds. (1986). *Software Specification Techniques*. Wokingham: Addison-Wesley

Genesereth, M.R. and Nilsson, N.J. (1987). *Logical Foundations of Artificial Intelligence*. Los Altos, CA: Morgan Kaufmann

Gerhart, S. and Yelowitz, L. (1976). Observations of Fallibility in Applications of Modern Programming Methodologies. *IEEE Trans. on Soft. Eng.*, **SE-2**(8)

Giannesini, F., Kanoui, H., Pasero, R. and van Caneghem, M. (1986). *Prolog*. Wokingham: Addison-Wesley

Goguen, J.A. and Meseguer, J. (1984). Equality, Types, Modules and Generics for Logic Programming. In *Proc. 2nd Int. Logic Programming Conf.*, (Uppsala, July), S. A. Tärnlund (Ed.), Uppsala: Uppsala University Press pp. 115–25

Goguen, J.A. and Meseguer, J. (1985). EQLOG: Equality, Types and Generic Modules for Logic Programming. In DeGroot and Lindstrom (1985)

Goguen, J.A., Thatcher, J.W. and Wagner, E.G. (1978). An Initial Algebra Approach to the Specification, Correctness, and Implementation of Abstract Data Types. In *Current Trends in Programming Methodology, Vol. 4: Data Structure*, (Yeh, R.T. ed.), Englewood Cliffs, NJ: Prentice Hall, pp. 80–149

Goldberg, A.T. (1986). Knowledge-Based Programming: A Survey of Program Design and Construction Techniques. *IEEE Trans. on Soft. Eng.* **SE-12**(7), 752–68

Gram, A. (1986). *Raisonner pour programmer*. Paris: Dunod

Green, C. (1969). Application of Theorem Proving to Problem Solving. In *Proc. IJCAI-69*, Washington, pp. 219–39

Gregory, S. (1987). *Parallel Logic Programming in Parlog: The Language and its Implementation*. Wokingham: Addison-Wesley

Gries, D. (1981). *The Science of Programming*. Berlin: Springer-Verlag

Guttag, J.V. (1977). Abstract Data Types and the Development of Data Structure. *CACM*, **20**(6), 396–404

Guttag, J.V. (1979). Notes on Types Abstraction. In Gehani & McGettrick (1986)

Hansson, A. (1980). A Formal Development of Programs. *PhD Dissertation*, The Royal Institute of Technology and the University of Stockholm, Department of Computer Science

Hansson, A. and Tärnlund, S.A. (1979). A Natural Programming Calculus. In *Proc. IJCAI-79*, Tokyo, August 1979

Haridi, S. and Sahlin, D. (1983). Evaluation of Logic Programs Based on Natural Deduction. *Logic Programming Workshop 83* (Albufeira, Portugal, June), Lisbon: University of Lisbon, pp. 560–74

Hayes, P. (1973). Computation and Deduction. In *Proc. 2nd MFCS Symp.*, Czechoslavak Academy of Sciences, pp. 105–18

Hecht, M. (1977). *Flow Analysis of Computer Programs*. New York: North Holland

Herbrand, J. 1930. Researches in the Theory of Demonstration. In *From Frege to Gödel: A Source Book in Mathematical Logic, 1879–1931* (van Heijenoort

J., ed.), pp. 525–81. Harvard MA: Harvard University Press

Hill, P.M. and Lloyd, J.W. (1988). *Analysis of Meta-Programs*. Report CS-88-08, University of Bristol

Hill, R. (1974). *LUSH Resolution and its Completeness*. DCL Memo No. 78, Dept. of AI, University of Edinburgh

Hoare, C.A.R. (1969). An Axiomatic Basis for Computer Programming. *CACM*, **12**(10), 576–83

Hoare, C.A.R. (1971). Procedures and Parameters: an Axiomatic Approach. In *Proc. Symp. on Semantics of Algorithmic Languages, Lecture Notes in Mathematics*, pp. 102–16. Springer-Verlag

Hoare, C.A.R. (1972). Proof of Correctness of Data Representation. *Acta Informatica*, **1**, 271–81

Hoare, C.A.R. and Shepherdson, J.C., eds. (1985). *Mathematical Logic and Programming Languages*. Hemel Hempstead: Prentice Hall

Hogger, C.J. (1981). *Derivation of Logic Programs. JACM*, **28**(2), 372–92

Hogger, C.J. (1984). *Introduction to Logic Programming*. London: Academic Press

Horiuchi, K. and Kanamori, T. (1987) Polymorphic Type Inference in Prolog by Abstract Interpretation. In *Logic Programming 87*, Furukawa *et al.* (Eds.), Berlin: Springer-Verlag, pp. 195–214

Howden, W.E. and Miller, E., eds. (1978): *Tutorial: Software Testing and Validation Techniques*. Long Beach CA: IEEE Computer Society Press

Huet, G. (1976). Résolution d' Equations dans les Langages d'Ordre 1, 2, . . . ω. *Thèse d'Etat*, Université Paris VII

IEEE Transactions on Software Engineering: Special Issue on Artificial Intelligence and Software Engineering. (1985). **SE-11**(11)

Jacquet. J. M. (1989). Conclog: A Methodological Approach to Concurrent Logic Programming. *PhD Thesis*, Institut d'Informatique, University of Namur, November 1989

Jaffar, J. and Lassez, J.-L. (1987). Constraint Logic Programming. In *Proc. 12th ACM Symp. on Principles of Programming Languages*, Munich, January 1987, pp. 111–119

Jaffar, J. and Michaylov, S. (1987). Methodology and implementation of a CLP-System. In *Proc. 4th Int. Conf. on Logic Programming* (Melbourne, May), Cambridge, MA: MIT Press, pp. 196–218

Jaffar, J., Lassez, J-L. and Lloyd, J.W. (1983). Completeness of the Negation as Failure. In *Proc. IJCAI-83*, Karlsruhe, pp. 500–6

Janssen, R.W. and Tonies, C.C. (1979). *Software Engineering*. Englewood Cliffs, NJ: Prentice Hall

Johansson, A.L. (1984). Using Symmetry for the Derivation of Logic Programs. In *Proc. 2nd Int. Conf. on Logic Programming* (Uppsala, July), S.A. Tärnlund (Ed.), Uppsala: Uppsala University Press, pp. 243–51

Johansson, A.-L. (1985). Using Symmetry and Substitution in Program Derivation. *PhD Thesis*, Computer Science Dept., Uppsala University

Johansson, A.L. (1986). *Simplifying Program Derivation using Program Schemas*. UPMAIL Technical Report, Uppsala University

Jones, C.B. (1980). *Software Development: A Rigorous Approach*. Hemel Hempstead: Prentice Hall

Jones, C.B. (1986). *Systematic Software Development Using VDM*. Hemel

Hempstead: Prentice Hall

Jones, N.D. and Sondergaard, H. (1987). A Semantic Based Framework for the Abstract Interpretation of Prolog. In Abramski & Hankin (1987), pp. 123–42

Kahn, K.M. (1982). A Partial Evaluation for Lisp Programs Written in Prolog. In *Proc. 1st Logic Programming Conf.*, Marseille, pp. 19–25

Kanamori, T. and Fujita, H. (1984). *Formulation of Induction Formulas in Verification of Prolog Programs.* Technical Report TR-094, ICOT Research Center, December 1984

Kanamori, T. and Horiuchi, K. (1987). Construction of Logic Programs Based on Generalized Unfold/Fold Rules. In *Proc. 4th Int. Conf. on Logic Programming* (Melbourne, May), Cambridge, MA: MIT Press, pp. 744–68

Kanamori, T. and Seki, H. (1986). Verification of Prolog Programs Using an Extension of Execution. In *Proc. 3rd Int. Conf. on Logic Programming* (London, July), New York: Springer-Verlag, pp. 475–89

Kawanobe, K. (1984). Current States and Future Plans of the Fifth Generation Computer Systems Project. In *Proc. Int. Conf. Fifth Gen. Comp. Syst.* (Tokyo, November), H. Aido (Ed.), Amsterdam: Elsevier/North Holland, pp. 3–17

Kleene, S.C. (1952). *Introduction to Metamathematics.* New York: van Nostrand

Kluźniak, F. (1987). Type Synthesis for Ground Prolog. In *Proc. 4th Int. Conf. on Logic Programming* (Melbourne, May), Cambridge, MA: MIT Press, pp. 788–816

Knight, K. (1989). Unification: A Multidisciplinary Survey. *ACM Computing Surveys*, **21**(1), 93–124

Knuth, D.A. (1968). *The Art of Computer Programming, Vol. 1: Fundamental Algorithms.* Reading, MA: Addison-Wesley

Komorowski, H. (1982). Partial Evaluation as a Means for Inferencing Data Structures in an Applicative Language: A Theory and Implementation in Case of Prolog. In *Proc. ACM Symp. on Principles of Programming Languages*, pp. 255–67

Kowalski, R.A. (1974). Predicate Logic as a Programming Language. *IFIP 74*, pp. 569–74

Kowalski, R.A. (1979). *Logic for Problem Solving.* Amsterdam: North-Holland

Kowalski, R.A. (1983). Logic Programming. *IFIP 83*, pp. 133–45

Kowalski, R.A. (1985). The Relation between Logic Programming and Logic Specification. In Hoare and Shepherdson (1985), pp. 11–28

Kowalski, R.A. and Kuehner, D. (1971). Linear Resolution with Selected Function. *Artificial Intelligence*, **1**, 227–60

Kunen, K. (1987). Negation in Logic Programming. *Journal of Logic Programming*, **4**(4), 289–308

Lassez, C. (1987). Constraint Logic Programming. *BYTE Magazine*, **12**(9). (Special Issue on Logic Programming)

Lassez, J-L., Maher, M.J. and Marriott, K. (1988) Unification Revisited. In Minker (1988), pp. 587–626

Le Charlier, B. (1985). Réflexions sur le Problème de la Correction des Programmes. *PhD Thesis*, Institut d'Informatique, University of Namur

Leroy, H. (1978). *La Fiabilité des Programmes.* Ecole d'été de l'AFCET, Note de cours

Levin, M. (1974). Mathematical Logic for Computer Scientists. *MAC TR-131*, Massachusetts Institute of Technology

Liskov, B.H. (1975). Specification Techniques for Data Abstractions. *IEEE Trans. on Soft. Eng.*, SE-1(1), 7–19

Liskov, B. and Guttag, J. (1986). *Abstraction and Specification in Program Development.* Cambridge, MA: MIT Press

Lloyd, J.W. (1987). *Foundations of Logic Programming*, 2nd edn. Berlin: Springer-Verlag

Lloyd, J.W. and Shepherdson, J.C. (1987). *Partial Evaluation in Logic Programming.* Report CS-87-09, University of Bristol

Lloyd, J.W. and Topor, R.W. (1984). Making Prolog more Expressive. *Journal of Logic Programming*, 1(3), 225–40

Loveman, D.B. (1977). Program Improvement by Source-to-Source Transformation. *JACM*, 24(1), 121–45

Macro, A. and Buxton, J. (1987). *The Craft of Software Engineering.* Wokingham: Addison-Wesley

Maher, M.J. (1988). Equivalences of Logic Programs. In Minker (1988), pp. 627–58

Maluszynski, J. and Komorowski, H.J. (1985). Unification Free Execution of Logic Programs. In *Proc. Symp. on Logic Programming* (Boston, MA, July), Silver Spring MD: IEEE Computer Society Press, pp. 78–86

Manna, Z. (1969a). The Correctness of Programs. *Journal of Computer and System Sciences*, 3, 199–27

Manna, Z. (1969b). Properties of Programs and First-Order Predicate Calculus. *JACM*, 16(2), 244–55

Manna, Z. (1974). *Mathematical Theory of Computation*, New York: McGraw-Hill

Manna, Z. and Waldinger, R. (1977): The Automatic Synthesis of Recursive Programs. In *Proc. Symp. on Art. Int. and Programming Languages*, Rochester (ACM). pp. 29–36

Manna, Z. and Waldinger, R. (1978). Is 'Sometime' Sometimes Better than 'Always'? Intermittent Assertions in Proving the Correctness of Programs. *CACM*, 21(2), 159–72

Manna, Z., Ness, S. and Vuillemin, J. (1973). Inductive Methods for Proving Properties of Programs. *CACM*, 16(8), 491–502

Mannila, H. and Ukkonen, E. (1987). Flow Analysis of Prolog Programs. In *Proc. Symp. on Logic Programming* (San Francisco, September), Silver Spring, MD: IEEE Computer Society Press, pp. 205–14

Marriott, K. and Sondergaard, H. (1988). Bottom-up Abstract Interpretation of Logic Programs. In *Proc. 5th Int. Conf. and Symp. on Logic Programming*, (Seattle, August), Cambridge, MA: MIT Press, pp. 733–48

Martelli, A. and Montanari, U. (1982). An Efficient Unification Algorithm. *TOPLAS*, 4(2), pp. 258–82

Mellish, C.S. (1981). The Automatic Generation of Mode Declaration for Prolog Programs. In *Proc. Workshop on Logic Programming for Intelligent Systems*, Los Angeles, pp. 1–16

Mellish, C.S. (1985). Some Global Optimizations for a Prolog Compiler. *Journal of Logic Programming*, 2(1), 43–66

Mellish, C.S. (1986). Abstract Interpretation of Prolog Programs. In *Proc. 3rd Int.*

Conf. on Logic Programming (London, July), New York: Springer-Verlag, pp. 463–74

Mellish, C.S. (1987). Abstract Interpretation of Prolog Programs. In Abramski and Hankin (1987), pp. 181–98

Meyer, B. (1984). *On Formalism in Specification.* Technical Report TRC 584–09. Dept. of Computer Science, University of California, Santa Barbara

Michie, D. ed. (1979). *Expert Systems in the Micro-Electronic Age.* Edinburgh: Edinburgh University Press

Mignon, B. (1988). Application et Evaluation d'une Méthodologie de Programmation Logique. *Mémoire de fin d'étude,* Institut d'Informatique, University of Namur

Mills, H.D. (1975). How to Write Correct Programs and Know it. In *Proc. Int. Conf. on Reliable Software,* Los Angeles, pp. 252–9

Milner, R. (1978). A Theory of Type Polymorphism in Programming. *Journal of Computer and System Sciences,* **17**, 348–75

Minker, J. (1982). On Indefinite Data Bases and the Closed World Assumption. In *Proc. 6th Conf. on Automated Deduction,* LNCS 138, New York: Springer-Verlag, pp. 292–308

Minker, J., ed. (1988). *Foundations of Deductive Databases and Logic Programming.* Los Altos: Morgan Kaufmann

Mishra, P. (1984). Towards a Theory of Type in Prolog. In *Proc. Int. Symp. on Logic Programming* (Atlantic City, NJ, February), Silver Spring, MD: IEEE Computer Society Press, pp. 289–98

Mishra, P. and Reddy, D. (1985). Declaration-Free Type Checking. *Principles of Programming Languages*

Mizoguchi, F., Ohwada, H. and Katayama, Y. (1984). Looks: Knowledge Representation System for Designing Expert System in a Logic Programming Framework. In *Proc. Int. Conf. on Fifth Gen. Comp. Syst.* (Tokyo, November), H. Aido (Ed.), Amsterdam: Elsevier/North Holland, pp. 606–11

Mycroft, A. (1984). Polymorphic Type Schemas and Recursive Definitions. In *Proc. Int. Symp. on Programming,* Springer-Verlag, pp. 217–28

Mycroft, A. and O'Keefe, R.A. (1983). A Polymorphic Type System for Prolog. *Logic Programming Workshop 83* (Albufeira, Portugal, June), Lisbon: University of Lisbon, pp. 107–122

Naish, L. (1985a). *MU-Prolog 3.2db Reference Manual.* Technical Report, Dept. of Comp. Science, University of Melbourne

Naish, L. (1985b). Negation and Control in Prolog. *PhD Dissertation,* University of Melbourne. Also published by Springer-Verlag, LNCS 238, 1986

Naish, L. (1985c). Automating Control for Logic Programs. *Journal of Logic Programming,* **2**(3), 167–83

Naish, L. (1986). Negation and Quantifiers in NU-Prolog. In *Proc. Int. Conf. on Logic Programming* (London, July), New York: Springer-Verlag, pp. 624–34

Naish, L. (1987). Specification = Program + Types. In *Proc. FST & TCS,* Peene, India. Published in LNCS. Springer-Verlag

Nakagawa, H. (1985). Prolog Program Transformation and Tree Manipulation Algorithms. *Journal of Logic Programming,* **2**(3) 77–91

Nakamura, K. (1986). Control of Logic Program Execution Based on the

Functional Relations. In *Proc. 3rd Int. Conf. on Logic Programming* (London, July), New York: Springer-Verlag, pp. 505–12

Naughton, J.F. (1986). Redundancy in Function-Free Recursive Rules. In *Proc. Symp. on Logic Programming* (Salt Lake City, September), Silver Spring, MD: IEEE Computer Society Press, pp. 236–43

Naur, P. (1966). Proof of Algorithms by General Snapshots. *BIT* **6**, pp. 310–16

Néel, D. ed. (1982). *Tools and Notions for Program Construction.* Cambridge: Cambridge University Press

Nordström, B. and Smith, J. (1984). Propositions and Specification of Programs in Martin-Löf's Type Theory. *BIT* **24**, pp. 288–301

O'Keefe, R.A. (1985). On the Treatment of Cuts in Prolog Source-Level Tools. In *Proc. Symp. on Logic Programming* (Boston, MA, July), Silver Spring, MD: IEEE Computer Society Press, pp. 68–72

Parnas, D.L. (1972). A Technique for Software Module Specification with Examples. *CACM*, **15**(5), 330–6

Parnas, D.L. (1977). The Use of Precise Specification in the Development of Software. *IFIP77*, North Holland, pp. 861–7

Parnas, D.L. (1983). *Software Engineering Principles.* UVIC Report No. DCS-29-IR

Partsch, H. and Steinbrüggen, R. (1983). Program Transformation Systems. *Computing Surveys*, **15**(3), 199–236

Paterson, M. and Wegman, M. (1978). Linear Unification. *Journal of Computer and System Sciences*, **16**(2), 158–67

Pereira, L.M. and Porto, A. (1982). Selective Backtracking. In Clark (1982), pp. 107–16

Plaisted, D.A. (1984). The Occur-Check Problem in Prolog. In *Proc. Int. Symp. on Logic Programming* (Atlantic City, NJ, February), Silver Spring, MD: IEEE Computer Society Press, pp. 272–80

Poole, D.I. and Goebel, R. (1986). Gracefully Adding Negation and Disjunction to Prolog. In *Proc. 3rd Int. Conf. on Logic Programming* (London, July), New York: Springer-Verlag, pp. 635–41

Porto, A. (1982). EPILOG: A Language for Extended Programming in Logic. In *Proc. 1st Int. Conf. on Logic Programming*, Marseille, pp. 31–7

Przymusinski, T.C. (1988a) On the Declarative Semantics of Deductive Databases and Logic Programs. In Minker (1988), pp. 193–216

Przymusinski, T.C. (1988b) Perfect Model Semantics. In *Proc. Fifth Int. Conf. and Symp. on Logic Programming* (Seattle, August), Cambridge, MA: MIT Press, pp. 1081–96

Reddy, V.S. (1984). Transformation of Logic Programs into Functional Programs In *Proc. Int. Symp. on Logic Programming* (Atlantic City, NJ, February), Silver Spring, MD: IEEE Computer Society Press, pp. 187–96

Reiter, R. (1978). On Closed World Data Bases. In Gallaire and Minker (1978), pp. 55–76

Ringwood, G.A. (1988). SLD: A Folk Acronym? *Logic Programming Newsletter*, **2**(1), pp. 5–7

Robinson, J.A. (1965). A Machine-Oriented Logic Based on the Resolution Principle. *JACM*, **12**(1), 23–41

Robinson, L. and Levitt, K.N. (1977). Proof Techniques for Hierarchically Structured Programs. *CACM*, **20**(4), 271–83

Royce, W.W. (1970). Managing the Development of Large Software Systems: Concepts and Techniques. In *Wescon Proc.*, August 1970

Sakai, K. and Miyachi, T. (1983). *Incorporating Naive Negation into Prolog.* ICOT Research Center, Technical Report TR-028, October 1983

Sannella, D.T. and Wallen, L.A. (1987). Calculus for the Construction of Modular Prolog Programs. In *Proc. Symp. on Logic Programming* (San Francisco, September), Silver Spring, MD: IEEE Computer Society Press, pp. 368–78

Sato, T. and Tamaki, H. (1983). *A Transformation System for Logic Programming which Preserves Equivalence.* Technical Report TR-018, ICOT Research Center, August 1983

Sato, T. and Tamaki, H. (1984a). Unfold/Fold Transformation of Logic Programs. In *Proc. 2nd Int. Logic Programming Conf.* (Uppsala, July), S.A. Tärnlund (Ed.) Uppsala: Uppsala University Press, pp. 127–38

Sato, T. and Tamaki, H. (1984b). Transformational Logic Program Synthesis. In *Proc. Int. Conf. on Fifth Generation Computer Systems* (Tokyo, November), H. Aido (Ed.), Amsterdam: Elsevier/North Holland, pp. 195–201

Sato, T. and Tamaki, H. (1986). *A Generalized Correctness Proof of the Unfold/Fold Logic Program Transformation.* Technical Report No. 86-4, Ibaraki University, Japan, June 1986

Sawamura, H. and Takeshima, T. (1985). Recursive Unsolvability of Determinacy, Solvable Cases of Determinacy and their Application to Prolog Optimization. In *Proc. Symp. on Logic Programming* (Boston, July), Silver Spring, MD: IEEE Computer Society Press pp. 200–7

Sawamura, H., Takeshima, T. and Kato, A. (1985). *Source-Level Optimization Techniques for Prolog.* IIAS R.R No. 52, International Institute for Advanced Study of Social Information Science, Fujitsu Ltd., Numazu, Shizuaka, Japan

Scheifler, R.W. (1977). An Analysis of Inline Substitution for a Structured Programming Language. *CACM*, **20**(4), 647–54

Schoenfield, J.R. (1967). *Mathematical Logic.* Reading, MA: Addison-Wesley

Sebelik, J. and Stepanek, P. (1982). Horn Clause Programs for Recursive Functions. In Clark (1982), pp. 325–40

Seki, H. and Furukawa, K. (1987). Notes on Transformation Techniques for Generate and Test Logic Program. In *Proc. Symp. on Logic Programming* (San Francisco, September), Silver Spring, MD: IEEE Computer Society Press, pp. 215–23

Shapiro, E. ed. (1987). *Concurrent Prolog: Collected Papers.* Cambridge, MA: MIT Press

Shepherdson, J.C. (1984). Negation as Failure: A Comparison of Clark's Completed Data Base and Reiter's Closed World Assumption. *Journal of Logic Programming*, **1**(1), 51–79

Shepherdson, J.C. (1985). Negation as Failure II. *Journal of Logic Programming*, **2**(3), 185–202

Shepherdson, J.C. (1988). Negation in Logic Programming. In Minker (1988), pp. 17–88

Smith, D.R. (1984). The Synthesis of LISP Programs from Examples: a Survey. In Biermann *et al.* (1984), pp. 307–24

Smith, D.R. (1985). The Design of Divide and Conquer Algorithm. *Science of*

Computer Programming, **5**, 37–58

Soham, Y. and McDermot, D.V. (1984). Directed Relations and Inversion of Prolog Programs. In *Proc. Conf. on Fifth Generation Computer Systems* (Tokyo, November), H. Aido (Ed.), Amsterdam: Elsevier/North Holland, pp. 307–16

Sommerville, I. (1989). *Software Engineering. 3rd* edn. Wokingham: Addison-Wesley

Sondergaard, H. (1986). An Application of Abstract Interpretation of Logic Programs: Occur-Check Reduction. *Proc. ESOP-86*, LNC 213, Springer-Verlag, pp. 327–38

Stepankova, O. and Stepanek, P. (1984). Transformations of Logic Programs. *Journal of Logic Programming*, **1**(3)

Sterling, L. and Shapiro, E. (1986). *The Art of Prolog: Advanced Programming Techniques.* Cambridge, MA: MIT Press

Stoy, J. (1982). Some Mathematical Aspects of Functional Programming. In Darlington (1982), pp. 217–52

Summers, P.D. (1977). A Methodology for LISP Program Construction from Examples. *JACM*, **24**(1), 161–75

Swartout, W. and Balzer, R. (1982). On the Inevitable Intertwining of Specification and Implementation. *ACM*, **25**(7), 438–40

Takeuchi, A. and Furukawa, K. (1985). Partial Evaluation of Prolog Programs and its Application to Meta Programming. Technical Report TR-126, ICOT Research Center, July 1985

Takeuchi, A. and Furukawa, K. (1986). Parallel Logic Programming Languages. In *Proc. 3rd Int. Conf. on Logic Programming* (London, July), New York: Springer-Verlag, pp. 242–69

Tärnlund, S.A. (1977). Horn Clause Computability. *BIT* **17**, pp. 215–26

Tärnlund, S.A. (1981) *A Programming Language Based on a Natural Deduction System.* UPMAIL Technical Report No. 6, November 1981

Thatcher, J.W., Wagner, E.G. and Wright, J.B. (1982). Data Type Specification: Parametrization and the Power of Specification Techniques. *ACM Trans. on Prog. Lang. and Syst.*, **4**(4), 711–32

Topor, R.W. and Sonenberg, E.A. (1988). On Domain Independent Databases. In Minker (1988), pp. 217–40

Turner, D.A. (1982). Functional Programming and Proofs of Program Correctness. In Néel (1982), pp. 187–209

Ueda, K. (1986a). Guarded Horn Clauses. *Doctoral Thesis*, Information Engineering Course, Faculty of Engineering, University of Tokyo, March 1986. (To be published by MIT Press.)

Ueda, K. (1986b). Making Exhaustive Search Programs Deterministic. In *Proc. 3rd Int. Conf. on Logic Programming* (London, July), New York: Springer-Verlag, pp. 270–82

van Emden, M.H. and Kowalski, R.A. (1976) The Semantics of Predicate Logic as a Programming Language. *JACM*, **23**(4), 733–42

van Emden, M.H. and Lloyd, J.W. (1984) A Logical Reconstruction of Prolog II. In *Proc. Int. Symp. on Logic Programming* (Atlantic City, NJ, February), Silver Spring, MD: IEEE Computer Society Press, pp. 35–40

Van Hentenryck, P. (1989). *Consistency Techniques in Logic Programming.* Cambridge, MA: MIT Press

Van Hentenryck, P. and Dincbas, M. (1986). Domains in Logic Programming. In

Proc. AAAI-86, Philadelphia, pp. 759–65

Van Hentenryck, P. and Dincbas, M. (1987). Forward Checking in Logic Programming. In *Proc. 4th Int. Conf. on Logic Programming* (Melbourne, May), Cambridge, MA: MIT Press, pp. 229–56

Vasak, T. (1986). Towards a Methodology for Logic Programming. *PhD Dissertation*, University of New South Wales, Kensington, Australia

Vasak, T. and Potter, J. (1985). Metalogical Control for Logic Programs. *Journal of Logic Programming*, **2**(3), 203–20

Vasak, T. and Potter, J. (1986). Characterization of Terminating Logic Programs. In *Proc. Int. Symp. on Logic Programming* (Salt Lake City, September), Silver Spring, MD: IEEE Computer Society Press, pp. 140–7

Vasey, P. (1986). Qualified Answers and their Application to Transformation. In *Proc. 3rd Int. Conf. on Logic Programming* (London, July), New York: Springer Verlag, pp. 425–32

Venken, R. (1984). A Prolog Meta Interpreter for Partial Evaluation and its Application to Source-to-Source Transformation and Query Optimization. *ECAI-84*, pp. 91–100

Voda, P.J. (1986). Choices in, and Limitations of, Logic Programming. In *Proc. 3rd Int. Conf. on Logic Programming* (London, July), New York: Springer-Verlag, pp. 615–23

Waem, A. (1988). An Implementation Technique for the Abstract Interpretation of Prolog. In *Proc. 5th Int. Conf. and Symp. on Logic Programming* (Seattle, August) Cambridge, MA: MIT Press

Wand, M. (1980). Continuation-Based Program Transformation Strategies. *JACM*, **27**(1), 164–80

Warren, D.H.D. (1977). *Implementing Prolog – Compiling Predicate Logic Programs*. DAI Research Reports 39 and 40, Department of Artificial Intelligence, Edinburgh University

Warren, D.H.D. (1979). Prolog on the DECsystem-10. In Michie (1979), pp. 112–21

Warren, D.H.D. (1980). An Improved Prolog Implementation which Optimizes Tail Recursion. *Logic Programming Workshop 80* (Dreceben, Hungary), Tärnlund (Ed.)

Warren, D.H.D. (1981). Higher-Order Extensions to Prolog: Are they Needed? In *Proc. 10th Int. Machine Intelligence Workshop*, Cleveland, Ohio

Warren, R. and Debray, S.K. (1988). On the Practicality of Global Flow Analysis of Logic Programs. In *Proc. 5th Int. Conf. and Symp. on Logic Programming* (Seattle August), Cambridge, MA: MIT Press, pp. 684–99

Wegbreit, B. (1976). Goal-Directed Program Transformation. *IEEE Trans. on Soft. Eng.*, **SE-2**(2), 69–86

Winsterstein, G., Dausman, M. and Persch, G. (1980). Deriving Different Unification Algorithms from a Specification in Logic. *Logic Programming Workshop 80* (Dreceben, Hungary), Tärnlund (Ed.), pp. 274–85

Yardeni, E. and Shapiro, E. (1987). A Type System for Logic Programs. In Shapiro (1987), pp. 211–44

Zanioli, C. (1984). Object Oriented Programming in Prolog. In *Proc. Int. Symp. on Logic Programming* (Atlantic City, NJ, February), Silver Spring, MD: IEEE Computer Society Press, pp. 265–76

Zave, P. (1984). The Operational versus the Conventional Approach to Software

Development. *CACM*, **27**(2), 104–18

Zelkowitz, M.V. (1978). Perspectives on Software Engineering. *Computing Surveys*, **10**(2)

Zobel, J. (1987). Derivation of Polymorphic Types for Prolog. In *Proc. 4th Int. Conf. on Logic Programming* (Melbourne, May), Cambridge, MA: MIT Press, pp. 816–38

Index

This index includes authors' names, notations and procedures not referred to in the Appendix. For multiple entries, **boldface** page numbers refer to the definition or the main source of information about the subject.